Cuban Émigrés and Independence in the
Nineteenth-Century Gulf World

Envisioning Cuba

Louis A. Pérez Jr., *editor*

Envisioning Cuba publishes outstanding, innovative works in Cuban studies, drawn from diverse subjects and disciplines in the humanities and social sciences, from the colonial period through the post–Cold War era. Featuring innovative scholarship engaged with theoretical approaches and interpretive frameworks informed by social, cultural, and intellectual perspectives, the series highlights the exploration of historical and cultural circumstances and conditions related to the development of Cuban self-definition and national identity.

Cuban Émigrés and Independence in the Nineteenth-Century Gulf World

....

DALIA ANTONIA MULLER

The University of North Carolina Press   Chapel Hill

This book was published with the assistance of the
Authors Fund of the University of North Carolina Press.

© 2017 The University of North Carolina Press
All rights reserved
Set in Charis and Lato by Westchester Publishing Services
Manufactured in the United States of America

The University of North Carolina Press has been a member
of the Green Press Initiative since 2003.

Library of Congress Cataloging-in-Publication Data
Names: Muller, Dalia Antonia, author.
Title: Cuban Émigrés and independence in the nineteenth-century
  Gulf world / Dalia Antonia Muller.
Other titles: Envisioning Cuba.
Description: Chapel Hill : University of North Carolina Press, [2017] |
  Series: Envisioning Cuba | Includes bibliographical references and
  index.
Identifiers: LCCN 2016039786| ISBN 9781469631974 (cloth : alk. paper) |
  ISBN 9781469631981 (pbk : alk. paper) | ISBN 9781469631998 (ebook)
Subjects: LCSH: Cubans—Mexico—History—19th century. | Cubans—
  Political activity—Mexico—History—19th century. | Political refugees—
  Mexico. | Political refugees—Cuba. | Cuba—History—Revolution,
  1895-1898. | Cuba—History—1810-1899. | Caribbean Area—
  History—1810-1945.
Classification: LCC F1392.C8 M85 2017 | DDC 972.91/05—dc23 LC record
  available at https://lccn.loc.gov/2016039786

Cover illustration: "Map of the Straits of Florida and Gulf of Mexico. To
accompany a report from the Treasury Department of Israel D. Andrews
in obedience to the resolution of the Senate of March 8th, 1851" by Israel
de Wolf Andrews (Wikimedia Commons).

For Lucie, Dalia, and Isa

Contents

Acknowledgments, xi

Introduction, 1
A Case Apart?

1 Nineteenth-Century Cuban Migrants in the Gulf World, 15

2 Cuban Communities in Late Nineteenth-Century Mexico, 43

3 Cuban Revolutionary Politics in Diaspora, 83

4 Internationalizing *Cuba Libre*, 132
Cuban Insurgent Diplomacy and the Building of Transnational Solidarities

5 Spanish Immigrants, the Mexican State, and the Fight for *Cuba Española*, 168

6 Affirming Americanismo, 210
Desespañolización and the Defense of America

Epilogue, 245
The Legacies of Cuban-Mexican Solidarities

Notes, 259

Bibliography, 281

Index, 295

Map, Tables, and Figures

Map

1.1 Major migratory routes of nineteenth-century Cuban émigrés in the Gulf World, 21

Tables

1.1 Place of departure in Cuba, 1895–1898, 32
1.2 Places of arrival in Mexico, 1895–1898, 32
3.1 Occupation of ANERC applicants from Mexico, 86

Figures

4.1 Image of Antonio Maceo, *El Continente Americano*, 21 June 1896, 163
6.1 "Se Completó el Mapa," *El Hijo del Ahuizote*, 2 May 1897, 214
6.2 "Su Medio de Oro: Tres Americanos Ilustres Premian el Triunfo de Tio Samuel" (Juárez, Xicotencatl, y Cuauhtemoc), *El Hijo del Ahuizote*, 1898, 234
6.3 "El A, B, C de la democracia," *El Hijo del Ahuizote*, 8 January 1899, 235

Acknowledgments

This book is dedicated to three incredible women, all of whom built and sustained friendships and solidarities across oceans and borders. Lucienne Muller, Dalia Justo, and Isabel Portilla Flores have served as enduring inspiration for as long as I can remember. They taught me the power of dreaming, the virtue of hard work, the value of perseverance, and the importance of *solidaridad*. This work is for them.

I remember the moment I fell in love with the study of history. It was in a ninth-grade history class taught by Mrs. Stearn. Her lectures are still vivid in my mind, and I hope they remain so always. In a way, I also owe this book (and my career) to her. Sadly, she is not able to read this book, but I'd like to think she would have enjoyed it.

In the time it has taken me to conceive of, research, write and rewrite this book, I have accumulated many debts to many people. These acknowledgments only begin to express my gratitude to them. At Yale and then at Berkeley I had the opportunity to study with brilliant historians and scholars and to benefit from strong mentorship. During my time at Yale, Gilbert Joseph, Stuart Schwartz, Raymond Craib, and Rick López helped me gain footing in the field, while Jonathan Spence and John Demos instilled in me a love of narrative history I will never lose. Many thanks to my advisor at Berkeley, Margaret Chowning, whose faith in me never waned. I have yet to find a more keen and critical eye than hers. Thank you to William Taylor as well. He saw the full potential of my project long before I did. And to Julio Ramos: this book was quite literally born in your seminar. Others at Berkeley who cannot go without mention for the support they provided are Mark Healy, José David Saldivar, Eugene Irschick, James Vernon, and Tyler Stovall. My time at Berkeley drew me, unexpectedly, into a different community of like-minded people. Thank you to my friends at UCMAP for testing my limits and for catching me when I fell. The same goes for the John Machado Academy in Los Angeles, where I learned how to move through life differently.

In Spain, Mexico, and Cuba, many scholars, librarians, and archivists helped me during two years of rigorous research. Special thanks to the staff and archivists at the Secretary of Foreign Relations in Mexico, the Hemeroteca and Biblioteca National, the Instituto Mora, El Colegio de México, Condumex, the Archivo General de la Nación and the state and municipal archives in Veracruz and Mérida. In Cuba, I owe thanks to the Fundación Antonio Nuñez Jimenez, and especially its director Reinaldo Funes Monzote for sponsoring research visas over the years. The Instituto de Historia, where I presented early versions of this work, and the archivists and librarians at the Archivo Nacional de Cuba and the Biblioteca José Martí deserve special mention as well. At the Archivo Nacional de Cuba, the support of Jorge Macle Cruz was absolutely indispensible. I can say the same for Enrique López Mesa, researcher at the Instituto de Estudios Martianos, whose intelligence is only matched by his kindness. Our fateful meeting in Chile in 2003 marked the beginning of more than a decade of rich intellectual conversations and exchanges, all of which have shaped this work. My research assistant Claudia Martínez made it possible for me to work even when I was not in Cuba—a luxury, to be sure. Other scholars in Mexico, Cuba, and Spain who have provided support and inspiration are Conseulo Naranjo Orovio, Leida Fernández Prieto, Josefina Toledo, René González Barrios, Yoel Cordoví Nuñez, Santiago Portilla, Laura Muñoz Mata, Johanna Von Grafestein and Margaret Shrimpton.

In both Mexico and Cuba, family connections made coming home from the archive each day sweet. In Cuba, my namesake, Dalia Justo, and her family embraced me as if I had always been there. Dalia's stories of growing up in Puerto Padre, of her participation in the Revolution, of the trials of the Special Period, and of the correspondence she sustained with my mother over five decades gave me much food for thought over many meals shared. Her nieces Valia and Miosotis have always been especially kind. Thanks also to Tia Tina in Mexico, and to my godparents Isabel Portilla Flores and Jorge Flores and their daughter Jimena. They taught me how to live in and to love Mexico City, which is no mean feat. In Spain, Conseulo Naranjo Orovio opened doors for me professionally, and also opened the doors to her home. Gracias.

Back in the United States, many scholars have supported me along my journey by reading drafts of chapters, entertaining wild queries, and engaging in intellectual conversations. Rebecca Scott stands out among a group of fantastic Latin Americanists who have offered guidance. She has done everything, from peering over my shoulder at documents, to helping me unearth hidden gems and resolve stubborn mysteries, to inspiring me with her pioneering methods and brilliant scholarship. Conversations with

Christopher Schmidt-Nowara have shaped this work in important ways over the better part of a decade. RIP. Elliott Young has provided continuous support and insight over the years. Thank you to Mauricio Tenorio-Trillo for a fateful and illuminating exchange at the very first Tepotzlan Institute conference. There are many, many colleagues across the academy on whom I have counted at many levels. In no particular order I would like to thank David Satorius, James E. Sanders, Raymond Craib, Kris Lane, Pamela Voekel, Lawrence Powell, Jane Landers, Barry Carr, Ada Ferrer, Michele Reid-Vázquez, John Lawrence Tone, Louis A. Pérez, Eric Zolov, Alejandro de la Fuente, Michael Gobat, Alicia Partnoy, Michael Alderson, Nancy Raquel Mirabal, Christine Arce, Celso Castilho, Jessica Delgado, Cuco de la Torre Curiel, Rachel Moore, and David J. Bertuca.

At the University at Buffalo, I have had the pleasure of working with fantastic colleagues. I would like to thank my fellow historians for welcoming me into an unusually collegial and supportive department. Individuals in History and across the College of Arts and Sciences who have offered advice and support for this project in particular include Hal Langfur, Camilo Trumper, Sasha Pack, Gwynn Thomas, Marion Werner, Ana Mariella Bacigalupo, James Bono, Erik Seeman, Cecil Foster, Susan Cahn, David Herzberg, José Buscaglia, Victoria Wolcott, Roger Des Forge, Tamara Thornton, and Patricia Mazón. Thank you to PhD student Amanda Magdalena for helping me tie up loose ends in Mérida. In my wider Buffalo community, Ellen Berrey, Steve Hoffman, Jordan Geiger, Miriam Paeslack, Eric Walker, Jaume Franquesa, and the people of Claremont street have helped make my time away from work rich and rewarding.

Thank you to Elaine Maisner and Louis A. Pérez at UNC Press. To David Sartorius and Elliott Young, who read and critiqued the manuscript twice, a thousand thanks. To Michael Needham and Humanities First, as well as Kim Singletary, D. Ohlandt, and Susan Storch, thanks are also due.

Institutions, departments, and programs that have supported this research are the SUNY Faculty Diversity Program, the UB History Department, the UB Humanities Institute, the Dr. Nuala McGann Drescher Affirmative action/Diversity Leave program, the Caribbean and Latino/American Studies program at the University at Buffalo, the UC Berkeley Visiting Scholars Program, the Henry Morse Stephens Memorial Traveling Fellowship and the Eugene Cota Robles Fellowship.

I reserve the last note for my family. To those in my most intimate circle—Lucie, Paty, Rich, Jorge M., Rayén, Nahuel, Myrna, Norma, Chris, Teresa, Jorge Flores, Isa, Jimena—thank you for your constant love and encouragement. To my compadres Jessica Pelgado, Celso Castilho, Ellen Berrey, and Steve Hoffman, thank you for helping me care for what is most dear. To Camilo, I hardly know what to say because words cannot describe. You are and will be my partner in everything, always and forever. Abuela and my little Enanito thank you for watching over me. I'll see you again. Amaya and Simón, you have my heart. Escaping with you each day to enchanted worlds in books very different from the one I have written has been an indescribable joy.

Cuban Émigrés and Independence in the Nineteenth-Century Gulf World

Introduction
A Case Apart?

In 1909, the journalist Manuel Márquez Sterling criticized Cuban publicists for framing the Cuban independence movement as "a case apart . . . disconnected from the common problem of Spanish America . . . with no discernable relationship to the nations of the South."[1] The year 1909 marked the end of the second U.S. intervention in Cuba. Just over ten years earlier, the United States had declared war on Spain, "liberated" Cuba, and subsequently placed the island under colonial control. While U.S. territorial occupation would come to an end in 1902, Cuba's adoption of the Platt Amendment—the condition set by the United States for its withdrawal—ensured Cuba's continued subordination. It would not be long before political crisis brought U.S. navy ships back to Cuban harbors, in 1906. Manuel Márquez Sterling would characterize the second intervention between 1906 and 1909 as "a time of sad deception . . . when we believed we had seen our nationality forever unmade."[2] The first decade of Cuba's independent life as a republic was not what most Cuban revolutionaries had imagined.

Many were blamed for Cuba's grim fate. Some blamed the United States for intervening. Others blamed the insurgent army for laying down its arms too soon. For others, it was Cuba's political elite that had betrayed the Cuban people who had fought so earnestly for independence. Finally, Cubans blamed Latin America for the diplomatic neglect that left insurgent Cuba adrift on a dangerous sea in its hour of need. While the United States' blatant violation of Cuban sovereignty in and after 1898 was deeply disappointing, it was not surprising. Much more shocking for Cubans like Manuel Márquez Sterling was Latin American states' refusal to support the Cuban independence movement as the insurgents fought doggedly to sever the island's ties to Spain between 1895 and 1898. The framing of Cuban independence as a "case apart," disconnected from Latin America, was thus a defensive response to Latin America's abandonment of Cuba. As Esteban Borrero y Echeverria, a Cuban Revolutionary Party agent in Costa Rica pled with the president of that nation to recognize the validity of the insurgent's struggle against Spanish colonialism, he wrote "Cuba, stained with the blood of the last battle turns her eyes naturally to [Latin America], as if she were looking for her own place in the home that the generous hand of Bolivar made for all."³ His pleas were met with silence. Shortly after, with the United States already determined to declare war on Spain, Borrero's hope gave way to disillusionment, and in another letter he wrote that "Washington has been dearer to us than Bolivar."⁴ The descendants of George Washington may not have been entirely trustworthy, but Borrero was forced to admit that they had nonetheless taken a stand in support of the Cuban struggle against Spain, whereas the Latin American descendants of the famed liberator of South America, Simón Bolivar, including the president of Costa Rica to whom he had appealed, remained silent. Borrero, Márquez Sterling and other Cubans' deep disillusionment, often expressed as heartless and incomprehensible betrayal, points not to their naiveté or their own irrational and excessive feelings, but to the fact that by the late nineteenth century, Cubans had come to think of Latin America and Latin Americans as central to their own fate and future. So, why has Latin America been left out of the history of Cuban Independence?

The tendency to treat Cuban independence as a case apart from Latin America is especially prominent in the U.S. academy where U.S.-Cuban and Cuban nationalist frameworks of analysis prevail. Cuba's orientation toward the United States, especially from the 1850s forward, is undeniably important to any study of the Cuban independence process, as well as the formation of Cuban national identity, and the particular evolution and challenges of republican statehood in Cuba. However, to frame Cuban independence as a process that evolved in Cuba and in relation to the United States alone is to constrain the past. In so doing, scholars reaffirm the original erasure of Latin America from what is a much broader history of Cuban independence.

Manuel Márquez Sterling's critique of the idea that Cuba was a "case apart" is the starting point for this book, which examines the Cuban independence struggle in a Gulf World context and takes seriously the space in and in between Mexico, Cuba and the United States as both the sphere of action and the resonance chamber of Cuban independence. To be sure, the Cuban independence movement was carried forth and echoed throughout the Caribbean, the Americas, and the Atlantic world; however, the Gulf World shaped, and was intimately shaped by, the Cuban independence conflict during the nineteenth century.

The wars of Cuban independence spanned thirty years, but the struggle for Cuban independence extended across a century. As Spain's mainland colonies rose up against the metropolis during the Age of Revolution, Cubans looked on with fear and anticipation. Among the many who remained "ever faithful," there were those who dreamed of independence.⁵ Plots and conspiracies to liberate the colony began as early as 1812 and gained force and number in the 1810s and 1820s.[6] But the forces in favor of colonialism would prove resilient, and it would take three military conflicts over thirty years to finally break Spain's hold on the colony.

From the early nineteenth century forward, the theater of Cuban independence was not limited to the island of Cuba but was international in scope. Its condition as an island, together with the strength, reach, and resilience of Spain's nineteenth-century colonial regime, made it critical for Cuban patriots to seek shores near and far from where to plan and plot revolution. Handfuls of exiled conspirators circulating throughout the Gulf, Caribbean, and Atlantic worlds in the early 1800s became thousands of migrants, refugees, and exiled dissidents during the three military conflicts that spanned the last thirty years of the nineteenth century: the Ten Years' War (1868–1878), the Little War (1879–1880), and the War of Cuban Independence (1895–1898). The majority of these migrants sought refuge in the United States and Mexico, while others found themselves on Caribbean islands, or along circum-Caribbean coastlines in Central and South America, as well as in the Southern Cone and Europe. From the 1820s through the 1890s, Cuban migrants, refugees, and political exiles circulating in and beyond the Gulf World forged connections and solidarities, and along with their allies conceived of Cuban independence in Bolivarian terms as a movement of continental significance. Indeed, Cuban independence was seen as the "*último cañonazo*," the last cannon shot in a long war against Spanish colonialism in America.

The first half of this book centers on the migrations and the lives of Cuban men and women, rich and poor, white and nonwhite, who chose Mexico as a safe haven during the turbulent years of war that marked Cuba's final push for independence. Early chapters detail Cuban migrants' travels to and beyond Mexico in the networked space of the Gulf World while examining their insertion into long-standing diasporic migrant communities and exploring their political activity and revolutionary self-fashioning. The first half of the book which is a social and political history of travel, migration, circulation, and politics in diaspora, frames the Gulf World as a space of migration. The fourth chapter serves as a hinge connecting the two halves of the book. Cuban migrants circulating in the Gulf World and engaging in revolutionary activity were anything but insular. Rather, they opened the intimate spaces of their political clubs and associations to foreigners, eagerly seeking solidarity and encouraging supporters to make the Cuban independence cause their own. Far from the traditional exile community turned in on itself, Cuban migrant communities in Mexico and in Latin America nurtured a nationalist revolutionary politics that was outward-looking.

The social and political history of Cuban exile and migration in Mexico is also a history of transnational solidarities forged in private and public gathering places throughout the nation. Mexican citizens, from railroad workers to federal deputies, pledged their support and allegiance to the Cuban cause. They came to identify with the movement by interacting with Cuban migrants, belonging to their political clubs, co-organizing and attending public events for the cause, and engaging with the Mexican pro-Cuban independence press. But Cubans were not the only foreigners interested in Cuba's fate. Spaniards, who were present in significant numbers in Mexico at the end of the nineteenth century, were as vigorous and determined to be heard and to advance their own project for the preservation of Spanish rule in Cuba. As a result, Mexico became a battleground where Cubans, Spaniards, and Mexicans fought over the fate of Cuba and the future of the Gulf World. As Mexicans took up the cause of *Cuba Libre* (Free Cuba) or *Cuba Española*, they used it to refocus and invigorate their own national struggles. The Cuban cause became a prism through which Mexican politics was refracted. Mexicans all across the political spectrum weighed in on the meaning and impact of Cuban independence for Mexico and Mexico's place in the Gulf World.

Thus, the second half of the book shifts register into that of political, intellectual, and diplomatic history and considers the Gulf World as contested geopolitical space to which Mexico, Spain, the United States, and Cuban insurgents all lay claim. As a body of water bordered by the United States, Mexico, and the Spanish colony of Cuba, the Gulf of Mexico became a theater for competition between states and peoples who saw the space as both a vulnerable borderlands and profitable frontier zone. The diplomatic maneuverings of competing states gave rise to competing visions of the region. U.S. imperialists figured the Gulf as an "American Mediterranean," a space it was destined to dominate. This vision had largely become reality by the mid-nineteenth century. Spain, a victim of the United States' westward expansion and of the anti-colonial revolutions that shattered its empire in the 1820s, saw the Gulf as a bitter reminder of its own imperial decline and clung to its remaining imperial fragments, vowing to commit the "last man and the last peseta" in defense of its dwindling empire.[7] Mexico's presence in the Gulf had also shrunk when it lost its territory bordering the Gulf of Mexico east of the Rio Grande as a result of the Mexican-American War. For Mexico, the Gulf that bore its name as the "seno Mexicano," or Mexico's bosom, was first and foremost a space of vulnerability and defense, but it was also seen as a space of commercial opportunity and imperial projection.⁸

Cuban insurgents were keenly aware of Cuba's position as the *"llave del Golfo,"* the key of the Gulf. Cubans in exile played an at once savvy and risky game of politics and diplomacy as they sought profitable solidarities in the interest of the independence cause. By framing Cuban independence as more than a national struggle, they permitted—even encouraged—non-Cubans to appropriate and resignify the Cuban cause for their own ends. The price of this strategy would be dear in the United States, where Cuban diplomacy gave U.S. Americans a language of solidarity and benevolence with which to simultaneously promote and disguise blatant imperialism. In Mexico, Cuban insurgent diplomacy failed. As Cubans saw it, Mexico left them to face a battle of titanic proportions and continental implications on their own.

As the war between Spaniards and Cubans progressed on the island, the battle in Mexico between Spanish immigrants, Cuban migrants, and Mexican nationals intensified. Disagreements led to heated debates in the press, some of which resulted in incarceration, others of which led to physical altercations in the streets. Brawls broke out in cantinas, theaters, and restaurants.

Spanish immigrants who participated in and observed these conflicts felt affirmed by the positive official response they received from the Mexican government and certain sectors of Mexico's political elite, but they felt aggrieved by the Mexican people, whose hostility toward them was palpable. Spaniards regularly complained that their honor was violated by Mexicans who were favorable to the Cuban cause. In contrast to Spaniards, Cubans in Mexico were bitter about the failure of their diplomacy, but took consolation from the popular solidarities they acquired during the course of the war, solidarities that were in no small measure due to their own active organizing and the capaciousness of their vision of the transnational significance of Cuban independence. The conflict over Cuba came to a dramatic end in 1898. Many Cubans returned to rebuild their homes and communities that had been devastated by war, while others stayed abroad by choice or out of necessity. In Mexico, Spanish immigrants grew in number in the first decade of the twentieth century, as did *hispanismo*. Dissent and opposition to Díaz's policies, including his pro-Spanish position, simmered and then boiled over in 1910.

This book ends where it begins, with Manuel Márquez Sterling's reflections on Cuba's isolation from Latin America. For Márquez Sterling, the Cuban movement in Mexico and in Latin America represented not a failure but a victory. A victory not for political elites and their narrow nationalist agendas, but a victory for *americanismo*, an ideal that could unite Latin Americans across national borders, and, at times, across race, class, and gender in the defense of values and principles they held in common. *Americanismo*, a forerunner to the anti-imperialist *latinoamericanismo* of the twentieth century, has, like the broader story of Cuban independence, been overshadowed. The tendency to consider U.S.-Latin American relations at the turn of the century as a struggle between a conquering Anglo race and a beleaguered Latin race left Pan-Hispanism as the central option for those who would take a stance against U.S. imperialism. This position, however, does not leave room for the recognition of an ideology of solidarity like *americanismo* rooted in a vigorous rejection of both Spanish and U.S. imperialism.

The Gulf World as a Framework

The last letter Cuban revolutionary José Martí wrote before he died in battle was addressed to his longtime friend and confidante, the Mexican lawyer and statesmen Manuel Mercado. In it he famously articulated the struggle between Cuba and the United states as the contest between David and Goliath. Less well-known in the same letter is Martí's call to Mexico, which reveals what he saw as Mexico's role in aiding and safeguarding Cuban independence. "And Mexico," he wondered, "will it not find a wise, effective and immediate way of helping, in due time, its own defender?"[9] The idea that the fates of Cuba and Mexico were intertwined, and that Cuba's independence was critical for the safeguarding of Mexican sovereignty, was commonly espoused by Cuban migrants affiliated with the revolutionary cause in Mexico and by the Mexicans who stood in solidarity with them.

Because of its geographical and geopolitical position, Mexico provides a unique laboratory in which to examine the development of Cuban independence politics in the Americas during the late nineteenth century. Forming a bridge (or buffer, depending on one's perspective) between the United States and Latin America, Mexico was at the center of a mobile world marked by the constant circulation of goods, people, and ideas both within Latin America and between the United States and Latin America. Cuba functioned in much the same way via an intimate relationship with the United States that was cemented throughout the nineteenth century through economic ties. Both countries were border states in an increasingly polarized hemisphere. Examining the lives of Cuban migrants in Mexico therefore illuminates a Gulf connection between the United States, Cuba, and Mexico, and offers the opportunity to observe the particular characteristics of a Cuban revolutionary politics formed in the shadow of the United States. As Cubans and Mexicans came together, or came into conflict over Cuba's fate, the United States always loomed in the background.

Numerous scholars have challenged narrow conceptions of the Caribbean as well as the dominance of nation-state frameworks in the study of Mexican history, Cuban history, and the history of U.S. Gulf South. U.S. Gulf South scholars now foreground the complexity of the region, examining in detail the South's relationship to Mexico, Cuba, and the Caribbean.[10] Similarly, Latin Americanist historians, as well as literary and cultural studies scholars examining transnational linkages within the greater Caribbean, define the region expansively as a space uniquely shaped by various modes of U.S. imperialism and resistance to them.[11] A slightly different formulation has been developed by historians in Mexico who study Mexico's integration into the Caribbean. These scholars understand the Caribbean as a *"complejo Golfo-Caribe,"* or Gulf-Caribbean complex, a "mobile frontier that like a contact zone rather than a political border expanded and contracted depending on the circumstances."[12] This frontier, or contact zone, was the site of multiple exchanges and interactions between Mexico and a broader Caribbean and Gulf world, some of which were the result of increasing presence of the United States, and some of which were due to well-established regional connections and dynamics. For Mexico throughout the past five hundred years Cuba has been the place in the *Golfo-Caribe* to which it is most intimately connected. In the years after Mexican independence, the island, which had once been a part of the administrative unit of New Spain, became a launching pad for Spain's efforts to reconquer its lost colony, Mexico. Decades later, as the nineteenth century came to a close, and as sovereignty in Cuba passed from Spain to the United States, Mexican politicians understandably feared that Cuba would remain a danger to Mexico. The empire changed, but the threat remained the same.

While the scholars who formulated the idea of the *Golfo-Caribe* recognize it as an integrated region, they insist that the Gulf is a space unto itself that sustains intimate connections with the Caribbean. Similarly, I recognize that Cuban independence had ramifications far beyond the Gulf, but argue that the Gulf World is a useful framework of analysis because, despite many intimate connections with the Caribbean and Central and South America, it was in the Gulf World that the largest number of Cuban migrants, refugees, and exiles circulated in the nineteenth century, establishing communities linked in diaspora. It was in the Gulf World that Cubans centered their most important diplomatic projects, and it was the Gulf World that was the first theater of a struggle between empires and nations that would change the course of history in the Americas. A history of Cuban independence framed by the Gulf World inspires us to consider not only how Mexico was a site of Cuban organizing and a theater of conflict over the Cuban Question, but also the dynamic linkages between the United States and Mexico created by traveling migrants and by those whose political thought was framed by the spaces between Mexico, Cuba, and the United States. But just as a Gulf World frame offers new perspectives on the histories of migration, exile, geopolitics, and diplomacy, as well as on transnational connections and solidarities, it can also give us ways to reconsider both Cuban and Mexican national histories.

Cuban History Reconsidered

Notable historians in the United States, Cuba, and Spain have expanded our understanding of the Cuban independence struggle, approaching the topic from the vantage point of social, political, cultural, diplomatic, military, or environmental history while also foregrounding the importance of race, class, and gender.[13] Many of these scholars have challenged the erasure of Cubans as protagonists of their own independence process, a legacy of U.S. intervention and imperialism.[14] Others have subjected Cuban nationalist historical traditions to rigorous scrutiny, noting that when the complexity of the past renders history resistant to nationalist narratives, it is the history that is amended.[15] The role that Cuban exile networks played in fomenting and sustaining a national struggle for independence is acknowledged, but studies of Cuban communities in the United States still dominate the literature.[16] In these works, the history of Cuban migrants and exiles is often told as a history of the machinations of a handful of pro-U.S. political elites with annexationist tendencies who took control of the independence movement at the expense of a large popular and democratic base of true patriots that included Cuban tobacco workers in Florida and poor and black insurgent soldiers in Cuba. These Cuban elites envisioned an independent republic modeled on the United States with close ties to its northern neighbor. While recent studies have rendered this straightforward narrative more complex, especially by exploring the role of Afro-Cuban political actors in exile, a history that focuses only on events as they unfolded in and between the U.S. and Cuba misses critical aspects of the broader history of inter-American relations and transnational dynamics that is itself an important part of Cuban national history.

These are linkages that Cuban, Mexican, and other Latin American scholars have been busy tracing for decades. Numerous publications over the past twenty years have borne the fruit of collaborative work between Cuban and Latin American scholars interested in recovering the histories of various moments of Latin American solidarity in the Americas that may have responded to the rise of U.S. imperialism but were not exclusively defined by it.[17] Drawing critical inspiration from these collaborative works, this book seeks to further expand and deepen the commitment to critically engaging the forces of U.S. imperialism, while being mindful of the long shadow that U.S. imperialism has cast over histories of the Americas.

This history, like the broader studies from which it draws inspiration, seeks to understand the impact of Cuban independence beyond Cuba's borders. It also endeavors to make a contribution to Cuban history by exploring the ways the transnational solidarities forged by Cubans reaffirmed the nation rather than decentered it. "Nation" was, or became, the core aspiration of Cuban migrants affiliated with the revolutionary movement. However, their conception of the nation was shaped by a revolutionary politics made abroad. In part, their revolutionary politics was influenced by their membership in a Cuban diaspora, which after 1892 was increasingly coherent and self-conscious. But the migrants' idea(s) of Cuba were also dynamically shaped by the particular contexts in which they lived. *Cuba Libre* was envisioned differently by Cubans inhabiting different societies throughout the Americas. As migrants returned to Cuba, they carried these differing and sometimes competing visions with them, and interpretations of *Cuba Libre* formed in Latin America, like those that emanated from the United States, also impacted the development of Cuban politics in the twentieth century.

The significance of the expansive and connected Cuban migrant networks, including their revolutionary labors and their diverse national visions, is minimized when we limit ourselves to the study of Cubans in the United States. The spirited debate over Latin America's responsibility toward the nascent republic is also minimized under these circumstances. Cubans in the United States also debated the United States' responsibility toward Cuba, but the context and the stakes were not the same. Cubans and their allies and critics in Latin America fervently believed that the formation of an independent republic in Cuba was the key to safeguarding the independence of Latin America, especially given the rising power of the United States.[18] Thus, a deep sense of Cuba's transnational importance was embedded within Cuban nationalism, especially but not exclusively in the minds of revolutionary elites. This transnational dimension of Cuban nationalism is obscured if we focus only on Cuban independence within a U.S.-Cuba binary relationship, because in this context, the central drama of Cuba's modern history becomes the effort to secure, undo or otherwise come to terms with the "ties of singular intimacy" that bind it to the United States.[19] Seen from Latin America, however, Cuba's nationalism emerges as a "trans-nationalism" deeply embedded in and informed by conceptions of time, space, and history not bound by the nation-state or determined by the United States. The exceptionalist narrative of Cuba as a "case apart" is disrupted, and the power of the narrative of an exceptional relationship between the United States and Cuba is attenuated. "At some point in the nineteenth century Cubans developed the capacity to adopt an external vision of themselves as a perspective on themselves," Louis A. Pérez writes, "to see themselves from the outside as a way to both contemplate the world at large and take measure of their place in that world."[20] As Cubans contemplated the world and Cuba's place within it, they did so alongside and in dialogue with Latin Americans. These other intimate ties must be explored if we hope to fully understand nineteenth and twentieth-century Cuban history.

The Cuban independence movement was more than a national conflict over the future of one island, more than the final chapter in the history of Spanish colonialism, and more than a critical moment in the development of U.S. overseas imperialism. When seen from Mexico and from Latin America more generally, it becomes clear that the Cuban independence movement represented a critical chapter in Latin American and hemispheric American history.

Mexican History Reconsidered

Cuban independence studied from a Gulf World perspective makes critical contributions to Mexican history and historiography as well. For example, the Cuban Question sharpened the critique of both students' and journalistic opposition to the regime of Porfirio Díaz. Journalists used the Cuban Question to mask dissent, tying the regime's rejection of Cuba to the rise of conservatism and the betrayal of Mexico's liberal tradition, which was represented by the mid-century Liberal reform movement. These doctrinaire liberals went head to head with the new brand of conservative liberals who came to dominate Mexican politics in the second half of the Porfirian dictatorship. The Cuban call for the universal recognition of their belligerency rights gave Mexican sympathizers a legal cause and argument to press for change in Mexico's foreign policy. Mexico's refusal to recognize the Cuban insurgents as legitimate belligerents with rights to safe landing in surrounding ports during the nineteenth century not only signaled the regime's betrayal of Mexico's sacred liberal tradition but was also an indication of the corruption of the regime and of Mexico's weakness vis-à-vis both the United States and Spain, the two powers that were most actively determining Cuba's future and with it the future of the Gulf World. Mexican liberals in opposition to the regime used the Cuban Question as a public stage on which to discredit the regime's stewardship of the nation at a time when the price of blunt critique could be incarceration or death.

An examination of how the cause of *Cuba Libre* was used by Mexican doctrinaire liberals in the late nineteenth century to bolster their position reveals something about the strategies of the opposition to the Díaz dictatorship that was coalescing in the 1890s. At the same time, a close study of the ideological and intellectual arguments that undergirded the Mexican state's neutrality and de facto rejection of Cuban independence shows the close relationship between the transformation of liberalism in Mexico and the rise of Pan-Hispanism. The Cuban Question represented a serious trial for a nation that had elevated its own independence struggle and its wars to consolidate its liberal regime to the status of a cult.[21] Public or official rejection of the Cuban movement—an anti-colonial movement for the establishment of a liberal and democratic republic—was a considerable challenge, and it required skilled political acrobatics. We can see in the maneuverings of the Díaz regime as it formulated its Cuba policy how late nineteenth-century Mexican political elites reconciled the idea that the Díaz regime represented the continuation and consolidation of the mid-century liberal political reform movement with the reality of the Mexican state's growing conservatism, its embrace of Hispanism, and an economic liberalism purchased at the expense of the political liberties and constitutional guarantees of its citizens.

Finally, this history of Cuban Independence can help us gain a nuanced understanding of the rise of anti-Hispanism in Mexico. The Porfiriato has been seen as a period of relative peace and harmony between Mexicans and Spaniards when compared to earlier and later historical periods. However, the lens of the Cuban Question allows us to see a strong current of anti-Hispanism emerging during the 1890s. It should be said that, rather than a blanket rejection of Spaniards and Spanish culture, however, the anti-Hispanism expressed by advocates of Cuban independence is more accurately described as *anti-gachupinismo*. "*Gachupin*" was a favorite derogative term for those Spaniards to whom Mexicans objected. Mexicans critical of Spain drew a firm distinction between what they called hard-working, honest immigrants on the one hand and haughty, entitled, avaricious individuals who manifested clearly imperialistic attitudes on the other. Not only would Mexican supporters of Cuban independence embrace honest and hard-working Spanish immigrants, but they also venerated the fallen Spanish republic and embraced Spanish republicans in their midst. The complicated ways in which Mexican supporters of Cuban independence both embraced and rejected Spaniards is flattened when we see the Cuban conflict in stark oppositional terms as a battle between Pan-Americanism and Pan-Hispanism. The diversity of interpretations of what it meant, or might mean to be Spanish, or Hispanic in the late nineteenth- and early twentieth-century Mexico offers us the opportunity to begin to reexamine the history of Hispano-Mexican relations at that time. Analyzing the impact of the Cuban Question in Mexico forces us to draw the Porfiriato into the Gulf World, which, in turn, enables us to reflect differently on Porfirian domestic and international politics at the turn of the twentieth century.

A Note on Sources and Methods

Tracing Cuban migrations and movements around the late nineteenth-century Gulf World, exploring their solidarity-building efforts, and assessing the impact of the Cuban Question in Mexico is challenging work. This transnational and Gulf World study of Cuban independence is grounded in research done in archives and libraries spanning Cuba, Mexico, the United States, and Spain. The documents of the Cuban Revolutionary Party (PRC) and the National Association of Cuban Revolutionary Émigrés (ANERC)—two collections housed in the Cuban National Archives—are particularly important for the information they provide regarding Cuban migrants' demographic characteristics, their travels and circulations, and their political activities and revolutionary affiliations. The first of these collections is well-known and well used. The second is hardly referenced in the existing literature. This may have something to do with the fact that the documents of the ANERC are divided between two collections, the Registro de Asociaciónes and Donativos y Remisiones. The individual applications of Cuban migrants claiming to be revolutionary émigrés are gathered in the latter of these two collections, which is arranged so that a researcher must locate individuals by name. The ANERC's documents offer the patient researcher a rare opportunity to trace the Gulf World and Caribbean networks of Cuban revolutionary émigrés during the 1890s, because the documents record the city of origin, point of departure, city of arrival, and city of return, as well as the year of departure and year of return of individual migrants.

The prevalence of Gulf World trajectories among the Association's applicants likely reflects the location of the Association's main headquarters in Havana. The majority of the ANERC's members were Havana residents who had departed from Havana when they left Cuba during the war. The transportation networks and traditions of circulation linking Havana to ports along Mexico's Gulf Coast, as well as to places like New Orleans, Tampa, and Key West, explains, in part, the trajectories of the ANERC members. In addition to information that allows us to trace Gulf World migrations, the ANERC records offer critical insight into the political affiliations of the migrants and their involvement in the revolutionary struggle, which enables us to examine political linkages within Mexico and the United States. Reading these documents alongside the letters written by Mexico-based Cubans collected in the Cuban Revolutionary Party archive, we can see a world emerge, one populated by Cubans connected in diaspora, developing revolutionary politics in movement.

Due to the nature of the ANERC and its policies and practices in early republican Cuba, its membership tended to be elite, a tendency that became more pronounced over time. The elite character of the migrants whose stories can be recovered from the letters they wrote to the Cuban Revolutionary Party is equally pronounced, since these migrants were usually, although not exclusively, educated middle-class professionals. The ANERC documents and the letters written by Cubans in Mexico to the PRC together provide a detailed look at the lives of 298 Cubans—largely white, male, elite, and middle-class individuals—who lived in Mexico during the 1890s. However, by pairing these documents with others, including Spanish and Mexican consular reports, the meeting minutes of individual Cuban patriotic clubs in Mexico, Cuban newspapers published in Mexico and the United States, Mexican newspapers published in numerous cities throughout the republic, and memoirs, we gain a fuller picture of the experiences of a broader set of migrants in Mexico, a set that includes workers, women, and non-white Cubans. What emerges from the juxtaposition of these diverse sources is a rich and textured history of the dynamic relationships between Cubans abroad and their allies and enemies in Mexico as they struggled to envision Cuba's future and, in so doing, shape and contest competing visions of the Gulf and of the Americas.

While Spanish consular records, Cuban club documents, and letters all provide information about Cuban-Mexican solidarities, newspapers are perhaps the richest and most surprising founts of information, especially when read as repositories of details about mundane aspects of Cuban and

Mexican daily life. In Mexico, press houses and newspapers became spaces where Cubans and Mexicans communicated daily. They used newspapers to share information like last-minute changes in the schedule of Cuban club meetings, but they also used press houses as meeting places and distribution sites for revolutionary materials. Both the papers and the buildings became spaces of dissent when they displayed symbols of Cuban nationalism, like the Cuban flag or depictions of Cuban revolutionary heroes. The press's role in forging solidarities extended to far-flung destinations across Mexico. A handful of widely circulating newspapers linked individual Cuban and Mexican sympathizers from Chihuahua to Yucatán and from Guerrero to Veracruz, engaging them in reciprocal exchanges about the central issues of Cuban independence and building a sense of community and connection in the process. These same papers were read in cities across the Americas, from New York City to Santiago, Chile. The constant reproduction and circulation of articles in national and local newspapers in and beyond Mexico suggests the existence of a hemispheric community of readers engaged with the Cuban Question.

As one reads through consular records, club records, private and official letters, ANERC applications and published memoirs, a tapestry of tightly woven networks and linkages suturing together the Gulf World begins to emerge. While drawing together these sources and drawing out the connected histories they contain, I have reflected on José David Saldivar's call to "look awry" at histories of U.S. Imperialism and to be wary of what they conceal.[22] Using a Gulf World framework rather than a U.S.-Cuba binational framework allows us to do just that, rendering the intimate interconnections between the histories of nineteenth-century Cuban migration, Cuban independence, U.S. imperialism, Pan-Hispanism, and the emergence and consolidation of opposition to Porfirio Díaz's dictatorship in Mexico not only visible but unavoidable.

Shifting away from U.S.-dominant and Cuban national perspectives also allows us to see and appreciate an important contribution made by Cuban migrants and the Latin Americans who stood in solidarity with them, a contribution measurable not in financial terms so much as ideological ones, and made not only to revolutionary Cuba, but to the Americas generally. As Cubans and Mexicans joined hands and conjoined their struggles, they expressed a commitment to fighting imperialism, oppression, and inequality across borders in the Americas, affirming a deep and enduring *americanismo* that can, and should, inspire our common struggles in this hemisphere well into the future.

1 Nineteenth-Century Cuban Migrants in the Gulf World

In March of 1897, Gabriel López García arrived to the bustling port city of Veracruz, Mexico. In the preceding two years he had left his home in Cuba for foreign shores not once but twice, due to the war of Cuban independence. Gabriel joined the revolutionary movement in 1894 in his home province of Pinar del Rio. When the revolutionary plot in which he was involved was discovered, he fled to Tampa, Florida, to evade capture by Spanish colonial authorities. Tampa and Key West were hotbeds of revolution at the time, where Cuban migrants gathered arms for the insurgents and outfitted filibustering expeditions to transport supplies to Cuba. On 12 March 1896, the Three Friends expedition left Jacksonville, Florida, under the command of insurgent general Enrique Collazo, with Gabriel on board. The expedition landed safely several days later, delivering a full load of men, arms, and munitions in the province of Matanzas.[1] Instead of remaining with Collazo and his men, Gabriel made his way to Pinar del Rio soon after the insurgents made landfall, intent on joining Antonio Maceo, the Cuban general who was leading the revolution in that province. Changing between insurgent companies numerous times to achieve his objective, Gabriel finally arrived at the Spanish military line that separated Cuba's westernmost province from the rest of the island. Extensive reconnaissance proved the line to be uncrossable except by sea. Frustrated, Gabriel turned back toward the capital, Havana, where he took a civilian position within the revolutionary movement. Gabriel's dreams of military glory were foiled, and he was unable to thrive in a civilian position, where he butted heads with his superiors, so he left Cuba again, this time to return to the family he had left in Tampa.[2] Cuba, though, had changed radically since Gabriel's first departure in 1894. Between 1894 and 1897, the island had been ravaged by a remarkably destructive war that had dislocated hundreds of thousands of civilians. In 1897, Spanish general Valeriano Weyler y Nicolau was desperate to crush the insurgency, but victory eluded him. Keenly aware that Cubans just across the straits were redoubling their commitment to fuel the revolution, Weyler watched maritime traffic between Florida and Cuba closely. For this reason, Gabriel chose to depart for Veracruz rather than Tampa in 1897, and he knew that he would find his way east before long.

Gabriel López García's story illustrates how nineteenth-century Cuban exiles and migrants concentrated in the Gulf World shaped the Cuban independence process and were, in turn, shaped by the Cuban independence wars. This chapter explores the relationship between Cuban independence, war, exile, and migration in the context of the nineteenth-century Gulf World. During the nineteenth century and especially during the three decades of the Cuban independence process (between 1868 and 1898), Cubans made their way to near and distant shores as migrants, exiles, and refugees. Cubans could be found as far north as Buffalo, New York; as far south as Buenos Aires, Argentina; as far east as Paris, France; and as far west as the State of Oaxaca in Mexico. They could be found in centers and hubs in the greater Caribbean by the thousands and in farther removed locations like the northern mining region of Chile in small handfuls. Although Cuban migrations were Atlantic in scope, the Gulf World was the critical center of Cuban revolutionary activity in the nineteenth century.

After a brief exploration of the Gulf World as a uniquely connected region sutured together by centuries of circulation, this chapter examines the long history of Cuban political exile, beginning in the 1820s. The decades of the 1820s through the 1850s saw the migration of small groups of generally, although not exclusively, elite Cubans. During the thirty-year Cuban independence conflict, tens of thousands of Cuban men, women, and children, rich and poor, black and white, left the island. Some left looking for temporary refuge, while others hoped to build new lives and leave old ones behind. Still others used the space of exile as ground on which to prepare revolution, irreverently crossing and recrossing national and imperial borders and legally and illegally remapping the Gulf in new ways. During the Ten Years' War, which spanned 1868 to 1878, Cubans abroad created and sustained migrant centers across the Americas. When war erupted again in 1895, new migrants were welcomed in established communities.

The final section of this chapter focuses on the 1895 War, with a close look at the relationship between war and migration. The unique brutality of the 1895 conflict and its short duration distinguished it from the Ten Years' War. Tens of thousands of Cubans abandoned Cuba in the peak years of the conflict, especially in 1896 when General Weyler's reconcentration policies went into force. By analyzing the cases of 200 Cuban exiles, refugees, and migrants in this chapter and placing them in relation to the spatial and temporal geography of the 1895 War, we can see how the military strategies of both insurgents and royalists shaped internal and external Cuban migrations, resulting in their exodus and determining to some degree their destinations.[3] The conditions of the 1895 War, the emergence of an ever more connected Gulf World, and the existence of long-standing communities of Cuban migrants fundamentally defined the character of Cuban migration during the 1890s. As we will see in subsequent chapters, it also shaped the evolution of Cuban migrant communities in the Gulf and the development of their revolutionary politics.

The Gulf World

The Gulf World, extending from the Straits of Florida to those of Yucatán, bordered on the north side and on the southeast by what are today the states of the U.S. Gulf South, on the west by the Gulf coast states of Mexico, and on the south side by the western portion of the island of Cuba, has been a space of exchange and connection for centuries. Long before the Europeans arrived in the New World, native groups—among them the Maya, Arawaks, and Caribs—explored, navigated, and established trade from the Orinoco to the Gulf of Honduras and out into the Gulf of Mexico.[4] A recent study by archeologists suggests the strong possibility that on the other side of the Gulf native inhabitants of the Florida peninsula developed networks of exchange between the mainland and the island of Cuba.[5]

Columbus's voyages and the age of discovery they inaugurated changed the character of the Gulf and made it a key region in an emerging Ibero-Atlantic world. Within half a century, the Gulf of Mexico was dominated by Spain, which had established the sprawling viceroyalty of New Spain, an administrative unit that included what is today Mexico, the U.S. Southwest, California, Florida, Cuba, Puerto Rico, Hispañola, the Philippines, Central America north of Panama and parts of Venezuela. The Spanish presence in the Gulf radically restructured old pre-Columbian trade routes. The port cities of Havana and Veracruz became critical hubs in Spain's transatlantic economy during the sixteenth century, as ships moving between the ports transported goods to and from the Americas and Spain. But even as Spain drew the Gulf into an emerging Atlantic world, it also facilitated the creation of new interregional dynamics. The intercolonial trade that ran parallel to the transatlantic trade resulted in myriad exchanges between the island colony of Cuba and the mainland of New Spain throughout the sixteenth, seventeenth, eighteenth, and early nineteenth centuries.[6] For example, there are records of boats bringing contraband trade goods to

Cuba from Campeche as early as 1520.[7] More than 370 years later, the Spanish foreign minister and Spain's consuls in Mexico would complain of the small fishing vessels called *viveros* that plied the poorly defined and even more poorly patrolled waters between Yucatán and Cuba's coasts, running men and supplies to the insurgents in Cuba.[8]

Between the late seventeenth and eighteenth centuries the Gulf World changed again as imperial competition chipped away at Spanish hegemony. The French founded Louisiana at the end of the 1690s. Established in 1718, New Orleans would quickly become one of the most dynamic ports in the Gulf World.[9] Meanwhile, the British had been expanding their presence in the new world at Spain's expense throughout much of the seventeenth century. After establishing colonies along the eastern seaboard of North America, between 1607 and 1732, they took Jamaica from the Spanish in 1655, and several other island territories as well. During the Seven Years' War, which ended in 1763, Britain occupied Havana, holding Spain's most important western port hostage until the conclusion of the war, when, by the terms of the treaty of Paris, Britain returned Havana in exchange for control of Florida. Among other territories, Britain also gained the eastern part of Louisiana from the French. At this time, France gave Spain Louisiana west of the Mississippi in order to avoid a complete British takeover. New Orleans as a city grew under Spanish dominance and cultural and commercial connections between the new mainland colony and Spain's colonies in Mexico and Cuba intensified.[10] The Spanish period in Louisiana lasted a mere forty years, and in 1802 the colony was reclaimed by the French and promptly sold to the United States. By the end of the eighteenth century, the Gulf of Mexico, once a Spanish lake, was contested by three imperial rivals and one nascent republic.

During the first half of the nineteenth century, anticolonial wars and processes of emancipation fundamentally reshaped the Gulf World again. The independence of Britain's North American colonies in the 1770s was followed by the independence of much of Latin America between 1800 and the 1820s. By the mid-nineteenth century, British, Spanish, and French empires in the Americas had been greatly reduced, and the fledgling United States of America had secured a dominant presence in the Gulf. The new nation of Mexico still controlled the westernmost portion of the Gulf up through Texas, although it would lose this territory to the United States in the Mexican American War. Cuba was greatly coveted by the United States, which made numerous attempts to acquire the island while blocking several plots organized by Latin American states to liberate it. U.S. imperialists saw the

Gulf of Mexico as an American lake and the Gulf Region as an "American Mediterranean" throughout which the United States would project its power. For Southerners intent on preserving slavery, the "American Mediterranean" shone as a promised land, especially before and during the Civil War.[11] Just as slave masters leaving Haiti in the wake of revolution envisioned the U.S. South as their salvation as they sought the best way to secure their personal fortunes and way of life, U.S. Southern slave masters looked to Cuba during and after the Civil War. Some of them even absconded with freemen, women, and children they anticipated re-enslaving.[12] The Gulf in the age of emancipation was crossed and recrossed by those intent on preserving slavery, but it also offered refuge to those escaping it and to those who, after emancipation, sought rights and dignity.[13] Slaves in British territories found their way to Spanish Florida, seeking greater freedom in the eighteenth century, and freedmen and women in Florida traveled further south to Cuba to preserve their freedom when the territory became part of the United States in 1821.[14] Simultaneously, slaves in the United States left Texas and Louisiana for Mexico after the abolition of slavery there in 1829.[15]

As of 1850, advances in steamship technology and the demands of the second industrial revolution, which intensified in the second half of the nineteenth century, led to the multiplication of trade and transportation networks in the Gulf World. U.S. shipping companies were the most numerous, but British, French, Spanish, Danish, and Mexican companies stationed agents at key Gulf ports, including but not limited to New Orleans, Havana, and Veracruz.[16] Although the export and import of material goods was their primary business, steamships increasingly began to transport passengers, among them migrants of many kinds—some free and some not so free.[17]

Claimed, lost, reclaimed, and contested by diverse European powers and countries in the Americas for centuries, the Gulf World has always been home to communities of peoples who have lived cross-border lives, from the Arawaks and Caribs who navigated and explored the Gulf of Honduras and crossed into the Gulf of Mexico, to the native Floridians who sent commissions to Cuba during the Spanish colonial period, to the fishermen who lay claim to the waters between Pinar del Rio and Campeche for nearly four hundred years, to the free and enslaved people of color who fled across borders in the Gulf World looking for freedom and dignity in the nineteenth century, to the itinerant Cuban revolutionaries who traveled as exiles, migrants or stowaways. The people of the Gulf World, exiles, refugees, runaways, and migrants, took possession of a region linked by centuries of dense connections and made it their own, appropriating established routes and paving new ones, often circuitous, sometimes counterintuitive.

Nineteenth-Century Cuban Exiles and Migrants in the Gulf World

Historian Henry Kamen has argued that exile is and always has been a fundamental pillar of Spanish society, which has for centuries defined itself through exclusion rather than inclusion.[18] Beginning in the eighth century with the expulsions of Jews and Muslims and continuing throughout the twentieth century, Spain has routinely removed those it deemed heretics or dissidents. Spaniards carried this practice with them to the Americas in the fifteenth century, and it left an indelible mark not only on the Spanish colonies but also on the societies that emerged after the dissolution of the Spanish Empire in the early nineteenth century. Indeed, exile became a fundamentally distinguishing characteristic of Latin American culture and politics.[19] Although not independent until later in the nineteenth century, Cuba was no exception in Latin America. In some ways, Spain's nineteenth-century colonies offer the best example of the use of translocation as a strategy to remove dissidents from the body politic. Throughout the nineteenth century, dissidents and rebels from Cuba and Puerto Rico were continually banished, sent back to Spain, to Spain's penal colonies in Africa, or elsewhere in Latin America, especially Mexico. To the exiled and deported we must add those who self-exiled for political reasons, those fleeing successive wars as refugees, and those who became migrants seeking employment abroad when work at home was scarce. The nineteenth century in Cuba was defined in large part by the struggle to resolve Cuba's colonial crisis. This crisis stimulated an unprecedented exodus of Cubans from the island; the vast majority of these migrant Cubans found temporary refuge in the Gulf World along Mexico's Gulf Coast or in the southern United States. Mexico had long been connected to Cuba, from the earliest days of the Spanish colonial period, and Cuba's dependence on the United States grew steadily from the late eighteenth century forward. Thus it is no surprise that these two countries became centers of Cuban migrant life and revolutionary activity. However, historical studies of Cuban migrants persistently look at the migrations within a frame limited to the United States and Cuba. Viewed from the vantage point of an integrated Gulf World, the breadth, diversity, and connectedness of Cuban migrations and their diasporic cross-border revolutionary activity from the 1820s forward come into

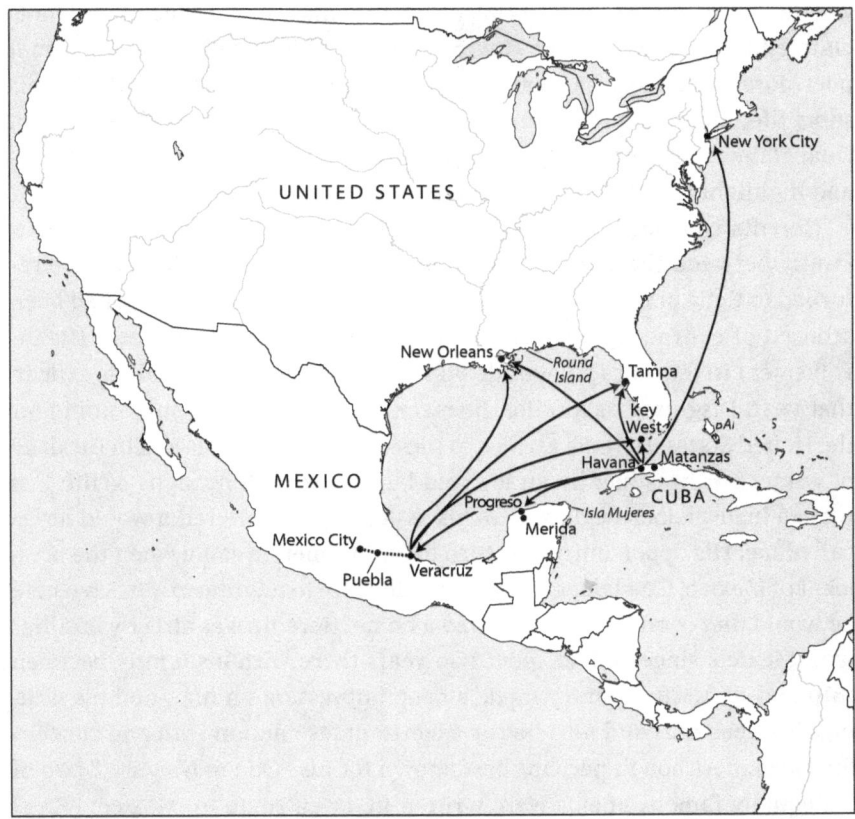

MAP 1.1 Major migratory routes of nineteenth-century Cuban émigrés in the Gulf World

sharp relief. Map 1.1 depicts the more common migratory routes of Cubans who traveled to, from, and between Cuba, Mexico and the United States.

José María Heredia, Latin America's first romantic poet, is one of the two most notable and recognized Cuban political exiles of the early nineteenth century. He was forced to leave Cuba in 1823 for his participation in the Soles y Rayos de Bolivar conspiracy, which aimed to liberate Cuba. Another exile is Felix Varela, who was sentenced to death in that same year for advocating for the independence of Latin America and the abolition of slavery in Cuba. Varela and Heredia both lived as exiles in the United States. Varela has the distinction of having established the first Spanish language newspaper in the United States, while Heredia is known as the "Cantor de Niagara" for his poem by this name, which immortalized Niagara Falls. While his time in the United States was formative, Heredia's time in Mexico was far more important in terms of his life and work. In fact, Heredia is claimed today by Cuba and Mexico, both of which see him as a national poet. José María Heredia spent a total of sixteen years in Mexico during his short life, married a Mexican woman, and died and is buried in Mexico. Dual claims to the poet signal the profound impact he had in both nations and highlight his life lived between two *patrias*.

Heredia was born in Cuba, but spent his childhood traveling with his family between the Dominican Republic, Venezuela, and Mexico. He returned to Cuba in 1821, but his stay was short. Within two years he had been accused of conspiring against Spain and was sentenced to death. His involvement in the Soles y Rayos de Bolivar conspiracy motivated his exile in that year. Disguised as a sailor, he made his way aboard a ship sailing for the United States. Heredia arrived to the coasts of Massachusetts in the dead of winter and was met by an icy cold landscape with no signs of life.[20] It was an inauspicious beginning to his exile, in a place Heredia would never call home. His opportunity to return to Latin America came when the president of Mexico, Guadalupe Victoria, invited him to migrate to Mexico where he would find community, work, and a home. Heredia was already familiar with Mexico, since he had spent two years there with his family between 1819 and 1821. The country made a deep impression on him, and his writings between 1821 and 1823 betray a constant fascination with and concern for Mexico. Although perhaps best known for his "Ode to Niagara," two of his equally famous poems were written in, or en route to, Mexico: "En el Teocalli de Cholula" (1820) and "El Himno del Desterrado" (1825), the latter composed as he traveled from New York to Veracruz and caught sight of the coasts of his beloved Cuba.

Between 1825 and his death in 1836, Heredia lived in Mexico and served in numerous government positions, working at one point as the secretary of Antonio López de Santa Ana. Although Mexico was his home, Heredia remained connected to Cuba. He played a key role in the creation of the Junta Promotora de la Libertad de Cuba, an organization founded in 1825 to promote Cuban independence.[21] The Junta was closely tied to the Xalapa-based secret society, the Gran Legión del Águila Negra, which set the independence of Cuba as its goal. In the early nineteenth century, Xalapa, although forty miles from the sea, was intimately connected to the Gulf of Mexico and the Atlantic World.[22] Thus, Heredia continued to be associated with efforts to liberate his homeland. The outpouring of grief in Mexico after his premature death in 1836 included numerous statements claiming Heredia as a son of Mexico. One Mexican journalist quipped that in her tribute to

Heredia, Gertrudis Gómez de Avellaneda, the poet and future author of Cuba's first antislavery novel, *Sab*, simply stated that it was a shame that he died on foreign soil, failing to mention the importance of Mexico in his life.[23]

Soon after the inauguration of the first republic in Cuba in 1901, a controversy about the exact location of Heredia's remains erupted in Cuba. As the Cuban republic emerged from the ashes of war and intervention, Cuban nationalists immediately set about recovering Cuba's *historia patria*. Heredia was one of Cuba's early and most famous revolutionaries, and recovering his remains became an obsession in the early twentieth century. There were three possible cemeteries in Mexico where the poet's remains might be. Shortly after his death, Heredia's wife had had her husband's remains moved from his first resting place in the cemetery of Nuestra Señora de los Angeles to the cemetery of Santa Paula. The family then returned to Cuba. Since there wasn't any kin to call upon, Heredia's remains were mixed with those of other deceased when the Santa Paula cemetery was closed. The remains were then moved to a cemetery in Tepeyac, north of the city center.[24] In 1844, José Maria Heredia's mother made an effort to repatriate her son's remains, but the Spanish colonial government, which in that tumultuous year had no interest in permitting the return of the ashes of a revolutionary figure of that stature, refused. Had she been successful, perhaps the controversy would have never erupted, for at that point Heredia's remains were still in the Santa Paula cemetery. Heredia remained in exile after his death as he did in life, unable to return to his beloved Cuba. As Cubans looked to reclaim their national heroes after independence, the lack of certainty regarding Heredia's final resting place was deeply troubling. Yet, the fact that Heredia remained in Mexico, the land he adopted as his own, is also fitting. As Cuban poet and journalist José Manuel Carbonell said in a speech given in Mexico in honor of Heredia in 1926, "José Maria Heredia . . . served and honored Mexico with same burning passion with which he served his own nation . . . [In Mexico] he found Glory. He fought, he sang, he loved. He exhaled his last breath. He enveloped . . . in his gaze both the fatherland of his birth . . . and the beloved adopted nation that bade him drink from its fragrant fraternal cup."[25]

The United States and Mexico were also key destinations for Cubans exiled from the island in the 1840 and 1850s. During the 1840s Cuba was rocked by numerous slave rebellions and anticolonial conspiracies, which were met with brutal repression. Given the climate of instability in Cuba, colonial authorities had good reason to deny the request of Heredia's mother to repatriate his remains. The return of a native son and revolutionary could only spell trouble. The colonial response to deep unrest brought widespread censorship and repression that affected all classes and resulted in both voluntary and forced exile of suspected dissidents. Cuban elites like Cirilo Villaverde, Juan Clemente Zenea, Gaspar Betancourt Cisneros, and Pedro Santacilia were among the most prominent exiles who established themselves in the United States during these decades. This group of white elites in exile was defined by their strong stance against Spanish colonialism, but most of them remained either proslavery, or indifferent to the question of slavery. Another seemingly contradictory characteristic of these advocates for independence was their support for the U.S. annexation of Cuba.[26] The most radical wing of the annexationist movement was composed of Cuban migrants who were deeply allied with the interests of the master class in the U.S. South and who supported the extension and preservation of the institution of slavery in a time of emancipation.[27] The crowning achievements for the alliance between Cuban exiles and Southern planters were the famous filibustering expeditions of Narciso López. Other Cuban annexationists, Pedro Santacilia among them, were less drawn to Southern planters, and their annexationism was tied to their admiration of modernization in the United States. With the close and ever-growing economic relationship between the United States and Cuba, annexation to them seemed to be a natural step.

Like José María Heredia, Pedro Santacilia, is known principally for his literary works published in the United States, especially "El Arpa del proscrito" and "El Laúd del desterrado," which appeared in print in the New York in the 1850s. However, his actions in the realm of politics are equally fascinating and direct attention toward the Gulf. Although Santacilia collaborated with and supported projects that aimed to annex Cuba to the United States in the early 1850s, like the filibustering expedition of Narciso López, his political inclinations began to change when he moved to New Orleans in 1853. He came to embrace full independence for Cuba, including a stance against slavery. In New Orleans, Pedro Santacilia met Benito Juárez, who was in exile and preparing to return to Mexico to challenge the conservative regime that had ousted him. The two men developed a close relationship that lasted a lifetime. Santacilia supported Juárez remotely by supplying him with arms against Mexican conservatives during the civil war. Later, in 1861, Santacilia joined Juárez in Mexico, eventually securing a position as his personal secretary. Personal ties were joined to political ones when Santacilia married Juárez's oldest daughter. Pedro Santacilia remained loyal to his father-in-law throughout the struggle against the French occupation of Mexico in the mid-1860s, and he defended Juárez's legacy until his own death in 1910. Santacilia was not alone in his admiration for Juárez and Mexico's liberal struggle. Two of the most prominent Cuban exiles in Mexico at the time, Rafael and Manuel Quesada, fought alongside Juárez in Mexico's civil wars, achieving distinction and being rewarded with promotions in the Mexican army.[28] During Cuba's first independence war, which erupted in 1868, Manuel was named general-in-chief of the insurgent army by Carlos Manuel de Céspedes. The brothers would be remembered in Cuba as the "Juarista Generals."[29]

Santacilia and the Quesada brothers never abandoned their commitment to the liberation of Cuba from colonial rule. They advocated and fought vigorously for Cuban independence, especially during the Ten Years' War, which erupted in 1868, one year after the Mexican Liberals' ousting of Maximilian. It was easy to draw parallels between Mexico's fight to dislodge a European monarchy and Cuba's fight against colonial Spain, as both were seen as struggles against European dominance in the Americas. It is beyond a doubt that Pedro Santacilia played a role in convincing Juárez to open Mexico's ports to Cuban insurgent vessels at that time. Thus, although scholars focus centrally on Santacilia's intellectual production during his exile in the United States, his time in and connections with Mexico as well as his active diplomacy in that country reveal that Santacilia was, like Heredia, a figure who moved through the Gulf World between ports like Havana, New Orleans, and Veracruz, drawing them together in webs of political and revolutionary intrigue.[30]

Men like Heredia and Santacilia were not the only Cubans circulating between Cuba, Mexico, and the United States and making alliances in the first half of the nineteenth century. From the 1812 Aponte uprising forward, rebels accused of conspiring against Spanish colonial authority or against the institution of slavery in Cuba were subjected to execution or forced deportation. Deportation was often a death sentence; victims languished in colonial prisons in Spanish colonial Florida or Spanish Africa.[31] The near-constant slave uprisings during the 1840s in Cuba caused a hardening of the colonial regime there. Spanish authorities targeted not only slaves and free people of color suspected of participating in uprisings but also white Creoles who were critical of the colonial regime. As we have seen, prominent men of letters like Villaverde, Santacilia, Tolón, Betancourt Cisneros, and others fled Cuba as a result of the harsh climate of repression that affected all classes. But, among those deported or pressured to leave Cuba in this period, we find the fascinating cases of 416 free men of color who relocated to Mexico.[32] Michele Reid-Vázquez details how, in the aftermath of the Escalera, an alleged conspiracy to end slavery and colonial rule in Cuba, thousands of free and enslaved Afro-Cubans were tortured, executed, deported, and incarcerated. Captain General Leopoldo O'Donnell devised a strategy to ensure the long-term stability of Cuba by offering free passage and documents to any free Cubans of color who wished to leave the island. Scholars estimate that 739 individuals availed themselves of this option, and 416 of these chose Mexico as their destination. Far fewer chose to relocate to the United States. Mexico had abolished slavery in 1829 and was perceived as a society more amenable to individuals of African descent, as the cases of slaves escaping the United States from Texas and Louisiana bound for Mexico in the late 1830s demonstrate.[33] Both U.S. and Spanish officials expected the Mexican government to cooperate by returning slaves in the case of runaways or by interning free Cubans in the case of O'Donnell's expatriates. While Mexican officials offered partial compliance with internment of the Cubans, they refused on principle to return runaway slaves to the United States.

It is harder to glean why the forty or so freemen who settled in the United States would chose a republic where slavery persisted over Mexico, but it may have to do with their financial resources and political aspirations. The migrants had significant financial resources and forged broad connections that spanned New York, New Orleans, Philadelphia, and Baltimore. Although evidence of connections between white elite Cuban exiles and the Cuban free men of color who relocated to the United States in the 1840s is sparse, historians speculate that the different groups collaborated at some level.[34] Spanish authorities in the United States and Mexico enacted close vigilance of exiled free men of color, convinced that they were conspiring against colonialism and slavery from afar.

The clandestine Cuban networks linking Louisiana, Veracruz, and Florida were particularly dense from the 1840s forward, but the conditions were not ripe for armed struggle until the 1860s. The Grito de Yara, issued by Carlos Manuel de Céspedes, inaugurated the first Cuban independence war. The Ten Years' War was a drawn-out conflict that never succeeded in spreading rebellion beyond Cuba's eastern provinces. The timorous attitude of the Creole elites at the helm was, in large part, to blame. Ultimately, the Creole leadership was looking for a path to reform, not radical social change. They hoped to convince the western sugar planters to join them by promising to protect their material and human property, but the western planters remained suspicious of their eastern counterparts, and so they remained loyal to the colonial regime. The insurgency gradually diminished and was brought to a conclusion with the Pact of Zanjón, which promised colonial reform. While some insurgents, exhausted and demoralized by the war, jumped at the chance to work toward reform, others, angry and determined, abandoned Cuba for exile where they would prepare another rebellion.

Cubans left during and after the Ten Years' War as political exiles and migrants. While the wealthiest settled in Europe, and middle-class and professional Cubans migrated to cities like New York, Boston, Philadelphia, Mexico City, and Puebla, Cubans of less means looked for refuge along the coasts of the Gulf of Mexico in cities like Tampa, Key West, New Orleans, Veracruz, and Mérida, among others. In her comparative history of Louisiana and Cuba, Rebecca Scott underscores the importance of the city of New Orleans for Cuban migrants. During the 1880s, insurgent generals Antonio Maceo and Máximo Gómez traveled to the city to gather support for the revolution. She surmises that African American activists struggling to secure and defend basic civil, political, and public rights may have crossed paths with the great generals, whose choice to stay together in the same lodging must have created a stir in a deeply segregated society.[35] Cities along the Gulf like Matamoros and Veracruz were home to some of the oldest Cuban *juntas*, established in 1868 and 1870 respectively. In their naturalization records, Cubans who sought Mexican citizenship in this period often referred to Mexico's liberal laws and institutions and to the ability to live freely under these laws as reason for their migration to Mexico. However, not all of these migrants were revolutionary activists. Many Cubans, desperate to find a way to make a living, were driven into exile by the length and intensity of the Ten Years' War, the shorter Guerra Chiquita (1879–1880), and the economic crisis, which brought crushing unemployment and empty promises of reform. As we will see in subsequent chapters, new Cuban communities were established and old communities were nourished by the wars and by economic conditions in Cuba that brought new migrants. These communities, especially those in the Gulf, became increasingly connected to each other as migrants used the vast trade and transport networks of the region to move between migrant centers and to establish and nurture connections.

The Ten Years' War of Cuban independence may have ended in a pact at Zanjón, but Cuban separatist activities in the Gulf continued without interruption. Furthermore, during the 1880s and 1890s, Cuban communities swelled as economic migrants fleeing the vagaries of the Cuban economy joined refugees and exiles. Thousands of cigar workers in particular moved to Florida looking for work during the last two decades of the nineteenth century. So close were the linkages between cigar workers in Florida and western Cuba that Louis Perez has referred to them as belonging to a "single universe."[36] Spanish consuls kept close tabs on growing migrant communities and on the exile networks that linked them, increasingly aware that a formidable threat to the colony's stability was coalescing outside of its borders. In Mexico, Cubans like Nicolás Domínguez Cowan, future regional head of the Cuban Revolutionary Party in Mexico, Andrés Clemente Vázquez, the man who would be Mexican consul in Havana during the 1895 War, and Emilio Núñez, the Ten Years' War general, were among those closely surveilled by Spanish and Mexican authorities throughout the 1880s and 1890s.[37]

Often the activities of exiles and insurgents seemed benign enough, but then again, the ability of the insurgents to maneuver and advance their struggle in the Gulf World often exceeded the capacities of the Spanish to deter them. More revolutionary plots and filibustering expeditions failed than succeeded, but the Spanish cannot be given credit for their undoing. Financial, environmental, or political obstacles were more significant. Yet, Cubans persisted and they collaborated across borders. In Veracruz, for example, the efforts of Cuban patriot general Angel Maestre to launch a filibustering expedition from Veracruz with a boat acquired in New Orleans in the mid-1880s caught the attention of the leader of the insurgent army, General Máximo Gómez, who sent General Antonio Maceo to Mexico in 1884 to support Maestre's mission.[38] Maceo traveled to Mexico and established contact with Maestre, founded revolutionary clubs, and collected funds for the revolution.[39] He even boldly sought official governmental support and an audience with Mexico's president Porfirio Díaz, but failed in the endeavor.

Díaz may not have agreed to sit down with that Cuban rebel, but he accepted the invitation of another in 1894, shortly before the outbreak of the final independence war. It wasn't José Martí's first time in Mexico. Like José María Heredia and Pedro Santacilia, Martí is still mostly recognized for the time he spent in the United States and the influence of that country on his political thinking and his literary works. Also like these men, Martí had deep and intimate connections to Mexico, where he spent formative years of his life. Martí was firm in his faith in Cuban communities in Mexico. Notably, he called Veracruz the "fraternal home of all Cuban pilgrims" and insisted that "there are no Cubans more worthy than those of Veracruz."[40] Indeed, Mexico was of particular importance in shaping Martí's thinking, as we will see in a later chapter.

Martí traveled to Mexico in the mid-1870s, when he spent two years living there, and again in 1894, when he came to Mexico for a short, strategic visit. In the earlier period, he came to Mexico to join his family that had fled Cuba for safer shores. Martí's two-year stay in Mexico City was one of many first encounters. While Martí had written and published articles in newspapers before, it was in Mexico that he became a journalist. The young Cuban had certainly cast a critical eye toward the United States, but it was in Mexico that he became an anti-imperialist. Finally, despite his deep knowledge of the history of the Americas, it was in Mexico that Martí first discovered Latin America.[41] After his departure in 1876, Martí did not return to Mexico until 1894, when, as leader of the Cuban Revolutionary Party, he came on official business, seeking the direct support of Mexico's president Porfirio Díaz for Cuba's revolutionary struggle, as Maceo had done some years earlier. Drawing from his predecessors' examples and also from a deep well of collective and collaborative traditions, Martí called for the unity of Latin America in defense of Cuban independence, convinced that unity in Latin America was indispensable to inhibiting the advance of the "giant in seven-league boots." If unity was critical, however, so was speed. Cuba had to win its independence in a short and effective war. That war broke out in 1895, and Martí was among the first casualties. Curiously, Martí's parting words—in the last letter he wrote before his death in battle in 1895—include a longing and hopeful reference to Mexico, and the role the republic might play in Cuba's future.

The story of Gabriel López García that opens this chapter reminds us that by 1894 Cuban exile networks were established enough to give rise to the revolutionary initiative that Martí and others were crafting, an initiative that would emanate from outside Cuba. So important were the exile communities in the Gulf World that when the revolutionary uprising Gabriel was involved in failed in 1894, he sought cover not in mountains or in the Cuban *manigua* but in Florida, a safer and perhaps even more strategic place from which to launch another revolutionary strike. The transnational dimensions of Cuban independence would encompass far more than the United States. By 1897, when Gabriel departed from Cuba a second time, the island had been thoroughly ravaged by war. After struggling unsuccessfully to find a place in the revolution in a new context, Gabriel made the decision to return to Tampa and to his family. The route to Tampa passed through Veracruz for Gabriel and for many other insurgents and migrants in that year. In the 1895 War, insurgents like Gabriel drew on a decades-long tradition of cross-border organizing, relying on the structures, institutions, and communities that their countrymen and women had established and maintained since the early decades of the nineteenth century. For migrants leaving Cuba during the 1890s, cities like Veracruz, Tampa, Key West, New Orleans, and others in the Gulf World were imaginable destinations, places where Cubans were confident they would find communities they could depend on and where they could either bide their time or make lives anew.

The 1895 War

The final war of Cuban independence was officially inaugurated on 24 February 1895, in eastern Cuba. Since the Spanish forces were slow to respond to the uprising, the insurgency spread rapidly, engulfing eastern provinces by the summer of that year. The Spanish colonial authorities had no reason to fear that the 1895 uprising would be any different than the many failed movements in previous decades, including the unsuccessful Ten Years' War. Despite the calm attitude of colonial elites, news of insurgency in the east was frightening Cubans as far away as Havana. Three months after the outbreak of war in 1895, Andrés Clemente Vázquez, the Mexican consul in Havana, wrote, "It is rare the day that I do not receive a petition from a person or family asking me to facilitate their migration to Mexico."[42] So eager were Cubans to leave early in the war, the consul reported, that the city seemed abandoned. By the end of the first year of the war, refugees came pouring onto the city, fleeing nearby towns and provinces. Clemente Vázquez, remembered vividly how refugees—especially women and children desperate to escape the ravages of the war—arrived daily to Havana by train, horse drawn-carriage, or on foot from other areas of western Cuba.[43] In January of 1896, he reported that collections were being taken up to offer some support to the "many people from the surrounding areas that are taking refuge in the capital."[44] Passenger lists for ships entering Mexico during the Cuban war record a spike in the migrations of entire families, especially in the two most intense years of the war, 1896 and 1897.[45]

The War of Cuban Independence of 1895 generated an explosion of the refugee populations, especially in the Gulf of Mexico. The extension of the war engulfed the whole country and the unique brutality of the 1895 conflict, which included "scorched earth" tactics by the insurgents and the Spaniards' equally merciless responses, distinguished it from the Ten Years' War. The conflict drove the wealthy and the poor, including entire families, into exile. Cuban men, women, and children traveled along established routes, and existing Cuban migrant communities around the Gulf of Mexico swelled, causing a meaningful demographic shift. The observations in the following pages are based on the experiences of two hundred Cubans who traveled to Mexico or between Mexico and the United States during the War of Cuban Independence. The voyages and experiences of these migrants are recorded in the files of the National Association of Cuban Revolutionary Émigrés (ANERC), a patriotic organization established in Havana after the war, which recorded information about the departure and arrivals of Cuban migrants. The members of the ANERC were disproportionately professionals and educated elites, so this sample is broadly representative of the experiences of elite migrants, many of whom were highly mobile. That said, a small number of ANERC applicants were tobacco workers and farmers and, though few, their stories are also recovered here and throughout the book.

Exploring Cuban emigration out of Cuba between 1895 and 1898 in the context of the temporal and political geography of the war demonstrates the close relationship between war and emigration in the 1890s. Royalist and insurgent military strategies shaped emigrations out of Cuba and in some cases even determined the destinations to which Cubans traveled. These factors, along with the transportation networks that crisscrossed the region, the historic connection between key port cities, and the history of Cuban circulation within the Gulf World shaped Cuban migrations during Cuba's last independence war.

The documents collected by the ANERC offer a unique opportunity to track the movement of Cuban migrants, both individually and *en masse*. Havana was the most common departure point for Cubans leaving the island after 1895, followed by Matanzas. The most common port of arrival was Veracruz. Tables 1.1 and 1.2 show the distribution of ports of departure and arrival for migrants whose records are preserved in the ANERC files.

The fact that we find a strong relationship between the western ports of Havana and those of Matanzas and other Gulf port cities like Veracruz is not surprising and reflects the extent of the trade and transportation networks that linked these cities. Further evidence of the connection between Havana and Veracruz is found in the fact that in table 1.2, fourteen of the nineteen travelers with multiple destinations spent some time in Veracruz. Furthermore, twenty-five of the two hundred migrants traveled beyond Mexico to other destinations in the Gulf World like Tampa, Key West, New Orleans, and Galveston, although these data are not reflected in the tables above. As we have seen, these Gulf ports were linked by Cubans traveling to and conspiring between them as early as the 1820s.

TABLE 1.1 Place of departure in Cuba, 1895–1898

Place of departure in Cuba	Number of migrants
Havana	101
Matanzas	33
Santa Clara	25
Pinar del Rio	10
Puerto Principe	8
Santiago	5
Unidentified	18
Total	200

Source: Archivo Nacional de Cuba, Donativos y Remisiones, Asociación Nacional de los Emigrados Revolucionarios Cubanos (ANERC).

TABLE 1.2 Place of arrival in Mexico, 1895–1898

Destination in Mexico	Number of migrants
Veracruz	127
Yucatan	32
Mexico City	11
Multiple destinations	19
Other	11
Total	200

Source: Archivo Nacional de Cuba, Donativos y Remisiones, Asociación Nacional de los Emigrados Revolucionarios Cubanos (ANERC).

As with previous periods of migration, Cubans leaving Cuba during the 1895 War were a mix of exiles, refugees, and economic migrants. Ramón Martínez Álvarez, who participated in the failed "la Luz" conspiracy in Matanzas in 1895, reports having been deported. So does Gerónimo Lobe y Figueroa, who was an active revolutionary collaborator in Havana before and during the war. José Castillo Rodríguez was a soldier in the insurgent army who was captured and deported, while Segundo Corvisión y Cabello and Emilio Cancio Bello both indicate that they were forced into exile for their political beliefs and activities.[46] Gabriel López García, whose story opens this chapter, left Cuba first as an insurgent and traveled along the well-worn pathways carved out by other revolutionaries like him. During his second voyage, however, he traveled as a migrant looking to escape Cuba and rejoin his family.

Thus, while insurgents and revolutionaries, many of them influential figures who were part of revolutionary networks, circulated in the Gulf, the vast majority of those traveling were civilians. Of the two hundred cases explored here, only a minority indicated that their migrations were motivated by direct persecution. The majority omitted any explanation of the circumstances that motivated their departures. The dearth of self-identified political exiles in this sample is indicative, because Cubans applying to the ANERC would have had every reason to list their contributions to the revolutionary cause had they made them: involvement in the independence movement before exile only strengthened the cases of Cubans seeking admission to the ANERC.[47] For example, émigré Luis Lagomasino y Alvarez detailed his services to the revolution at length in his application, noting how he had been involved in early conspiracies in Cuba, had served in the insurgent army and been an active revolutionary in Florida before arriving in Mexico in the late 1890s. Men like Guillermo Valdes Coroalles and Gabriel Valdes Pinto, traveled to Mexico first before migrating to Tampa, from where they joined revolutionary expeditions that took them to Cuba as insurgents. They both made sure to include their active participation in the military struggle, but also underscored their revolutionary labors in exile. The existence of so few ANERC members who reported being active revolutionaries upon arrival in exile, alongside the reports of the Mexican consul in Havana that point to the exodus of refugees by the hundreds, provide strong evidence that many Cuban migrants leaving the island fled the war itself.

If Cubans leaving Havana in 1895 and 1896 before the war engulfed the city were either political exiles fleeing persecution or frightened individuals anticipating that war would eventually come to the capital, those who left Santa Clara and Matanzas in those years were more than likely fleeing the conflict, which had already engulfed the province. Santa Clara was the first western province to be affected by the insurgent advance. While minor conspiracies were identified during the early 1890s and small bands of insurgents coalesced in Los Guaos as early as February of 1895, it was in mid-July of that year, when insurgent General Serafín Sánchez's forces landed on the coasts of Santa Clara, that the insurgency gained momentum. Owners and managers of sugar estates in Santa Clara were unnerved by the insurgents' orders to burn down estates whose owners refused to stop grinding cane, but workers on these estates who chose not to join the insurgent ranks were nervous, too, since their livelihoods hung in the balance. The formal arrival of the insurgent army from the east in late fall of 1895 intensified tensions in the region.[48] In November 1895, the insurgents achieved what in the 1860s and 1870s had been impossible: they managed a sustained invasion of western Cuba and crossed the Morón-Júcaro Trocha, the heavily fortified and patrolled military line dividing east and west that had held during the Ten Years' War. The insurgents moved quickly, sweeping westward into Santa Clara and eventually Matanzas, Havana, and Pinar del Rio. The invasion of Santa Clara was a major military achievement for the insurgents. Santa Clara, which produced 40 percent of the island's sugar, was of critical importance to both sides in the conflict, economically, geographically, and strategically. The province quickly became a contested frontier as Spanish forces struggled to push the insurgents back into eastern Cuba.[49]

The dislocation that resulted from the insurgents' policies as Gómez's and Maceo's forces pushed the insurgency westward across the province, and the brutal retaliation of the Spaniards, provided compelling reasons for any individual to leave. This may well have been the case of Mercedes Perlamo de Chirino when she made her way to Havana in 1895. Another migrant who left from Cienfuegos in 1895 described departing on *La Ciudad Condal*, a Spanish steamship. Fernando Echermendia Flores indicated in his AN-ERC file that he had supported the Revolution through his "patriotism and his contributions" in advance of the outbreak of the insurgency, although he did not consider himself a political exile upon departure. In discussing his flight from Cuba, he cited the fact that he belonged to "no armed company" and was thus vulnerable to persecution. By not enlisting, yet still being an insurgent sympathizer, Echermendia Flores worried that he would be vulnerable as a civilian and would not have even the minimal protection that membership in an insurgent company might provide.[50] The Cuban independence war took an incredible toll on the island's civilian population. War is destructive by nature, but during the 1895 War, insurgent and royalist armies pursued policies that intentionally targeted the livelihood and claimed the lives of Cuban civilians.

The Cuban insurgent army included between forty and fifty thousand men at its height. While the presence of Cuban men of color in positions of power within a cross-racial army drew many Afro-Cubans to join the struggle, other Cubans of color were conflicted about the risks and advantages of joining the movement.[51] As Rebecca Scott reminds us, "alongside and within the formal struggle for national independence were thousands of individual struggles for survival."[52] Cuban recruits were nervous about leaving their homes and families, especially during the march westward when they were required to leave known worlds for provinces that were utterly foreign.[53] Indeed, General Gómez knew that Cubans would need to be incentivized, and his "scorched earth" policy was carefully crafted to draw recruits for the insurgent army while depriving the Spanish of critical resources.

Gómez's strategy of burning cane fields and mills to bring Cuba's economy to a halt was especially effective in western Cuba, home to the vast majority of the sugarcane plantations and mills. In 1894, the province of Santa Clara produced one million metric tons of sugar.[54] As "sugarfields became battle fields," Spaniards lost critical resources and civilians were deprived of work and a means of survival.[55] The insurgent army also needed to be fed, and it relied on destitute local populations for sustenance. With no employment, civilians—particularly women, children, and the elderly—had few options. Those who did not join the insurgents either crafted precarious lives on the few remaining functioning sugar estates or on their margins, sought protection in Spanish-controlled towns, or, when possible, left Cuba for safer shores. For those Cuban planters whose fields had not gone up in smoke, making sugar was risky business. Losing even one crop of cane could be the difference between survival and economic collapse. Those who could not accept these financial consequences, or could not afford private guards to protect their estates, fled Cuba.[56] Western Cuba was more thoroughly connected by rail than the east, largely due to the sugar industry. Railroad lines linked agricultural hinterlands to port cities; thus, migrants in Santa Clara, Havana, and Matanzas were able to ride trains (when the tracks were not tactically destroyed by insurgents) as they fled the war.[57]

The reaction to the invading insurgents across Cuba, especially in the west, differed by class, race, and region. The army was largely composed of easterners, most of them Afro-Cubans and poor cane cutters or small farmers. Cubans from the western provinces, where residents were whiter and wealthier, were more likely to see the insurgents as foreign invaders and resist or avoid them. Yet, civilians in neither the west nor the east joined the insurgent army en masse. Many more fled to safety, or tried—and often failed—to stay out of the conflict altogether. By late 1895 and early 1896, Spanish-held towns and cities like Havana, Matanzas, Pinar del Rio, and many others, swelled with refugees. Andrés Clemente Vázquez reported that "the emigration of civilians continues to grow and each steamship takes entire families to Mexican ports."[58] Later that month, the consul again reported a notable rise in the volume of emigration to Mexico and elsewhere. "The migration of the sons of this country (men and women) continues to grow at an extraordinary rate especially to Mexico, New York, New Orleans and Florida," he noted.[59] Vázquez's general observations confirm the importance of the Gulf World as a space of circulation for Cuban migrants.[60] As he contemplated the capital city in June of 1896, the consul described the streets as all but deserted, the theaters closed, and commercial businesses announcing liquidation sales advertised by Cubans desperate to leave the island.[61]

As early as December of 1895, Cubans from Matanzas began arriving in Havana as refugees; they spoke of darkening skies as ashes from burning fields and towns filled the air.[62] Matanzas, like Santa Clara, was particularly devastated by the totality of the war, but this province was doubly ruined by the dissolution of the revolutionary faction after Gómez was forced to fall back to Santa Clara in the spring of 1896. As the insurgency fell apart in Gómez's absence, many insurgents turned to banditry, robbery, and pillage.[63] The combination of the assault on Matanzas and the chaos that ensued after the disbanding of the revolutionary forces likely explains the dramatic rise in emigration of Matanceros to Mexico in that year. While we have no way of knowing exactly how many of these migrants fled the war and how many were fleeing persecution, the sheer devastation visited upon this province provided ample impetus for emigration.

According to Andrés Clemente Vázquez, political persecution and sheer survival were certainly important causes of emigration, but he also believed that there was an additional motivation as of 1896. In one report he described the migrants' motivations as "either a mute protest against Spanish domination, a reaction born of fear and inspired by rumors of the persecutions that General Weyler intends to mete out, or because here they no longer have the means to survive."[64] So, in addition to the economic and political reasons for emigration, Vázquez added the public's fear of one man: General Valeriano Weyler y Nicolau, also known as "the butcher." When it became clear that the then captain-general of Cuba, Arsenio Martínez Campos, was incapable of crushing the insurrection, the Spanish government decided to replace Martínez Campos with General Weyler. Weyler was no stranger to Cuba. In fact, he had led troops against the insurgents in the Ten Years' War and was remembered for his exceptional brutality. The General returned to Cuba eager to face both Gómez and Maceo, formidable adversaries he knew well from the Ten Years' War.

Weyler met the insurgents' military strategies with even more violent policies. Although most infamous for mandating the relocation of civilians into garrisoned towns and concentration camps, Weyler also presided over the mass deportations of individuals who were deemed troublesome. In a move that recalled the policies of Leopoldo O'Donnell, Weyler deported hundreds of Cubans on the mere suspicion of involvement. Others simply fled in terror, for Weyler's reputation for violence and repression preceded him. In the first two months of Weyler's appointment, two thousand Cubans fled for Europe. In February of 1896 alone, another thirteen hundred Cubans fled the island.[65] As a result, many Cuban civilians and some revolutionaries found themselves on ships bound for various exile destinations, the most feared of which were Spain's penal colonies in Africa.[66] Puzzled and visibly distressed by this strategy, Andrés Clemente Vázquez wrote the following in his report on 4 January 1897: "The government of the island of Cuba continues, without hesitation, to deport large numbers of Cubans and Latin Americans who do not demonstrate love for Spain. . . . It makes no sense that the government of Cuba would continue this practice . . . when its newspapers announce that the insurgency has been crushed in Pinar del Rio."[67] Although Vázquez does not record observations about the deportees' socioeconomic class, we know that large numbers of the displaced were Afro-Cubans accused of being *ñañigos*, members of an Afro-Cuban secret society, and tobacco workers with or without revolutionary sympathies. Members of both these groups often found themselves bound for Africa.[68] Detectives working for the chief of police and the civil governor of Havana were charged with the responsibility of rounding up undesirables in the capital city in 1897. Manuel M. Miranda, a revolutionary tobacco worker from Havana, was one of their victims. Just before he was captured, Miranda had finalized arrangements for his escape to Mexico—a destination he would never reach.[69]

None of the 200 ANERC applicants considered here ended up in Spanish Africa. Two migrants indicated how fortunate they were to escape deportation to the Chafarinas Islands or to the island of Fernando Po.[70] Yet it is unlikely that good fortune had much to do with it. There is ample evidence to suggest that more favorable exile destinations were offered to those from wealthy and/or connected families who had important contacts within the Spanish administration. Of those Cubans forcibly deported to Ceuta in Spanish North Africa between 1895 and 1898, 60 percent were peasants or wageworkers.[71] Lisardo Muñoz y Sañudo and Ignacio Martín Arbona y Domínguez both had important royalist connections and thus benefitted from the kind of Spanish translocation practices applied to elites throughout Spanish territories across the Americas during the colonial period. In some cases, Weyler's reign of terror was responsible for a migrant's choice of destination. In the cases of Gabriel López García, Lisardo Muñoz y Sañudo, and José Antonio Caiñas, for example, Weyler's close vigilance of travel between Havana and Florida caused the men to reroute their travels through Veracruz. Explaining his decision to migrate to Mexico, Caiñas wrote, "If I asked for a passport to any destination in the United States I would have been jailed."[72] Recounting the story of his exile in another letter, he explained that Veracruz was a safer choice than any destination in the United States because "the Spaniards take Mexico for their colony" and thus were not quite as vigilant in Mexico.[73] If Veracruz presented less risks, there were also some rewards. All three men knew that dynamic Cuban communities where they could find an insertion existed in Veracruz. They also knew that they could get to Florida from Veracruz. Using intentionally and strategically circuitous routes to navigate the Gulf World was one of many clandestine practices commonly engaged in by Cuban revolutionaries in the nineteenth century.

If Weyler used deportation as a way to control and intimidate his enemies, he used *reconcentración*, the forced relocation of Cuban civilians into garrisoned towns, to ensure their submission. The first *reconcentración* orders were issued for Santiago de Cuba, Puerto Principe, Sancti Spíritus, and Santa Clara. Between October 1896 and January 1897, Weyler issued *reconcentración* orders for Havana, Matanzas, Pinar del Rio, and the rest of Santa Clara. Some 140,000 civilians were reconcentrated in Santa Clara, while historians speculate that in Havana 120,000 civilians were herded together. Available statistics for Matanzas indicate that approximately one hundred thousand were reconcentrated there and another forty-seven thousand in Pinar del Rio.[74] While the numbers are dramatic, *reconcentración* in the western provinces was less devastating than it was in the central province of Santa Clara. John Lawrence Tone argues that this is largely because the Spanish had pacified the western provinces before *reconcentración* was fully implemented. Santa Clara, in contrast, was a hotly contested no-man's-land in 1897, which meant that the impact of war and *reconcentración* was particularly devastating there. By forcing Cubans into camps, garrisoned towns, or out of Cuba altogether, Weyler hoped to starve the insurgency of food, supplies, and recruits.

Migration to Mexico declined during and after 1897 as a result of the combination of insurgent battle tactics and Spanish repression. Reconcentration in particular terrified Cubans, as the reports of the Mexican consul attest. Cuban migrants in Mérida confirmed this observation when they indicated that the rise in emigration to Merida in 1895 and 1896 was directly attributable to "the violent methods used by the Spanish government."[75] Cubans got out while they could. Among those who remained mobile during and after 1897, we find numerous migrants with revolutionary and royalist connections that allowed them to navigate the hostile terrain of war-torn Cuba. Luis Castillo Sánchez, a young man from a family of insurgents, was among those lucky enough to escape at the height of the Spanish crackdown on Santa Clara. He reports being run out of his hometown in 1897, when Spanish authorities mandated the evacuation of all those sympathetic to the insurgency (a precursor to *reconcentración*). Castillo Sánchez left for Havana to join his brother, Brigadier General Adolfo del Castillo y Sánchez, who was leading the offensive in the capital. Unable to serve as a soldier due to chronic illness, the younger Castillo Sánchez purchased a third-class ticket on a steamer bound for Mexico later that year.[76]

If revolutionary connections proved invaluable, royalist connections could prove even more useful. Ignacio Martín Arbona y Domínguez and José Antonio Caiñas both availed themselves of royalist connections to escape Cuba. Arbona was imprisoned in Santa Clara, but was lucky enough to have his prison sentence commuted to exile. He credited his father's royalist contacts for the leniency he experienced after his arrest. Eventually, Arbona made his way to Veracruz.[77] José Antonio Caiñas also escaped Cuba and arrived in Veracruz in 1897. Caiñas was carrying out an important commission near the city of Pinar del Rio when he was caught and imprisoned along with his two sons. Using his contacts with influential Spaniards, he managed to have his and his sons' sentences commuted to exile, just like Arbona. Once freed, he made his way to Havana, easily crossing the Spanish military line that had proven an insurmountable obstacle for Gabriel López García in the same year. Lisardo Muñoz y Sañudo also owed his escape from Pinar del Rio to Spanish connections. He migrated to Mexico, leaving his family in Pinar del Rio sometime in 1897. In his letter he revealed that the only reason he was able to escape Cuba was because he was the nephew of a Spanish official in the civil guard who intervened when he was captured and helped save him from the "claws of Weyler who would have had me exiled to Chafarinas . . . but thanks to those two men, he only exiled me."[78] In sum, the *trocha* was not crossable, except by those who had authorization. While Lopez García, Castillo Sánchez, Caiñas, Muñoz, and Arbona demonstrate the power of revolutionary and royalist connections to facilitate escape from Cuba at just the moment when the island's civilian population was effectively immobilized, their examples also illustrate the triangular connections between Cuba, Mexico, and the United States via the port cities of Havana, Veracruz, and Tampa.

If 1897 saw reduced rates of migration, these were further diminished in 1898. Conditions for emigration were not optimal during these years due to external as well as internal factors. During the summer of 1897, events in Spain altered the fate of Cuba. On 30 July, Spain's prime minister, Antonio Cánovas del Castillo, was assassinated. The assassination allowed the Liberal Party in Spain to regain power, and with it a new plan for handling the Cuban insurgency came to the fore. The government of Práxedes Sagasta made a sincere effort to appease the rebels and end the war by recalling General Weyler and granting Cuba broad autonomy within the Spanish regime. The new government took formal control of Cuba on 1 January 1898, but it was too late. The Cuban revolutionaries, who insisted they would accept nothing short of full independence, organized vigorously in and outside Cuba. The liberal government's recall of Weyler allowed the insurgents an opportunity to regroup and regain strength. To make matters worse for the Spanish, they lost the support of the *integristas*, Spanish residents in Cuba who saw the new course of action as capitulation. They firmly believed in a Spanish military victory and hated the idea of compromising with the rebels. *Integrista* protests, which included attacks on U.S. property, ultimately brought the battleship *Maine* to Havana's harbor in late January. Less than three weeks later, the ship exploded, and two months after that explosion, on 25 April 1898, the United States declared war on Spain.[79]

Both the granting of autonomy and the U.S. declaration of war likely worked to dissuade Cubans from emigrating. Indeed, only two out of two hundred Mexico-bound ANERC applicants left Cuba for Mexico in 1898. By the early months of 1898, *reconcentración* had been revoked, but, ironically, it was the dismantling of the system, which began in November of 1897, that caused the greatest catastrophe. *Reconcentrados* had nowhere to go and no way to feed themselves once they were released, and they died by the thousands. Cuban separatists, who were leaving Cuba in protest of the proclamation of autonomy, would have most likely left at an earlier point in the war. Other Cubans changed sides, reconciling with Spain because they believed that autonomy was a reasonable compromise. Finally once the *Maine* steamed into Havana harbor, most Cubans came to the conclusion that Spain's defeat was assured. Rather than emigrate, large numbers flocked to the insurgent ranks or served as volunteers in the U.S. Army, where the risks were substantially reduced. Ricardo Sirven, a humble Cuban pharmacist residing in Orizaba, Veracruz, offered his services to the Revolution in July of 1898 when he wrote a letter to Tomás Estrada Palma, the leader of the Cuban Revolutionary Party. Sirven stated that he knew the conflict was coming to an end, but he still wanted to volunteer.[80] It is quite likely that some Cuban migrants looking to join the insurgency late in the summer of 1898 were looking either for a paid ticket home or to benefit from veteran status after the war—or perhaps both. While it is possible that a few revolutionaries left Cuba in protest of the U.S. intervention, those who were early critics of the U.S. would have been just as likely to stay in Cuba to push for an end to U.S. military rule as to leave the island. Potential migrants were either too poor and destitute to travel, had changed sides and now favored autonomy, or flocked to the insurgency or the invading army in the eleventh hour.

Conclusion

The Gulf World was dynamically connected in the late nineteenth century. The region had once been dominated by the Spanish empire, but the geopolitics of the Gulf began to change by the end of the seventeenth century. France and Great Britain, in particular, established a firm presence in the region by the end of the eighteenth century. By the nineteenth century, the French presence had receded due to the sale of Louisiana, as had the British presence due to the liberation of the thirteen colonies and the loss of Florida. Across the century, the Gulf World became a space increasingly defined by three processes: the westward expansion of the U.S., the emergence and consolidation of the Mexican state and nation, and the long fight for Cuban independence. As trade and transportation networks expanded across the century, an increasing number of steamships began to transport ever larger numbers of migrants, among them many thousands of Cubans escaping the war-torn island. Isolated handfuls—mostly elite conspirators like Heredia, Santacilia, and Martí—became thousands. Among the broader, more diverse, and lesser-known Cuban migrants, we find the 416 free Cubans of color who relocated to Mexico in the late 1840s, poor insurgents like Gabriel López García, civilians like Fernando Echermendia Flores—the man who "belonged to no armed company"—and women like Mercedes Perlamo de Chirino, who escaped Matanzas's "darkening skies" in late 1895. These migrants and others made their way across the Gulf to established Cuban communities in the United States and Mexico.

Between the 1820s and the 1890s, the pace and character of migration changed in relation to the intensity of Cuban politics and the availability of means of travel. After the 1860s, the number of migrants swelled due to the wars and periodic economic downturns in Cuba, which provided motivation for exodus, while the development of transportation technology, increasing economic opportunities, shifting attitudes toward immigration in receiving countries, and, eventually, the existence of established and thriving Cuban migrant communities drew Cubans to neighboring shores. As Cuban migrant centers in Veracruz, Florida, Louisiana, and other Gulf Coast states were called upon to incorporate waves of often destitute individuals, especially after 1895, racial and socio-economic tensions between Cubans rose, resulting in serious challenges for communities that prided themselves on the maintenance of unity and rigorous adherence to the nationalist cause, which they espoused. These challenges and the character of Cuban migrant communities in Mexico are the subject of the next chapter.

2 Cuban Communities in Late Nineteenth-Century Mexico

When Ignacio Martín Arbona y Domínguez joined the insurgency in January of 1896, Gabriel López Garcia was already in Tampa biding his time and eagerly awaiting the opportunity to return to the field of battle. As fate would have it, it would not be long before Ignacio, too, would find himself at sea. Unlike Gabriel, who had left Cuba voluntarily as an insurgent, Ignacio was forcibly deported after being captured and imprisoned by Spanish forces on 25 December 1896. The young insurgent might have ended up in Spanish West Africa, had it not been for his father's connections with prominent Spanish families in Santa Clara, which worked to his advantage. Ignacio was sent to Puerto Rico instead. He arrived sometime in April. From there he escaped to the Dominican Republic, where he spent two months. A fellow Cuban exile helped him fabricate a passport that allowed him to sneak back into Cuba traveling on the Spanish steamship *Maria Herrera* under the assumed name Antonio. Like Gabriel, Ignacio also found it difficult to rejoin the insurgency when he returned, although for different reasons. By the summer and fall of 1897, the province of Santa Clara, which had been bitterly contested by insurgent and royalist forces, had now also suffered the effects of Weyler's reconcentration policy. With less room to maneuver and worried that he would be apprehended again, Ignacio fled Cuba, this time to Veracruz in October of 1897. Like Gabriel, his ultimate plan was to travel to the United States, but he knew that to travel directly to Florida would be too much of a risk.

In Veracruz, Ignacio was embraced by a vibrant expatriate Cuban community and was offered membership in a Cuban revolutionary club. He spent only a few months in Veracruz before signing up to form part of a crew transporting arms, ammunition, and men to Cuba. This expedition departed Veracruz under the cover of night sometime in the late fall of 1897.[1] A number of complications left the packet boat *Oscar G* and its men stranded off the coast of Round Island, Mississippi. According to Ignacio, the men spent about a month at sea. Ignacio and the other men were eventually taken in by the U.S. Coast Guard and held at Scranton, Mississippi (today Pascagoula), where they remained until the Cuban Revolutionary Party headquarters was contacted. The Party leaders had the men transported to New Orleans, where they were incorporated into volunteer regiments at Camp Corbin, which was located at the fairgrounds "where there were many Cubans and Americans training for the blockade of Cuba and the taking of Santiago."[2] By this time it would have been late February or early March. The battleship *Maine* had exploded in Havana's harbor, killing 261 U.S. sailors and marines and giving the United States a perfect justification to wage war on Spain. As the nation prepared for war, volunteer regiments were mustered and trained in anticipation of the planned invasion of Cuba. At Camp Corbin, however, Ignacio and his close friend and fellow Cuban Mariano Martínez Ruíz decided that they did not feel comfortable pledging allegiance to the U.S. flag. The two men decided to abandon the camp, and, after neatly folding their uniforms, they left the site on foot. Ignacio and Mariano eventually found their way to Bayou Saint John, where they boarded a slow-moving logging barge destined for New Orleans.[3] The Cuban Revolutionary Party leaders in New Orleans put both men on a train to Tampa, from which point they eventually returned to Cuba.

Ignacio's experiences, which included being imprisoned, deported, exiled, shipwrecked, and mustered in the U.S. military, while traveling around the Gulf and the Caribbean on steamships, packet boats, barges, by foot, and by rail, would be incredible if they hadn't been so common. Insurgents like Gabriel, Ignacio, and many others circulated throughout the Gulf region and the Caribbean and became experts at navigating its waters, its transportation networks, and its geopolitical dynamics. The key to these various navigations, though, was not the ingenuity of an individual insurgents like Ignacio, but the resourcefulness of the migrant communities that stood behind them. In Ignacio's case, Cubans affiliated with the revolutionary struggle in Puerto Rico, the Dominican Republic, the United States, and Mexico provided him with everything from food and shelter to passports and train tickets. These migrant communities located throughout the Gulf and the Caribbean were long-standing, multigenerational and multiracial, cross-class, diasporic communities in which politics was at the center of daily life, and they were critical to the Cuban independence struggle.

Between 1895 and 1898, numerous waves of Cuban migrants set their course for Mexico, a place that seemed to offer something to both those escaping revolution and those looking for a place to continue to foment it. This chapter reconstructs critical elements of Mexico's foremost Cuban communities, exploring how they were shaped by race, class, generation, and connectivity. Beyond its attention to large communities, this chapter argues that smaller groups of Cubans and individual, highly mobile travelers were also important to building a diasporic community of émigrés in the Gulf World.

By the 1890s, Cubans established at Veracruz, Mérida, and Mexico City constituted the largest and most politically active communities in Mexico, although smaller concentrations of Cubans up and down the Gulf coast of Mexico and in places like Puebla and Orizaba were also significant. In the United States, sizable communities existed in Florida, Louisiana and New York, although there were a scattering of smaller groups throughout the Gulf and along the Atlantic coast. Numerous factors imparted unique characteristics to each Cuban community located in the Gulf World. Overall, the receptiveness of Gulf states to the migrants and refugees, as well as the length and character of Cuba's independence wars (which gave rise to successive waves of migration), facilitated the development of distinctly multigenerational communities in Mexico and the United States. In both cases, economic opportunities in host countries constrained and facilitated the migration of different groups of migrants at different points and times, but the economic realities of individual migrants leaving Cuba also set the conditions of possibility of their movements. For example, poorer migrants in the United States and Mexico tended to remain in the first port of call in the countries to which they escaped. At the same time, economic opportunities in the tobacco industry in both countries also ensured that larger numbers of working-class Cubans remained in the port cities, while wealthier individuals who were less dependent on factory or agricultural jobs migrated toward the interior of each country or further north to places like New York City and Mexico City.

These communities of Cuban migrants had certain characteristics in common, but they were also distinct from each other. Cuban communities in cities located along Gulf coasts like Veracruz, Mérida, New Orleans, Tampa, and Key West were on the whole larger and more diverse in terms of class and race than their counterparts located in the interior. Mexico City's Cuban migrant community, by contrast, resembled that of New York in its demographic profile more than it did that of Veracruz, which is to say that it was whiter and more elite. Comparing Mexico's major Cuban communities to Cuban communities in the United States reveals some core similarities among communities located in the Gulf and those in the interior, even across national boundaries. Additionally, such a comparison reveals those factors that made Cuban migrant communities in Mexico distinct from those in the United States. Most notably, Cuban migrants in Mexico shared language, history, and, to some degree, culture with their Mexican counterparts. These commonalities made the building of transnational Mexican-Cuban solidarity much easier than building U.S.-Cuban solidarity was in the United States. As we will see in chapter 3, the vast majority of Cuban clubs in Mexico had binational memberships. The fact that the founding members of Cuban clubs in Mexico were often both Mexican and Cuban is strong evidence that the most intimate spaces of Cuban revolutionary politics and organizing in Mexico were wrought through transnational collaboration. Cross-national collaboration certainly existed between Cubans and U.S. Americans at the club level, but it was far less pervasive. In part, this was the effect of cultural and linguistic differences, but it was also due to the fact that in areas where the number of Cuban migrants was significant, the migrants tended to draw on the resources of their own communities rather than reaching out to their U.S. neighbors.

While the experiences of Cubans in the United States and Mexico differed because of culture and language, they were both similar and different with respect to race and class. Of course, the differences in relation to race cannot be overstated. While Cubans struggled with racial tensions both in Mexico and in the United States, Cuban whites in Mexico did not have to defend their own whiteness in the same way that Cubans did in the United States. Similarly, Afro-Cubans in Mexico did not face the same kind of legalized discrimination that Afro-Cubans in the United States had to contend with; overall, the specter of Afro-Cubans involved in integrated associations and sharing social and public spaces with Cuban whites was less disquieting in Mexico than it was in the United States. Yet, racism was prevalent among Mexican elites, as was the notion that the greatest obstacle facing a future independent Cuba was the probability of a black revolution. Indeed, the possibility that Cuba might become another Haiti was as frightening to Mexican elites as it was to U.S. elites. Although in Mexico Cubans were not under pressure to maintain unity in a segregationist society, they did engage in social segregation and certainly worked to portray to Mexican audiences a vision of Cuba that was, if not anti-black, pro-white and pro-elite. At upper-class gatherings of revolutionary patriots in Mexico, poor, black Cubans were not welcome. While they painstakingly conjured an image of *Cuba Libre* securely in the hands of a white elite, Cuban elites in Mexico expressed their disdain for poor, non-white Cubans through subtle exclusions and by attacking their patriotism. By questioning the patriotism of new migrants, who were disproportionally poorer and non-white, Cuban elites in Mexico's Cuban migrant communities found an acceptable language with which to police the boundaries of the revolutionary community and established a hierarchy of membership. So, on the one hand, bonds of culture, language, and history paved the way for extensive cross-national solidarities between Mexicans and Cubans, but, on the other hand, these solidarities were still riven with class distinctions that overlay racial ones in complicated ways.

Cuban communities in Mexico City, Veracruz, and Mérida shared an intimate connection with each other and with their U.S. counterparts as part of a dynamically connected Gulf World, but each city had a different point of entry into the revolutionary struggle, based on its geographical location and the size and character of its migrant populations. Veracruz, for example, was an alternate destination for Cuban insurgents looking to return to Cuba, while Yucatán's remote coasts provided an advantageous location for distressed filibustering expeditions. Mexico City, somewhat more removed from the coast, became a key center of Cuban insurgent diplomacy. Thus, the size, character, and location of a given community of Cuban migrants determined its role in the revolutionary struggle. The same, of course, was true for Cuban communities in the United States, which also played different roles in the revolutionary struggle, depending on geography and the size and character of their Cuban migrant populations.

Although Veracruz, Mérida, and Mexico City are at the heart of this chapter, significant attention is also paid to smaller groups of migrants and lone Cuban travelers who lived along Mexico's Gulf Coast or deeper in the nation's interior. Close consideration of the impact of highly mobile travelers who linked disparate Cuban communities within and beyond Mexico grounds a central contention of this chapter; that travel and circulation between centers of migration within and beyond Mexico shaped the lives of Cuban migrants during the late nineteenth century, from the most famous itinerant revolutionary leaders like José Marti, Antonio Maceo, and Máximo Gómez to the many more unknown and unnamed workers and middle-class migrants and their families who sought refuge abroad in late nineteenth century. Individuals like Ignacio Martín Arbona y Domínguez, whose incredible odyssey begins this chapter, linked three of the most significant centers of Cuban organizing in the Gulf World: Veracruz, New Orleans, and Tampa. Whether they remained in their Gulf port cities of arrival and interacted with a constant stream of arriving migrants or traveled beyond them like Arbona and so many others, most Cubans affiliated with the revolution were meaningfully connected to a highly politicized and active Cuban diaspora.

This chapter takes a close look at the roles that war, diasporic connections, and economic factors played in the evolution of Mexico's Cuban migrant communities into multigenerational, cross-class, cross-race, diasporic communities. The following pages offer a partial profile of Cuban migrant communities in Mexico and explore the characteristics that made them both unique and integral to a dynamically connected Gulf World. This chapter adds letters written by 110 self-identified Cuban revolutionaries to the 200 ANERC files explored in chapter 1. After accounting for overlap between the two sources, these records capture the stories of 298 individual Cubans, and their stories form the basis of this chapter and of those that follow. These 298 Cubans represent a disproportionately elite fraction of the larger population of Cubans in Mexico estimated to have consisted of around 2,700 individuals in 1900, but that was certainly far larger in the previous decade.[4] By complementing personal and semi-official letters and ANERC files with other sources, including newspapers, consular records, and petitions, however, we can catch a glimpse of wider communities and of the internal divisions they struggled with.

Veracruz, "the Key West of Mexico"

Connections

When he traveled to Veracruz in 1897 on a special mission for the Cuban Revolutionary Party, Gonzalo de Quesada called Veracruz the "Key West of Mexico."[5] He was doubtlessly struck by the similarities between the two Gulf port cities teaming with Cuban migrants, awash with Cuban culture, dotted with Cuban businesses, and home to organized and active Cuban revolutionary populations.

This comparison between Veracruz and Key West reflected similarities that stemmed from the geographical location of both port cities in the Gulf of Mexico. Long before Veracruz became associated with the U.S. Florida port city in the minds of Cuban revolutionaries, both Mexico and Florida, as well as the Gulf in between them, were part of the Spanish empire. Veracruz was crucial to the Atlantic economy because it was the city where precious metals from Mexican mines and other goods were loaded onto Spanish vessels for export from the mid-1500s forward. These ships, laden with riches, then traveled through the Florida straits to Spain. Thus, Florida had a certain geostrategic significance for Spain because of its location at the exit of the Gulf of Mexico. Despite the change in political sovereignty over Florida in the early nineteenth century, the long traditions of circulation and exchange between Cuba and Florida continued and even intensified across the decades. The Florida Keys, as well as Tampa and other Florida cities, may have been part of the United States, but they continued to be marked by a distinctively Latin presence. As the destination for thousands of workers in the later nineteenth century, these cities became centers of revolutionary activity for Cuban exiles. On the other side of the Gulf, Mexico's changing political landscape in the early nineteenth century also failed to disrupt linkages between Mexico and Cuba. To the contrary, Spain used Cuba as a staging ground for a series of attempts to reconquer Mexico. Indeed, Cuba was a place that newly independent Mexico could hardly afford to ignore in the early nineteenth century.[6] Even as the danger of Spanish invasion receded, Veracruz continued to be intimately linked to Havana through many networks of exchange.

The specific linkages between Veracruz, Tampa, Key West, and New Orleans developed later as Cubans recognized the value of transiting between Mexico and the United States. Insurgents like López and Arbona found themselves enmeshed in a network of travel in which points like Tampa, Key West, Veracruz, New Orleans, and Havana were intimately connected. Veracruz was known to Cubans in Cuba as a center of Cuban revolutionary activity and as a place connected to Florida. Not only did the vast majority of the Mexico-based ANERC applicants settle in Veracruz, but two-thirds of the Veracruz-based migrants indicated in their files that they traveled to more than one destination in the Gulf, linking Veracruz with Tampa, Key West, or New Orleans. The majority of these travelers were insurgents. The Cuban Revolutionary newspaper, *Patria*, which was published in New York City and circulated in all the migrant communities, had a section called "Correspondence from Veracruz," which appeared regularly and more often than news emanating from other migrant centers. The existence of a permanent section dedicated to correspondence from Veracruz was a testament to the centrality of the city as a conduit of news and information arriving directly from Cuba and circulating throughout the diaspora.

Community

If Cubans saw Veracruz as a gateway to Florida, they were also aware of the long-standing Cuban migrant community there. Indeed, for Cuban migrants, the existence of restaurants, voluntary associations, hotels, and other Cuban-owned businesses made Veracruz a compelling destination in its own right. The existence of a resourceful political community provided support for revolutionaries and insurgents who seamlessly continued their revolutionary labors from the city. For those fleeing Cuba as financial or wartime refugees, a large and established community was no less important. Such a community provided cultural continuity and networks that could help secure employment. Indeed, the Havana tobacco worker José Martín Bello remembers how José Miguel Macias, the revered veteran of the Ten Years' War and leader of the Veracruz Cuban community, took Bello under his wing and helped him get on his feet in a new and unfamiliar context.[7] In addition to the support offered by prominent individuals, Cuban-owned hotels like the Telégrafo provided a place to sleep for countless migrants newly arrived in the port city. Eateries like El Aguila Mexicana and La Juventud Veracruzana both offered familiar Cuban cuisine and served as key gathering places for Cubans during the years of peak migration. The furniture shop La Favorita, owned by J. I. Izazola, and Nicolás Valverde's sewing shop, La Puntualidad, were two of several businesses owned by Cuban migrants involved in independence politics. These businesses served as meeting places and important reference points for community members.[8]

Cubans who lived in Florida, like Juan José Cassasús, noted the strong presence of Cuban people and Cuban businesses when describing Key West: "The coffee seller . . . is Cuban, the reader in the tobacco factory is Cuban, and even the store owner, the butcher, the washer and the barber." Cassasús went on to observe that there were Cubans who lived twenty years in Florida without speaking a word of English.[9] The Spanish consul in Key West complained to his superior that "the émigré colony lives isolated from the rest of the population on the island, making it difficult to penetrate their tight circle."[10] The same was true of Ybor City in Tampa. Ybor City was named after a cigar manufacturer by the name of V. M. Ybor, who relocated his business there from Cuba. Ybor City was a closed world unto itself. As Susan D. Greenbaum notes, underscoring the fluidity of the U.S.-Cuba "borderlands," Ybor City was "much more a satellite of Cuba than a suburb of Tampa."[11]

TOBACCO

Like Key West and Tampa, Veracruz also had a significant working class Cuban population that coalesced around the tobacco industry. Of course, the scale of the tobacco industry in Florida dwarfed its counterpart in Veracruz. By 1885, there were ninety factories in Key West employing 2,811 Cubans.[12] Cuban cigar manufacturers began to move their production north after the Ten Years' War to avoid the high tariffs on the import of Cuban cigars. Tobacco leaves could be imported without penalty, so all entrepreneurial Cuban elites like V. M. Ybor had to do was move their factories across the border.[13] The workers, facing rising unemployment in Cuba, followed, looking for opportunities in Florida. Cuba and Mexico did not share the profound economic relationship that Cuba and the United States did. Neither did Mexicans have the infrastructure of economic development in the tobacco industry to support major Cuban operations, as historian José G. González Sierra demonstrates.[14] Still, Cuban technicians and workers were critical to the development of the tobacco industry in Mexico, and it was the growth of this industry that, in turn, made Veracruz a viable destination for Cuban exiles, migrants, and refugees.

Mexicans had always cultivated tobacco for local consumption. In colonial Mexico, the tobacco industry, which was concentrated in Veracruz, was one of the largest organized industries. In 1790, the industry employed some twenty thousand people, and tobacco revenues were the largest source of income around that time, after the silver tithes. The industry received its boost when Spain reoccupied Louisiana in the 1760s and used the colony to supply tobacco leaves to factories in Mexico cementing linkages between the ports of New Orleans and Veracruz. Tobacco production did survive the destructive period of the independence wars, but just barely; it did not, however, recover its remarkable profitability.[15] But during the 1880s, the Mexican tobacco industry, which had struggled since the independence wars, was revived due to events in Cuba. While the independence war destabilized production on the island, creating some incentive and opportunity for Mexican production, the same conflict drove civilians, among them skilled laborers, out of Cuba to neighboring countries looking for work. This, along with the Díaz government's interest in fomenting immigration, colonization, and agriculture, and the support of foreign tobacco experts including many Cubans, created an ideal climate for the revival of the Mexican tobacco industry.[16] Andrés Clemente Vázquez, Mexican consul in Havana, worked to increase the immigration of skilled professionals, including *tabaqueros*, to Mexico from war-torn Cuba. As was the case in other nations in Latin America, the late nineteenth century was a period in which political elites placed significant importance on the growth of populations through immigration. Immigrants, in particular European migrants, were seen as a civilizing force that could add to the prosperity of the nation while accelerating its modernization. In Veracruz, owners of tobacco factories, skilled workers, and others who brought technological know-how were welcomed.

The increasing demand for workers in Veracruz in the 1890s can explain, in part, why Cuban émigrés chose to settle there. One month after the outbreak of war in Cuba, the Spanish foreign minister reported to the governor of Cuba that there were approximately two hundred Cubans in the city of Veracruz, the majority of whom were tobacco workers and all of whom were affiliated with the revolutionary movement.[17] As we have seen, Veracruz's Cuban population would swell during the subsequent two years as refugees and exiles fled Cuba. Cuban tobacco workers from Veracruz also migrated further inland to the Valle Nacional de Oaxaca, where their employers took advantage of the region's cheap land. Indeed, the Valle became a new center for tobacco cultivation by the 1890s. The Valle was notorious for being a place where kidnapped and coerced workers labored, and it is difficult to ascertain how many Cubans went of their own free will.[18] While no reference to the Valle can be found in the letters written by Cuban migrants and the ANERC files, Cuban and Mexican newspapers record financial contributions collected among workers in the Valle that were destined for the coffers of the Cuban Revolutionary Party in New York City. The contributions range from one hundred pesos to less than one peso, suggesting that both wealthier *tabaqueros* and workers were contributors.[19] Among the names attached to the report, the pseudonyms "Mambi" and "un Cubano" provide further evidence of presence of Cubans among the workers in the Valle.

Despite their far smaller numbers, tobacco workers in Veracruz, like those in Key West or Tampa were intimately associated with the revolutionary movement. In the years after the end of the war during the U.S. intervention in Cuba, which extended from 1898 to 1902, tobacco workers from all three cities in both countries appealed to Cuban state authorities seeking repatriation on the basis of their patriotic labors during the war. As numerous scholars have shown, Cuban tobacco workers in Florida became the backbone of the Cuban revolutionary movement from the 1870s forward, offering critical financial aid to the movement. Although fewer, their counterparts in Mexico were no less fervently committed to the cause and they bolstered the movement with their financial contributions as well. What they lacked in numbers, they sought to make up for by forging solidarities with Mexicans who also offered aid to the insurgents and the revolutionary party.

RACE

For all their geographical proximity, Cubans in Cuba and in Florida lived in, and engaged with radically different cultural worlds. Reflecting on the Cuban migrant community in Key West, Juan José Cassasús observed that white Cubans were more likely than their Afro-Cuban counterparts to become naturalized U.S. citizens, participate in politics, and enmesh themselves in local society.[20] Cassasús insisted, however, that the white Cuban never became a "gringo." Only Spaniards in Florida might aspire to be considered white, and not always. If full immersion in the United States was unavailable to the white Cuban, it further eluded Cubans of African descent who could not count on a path to citizenship. Indeed, Afro-Cubans had to contend not only with cultural and linguistic differences, but also with racial segregation of a kind that did not exist in Cuba. Surely, the stark racism of the southern United States led to a hardening of racism against Cuban blacks within the Cuban community over time, but the effect was inconsistent. On one hand, Cassasús noted that an "absurd division" existed between whites, who were themselves further segmented into "rich" and "poor," and blacks, who were internally divided into "radicals" and "those who adore the whites." Tampa had a segregated all-black mutual aid society, while in Key West, Afro-Cubans developed their own associations such as the *Colegio Unificación* established in the 1870s and the *Sociedad el Progresso* founded a decade later.[21] Cuba had a long tradition of Afro-Cuban associations from which these exile societies drew. On the other hand, integration was also common. Integrated revolutionary associations were ubiquitous and the layout of Ybor City featured working-class, mixed-race housing.[22]

The co-presence of integration and segregation among Cuban migrants in Florida suggests that Cuba's particular culture of race relations was carried across the Gulf. Over time, however, the pressure of the culture of segregation in the South would harden the divide between white and Afro-descended Cubans as Susan D. Greenbaum demonstrates in her study of Afro-Cubans in Tampa. A man like V. M. Ybor was caught between his own economic interests, which tied him to the white American Tampa elite, and his sense of cultural distinctiveness, even superiority to them. It is likely that Ybor's decision to craft an integrated working class community around his factory was driven less by the cultural community he shared with the Cubans who worked for him than it was by his need to control his labor force and stifle the labor activism of his workers.[23] Even as they celebrated the unity of all Cubans during the 1890s, white Cuban migrants in Florida worked hard to disassociate themselves from their poorer compatriots and the mixed-race workers. They were loath to be subsumed in the label "Latin" by their white counterparts in the United States when "Latin" meant "anything other than completely white." Within the confines of the Cuban migrant community, though, the same elites promoted the idea of racial harmony. After providing evidence of social segregation as well as racial tensions in his study of Florida's Cuban communities, Cassasús quickly dismissed its importance and celebrated how Cubans came together as one behind the nationalist cause.[24] Juan Cassasús's book, *La emigración cubana y la independencia de la patria*, was declared the best history of the Cuban emigrations in a competition organized by the ANERC in 1953. Five decades after the war, Cubans maintained the myth of racial solidarity that had been constructed by Cuban patriots during the late nineteenth century.

Compared to Key West, Veracruz presents a slightly different story, although overt similarities between the two cities exist. For example, de facto segregation between blacks and whites existed in Veracruz. The moratorium on talk of racial divisions imposed by the Cuban Revolutionary Party after 1892 as it sought to unite Cubans behind the nationalist movement makes it difficult to discern racist practices in documentation of an official or semi-official nature. However, just as the musings of Cassasús reveal much about complicated racial dynamics in Florida, so does a small slip made by the leader of the Cuban community in Veracruz in his correspondence with Cuban Revolutionary Party leaders in New York City. In a standard report to his superior, José Miguel Macias listed the Cuban clubs in Veracruz. The presidents of three of the associations were identified by race: "Hijas de America, presidenta—Julia Alvarez de Xiques (negra), Angel Mestre, presidente- Rufino Alorda (negro), Benito Juárez, presidente- Antonio Sorio (negro)."[25] The other clubs referred to in the letter, Poesia and Bartolomé Maso, are also described, but here Macias described the migrants of the two organizations respectively as "poor" and "newly arrived." The choice to identify the three clubs by the race of their presidents was uncommon in this period, given that the Revolutionary Party worked hard to project an image of racial harmony and eschewed race-based discrimination. Other clubs in Veracruz surely had mixed-race memberships, but what seemed important to Macias about these particular clubs is that they were presided over by black Cubans. Presidents of all Cuban clubs presumably had equal membership and status in the Cuerpos de Consejo, which were the intermediary bodies between the mass of clubs and the Cuban Revolutionary

Party leadership in New York City. Cubans of color had been promoted to prominent positions within the Cuban insurgent army, and certainly there were figures like Juan Gualberto Gómez, the Puerto Rican journalist Sotero Figueroa, and Rafael Serra, both in Cuba and in exile, who had positions and influence within the PRC, yet the specter of Cubans of color of any station participating equally in politics alongside whites was potentially more intimidating.[26] As we will see in chapter 3, Cuban migrants would work over the course of the war to define the unique role of the émigré in the movement. The émigré was seen as a bearer of civilization, a figure who after experiencing life in other republican and "free" nations could bring lessons home to Cuba to help rebuild the island after the war. While the Cuban Revolutionary Party created spaces for Afro-Cuban women to become democratically elected presidents of Cuban associations, women like Julia Alvarez de Xiques would not fit the mold of the idealized émigré that PRC leaders imagined would play a key role in Cuba's future. In this context, Macias's flagging of black presidents is meaningful because it belies the idea that all Cubans regardless of race could participate equally in the struggle.

Macias's slip reveals the existence of race-based exclusion and de facto segregation among Cubans in Mexico. In a memoir, Cuban migrant Leandro Cañizares Gómez remembered the sensation caused by the arrival of a young Afro-Cuban woman to Orizaba in 1896. The story of this woman, a servant traveling in the company of a white family, made a particular impression on Cañizares Gómez. According to Cañizares Gómez, she was such a novelty in Orizaba with her dark skin and distinctive features that Mexicans stopped to stare at her constantly. Deeply ashamed, she began to restrict her movements so as not to draw as much attention to herself. Ultimately, the story tells us more about Cañizares Gómez than it does about the experience of Afro-Cubans in Orizaba. His description of the young girl stands out for two reasons. First, she is figured as odd and out of place. Second, her demeanor is demure and self-deprecating. In sum, she is a harmless oddity.[27] In a strange way, the attention Cañizares Gómez gives to this Afro-Cuban woman in his narrative reminds us of the undue attention that José Miguel Macias gave to the "black" presidents of the Cuban clubs on his list.

Cañizares Gómez's racial views become clear in an 1898 article he published in a Mexican newspaper called *El Continente Americano* titled "The Black Race in Cuba." The article sought to disprove the idea that the insurgent army was made up of "vulgar black men . . . in a state of semi-barbarism."[28] He argued that this was a misrepresentation, but rather than defend Afro-Cubans from racist caricature, Cañizares Gómez assured his readers that in Cuba, unlike Haiti and Jamaica, there were fewer individuals of African descent relative to whites. Those who did exist, he insisted, strove through unions with whites to lighten the race. Cañizares Gómez took the racial inferiority of Afro-Cubans for granted and emphasized the idea that over time they would simply be bred out of the population. After indicating that black Cubans sought out miscegenation as a way to better the race through whitening, Cañizares Gómez insisted that "the same zeal to better his color and his intellectual and moral condition can be seen in the mulato, who in unions with others of his kind or with whites succeeds in perfecting himself and contributing to the extinction . . . of the race of color in Cuba."[29] In a way, there is a correlation between Cañizares Gómez's conviction that the black race was doomed to extinction in Cuba and his representation of the Afro-Cuban girl in Orizaba shamed into silence. Both of these representations stand in stark contrast to the figure of Julia Alvarez de Xiques as a public female figure of African descent in Veracruz's Cuban political scene. Cañizares Gómez's portrayal of the girl who recedes into the shadows, like his racist suggestion that the disappearance of Cuba's Afro-descended population was inevitable, are evidence of the deep unease that white Cubans felt when confronted with black power and of their desire to keep Afro-Cubans in a subordinate position.

In Mexico as in the United States, the tension between inclusion and exclusion could be mapped directly on to race, class, and gender. In Mexico, however, the racism of figures like Cañizares Gómez and Macias notwithstanding, Cubans of color had access to a path to Mexican citizenship in a way that they did not in the United States. In his history of Cuban migrants in Florida, Juan José Cassasús noted that naturalization was available primarily to white Cubans. In Mexico, however, Afro-Cubans were among those who sought naturalization and were granted citizenship. In fact, not only did they naturalize, but they often used the process of naturalization to reinvent themselves. Historian Erika Pani has found that Afro-Cubans regularly chose new names, often modifying existing names by adding "y" and "de la" between two surnames to make them seem more aristocratic and to remove the stigma of slavery.[30] Like all immigrants, Cuban migrants who sought naturalization in Mexico were required to include a phenotypical description. Those who did not self-describe as white (*Blanco*) described themselves as either *trigueño* or *Pardo*. Like those who changed their names, Cubans of color who did not include photographs of themselves likely used descriptors that made them appear less black. In fact, it was rare for a Cuban to self-identify as *moreno* or *negro*, although these files exist.[31] If Cubans of color in Mexico did not confront legal segregation as they did in the southern United States, they were still subject to the racist pseudoscientific discourses of the era to which both Cuban and Mexican elites subscribed. The need to remove the stigma of slavery or to appear less black in their naturalization applications is clear evidence of the advantages of "whitening" in Mexico. This is not surprising, as, Mexican elites like most of their Latin American contemporaries harbored great anxiety about the "blackening" of their society in the late nineteenth and early twentieth centuries. In fact, in Mexico a core argument against the briefly popular campaign to annex Cuba to Mexico was that doing so would raise Mexico's black population significantly and thus hinder its march toward "civilization."

CULTURE

In Florida, Cubans existed in relatively insular communities, whose isolation would only begin to breakdown in the twentieth century, Veracruz, by contrast, was a society that by the turn of the twentieth century was discernibly Cubanized. The impact of Afro-Cuban cultural forms, from music to cuisine, was palpable in the city by the late nineteenth century. Indeed, Veracruz, along with Havana, Cartagena, and other cities in the Caribbean, was a key center of Afro-Caribbean diasporic culture by the late nineteenth and early twentieth centuries.[32] As we have seen, Afro-Cuban migrants had been arriving to Veracruz in significant numbers since the 1840s, bringing with them their culture and traditions. Thus, from the mid-nineteenth century forward, the influx of Cuban migrants gradually left an imprint on the port city of Veracruz.[33] Evaluating the impact of Cuban emigrations in Mexico overall, Bernardo García Díaz argues that, although Cubans represented only 0.02 percent of the Mexican population, their impact in Mexico was significant because of their concentration in the state of Veracruz, and they had a lasting and visible impact on its culture. When questioned in 2004 about the origins of Afro-Mestizos in Veracruz today, one local resident of San Andrés Tuxtla insisted that "Afro-Mestizo refers to the synthesis of Africans, Cubans and Indigenous Mexicans." So deeply intertwined were the histories of Cuba and Mexico, and so much a part of Veracruz culture had Cuba become that what it meant to be Mexican in Veracruz, at least for an Afro-Mestizo was to be in part Cuban as well.[34]

Studies centering on cultural exchanges seek to explain the persistence of Caribbean cultural elements, like musical and dance forms that are still identifiable in Veracruz today.³⁵ *Danzón* is an example of a music and dance form that Cuban migrants introduced to Mexico, although Mexicans came to claim it as their own by the early twentieth century. Prior to the 1890s, the *danzón* in Cuba was associated with the Afro-Cuban community. White Cubans were deeply critical of the form and uncomfortable with it, especially because public dances were a site of race mixing. Havana saw at least fifty dances on any given night by the turn of the nineteenth century, many of which featured Afro-Cuban bands and performers. During the last decades of the nineteenth century, however, the *danzón* was adopted by white Creole Cubans and was recast as a hybrid musical form in which European elements dominated. It became associated with *Cubania* and with national culture and the independence struggle. *Danzón* traveled across the Gulf to Mexico as early as the 1860s and became part of the musical culture of Veracruz and to a lesser extent Mérida as well. Music and dance were a regular feature of Cuban social life in exile and made their way into political spaces as well. For example, Regelio Mauresa y Silva, an émigré who lived in Veracruz between 1895 and 1899 remembered dancing to raise money for the revolutionary cause. He also "collected funds with songs" which were then transmitted to the revolutionary party.³⁶ Spaniards, who had always denigrated the form, sharpened their critique by associating it negatively with black Cubans in an effort to weaken the Cuban independence movement and the unity that Cubans had carefully constructed on the basis of the idea of racial harmony. Cuban revolutionaries simply worked harder to defend their movement against such attacks, and Leandro Cañizares Gómez's article is one example of an effort to counter the idea that the Cuban republic would be torn asunder by barbaric African and Afro-Cuban elements. The *danzón* became just another arena of struggle. This art form, embraced and claimed by white and black Cubans alike, traveled with migrants to Mexico during the last three decades of the nineteenth century. Mexican audiences were enraptured by the *danzón* and, by the turn of the century, they claimed it as their own. "While for many in Cuba . . . [danzón] represented a sonic unity that came to symbolize a nascent political independence and fictive national brotherhood," Christine B. Arce argues, "for Mexicans it represented a familiar sound that was negotiated through the triangulated sonic renderings of a displaced African heritage."³⁷ Tracing the career of the Mexican singer Toña la Negra who was a sensation in and beyond Mexico in the early nineteenth century, Arce shows how she came to embody the triangular relationship between Mexico, Africa and Cuba (or Afro-Caribbean culture more generally). Mexicans could approach their own blackness, Arce argues, only by displacing that blackness onto Cuba and the Caribbean.[38] In this context, Toña la Negra was seen as both deeply familiar and irreducibly foreign.

The twentieth century saw the continuous presence of Afro-Cuban entertainers and performers in Veracruz either as permanent residents or as part of traveling companies touring from Cuba.[39] Over the course of half a century, Cubans and Cuban culture had insinuated themselves into the fabric of Veracruz in a way that would only be true of cities in Florida in the later twentieth century.[40] Cuban migrants certainly came to see Veracruz as, in José Martí's words, a "Casa hermana de todos los peregrinos Cubanos," a home away from home for all Cuban pilgrims, but the city and its inhabitants were indelibly marked by Cuban migration and Cuban culture to the degree that for some veracruzanos to be Mexican is to be part Cuban as well.

Generation

Veracruz was a city poised on the edge of the Caribbean, a city shaped by the constant flow of people and information, marked economically by the presence of Cuban tobacco planters and workers and culturally by Afro-Cuban cultural forms and simmering racial tensions, but it was also a multigenerational city. The co-presence of Cuban migrants from the decade of the Ten Years' War and those from the 1890s was perhaps one of the most visible and defining characteristics of the Veracruz community. A number of the most influential leaders of the Veracruz community were revolutionary veterans from Cuba's first independence war. The most recognized figure in the port city was José Miguel Macias, a pedagogue who had been active in the revolutionary struggle and had suffered imprisonment in Spain's West African penal colonies. Many members of the older generation, including Macias, had become naturalized Mexican citizens by the 1890s. For some of the migrants of the 1860s and 1870s generation, naturalization represented a rejection not of their Cuban identity but rather of their status as Spanish colonial subjects. Indeed, those Cubans who dreamed of a republican and democratic Cuba eagerly severed their ties to a colonial state that oppressed them in favor of citizenship in a land that celebrated the values they held dear and the rights for which they longed.[41] Furthermore, naturalization provided many revolutionaries with the flexibility and protection needed to continue their revolutionary labors abroad. Naturalization among Cuban migrants was a strategy used across the Americas and in Europe. For example, the Cuban Revolutionary Party's leader after 1895 and Cuba's future first Republican president, Tomás Estrada Palma, was one among many Cubans in the United States who understood citizenship as an asset to the revolutionary cause. Men like Estrada Palma did not feel they were any less Cuban for becoming U.S. citizens.

The newer and younger generation of migrants, those associated with the 1895 War, sought naturalization in far smaller numbers than had the older generation. For these migrants, citizenship may have been less urgent, less desirable, or less accessible. Less urgent because, rather than a long, drawn-out war, the 1895 conflict accelerated quickly and Cubans believed it would be a short and decisive war. Less desirable because these Cubans were integrated into extensive and long-standing communities, whereas their predecessors were pioneers in a foreign society, and for them citizenship and forging strong ties to host nationals would have been important to long-term stability and success. Less accessible because the naturalization process required resources that the generally poorer newer immigrants might not have had; for example, naturalization required that one be able to demonstrate financial solvency. Finally, a larger percentage of the 1890s migrants were refugees rather than committed revolutionaries who had been expelled for political beliefs, and so they may have lacked the motivations that had spurred earlier generation revolutionaries to naturalize.

Anecdotal evidence drawn from the letters of some of the more prominent members of the older generation supports the idea that new migrants were seen as desperate, poor, and often disloyal. Men of the older, revolutionary generation tended to characterize the newer arrivals as people without professions and with suspect revolutionary credentials; this reveals the tensions in regard to generation and class, and the conflation of the two. One older migrant drew distinctions between the generations by defining the 1860s generation of Cubans as intransigent patriots who had never trucked with the Spaniards and the newer Cubans as untrustworthy troublemakers out for personal gain. Men like José Antonio Caiñas and Ignacio Martín Arbona y Domínguez, both of whom only escaped Cuba due to their royalist connections, would surely have drawn scrutiny from the self-proclaimed intransigent patriots of the older generation. Yet, just as older migrants complained about new arrivals, new ones also voiced frustrations about the stubbornness, rigidity, and dogmatism of their elders.

The tensions between the two generations of Cubans were not unique to Mexico. In fact, generational conflicts among Cuban migrants throughout the Americas were so prevalent that resolving them and unifying older and younger Cubans became a central mission of the newly founded Cuban Revolutionary Party in the 1890s. Generational unity was seen as critical to the success of the war effort. In large part, the tensions were a product of the length of the Cuban independence struggle, which evolved over thirty years and produced multiple waves of migrants. As we have seen, the different circumstances of war were also important. In the peak year of 1896, when the full force of insurgent and royalist military strategies made life in Cuba unbearable for many, thousands fled to surrounding communities. The stage was set for generational confrontation as communities full of older migrants were challenged to receive and incorporate large numbers of arriving Cubans, many of whom were destitute, some of whom were women and children, and all of whom had escaped frightful circumstances. The lived reality of these migrants was very different from that of the previous revolutionary generation. The fact that most of the newer arrivals had not fought in the war itself was unsettling and raised suspicions among military veterans who believed that revolutionary loyalty was forged in the fire of battle.[42]

Generational conflicts reached a boiling point in Veracruz in 1897 and 1898, when a dispute between migrants of different generations resulted in formal denunciation and imprisonment. The members of the older generation involved in the Veracruz dispute were scandalized by the behavior of the younger generation Cubans whose comportment did not square with their definition of revolutionary patriotism. A number of Cubans representing four of the nineteen political clubs established in Veracruz accused the local leadership of offering the funds gathered at a Cuban event to the colonels Baldomero Acosta and Gerardo Portela, who were in Veracruz at the time. Nicolás Valverde, a member of the club Bartolomé Masó, accused the vice president of a local representative body, Aurelio Silvera, of acting in an arbitrary fashion without the consent of the entire body. The members of the clubs José de la Luz Caballero, Protesta de Baraguá, and Josefa Ortiz y García Pérez joined Valverde. These clubs refused to send their collections to the local body and sent them instead directly to the Cuban Revolutionary Party headquarters. On 12 August 1898, the local body convened and agreed to banish the four clubs from the organization, stating that "the aforementioned clubs have contributed to creating divisions among Cubans in this community . . . they have neglected to send their collections to the treasury of this Consejo . . . thereby discrediting this body."[43] The charge of fostering disunity was a serious one. Maintaining unity was one of the most sacred responsibilities of Cuban migrants affiliated with the revolutionary struggle. Another four clubs under the same accusations were also banished, as well as two migrants, Nicolás Valverde and Ignacio Zarragoita. Eleven days later,

Nicolás Valverde wrote to Estrada Palma, angrily accusing the venerable Macías: "Don Miguel Macías who, with the experience of age and culture should have been more judicious, has insulted me in print . . . calling me a slanderer . . . I am a poor man, but an honorable one, and the only mark I have ever received upon my name has been made by Silvera and Macías."[44]

The leadership of the local representative organization defended itself in a statement published in September of 1898. The representatives of the Cuerpo de Consejo wrote: "This honorable *Cuerpo de Consejo* [has been] offended and slandered by certain individuals who are only Cuban because they were born there, and who before the altar of the nation have fixed their eyes on the quickest way to serve their individual needs. . . . These men could not stand to see a group of patriots from the 68 emigration strongly united and working in favor of the independence cause without becoming envious."[45] The first two full paragraphs of the statement were venomous critiques of the rebel clubs and their members as crass opportunists.

Educated and literate, yet poor by his own admission, Valverde figured himself as victimized by a generation that "with the experience of age" should be more "judicious." On 8 October 1898, Valverde wrote Estrada Palma again, this time from prison, furious. Aurelio Silvera and José Miguel Macías had conspired to have him arrested for defamation. The older generation of respected revolutionaries in Veracruz proved intolerant of an upstart like Valverde and they came down hard on him.

There were other younger generation Cubans in Veracruz who refused to be part of the PRC and who defended their right to form associations that were not affiliated with it. Such was the case with the Cañizares Gómez brothers, who founded the Agrupación Cubana de Orizaba. Perhaps concerned about whether the Agrupación would be recognized for its participation in the independence movement, Juan Cañizares Gómez wrote to Estrada Palma in 1899, describing how the organization was founded and why the members had decided not to constitute a formal club. His reasons included the belief that Nicolás Domínguez Cowan, a senior member of Mexico City's Cuban migrant community and the Cuban Revolutionary Party's appointed agent in the capital, would have been jealous that the club had not been founded by a member of the 1868 revolution.[46] It is hard to say if Cañizares Gómez's reasoning is reflective of Dominguez's actual prejudices or his own resentments and distrust, but the comment highlights the existence of tensions between revolutionary generations.

Cañizares Gomez's comments, like those of the Veracruz leadership, reveal the deep generational divisions within Mexico's principal Cuban communities. The comments of Veracruz-based Cubans about the renegade clubs demonstrate that older émigrés thought the younger generation to be composed of aimless or self-interested individuals whose patriotism was questionable. Their perspectives were classed and the implication that newer migrants were less patriotic seems to be determined by the circumstances of the immigration of these new Cubans. Silvera and Macias did not think that the new Cubans were revolutionary sympathizers exiled for their political beliefs, and that automatically lowered their revolutionary credentials. Cañizares Gómez's comments about the jealousies of the older generation and Valverde's frustrations in his dealings with the Veracruz leadership, on the other hand, give us a vantage point from the other side. The new generation's perspective suggests that at least some younger Cubans were looking for ways to carve a place for themselves in exile, but they were caught in the shadow of veterans of the Ten Years' War.

Veracruz had a large, multigenerational and politically active Cuban migrant community that included a sizable mixed-race, working-class population, as did its counterparts elsewhere in the Gulf. Like in Key West, Cubans in Veracruz were divided along the lines of class and race, although in both places a unifying revolutionary ideology mandated that Cubans work together across these divides. In Veracruz and also in Florida, that unity was severely tested by generational conflicts in which old guard revolutionaries squared off against new migrants to ensure that, within a broad unity, a hierarchy of power and influence remained intact. As we will see, race, class, and generational tensions were most acute in cities that bordered the Gulf because these cities were the first ports of arrival for increasing numbers of destitute migrants departing Cuba. Indeed, Veracruz was intimately connected to the Gulf, the Caribbean, and the Atlantic. Constant traffic between Veracruz and Havana ensured that Veracruz received not only migrants but also the most current news about the war as it progressed. Accessibility, work opportunities, cultural similarities, and established networks all contributed to making Veracruz an important center of the nineteenth-century Cuban diaspora.

Mérida

Connections

Like Veracruz, Yucatán was an integral part of a uniquely connected Gulf and Caribbean world from early on. Connections between Yucatán and Cuba were forged by intercolonial trade, especially in the seventeenth and eighteenth centuries. Havana, a mere 200 kilometers from Yucatán, was in some senses a regional metropolis for Yucatecan elites, many of whom lived temporarily in the city to attend university, and who moved back and forth.[47] Yucatán's economy suffered visibly when commerce between Yucatán and Cuba was interrupted by the Mexican independence wars. Isolated from much of Mexico, Yucatán had grown dependent on trade with Cuba. By the mid-nineteenth century both contraband and legal trading connections resumed. This commerce was enhanced by the construction of a new port. During the first three decades of the nineteenth century there had been interest in creating a port closer to Mérida to facilitate trade, but the political instability of Yucatán in the years after Mexican independence made progress on the project impossible. Modest port development began around the middle of the nineteenth century. At first, Progreso was just an *embarcadero* for fishermen, and it supported local maritime commerce along the near coasts of Yucatán. More serious construction followed, and a formal port was inaugurated in the early 1870s with the authorization of a customs house. Soon, customs agents from Europe and the United States established themselves there. The port developed in tandem with the railroad, whose lines connected the coast to Mérida (a mere thirty-seven kilometers apart) as early as 1862. Due to its excellent location, Progreso was a convenient port for ships making long treks across the Atlantic and desirable for its access to Yucatán's prize commodities, especially henequen fiber. Ships carrying henequen were destined for New York, Le Havre, Seville, Cadiz, Liverpool, New Orleans, Boston, Hamburg, Barcelona, London, and Havana. In 1889 alone, Progresso saw 428 Mexican ships, 160 U.S. ships, 70 English vessels, and 11 Spanish ships. These ships transported a total of 3,769 Mexican passengers, 1,614 Spaniards (including Cubans), and 397 U.S. citizens. By 1898, Progreso was a town of 4,200 inhabitants.[48] In addition to henequen, exports from Yucatán included cattle, corn, cotton, rice, and, in one of the darkest moments of Yucatán's history, people.[49] In the wake of the Caste Wars, hundreds of Mayan rebels were sold to Cuban planters. The exchange was seen to be mutually advantageous, as Yucatán rid itself of its dissidents and Cuban planters acquired laborers in a moment when the slave trade was increasingly threatened.[50]

Although the Cubanization of Mérida might be less apparent than that of Veracruz in cultural terms, deep Cuban resonances can be detected in the *trova Yucateca* developed in the 1920s and 1930s, as well as in the *vaquerías* and *bombas* of the region.[51] Scholars also credit Mérida as a key site for the transmission of Cuban *danzón*. Although *danzón* has clear African roots, Mexican elites in Mérida first encountered it in white, elite Cuban circles and thus did not associate it with blackness. It was much later, when *danzón* reached Mexico City and became popular among the city's working classes, and as fears over the migration of British West Indian migrant workers rose, that the *danzón* came to be associated with blackness.[52] The association of *danzón* with only white Cubans underscores the existence of social segregation among Cubans in Mérida. As we have seen, *danzón* became a battlefield of race and respectability as Spaniards attacked the art form to weaken the insurgent movement. In all likelihood, revolutionary Cubans in Mérida, ever conscious of defending the insurgency and their own respectability, intentionally whitened the *danzón*, similar to the way the Orizaba-based Cuban migrant Leandro Cañizares Gómez rhetorically whitened the Cuban insurgent army and the Cuban populations as a whole in his newspaper article published in Mexico in 1896.

The Cubanization of Mérida and Veracruz was similar, but their strategic significance for the Cuban revolutionary struggle differed. While Veracruz's geographical position and place in trade and transportation networks made the city a key destination for insurgents and laborers, the isolation of a majority of Yucatán's Gulf and Caribbean coasts was the key to its significance for Cuban revolutionary activity. Dynamic port cities like Progreso notwithstanding, Yucatán's coasts were poorly surveilled, and this made it an enticing place from which to launch or provision filibustering expeditions.

Correspondence between Tomás Estrada Palma and his appointee in Mérida indicates that Cubans' interest in Yucatán as a strategic site for revolutionary activity was strong in the 1890s. The case of the *James Woodall* expedition illustrates the interrelationship between Gulf ports and the strategic significance of Yucatán. The steamship *James Woodall* left Baltimore destined for Progreso with the stated purpose of transporting workers from Florida to Mexico in early July 1895. One eyewitness testified to the fact that the vessel's true mission was to land men and arms in Cuba. The *Woodall* took on 153 men, including the Cuban generals Carlos Roloff and Serafin Sánchez, just off of Key West before heading for Cuba. Unable to find an appropriate landing spot, the ship remained at sea off the Cuban coast for several days. The *Woodall* took refuge at Isla Mujeres off the coast of Yucatán, where local Cubans offered critical aid and provisions to the insurgents. The *Woodall* landed its men in Cuba successfully and steamed to Progreso, where the vessel was searched by Spanish and Mexican authorities and the Captain interrogated for his suspicious landing at Isla

Mujeres.⁵³ The authorities were one step behind though, and unable to prove wrongdoing, so the *Woodall* was permitted to continue on its way. Once the *Woodall* cleared Progreso, the Cuban Revolutionary Party agent in Mérida wrote to the head of the Party in New York, reporting the details of the ship's emergency landing at Isla Mujeres.⁵⁴

In the wake of *Woodall*'s success, Estrada Palma wrote to Rodolfo Menéndez Peña about the possibilities of using Yucatán as a base of operations for expeditions to Cuba. Menéndez suggested an alternative that he felt trumped Yucatán: Belize. He noted that Belize was connected to Jamaica, New Orleans, and New York, not by telegraph but by ship. He emphasized its mixture of accessibility and isolation, and he also highlighted the fact that arms were readily available because the British sold them with regularity to Mayan rebels. On the other hand, Belize did not have the infrastructure of support that an established Cuban migrant community could provide. Indeed, in cities like New Orleans, Tampa, and Key West, Florida Cuban migrants did everything for the filibusters, from providing food and provisions to sewing clothing and buying arms.⁵⁵

While there were efforts to launch expeditions from Veracruz, the state's coasts dotted with many ports were more easily policed and traffic was more easily tracked. Veracruz's Spanish community was also larger and more influential than Mérida's, which meant that Spaniards in Veracruz were that much more successful at frustrating Cuban ambitions, including efforts to collect and transport weapons and supplies to Cuba. While the prospects of launching filibustering expeditions from Veracruz may have been dim, the opportunities for individual insurgents to make their way home from Veracruz were significant, in large part due to the connectedness of Veracruz to other Gulf ports. Yucatán's Cuban communities found the prospect of launching filibustering expeditions equally daunting. It was this lack of resources that led the PRC agent at Mérida to suggest Belize instead when he was prompted to deliver a report on Yucatán's potential as a filibustering center. The availability of arms and tradition of arms smuggling across the border between Belize and Mexico were clear advantages. At the same time, the relative isolation of the coasts of Yucatán provided excellent cover for Cuban expeditions—like the *Woodall*—that needed provisioning and supplies, and for small arms smuggling carried out by the *viveros* moving regularly between Mexico and Cuba's westernmost province.⁵⁶ Indeed, Spanish consular records during the 1890s show that Spanish authorities were anxious about Yucatán's unsupervised coastline. They expressed constant frustration at the Mexican government's inability or unwillingness to assist in the surveillance of the coast.

Community

As we have seen, Yucatán had long been connected to Cuba, and these connections took the form of economic and cultural exchanges and well as population movements. During the Ten Years' War, however, the migration of Cubans intensified. Historians have had difficulty finding population statistics for the migrant communities and so have had to rely on newspapers that listed Cuban passengers arriving in area ports. These documents indicate that, after 1869, entire families frequently arrived together. They were intellectuals, artists, professionals, planters, and also workers.[57] In 1889 and 1890, two Mérida newspapers indicated that Cuban workers including "mulatos" were migrating to Yucatán by the hundreds looking for work. This exodus corresponded to the difficult economic situation of the island of Cuba in these years, but it was supported by the prosperity of Yucatán and especially its reputation. *La Lucha* from Trinidad in Cuba reported that, on one ship, over 150 desperate and poor Cubans departed for Yucatán because its "admirable prosperity" was an irresistible draw.[58]

In 1895, the Cuban Revolutionary Party representative in the Yucatán, Rodolfo Menénde Peña, stated that Cuban migrants there were "few and isolated" but that, according to his own observation in 1896, the community had grown exponentially.[59] Cubans arriving to Mérida, especially in the 1890s, traveled from the ports of Progreso or Campeche to Mérida via rail. The Yucatán peninsula was uniquely connected by rail in the 1890s. In an excellent study of nationally owned railroads, Pedro Riguzzi indicates that the kilometers of track laid in Yucatán grew exponentially between 1880 and 1903, from 44 to 739.[60] The construction of the railroad was bankrolled by henequen elites representing four separate companies that eventually became consolidated as the Ferrocarriles Unidos de Yucatán in 1908. The primary purpose of these rail lines was to move henequen from plantations to the coast for shipment, and yet all four lines converged in Mérida. Two of these lines explicitly connected Mérida and Progreso and Mérida and Campeche, providing ample and regular travel opportunities for Cuban émigrés looking to move beyond costal ports of arrival.

For some migrants, family connections provided a substantial advantage. Carlos Bojórquez Urzaiz suggests that many émigrés came to Yucatán because they had family members established there, or had friends who knew of its many economic opportunities.[61] Yucatán's proximity to Cuba made the peninsula an important destination for insurgents and their families. For example, Fernando Urzaiz y Arrítola settled his family in Progreso before returning to the war. General Alberto Nodarse's family members migrated to Yucatán between 1889 and 1895, although he himself returned to the war. In fact, Nodarse's mother was among a handful of women who sent letters to Estrada Palma; Rita Bacallo Vida de Nodarse corresponded with the head of the Cuban Revolutionary Party regarding matters related to the political club that she belonged to, the *club de señoritas de Mérida, Cuba Libre*.[62]

Among Mérida's Cuban population there were a significant number of professionals, especially doctors. One of Mérida's most important Cuban political clubs was composed of medical doctors who specialized in collecting and transporting medical supplies to insurgent soldiers. Judging by the elite character of public events staged to support the Cuban cause during the war years, it is clear that Cubans sought to project an image of the future Cuban nation as modern and elite.

Gilbert Joseph and Allen Wells describe Mérida, Mexico's "white City," in the late nineteenth century as a "provincial echo of the national capital's style and substance."[63] Just as Mexico City was being modernized in the late nineteenth century, revenues from the henequen boom allowed elites to transform Mérida from a small colonial town into a modern city with tramways, public lighting, better sanitation, and a paseo imitating the famous *Paseo de la Reforma* in Mexico City, which was lined with tufted laurel trees imported from Cuba. Mérida was surely a capital where a wealthier, more professional set of migrants, many of whom likely enjoyed sumptuous lives in Havana or Matanzas, could imagine living. Cuban migrant Cloridiano Betancourt, a banker and owner of a Bon Marche selling *"novedades para caballeros"* (new fashion for gentlemen) in Mérida, certainly counted himself among Mérida's urban elite, for whom the latest in French fashion would be a necessity.[64] Yucatán's "admirable prosperity" likely was a boon to Cuban elites and may have provided employment for Cuban workers, but the observations of the Spanish consul in Mérida tell a different story, one of a community afflicted by poverty. The consul observed that Cubans were generally very poor: "None of them have money to spare, and furthermore, they are burdened with having to aid the numerous émigrés who arrive in a state of misery."[65] Not only were many newcomers poor, but wealthier members complained of being impoverished for many reasons, including the trials of making a life in exile, providing financial support for the independence struggle through financial contributions, and supporting the needs of poor Cuban refugees. The consul continued: "Many [Cubans] leave a few days after arriving because they cannot find work. Here, neither the day laborer, nor the artisan, nor the tobacco worker can find jobs. Some move on because they cannot adjust to working in the fields, others because there are no tobacco factories here."[66] He insisted that there was little of the work that most Cubans were prepared to do—by which the consul surely meant that there were not enough jobs in the tobacco and sugar industries.

Cuban migrants in Mérida and Progreso may have been impoverished and downright poor, but the poorest and most isolated migrants were those who lived outside of Mérida as indentured workers on the state's interior and its eastern coast. Indeed, the specter of elite wealth and mobility contrasted starkly with the immobility of scores of contract workers who signed on with colonization companies like the Compania Colonizadora de la Costa Oriental de Yucatán. Some of these contract workers did so to escape the 1895 War. As the demand for labor related to the henequen industry grew, colonization companies duped poor, rural Cubans into migrating to Yucatán, where they found themselves locked into semi-slavery on henequen plantations alongside Yaqui prisoners of war and contract laborers from China, Korea, Puerto Rico, and the Canary Islands.[67]

On 14 May 1896, a representative of the Spanish company contracted 110 Cubans to colonize San José de la Vega on the Yucatán peninsula.[68] The colonists were promised sustenance, land, and remuneration for their work. They were transported free of cost to Isla Mujeres and then to San José de La Vega. Shortly after their arrival, however, it became clear that the company did not intend to keep its promises. The colonists were kept in an "indescribable condition of famish and slavery, without pay and hard labor and bodily punishment, as well as without communication with the rest of the world." One colonist named Juan Ortega Manzano fled the farm, but when he tried to return for his wife and children, he was prohibited from doing so. He called on the Spanish consul and the Mexican authorities for help, but was ignored. Managing to return to Cuba, he petitioned the U.S. military governor John R. Brook for help. In a letter to the governor, Ortega Manzano stated that since his departure his wife had died of starvation, and he desperately wanted to "free my six children from barbarie and illegal servitude to which they are subjected by that Spanish company in Mexican territory." He pled with the governor for his family and the hundred or so other colonists languishing in the Vega de San José to be rescued.[69] The fate of those colonists remains a mystery, but evidence suggests that years later many remained in Yucatán under the same circumstances.

On 10 January 1900, J. Maresma wrote to Diego Tamayo, the Cuban secretary of state, about the plight of the Cubans stranded in Yucatán. He included a clipping from a contemporary issue of the newspaper *El Cubano*, which referred to the lamentable situation of Cubans in both Yucatán and Veracruz. Maresma was particularly concerned with the following statement in the article: "In the states of Veracruz and Yucatán, there are Cuban families that suffer from hunger and misery. These families were duped by the miserable companies who brought them to Mexico promising remunerated work when life in Cuba was unsustainable."[70] Maresma asked Tamayo to use his influence with the American authorities to repatriate these Cubans, arguing that the nascent republic desperately needed farmers to cultivate its own lands. Tamayo immediately forwarded this letter to the U.S. military governor, General Leonard Wood, asking him to order that U.S. consuls in Veracruz and Yucatán look into the matter. Were these the same colonists on whose behalf Ortega Manzano had intervened a year earlier? Perhaps. Four years later, complaints of Cubans suffering deplorable living and working conditions on the lands of the Compañía Colonizadora de la Costa Oriental de Yucatan surfaced again. On 16 February 1904, the Cuban minister in Mexico, Carlos García Vélez, wrote to the Cuban secretary of state, Carlos Zaldo, concerning an article that appeared in the Mexican newspaper *El Diario del Hogar*. The article referred to the death of several Cubans and Puerto Ricans on the lands of the Compañía.[71]

Ultimately, the indentured workers of Yucatán were not represented in the PRC documentation or among the applicants to the ANERC because they were isolated from the larger Cuban migrant community in Yucatán. It is hard to imagine that Mérida-based Cubans had no knowledge of them, yet they are not mentioned in party-related correspondence. Their existence raises important questions. How many Cuban refugees were relocated into lives of semi-slavery in other parts of the circum-Caribbean? And how can this relocation be compared, say, with the deportation of Cubans to Spain's African penal colonies during these same years?

While the Cuban Revolutionary Party urged unity across class differences for the sake of national struggle and invited all people to become part of the movement, class divisions remained strong during the war and were firmly reinforced in the new republic. Lillian Guerra refers to the practice among many elite exile women of sending luxury goods to men of pedigree who were insurgents in the war. Well-to-do generals and colonels might receive alcohol, chocolate, silk, and similar hard-to-procure items, while many foot soldiers were barely clothed.[72] Among the Mexico-based émigrés, at least one woman sent hammocks to the young girls of a children's club in New York City in lieu of sending something of use to the insurgents fighting the war.[73] These gestures suggest that for elite migrants and their kin, reinforcing their status was at times just as important as funneling resources into the war effort.

The occupation of the ANERC applicants and PRC letter writers, coupled with their literacy and their political connections, confirms their elite status. However, the same documents reveal the existence of the poor migrants and indentured workers struggling under exploitative labor conditions. This reminds us of the exploitation in the tobacco industry in Oaxaca, where Cubans in Veracruz were taken to work as well. The Valle was notorious for exploitation.[74] While the presence of Cubans in the Valle is confirmed by the report of their financial contribution to the revolutionary struggle, there is no evidence that the indentured workers in Yucatán were involved in the movement. As Ortega Manzano indicated, the colonists were "without communication with the rest of the world." When Ortega Manzano escaped the camp and made his way to Mérida, he called on the Spanish consul first. It is hard to ascertain exactly how much he knew of the events in his homeland in 1898, but it is possible that he emerged from the company's lands without a clear grasp of the course of the war. Rebuffed by the Spanish consul, he sought the support of the U.S. consul in Mérida. While the Spanish consul advised him to keep quiet about the affair, the U.S. consul told Ortega Manzano that he could not aid him without authorization from his superiors. With no representation abroad, Ortega Manzano's only hope was to appeal directly to the U.S. military governor in Cuba, which he did twice. Ortega Manzano filed two appeals over the course of five months, but there is no indication that his case was resolved.

The fact that we find no contract laborers among the ANERC applicants or letter writers can be explained by the isolation of such workers from political life in cities like Mérida and, to a lesser degree, Progreso and Campeche. Most of the documentation for Mérida specifically speaks of the involvement of elites in the political struggle. References to other Cuban workers are few, with the exception of a sizable group of men and women in Progreso who came together to make financial contributions to the revolution under the name "Obreros de Progreso." The presence of workers in the ANERC files for Veracruz likely reflect the larger number of migrants overall and the existence of a more politically active migrant working class affiliated with the tobacco industry in that state.

Generation

Mérida's Cuban community was composed of wealthy professionals who shouldered the burden of supporting waves of poor migrants who arrived through the ports of Campeche and Progresso and were dependent on the generosity of other migrant Cubans. These poor stayed if the conditions were favorable or moved on if they could not find work. Among these poor we also find the "colonists" in the interior who could not escape indentured servitude. The Cuban Revolutionary Party representative in Yucatán, Rodolfo Menéndez Peña, was conflicted about the growth of the Cuban population in Mérida, especially about the influx of poor and destitute migrants.[75] This increase was, in Menéndez Peña's opinion, a double-edged sword. On one hand, the growth of the community might provide fresh recruits and a firm base of the Cuban Revolutionary Party, but the new migrants could also be a burden. In a report to the leader of the Cuban Revolutionary Party dated January of 1896, Menéndez Peña strained to keep his composure as he complained about the newer and younger generation of Cuban migrants in the city: "The majority of the Cuban population is newly arrived and composed of the sort of riffraff that inspires fear. Gamblers and those without any purpose in life abound. Of the old émigrés, those men who are intransigent and who never have had dealings with Spain, who have preferred to live as exiles for the last twenty-six years suffering countless miseries rather than collaborate with the Spanish, few are left."[76]

Just like the older generation leadership in Veracruz, Menéndez Peña set up a dichotomy between the older migrants and the newer ones when he described the former as intransigent, courageous, and proud, and the latter as "*guatíbaro*" or riffraff. A *guatíbaro* was a person of low social standing, generally a peasant, or someone residing in the countryside.[77] Menéndez Peña seemed to chide the new arrivals for having remained in Cuba after the Ten Years' War rather than having emigrated in protest of the resolutions reached at Zanjón in 1878. In another complaint filed some months later, Menéndez Peña reported to Estrada Palma that a handful of recent arrivals had created a political club, which he dismissed as being of little importance. Troublingly, however, they also launched a newspaper in which they openly criticized the older generation. "These people created an insignificant rag," he wrote, "in which they publish all kinds of insults against

Cubans, particularly the older Cubans like us." Menéndez Peña continued, "What would you have us do with these insubordinate émigrés? . . . What we have done: ignore them and go on with our collections. Of course, these people do us harm in our work."[78] Who were these insubordinate young migrants? Were they young men like Nicolás Valverde in Veracruz, who was punished for calling into question the authority of the established older generation veterans of Veracruz? Did they have legitimate complaints against older migrants who had established a rigid revolutionary hierarchy that relegated them to the lowest rungs on the ladder?

Menéndez Peña alludes more than once in his correspondence with Estrada Palma to the fact that bridging the generational gap was a difficult task, while also claiming that he persevered for the good of the cause. Menéndez Peña's efforts reflect the Party's commitment to unity between revolutionaries in the interest of the war. Indeed, his outburst is atypical when seen in the context of the numerous letters he wrote to Estrada Palma over several years. Menéndez Peña's unusual complaint allows us to observe how tensions were simmering beneath a veneer of forced cooperation and tolerance in Mérida, just as they were in Veracruz. Curiously, while Menéndez Peña complains about the riffraff in the cities, he makes no mention of the struggles of Cuban workers like Juan Ortega Manzano suffering at the hands of Spanish exploitation not in Cuba but in the not so distant Vega de San José. The silence is curious if only because the exploitation garnered public attention in Mexico and Cuba each year from 1899 to 1904. Whether their ignorance of the suffering of Cuban compatriots in Mexico was honest or willful, the absence of any mention of the colonists provides evidence of the stark separation between Cuban elites located in the city of Mérida and laborers in the countryside.

Like Veracruz, Mérida was intimately connected to Cuba and had been for centuries. In fact, both cities were arguably more closely linked to the Caribbean, Gulf, and Atlantic worlds than they were to each other. As we will see, Cubans did travel between Veracruz and Mérida, but much more often they traveled to and from each city and ports in Cuba and the United States. The position of both cities with respect to the Gulf and Cuba shaped them and shaped the Cuban migrant communities to which they were home. As older revolutionaries and wealthy Cubans were called upon to integrate and provide support for large numbers of poor and mixed-race Cubans fleeing the war, tensions rose, straining the limits of a revolutionary rhetoric that advocated for the unity of all Cubans and for the right of every Cuban to belong to the future Cuban nation. Such tensions were less pronounced in interior cities like the Mexican capital, where the Cuban migrant population was far more homogeneous.

Mexico City

Connections

For all its distance from the coast, Mexico City was more integrated into the Gulf World in the 1890s than it had been just decades earlier. A journey from coast to capital that took weeks could now be completed in two days, with the advent of the railroad linking Veracruz and Mexico City in the early 1870s.[79] As a result, Mexico City became a more accessible destination for Cubans and other migrants and immigrants. Many scholars have written eloquently about the transformation of Mexico City during the three decades of the Porfiriato.[80] The city saw radical changes as it was remodeled to fit an idealized—and rather francophone—vision of modernity. The growth and modernization of the city, including its increased accessibility due to railroad construction, made the capital a destination for both foreigners and Mexicans. The fact that revenues from third-class tickets for the Mexican Railway were significantly larger than revenues from first-class tickets proved without a doubt that massive numbers of workers and non-elites rode the rails.[81] Such might have been the case for Cubans like Fernando Echermendia Flores, who traveled looking for work not only between Veracruz and Mexico City, but also up the Gulf Coast to Tampico as well. Destitute and dispossessed the rural Mexican poor flocked to the city in search of work, often settling in outer neighborhoods; at the same time, various groups of wealthy foreigners inhabited Mexico's city center and financial district.[82] Internal migration so dwarfed foreign migration that the influx of foreigners might have passed largely unnoticed, were it not for their concentration in the nation's capital, where they were involved in the business and financial sectors.

Community

Compared to that of Veracruz and Mérida, Mexico City's Cuban population was much more homogenous in terms of race and class. The Cuban migrants were generally white, educated professionals, including businessmen, doctors, journalists, students, and lawyers. In many senses, Mexico City's demographic profile was similar to that of New York City, where professionals and educated elites dominated politics.[83] Like New York and also Washington, D.C., where Cubans had strategically placed representatives to lobby congressmen, Mexico City was a center of political maneuvering and diplomacy more than it was a key site of grassroots organizing. In Mexico City, racial and class homogeneity minimized the tensions between older and younger revolutionary generations, which, as we have seen, often masked racial and class-based tensions.

Censuses taken in 1890, 1895, 1905, and 1910 allow us to get a sense of the relative size of the different foreign immigrant populations in the city. Spaniards and U.S. citizens were the two most numerous groups across all four periods, followed by the French, Chinese, and Germans. The sixth largest group (across all four periods), and the largest among Latin Americans, were the Cubans. In the 1890s, Cubans were also the largest immigrant group from Latin America in New York City, but there they also outnumbered Spaniards.[84] In Mexico City and in Veracruz, on the other hand, the Spanish immigrant population far surpassed the Cuban population at all times, a fact which made Cuban organizing much more difficult in Mexico in the United States, as we will see in a later chapter. The number of Cubans in Mexico City according to the census remained modest, rising from 123 in 1890 to 698 in 1910, but the greater number of Cuban migrants relative to other Latin American and Caribbean groups provides further evidence of the particular connection between Cuba and Mexico in this period—a unique connection forged over decades and nurtured by successive waves of Cuban migrants.[85]

Like the vast majority of foreigners, Cubans resided in the streets adjacent to the Zócalo. Their patterns of settlement similar to those of other Latin Americans and U.S. Americans. The similarity suggests the possibility of close associations between U.S. Americans and Cubans in financial and political matters. Indeed the main newspaper affiliated with the U.S. community was the *Mexican Herald*, which openly supported the Cuban independence struggle. Alfred Boisse, a U.S. American and longtime resident of Mexico, and professor at the Colegio Militar and Escuela Nacional Preparatoria, openly professed his love and support for Cuba. He had lived in Cuba for eighteen years before relocating to Mexico. Boisse wrote to Estrada Palma just as the Spanish-American War was coming to a close, offering advice on the benefits of teaching English to students of the future Cuban republic. Although he believed English acquisition would be critical for

Cuban youth, he cautioned that English should never replace Spanish. "Cuba . . . should never cease being Cuba," he insisted.[86] Boisse's own residence on Calle Reloj placed him in proximity to center of Cuban activity.

The central districts around the Zócalo were home to the majority of the hotels, which housed foreigners. Since renting was uncommon, and purchasing a place to live was impossible for many new arrivals, many came to reside in hotels for long periods of time.[87] Antonio Solar was one of many Cubans who took up residence at the famous and popular hotel Comonfort on Cinco de Mayo. From his modest accommodations there, Antonio wrote a hopeful letter to the secretary of the Cuban Revolutionary Party in New York, asking to be included in the next expedition to leave Cuba.[88] Solar was careful to indicate that he had the money to transport himself to the point of embarkation, wherever that may have been, which indicated his relatively privileged class status.

The capital of Mexico was a study in contrasts. It was the preferred city of residence for wealthy and professional foreigners, who were concentrated in its most modernized central districts, and also the destination of throngs of poor, destitute, and displaced workers looking for the means to survive. As we have seen, among those foreigners and residing in the same central areas were a significant number of Cubans. The ANERC and PRC letters provide little anecdotal information about Mexico City's Cuban residents. We do know, however, that the Mexico City Cuban émigré community was composed of former insurgents, doctors, pharmacists, and journalists. Some might also have been entrepreneurs deeply enmeshed in Mexico's financial sector and residing in the many hotels of central Mexico City. Certainly, the home of the agent of the Cuban Revolutionary Party in Mexico, Nicolas Domínguez Cowan, which was located in the center of the city, was a critical meeting point for revolutionary Cubans between 1868 and 1898. The press offices of the principal newspapers supporting Cuban independence were also located in this downtown core. The political center of Cuban activity was firmly ensconced in the areas where foreigners resided at the time.

Mexico City had long been a place where Cuban exiles conspiring against Spain had lived and sought alliance, from José María Heredia to Manuel Quesada and Perdo Santacilia. However, with the outbreak of insurgency in Cuba in 1895 and the creation of revolutionary agencies in capital cities across the region, Mexico City gained new importance as a center of Cuban revolutionary activity. Agents like Nicolás Domínguez Cowan acted as informal ambassadors. Men like Santacillia—who had served numerous terms as a deputy in congress and whose status was secured by his close affiliation with the revered Benito Juárez—and men like Carlos de Varona—an early generation migrant who had risen to become the president of Mexico's National Bank—continued to support the Cuban cause politically and financially.[89] Hardly the "integral outsiders" U.S. Americans proved to be and nowhere nearly as influential as Mexico City's wealthy and numerous Spanish communities, a small handful of Cubans (especially those who had resided in Mexico since the 1860s) were nevertheless tenacious in their efforts to gather funds and influence Mexican public opinion. These men took advantage of their memberships in literary, scientific, and political associations, where they engaged in literary criticism, played chess, and debated national and international questions alongside likeminded Mexicans. From these advantageous locations, they worked to shape the opinion of political elites whose support for the Cuban cause might translate into concrete advantages in the realm of international affairs.

Although linked via rail to Veracruz, Mexico City shared little with its Gulf and Caribbean coast counterparts when it came to the character of Cuban migrant communities. Where Veracruz and Mérida were cities that absorbed large numbers of poorer migrants, only Cubans of some means sought permanent residence in Mexico City. Furthermore, unlike Veracruz (or even New York City), Mexico City's distance from the coast made it a poor choice to launch insurgents seeking reentry into Cuba. Quite differently, Mexico City became a space of diplomacy and a center of elite transnational solidarities between Cubans and Mexicans who found common cause in the fight for *Cuba Libre*. Cubans in the capital still worked to sustain the revolutionary movement through the clandestine gathering and funneling of money, arms, and supplies, but Mexico City increasingly became a place where Cuba's international reputation was cultivated and defended, as we will see in subsequent chapters. With little demographic diversity, Cubans in Mexico City largely avoided the crippling internal divisions of the kinds that affected migrant communities in Mérida and Veracruz.

Gulf World Circulations: Multiple Migrations

Veracruz, Mérida, and Mexico City each offered different economic, cultural, and political benefits for the migrants who established themselves there, but Cubans were migrants in motion. Their lives were defined by their own constant circulations, or by those of the migrants around them. Cubans in Veracruz were uniquely and intimately linked to the Gulf World and the greater Caribbean by the steady stream of ships that called to the city's port, bringing newspapers, letters, and migrants with stories from home. Cuban migrant communities were anything but isolated. Progreso and Mérida were connected by a mere thirty-seven kilometers of railroad track, and, consequently, Cubans in Mérida felt nearly as linked to the Gulf World as those in Veracruz. Movement and circulation shaped the lives of those who remained sedentary, but it defined the lives of those who moved restlessly from place to place, circulating between Cuban migrant communities in Mexico and even traveling beyond Mexico altogether. The members of the group of Cubans residing in Mexico who applied to the ANERC after the war and those Cuban migrants we can track through their correspondence with members of the Revolutionary Party traveled to eighteen different cities within Mexico between 1895 and 1898: Veracruz, Alvarado, Tlacotalpan, Coatzacoalcos, Orizaba, Tampico, Tuxpam, Mérida, Progreso, Campeche, Mexico City, Puebla, Monterrey, Tula de Tamaulipas, Morelia (Michoacan), San Juan Bautista (Tabasco), Galeana, and San Lorenzo.

Despite the fact that most Cuban migrants settled in cities and towns along Mexico's Gulf coasts, 105 of 298 Cuban migrants identifiable from the ANERC documents and PRC letters—just over one-third of the sample—resided in interior cities, defined as cities which required travel inland from the coast, usually by rail.[90] This number increases to between one-third and one-half of the sample if we add the nineteen ANERC applicants who listed more than one city of residence in Mexico. In all likelihood, the mobility of the group corresponded to their relatively elevated social position.

Cities of residence for this group included Mexico City and Mérida, of course, but they also included cities like Puebla and Orizaba, both of which were connected by the Mexican Railway to Veracruz and Mexico City. Puebla was an important mini-center of Cuban revolutionary activity. The agent in Puebla, Antonio Hevia, sent detailed reports to the Cuban Revolutionary Party leadership discussing the many collections and events sponsored by the Cuban community there. Although there are only seven Cubans from Puebla listed in the ANERC files and PRC letters, this number is not representative of the city's full Cuban population. The directorship alone of Bravo y Maceo in Puebla registers fourteen members.[91] The elected positions in a club of a modest size might include four to seven members, by which we can assume that Bravo y Maceo of Puebla had dozens more. Orizaba, Veracruz, was another small center of Cuban revolutionary organizing located in the interior. The Cañizares Gómez brothers founded the Agrupación Cubana de Orizaba, the most important and organized association of Cuban migrants in that city. In a letter to Estrada Palma in 1896, Juan Cañizares Gómez reported that the Agrupación gathered all the Cubans of Orizaba, as well as a community of Mexican supporters into an integrated community. Between that year and the end of the war, the group sent regular financial contributions to the Cuban revolutionary leadership in New York throughout the duration of the war.[92]

Two-thirds of the ANERC applicants who reported residency in more than one city in Mexico traveled along the Mexico-Veracruz corridor, and a smaller minority traveled to Yucatán or Campeche as well. Travel between less directly connected regions like Mexico City and Yucatán was less common and more costly, given the logistical difficulties.[93] While travel between distant Mexican states was only undertaken by a minority, intrastate travel was a matter of daily practice. The travel of migrants between cities in Veracruz for the purpose of recruiting Cubans to political clubs, for the purpose of attending cultural celebrations, or to resolve disputes between community members is well documented.[94]

The listed occupations of highly mobile migrants reveal that they were largely professionals and included doctors, pharmacists, professors, and one sailor who worked for the U.S. and Cuban Mail Steamship Company, the Ward Line. Among those who did not list an occupation in their ANERC files, we find migrants who worked as journalists in exile—a common occupation of elite political exiles—and those who, judging by the extent of their travels to places like Paris, Madrid, and New York, were likely wealthy. One widely traveled individual boasted that he was an active member of twenty-two Cuban associations. Considering that active membership required payment of a monthly quota, membership in that many organizations could only be sustained by an exceptionally wealthy individual.

A few migrants traveled between states in Mexico for work-related reasons. Fernando Echermendia Flores traveled from Mexico City to Jalapa, Veracruz, and then to Tampico searching for employment, while Leandro González Alcorta left Mexico City to fill a position as a scribe for a customs house in the port of Campeche. Ricardo Sierra y García worked for the Ward Line and thus traveled constantly between Gulf, Caribbean, and Atlantic ports. All three men carried their political affiliations and commitments everywhere they went. So too did men like Rafael Rodriguez Acosta, the Cuban who belonged to twenty-two separate Cuban clubs, or Rafael Cuevas y Oliva, a member of clubs in Mexico City, Puebla, and Veracruz, both of whom forged enduring connections among political associations in distinct locations. Multiple memberships in clubs located in different cities were remarkably common among those Cubans with the means to sustain those memberships. Cesar Acosta O'Farrill, a resident of Mérida and Progreso, is another example. He belonged to one political club in each city. Likewise, Eduardo Colmo y Quintero maintained dual residence in Campeche and Mérida and membership in a political club in both cities.

Whether club business motivated their travels or club participation was a byproduct of their travels, all of these individuals served to link Cuban migrant communities within Mexico, much as the ships calling to port at Gulf Coast cities and the rail lines that linked those ports to interior cities facilitated the integration of Cuban communities into a world beyond Mexico's shores. The example of a Cuban known as "Dickens" is a case in point. In a letter to Estrada Palma, Rodolfo Menéndez Peña reported on the arrival of "Dickens," an ophthalmologist, who claimed to be related by marriage to Máximo Gómez. Dickens had come to Mérida carrying authorization from a Veracruz-based Cuban club to collect financial contributions for the independence cause. Menéndez was checking with Estrada Palma to make sure that the man could be trusted and that his authorization ought to be taken seriously.[95] This incident tells us three things: first, that financial contributions generally traveled through particular channels, either funneled to the party representative in Mexico City or remitted directly to the Revolutionary Party in New York. Dickens's mission was at odds with these practices. Second, the incident reveals that individual Cubans and individual clubs took up interregional collections, providing proof that interregional dynamic exchanges existed at the level of individuals, or individual club initiatives. Third, while Dickens's presence and activities are indicative of interregional connections, Menéndez's decision to communicate directly with the New York City–based leadership rather than settle the matter directly with the Veracruz club suggests that vertical hierarchies could often supercede horizontal connections.

Whether Cubans traveled on business related to the revolution, for work, or to reunite with families, their movements helped integrate Mexico's Cuban migrant communities, which facilitated an emerging diasporic consciousness. Within Mexico, Cubans who resided in Gulf port cities were never oriented only toward Cuba nor exclusively toward the Cuban diaspora beyond Mexico's borders; they were also oriented inward toward Mexico. They traveled between Mexican cities that were centers of Cuban activities and well beyond them. As we will see, Cubans' ability to nurture diasporic connections while building meaningful transnational solidarities in Mexico would shape Cuban politics in Mexico and play an important role in the broad popularity of the Cuban revolutionary cause in Mexico.

Conclusion

Ignacio Martín Arbona y Domínguez spent only a couple of months in Veracruz, but in that short time he became fully involved in the politics of the migrant community and a beneficiary of its social and revolutionary networks. He formed part of a revolutionary club, and when the opportunity arose to join a filibustering expedition and he volunteered, the Veracruz community made all the preparations so that he could return to the war. Whether it was manning and outfitting expeditions, aiding insurgents as they passed through ports, or restocking and provisioning filibustering expeditions en route to Cuba, the Cuban communities of Veracruz and Mérida provided critical services to the insurgent army.

What a transient visitor like Ignacio may not have seen were the cracks, fissures, and tensions that belied the veneer of perfect unity so vigorously defended by men like the head of the Veracruz CDC, José Miguel Macias, or the regional PRC agent in Mérida, Rodolfo Menéndez Peña. In the grander scheme of things, the tensions that did plague Cuban communities in Veracruz and Mérida may not have had significant tangible consequences for the revolution, like the major loss or diversion of funds, or the thwarting of expeditions bringing men and arms to Cuba. Still, the persistent tensions between old and young, black and white, and rich and poor, would have a deep and lasting effect on the new independent state of Cuba years after the war. Many Cuban migrants, especially those with means, would return to their country with a new, or a renewed sense of entitlement, and old inequalities would map easily onto new structures. But the harboring of inequalities would not be the only legacy that the vast Gulf and Caribbean network of Cuban migrant communities would bequeath to the revolution and later the republic. Indeed, the space of exile allowed Cubans of different walks of life to envision and lay the groundwork for a new Cuba. Their visions would be deeply influenced by lives lived in Mexico and in diaspora, as we will see in later chapters.

Dynamically connected Mexican coastal enclaves were linked to communities in the interior, like those in Mexico City, Puebla, and Orizaba, and together Cubans throughout Mexico worked alongside Mexicans to raise money and advance political and diplomatic projects in support of the Cuban cause. The efforts of settled migrants were further bolstered by those of itinerant and highly mobile Cubans who traveled between migrant centers, throughout the Gulf world and the Caribbean and even as far as New York City and Europe. Their travels served to suture together distant communities by transmitting news about the progress of the war and about revolutionary activities in different migrant centers. These travelers were often men, but not exclusively. Dominga Valdes Corovalles de Muniz strengthened the diasporic connection between Tampa, Florida, and Veracruz, Mexico, not just as a traveling migrant, but as a self-identified and politically active revolutionary émigré. It is to her story and to the twin forces of inclusion and exclusion in Cuban exile politics that we now turn.

3 Cuban Revolutionary Politics in Diaspora

Dominga Valdes Corvalles de Muniz emigrated to Florida and then to Mexico with her family sometime in the late 1880s.[1] Although her route was similar to that of Gabriel and Ignacio, her direction was reversed. Rather than make her way from Cuba to Mexico to Florida, she traveled from Cuba to Florida to Mexico, where she resided as of 1893. Ignacio and Gabriel's use of Mexico as a gateway to Florida had everything to do with their participation in the insurgency and the nature and progress of the war, and Dominga was neither an insurgent nor directly involved in the military conflict. However, like the experiences of both her compatriots, Dominga's migrant experience underscores the connectedness of Cuban revolutionary communities in the Gulf World, a place where Cuban migrants, insurgents, revolutionary sympathizers, and refugees circulated constantly.

As a young woman in Florida, Dominga had an active political life. She held an elected position in a Cuban political club in Key West. She carried her political affiliations across the Gulf and served as the secretary of a Cuban political club in Veracruz in the mid-1890s. What is curious about Dominga, however, is not the fact that she was politically active in the Cuban Revolutionary Party, nor that she held a prominent position in two Cuban clubs in two distinct migrant centers in the Gulf World; many other women, in fact, did both. What is unique about her is that she applied to the National Association of Revolutionary Émigrés after the war, and in so doing publicly claimed the status of a revolutionary. The applications of only three other Cuban female migrants from Mexico are conserved in the archives of the ANERC. Dominga's file also stands out for the way she staked a claim to her identity as a revolutionary. In her application she did not credit her father, brother, husband, or any other man for inspiring her revolutionary labors and sacrifices, and she did not indicate that her entry into politics was via collaboration with a male relative, as was customary for revolutionary women, who often figured themselves as auxiliaries to men.

While Dominga's migration reminds us that women and families were prevalent among Cuban migrants in the later nineteenth century, her story vividly illustrates the dual tendencies of inclusion and exclusion that marked

Cuban revolutionary politics in exile. On the one hand, Dominga's participation in the movement owes much to the structures of the Cuban Revolutionary Party, which encouraged the participation of women. Her determination to claim her revolutionary identity demonstrates that women not only embraced the opportunity to participate in the movement but also that they sometimes did so on their own terms. On the other hand, her isolation and the absence of the stories of the hundreds of other women who participated in the movement in Mexico make plain the practices of exclusion that were common both during the war years and afterward.

This chapter explores the inclusive and exclusive discourses and practices that shaped Cuban revolutionary exile politics in Mexico during the 1895 War and in Cuba after the war. It takes as its focus the Cuban Revolutionary Party (PRC), which was founded in Tampa and headquartered in New York City in 1892, and the party's successor organization, the National Association of Cuban Revolutionary Émigrés (ANERC), established in Havana in 1909. The Cuban Revolutionary Party, a nationalist party of international reach, was founded to coordinate the forces necessary to bring about the final struggle for Cuban independence, but the party's leaders also hoped that it might lay the groundwork for the emergence of a democratic Cuban republic. Building on lessons from Cubans' past revolutionary struggles, which were undermined by divisions within the revolutionary ranks, the party set as its primary mission the unification of Cubans on and off the island, across the divides of race, class, gender, politics, and generation, in support of a final push for Cuban independence. As we have seen, Cuban migrant communities, nourished over three decades by a steady stream of new migrants and networked together by travelers like Gabriel, Ignacio, and Dominga, were diverse and disaporic. The Cuban Revolutionary Party served to solidify existing linkages by providing additional channels of communication through interconnected institutional structures, international agents, special envoys, and newspapers that circulated between migrant centers. These structures supported the growth of a diasporic consciousness among Cuban migrants and brought émigrés together horizontally across borders while reorienting them vertically north toward New York City. In Mexico, the character of Cuban exile politics was specific to particular places. For example, as indicated in chapter 2, Veracruz was a space of working-class mobilization, while Yucatan was the site of smaller-scale elite mobilization. Mexico City, being the nation's capital, was a center of elite political action and *the* center of diplomatic projects. This chapter shifts the focus away from regional specificity and foregrounds cross-regional collaboration, while also highlighting the vertical nature of Cuban exile politics after the formation of the Cuban Revolutionary Party in 1892. A closer look at the politics of the PRC and an examination of how the party mapped itself onto existing communities with revolutionary traditions and diasporic connections allows us to see the PRC not as a foreign construct, but as something closely tied to the experiences of Cuban exiles and migrants.

The PRC was the product of the Cuban exile and migrant experience, but it also fundamentally reshaped the relationship of Cubans abroad to the revolutionary movement, albeit unevenly. By inviting Cubans abroad into the movement regardless of race, class, gender, age, or previous political affiliation, the Cuban Revolutionary Party fundamentally altered the status and self-perception of Cuban migrants, exiles, and refugees, offering them both a role in the struggle and a place in the imagined nation. However, even as every migrant was welcomed into the movement, the work of some was valued above that of others. Thus, while the PRC gave a broad range of actors—including women like Dominga, Afro-Cubans, and working class Cubans—the opportunity to participate in the revolutionary struggle, it also set limits on that participation, limits which became increasingly visible over time and as the war progressed. The fiction of perfect unity was belied by day-to-day discrimination on the ground. While the rhetoric employed to unite Cubans was one that envisioned all Cubans as members of the emergent nation, in practice white, male, educated elites— many of whom had revolutionary pedigree that extended back to the 1868 generation—were the most valued and celebrated members of the Cuban exile migrations. Ideal patriots were those with a respected revolutionary pedigree, those who could demonstrate unfaltering loyalty to the cause, and those who made what the PRC deemed valuable contributions to the revolutionary struggle. These preferences shaped Cuban revolutionary politics during the war, and they were reflected in both the official archives of the party and the practices of the party's successor, the ANERC.

The ANERC was founded in Havana in 1909 with the express purpose of continuing the legacy of the PRC. The ANERC's statutes include direct reference to three points drawn from the Manifesto of Montecristi, the guiding document of the Cuban Revolutionary Party. The organization pledged itself to the fulfillment of the following goals: to support the creation of a sincere and democratic republic; to ensure that the republic was for all Cubans equally; and to protect the republic from internal and external threats.[2] Even so, the archive of the ANERC suggests that the organization fell short of honoring the democratic and egalitarian ethos of the manifesto.

TABLE 3.1 Occupation of ANERC applicants from Mexico

Occupation	Number
Doctor	11
Journalist	10
Tobacco worker	5
Pharmacist	4
Day laborer	2
Tailor	2
Tobacco (owner)	1
Professor	1
Sailor	1
Banker	1
Photographer	1
Carpenter	1
Rancher	1
Circus performer	1
Total	42

Source: Archivo Nacional de Cuba, Asociación Nacional de los Emigrados Revolucionarios Cubanos.

First, the Cubans who applied to the ANERC as émigrés from Mexico were disproportionately from the elite and middle classes. Professional occupation is unevenly recorded in the ANERC files for Cuban migrants in Mexico, but, from available evidence for roughly one quarter of the sample, we know that 75 percent were elite or middle class and 25 percent were workers (see table 3.1).

By comparison with the ANERC data, only twenty-nine of the 110 Cubans residing in Mexico who wrote letters to the Cuban Revolutionary Party reveal their occupations. Of these, twenty-six were middle class or elite professionals and only three were workers. This statistic is not surprising given that those Cuban migrants who had direct access to the party leadership in New York City were bound to be disproportionately elite.

Further examination of the Mexico-based ANERC applications indicates that a majority of migrants returned to Cuba right after the war in the years 1898 and 1899. Thousands of Cubans across the Gulf and throughout the Caribbean were left stranded in exile after the war, trapped in crushing poverty. By comparison, the speedy return of the ANERC applicants from Mexico is evidence of their access to the financial resources necessary for repatriation. If there were few working-class members of the ANERC, there were even fewer women, a fact that further underscores the persistence of exclusion. Beyond membership, the organization's treasury documents for the period between 1920 and 1940 demonstrate that, decade after decade, more money was consistently spent on the beautification of the meeting hall than on aid to the organization's poor members. The reports of internal elections reveal how poor members were systematically disenfranchised. These exclusions within the association reached a peak during the dictatorship of Gerardo Machado, when all references to the Montecristi manifesto were ceremoniously removed from the statutes altogether.

The first section of this chapter explores the contradictions implicit in the Cuban Revolutionary Party and the organization that carried on its legacy in Cuba after the war. The second section examines the political practices of Cubans in Mexico, highlighting the ways in which Cubans, many of whom had fled Cuba as refugees and economic migrants, engaged with the party and the movement in order to affirm their emerging identity as Cuban citizens. By joining clubs, staging patriotic events, debating national questions, and defending democratic practices, Cuban migrants laid claim to membership in the future nation and "became Cuban."[3] While Cubans in Mexico displayed a high level of activity, they did not organize in isolation. They understood themselves as part of a Cuban Diaspora—a community of displaced citizens struggling together. As we have seen, individual Cubans traveled throughout the Gulf World, connecting key port cities in Cuba, Mexico, and the United States, but Cuban migrant communities in Mexico and the United States also shared news, information, and political practices across borders, forging revolutionary politics together in diaspora. Yet, beneath the tactical unity that Cubans worked hard to sustain across land and sea, divisions founded on exclusion persisted. Indeed, the tension within Cuban migrant communities explored in chapter 2 preceded the PRC and the independence war and persisted afterward. A close study of the spaces and practices of political participation lays bare the Janus-faced nature of Cuban exile politics. The final section of the chapter examines the ways in which Mexico-based Cuban migrants fashioned themselves as revolutionaries through their letters and their ANERC membership applications. A reading of these documents reveals the way in which those who had access to the party leadership through correspondence or who were able to apply to the ANERC worked to frame themselves as ideal revolutionary émigrés. The character of the ANERC membership, how ANERC members and Cuban letter writers imagined themselves and their participation in the war effort, and which migrants were fortunate enough to have their letters read and taken seriously reveal much about the politics of exclusion within the PRC and the ANERC.

The Cuban Revolutionary Party and Its Successor

The Cuban Revolutionary Party has been depicted by some scholars as an egalitarian organization whose vision of democracy was ahead of its time.[4] However, a wealth of scholarship on the history of democracy in Latin America makes clear that the Revolutionary Party's democratic vision and ethos owe much to a half century of similar efforts throughout the continent to construe democracy as broad and inclusive.[5] The founder of the Cuban Revolutionary Party, José Martí, drew on many influences as he developed his political thought during the 1870s, 1880s, and 1890s, and Mexico's liberal Reform Movement provided important inspiration. The significance of Latin America for Martí's political preparations, which would lead to the final Cuban independence war in 1895, will be discussed in chapter 4.

Although Martí envisioned the Cuban Revolutionary Party as embracing all Cubans—whether in Cuba or abroad—and bringing them into the revolutionary movement, the party itself was founded in a very specific place and time: Tampa, Florida, in 1891. With a collective population numbering in the thousands, Florida's enclaves of working-class Cubans had been hotbeds of revolution for years. Martí knew that any hope for a successful bid for Cuban independence relied on his convincing these workers to throw their support behind him and the Revolutionary Party. Martí's message was one that the workers very much wanted to hear: the new Cuban republic would be a place for all Cubans and for the good of all Cubans. The war and the establishment of a democratic republic, he insisted, were inseparable.[6]

As the traditional narrative goes, once Martí died and the leadership of the party passed to Tomás Estrada Palma, its democratic ethos was corrupted and the workers were sidelined, while a white, wealthy, and generally New York City–based Cuban elite took control of the party. As hundreds of middle-class white Cubans abandoned the island for New York City in the 1890s, the nationalism of the party's leaders and members in New York became more moderate. The stark difference between the moderate nationalism espoused by Cuban elites like those in New York City and the popular nationalism and social radicalism that characterized the views of Florida's working-class Cuban populations became increasingly apparent.

While there is certainly truth to the broad outlines of this story of the evolution of the PRC, there is more continuity between Martí and Estrada Palma's PRC than scholars have traditionally noted. Tomás Estrada Palma was conservative by comparison with Martí, and he was distinctly pro–United States. Yet, pinning the visibly exclusive practices of the PRC on Estrada Palma alone obscures the facts.

To begin with, the PRC under both Martí and Estrada Palma was simultaneously democratic and authoritarian. The base unit of the PRC was the democratically run Cuban political club. By the 1890s, there were hundreds of clubs spread across the Americas and Europe. The Cuban Revolutionary Party drew these established associations together and encouraged the creation of new ones, providing an international structure and unifying ideology for them. Beyond the grassroots base, however, the party's structure had always been hierarchical and fundamentally exclusionary. For instance, the only clubs that could vote within the organization were those with twenty or more active members. To be an active member required the payment of a monthly quota. So, smaller clubs with poorer members—of which there were many in Latin America—could not participate in the democratic process in the same way as larger clubs. In addition, qualifying clubs in larger Cuban migrant communities were organized into advisory bodies called Cuerpos de Consejo (CDC), which corresponded directly with the party's leadership in New York City. The CDCs were staffed by the presidents of the clubs in a given city, although clubs with female presidents were required to appoint a (male) surrogate. The most extensive network of CDCs existed in the United States, while outside of the United States there were far fewer CDCs. In Mexico, for example, there was only one CDC, in Veracruz, which limited the opportunity for Cuban clubs established in areas outside Veracruz to participate fully in the party's democratic structures.

The new system of agencies and agents created by Estrada Palma in his capacity as head of the Cuban Legation in and after 1895 addressed this problem. The appointed agent in Mexico City, for example, worked to galvanize and organize Cubans in areas removed from the CDC in Veracruz. However, these agents were appointees of the Cuban Legation and therefore not part of the carefully crafted PRC with its democratically run base clubs and CDCs. Thus, Cubans in Mexico outside of Veracruz, for whom the appointed agent was the main connection to the party, or those who ran clubs too small or too poor to be included in the CDC, experienced a party that seemed more hierarchical and less democratic. The power of the local councils was also limited. While the CDCs theoretically had the power to unseat the leader of the Revolutionary Party, to do so they would have had to gain the support of all existing CDCs, which would require coordination across borders throughout Latin America and Europe.

The incorporation of both democratic and authoritarian structures was a response to the perceived need for both in war, but there were other ways in which the needs of the war undermined the democracy Martí envisioned. As Yoel Cordoví Nuñez notes, the anti-democratic decision to suspend the practice of electing the leader of the party was a decision supported by the party's working-class base in Florida, who agreed that the suspension was a wartime necessity.[7] The Cuban provisional government's decision that the leader of the party would also be head of the newly constituted Cuban Legation was also a response to the needs of the war as it evolved. As head of the PRC, invested with the powers of a minister plenipotentiary, Estrada Palma's power was nearly limitless. If Tomás Estrada Palma never needed to fear that he might be voted out of his position by the CDCs, after the suspension of the election he was free to operate with complete autonomy, heeding or ignoring the advice of the councils as he pleased.[8] Thus, while the clubs continued to be run democratically, reflecting the value their members saw in democratic processes, the leadership of the party operated in a distinctly undemocratic fashion.

Another underexplored point of continuity between the PRC under Martí and under Estrada Palma was the vision of the role of the Cuban migrant in the revolutionary struggle. Both Martí and Estrada Palma saw the migrant-cum-revolutionary émigré as one of the "wings of the army," custodian of the nation after the war. In raising the status of the migrant to that of a revolutionary émigré, the PRC created an important distinction between the revolutionary soldier and the revolutionary émigré. During the war, the soldier's role was to fight for Cuba's liberation in the field of battle, while the émigré's role was to serve as an auxiliary to the soldier. After the war, however, the military veteran's primary role would continue to be martial, while that of the émigré would be primarily civil. That is to say, the veteran would be called to defend and protect the republic with the force of arms when necessary,[9] while revolutionary émigrés were expected to return to Cuba armed with the civic habits cultivated and nurtured in exile, habits that would help ensure the maintenance of the new nation's republican and democratic institutions.

The Manifesto of Montecristi, which was drafted and signed by José Martí and Máximo Gómez in the Dominican Republic just before the outbreak of the war, claimed that "Cuba is returning to the war with a democratic and cultured people, jealously aware of their own rights and of the rights of others."[10] Unlike the rest of Latin America, which emerged from colonialism to suffer not only the rule of *caudillos*, but also the slavish imitation of foreign ideas and doctrines, the perpetuation of feudal customs, and short-sighted reliance on single industries, Cuba would not fall victim to such problems. The revolutionaries believed that "these factors are by no means the problems of Cuban society," because

> at the crossroads of the world some brilliant sons—magnates or servants—are coming to Cuba from creative and sustaining work in the more capable nations of the world to enlist in the war, and they are bringing their own efforts on behalf of the country's misery and persecution. These are men who from the first age of adjustment (now overcome), among the heterogeneous components of the Cuban nation, went out to prepare, or on the island itself to continue to prepare, with their own perfectionism, the nationality to which they are today contributing with the stability of their industrious persons and the security of their republican education.[11]

The Cuban republic, the drafters of the manifesto insisted, would not suffer the same woes as its Latin American counterparts when her people broke their colonial chains, not only because they had the advantage of hindsight but because the Cuban people had already become democratic and cultured through their experience living in "more capable nations" where they learned industrious habits. Rich and poor Cubans together would bring the benefit of that experience back to Cuba to inform the development of the nation.[12]

If soldiers fought to bring into being a nation that would count them as citizens, migrants were encouraged to imagine themselves as displaced citizens waiting to return to a nation that would count on them for guidance. Between 1895 and 1898, Cuban revolutionary émigrés, working within the framework of the PRC, practiced, valued, and defended democratic citizenship, debated national questions, created patriotic rituals, and engaged in solidarity-building activities geared toward raising international awareness of the Cuban cause. In addition, José Martí and Tomás Estrada Palma encouraged migrants to see themselves as custodians of the nation abroad. Ultimately, both men viewed educated, middle-class professionals and elites as ideal representatives of the Cuban republic, although Martí had a broader vision of Cuban citizenship. In his address to the American people in 1896, Tomás Estrada Palma wrote, "The white man and the colored live in perfect harmony . . . the colored people of Cuba are industrious, intelligent and lovers of learning. . . . On the other hand, thousands of white persons, with the faculties their wealth offered them, have completed their education in foreign countries, especially the United States, where they have become accustomed to republican practices and to the exercise of their rights as free men, thus preparing themselves and their children for the exercise of those same rights in their native land when it shall be emancipated from Spanish domination."[13] Both the Montecristi manifesto and Estrada Palma's statement were firmly adhered to the cause of total and complete independence. Both also sought to assuage fears about the supposed ambitions of Cubans of color. Finally, both signaled the important role of Cubans educated outside of Cuba in the independence movement as well as in the future republic. Of course, the Manifesto indicated that that the individual embodying that salutary force from without could be a "magnate or servant," whereas Estrada Palma's statement clearly prioritizes the role of wealthy, white, educated Cubans.

These nuances meant little to the many Cuban migrants across the Americas who, empowered by the possibility of an expanded role in the independence movement and in Cuba's future, joined the PRC in large numbers after 1895, thereby becoming revolutionary émigrés. Before the onset of the war, the PRC was a modest organization in Mexico, but there was a veritable explosion of participation in the revolutionary struggle in Mexico after 1895. The CDC in Veracruz was among the first to be founded after the party was formed in 1892, a reflection of the importance of that community within revolutionary networks. However, from 1892 to 1895, the presence of the party was limited to the CDC in Veracruz and a handful of isolated clubs along the Gulf Coast, and in Mexico City and Puebla. In 1895, that changed radically. The influx of new migrants expelled by the war provided fresh recruits for both older and newly established clubs. Between 1892 and 1898, the total number of Cuban clubs in Mexico grew from four to eighty. By comparison, the number of clubs in Tampa, Florida, increased from two to fifteen, and in Key West from eight to sixty-two.[14] The clubs established in the United States far outnumbered those created in Mexico, but so too did the Cuban population. The proportion of clubs in Mexico to the size of the Cuban population (eighty clubs for what is estimated to be around 3,000 Cubans) was rather high. By comparison, the population of Cubans in Key West alone reached 5,000 in 1885 and far surpassed that number due to the influx of migrants during the War of 1895.[15]

The regional pattern of Cuban political club formation in Mexico followed the pattern of Cuban migration after 1895, concentrating in Veracruz, Mérida, and Mexico City and peaking in 1896 and 1897. Veracruz boasted the largest and most long-standing Cuban migrant community and, consequently, was home to the largest number of clubs. Mérida and Mexico City—the two other significant centers of Cuban émigré activity in Mexico—followed. We know the specific club affiliations of 181 of 200 ANERC members, and 55 of 110 PRC letter writers. The ANERC applicants registered participation in forty-one clubs, and data from the PRC letters and Cuban and Mexican newspapers confirm the existence of another thirty-nine clubs. All told, eighty clubs were constituted in at least fifteen cities across Mexico during the war years. This number is substantially higher than previously believed, making the explosion of club formation and enthusiasm for the Cuban cause between 1895 and 1898 that much more noteworthy.[16] Impressively, more than half of the ANERC applicants who list a specific club by name were members of two or more clubs within the same city or across regions, which indicates the existence of extensive networks within and between cities in Mexico. The reach of the clubs established in fifteen cities is significant, because only four cities in Mexico are recognized as centers of Cuban revolutionary activity during the period, leaving eleven cities, which contained smaller concentrations of Cuban revolutionaries linked to the PRC in New York City unrecognized.[17]

After the war, the Cubans who joined the ANERC committed themselves to the continuation of their labors in exile, but instead of sustaining a war effort, they participated in the construction of the new Cuban republic. Juan Ramón O'Farrill, a prominent figure in the Florida emigrations and one of the founding members of the ANERC, described the purpose of the organization as to ensure "the continuation of Cuban Revolutionary Party . . . and the perpetuation in the Republic and during peacetime, of the great work of Martí the Apostol and of the tobacco workers of Key West and Tampa."[18] O'Farrill's choice here and elsewhere to ignore the participation of émigrés outside of the United States would be costly as we will see. The ANERC's own statutes were more broad and inclusive stating that the organization was constituted with the purpose of celebrating the "still unrecognized revolutionary contribution of the emigrations in conferences, books, and other publications" that were meant to "serve . . . as stimulus and example, experience and lesson in the exercise and practice of civic responsibilities."[19] The ANERC's founding members' understanding of the purpose of the association perfectly reflected the one the PRC's leaders had envisioned for the émigrés. Also confirming the idea that the émigrés' role spanned the revolution and the republic, the governor of Havana described the ANERC as "that historic and patriotic association" that "has the glorious mission of bequeathing to its descendants the great labors begun in exile and continued in the republic."[20]

Despite its professed adherence to the Manifesto of Montecristi, however, within a decade of its founding, the ANERC had become an association that privileged elite, white, male migrants. The association's description of who qualified to be counted as an émigré was already broad at its founding in 1909 and became even broader and more all-encompassing with time, eventually including the children and other direct descendants of émigrés. At first glance, this openness might appear egalitarian; indeed, any Cuban who resided abroad and could demonstrate that he or she had belonged to a club and had made any financial contribution to the revolution qualified for membership. However, if we take into consideration the high and rising quotas charged to members on a monthly basis, and the fact that if a member neglected to pay on time, his or her membership would be revoked, and that once revoked it would be nearly impossible to reactivate, it becomes clear that not everyone could join the ANERC. In this context, the move to expand membership to include direct descendants served not only to extend the life of the organization (which existed until 1974), but also to perpetuate the influence of a select elite.

Women in the ANERC were at first part of a separate organization, a separation that underlay their lower status. As we will see, women ran their own political clubs during the war, participated in mixed-gender clubs, and held elected positions in both. Although women were later integrated into the main body of the ANERC and given full equal rights within the association, the first women to hold elected positions in the ANERC only appeared in the lowest rungs of the administration and not until the 1940s.

Racial exclusion is more difficult to trace, given that neither a phenotypical description nor a photograph were required by the ANERC of its members. Among 200 applicants from Mexico, only one, Juan Santa Cruz Benitez identified himself as "color mulato." This marker, which appears in a list of characteristics including age and marital status offered by the applicant, seems almost rote.[21] Yet, Benitez stands out as an exception not for being a Cuban of color, but for identifying himself as such. It is impossible to ascertain exactly how many other Cubans of color were admitted. The fact that not one of the two hundred applicants to the ANERC from Mexico belonged to any of the Cuban clubs identified as having black presidents suggests not only the racial homogeneity of the ANERC in early republican Cuba but also the segregation of black and white Cubans in exile during the war. If the ANERC did not begin as an exclusive organization, it certainly became one over time. The ANERC's early directorate included two prominent Afro-Caribbean figures—the Puerto Rican journalist Sotero Figueroa and the Cuban intellectual Juan Gualberto Gómez. But both men left the organization after 1911 with no explanation, perhaps due to a climate perceived as inhospitable.

Finally, the ANERC's early commitment to supporting the needs of the returning workers who formed the bulk of the migrations—needs for housing and employment, among other things—waned over time. For example, the association's treasury records for the 1920s show that the amount of money dedicated to paying the florist regularly exceeded that earmarked for the commission of beneficence, which was dedicated to supporting the needs of the organization's poor and sick members.[22]

Cuban Revolutionary Politics in Mexico

The Cuban political club was the heart and soul of revolutionary politics in Mexico and throughout the diaspora. These voluntary associations were the spaces where Cubans forged revolutionary identities, practiced civic habits, and came to understand themselves as citizens of a democratic republic in the making. It was in club spaces that national rituals were born. Indeed, Cuban patriotic traditions were forged as much in exile as they were in Cuba. Once the war was over, migrants returning home brought their exile traditions and their patriotic rituals with them.

Associational culture within Cuban civic life had emerged in Cuba as early as the late eighteenth century. Alfonso W. Quiróz attributes the gradual erosion of colonial authority in part to a developing "spirit of association" that was not explicitly tied to separatism.[23] Cuba's history of associational culture, the stability promoted by its remarkable economic growth in the early nineteenth century, its place in the Atlantic world at the crossroads of many influences, and the openings provided by Spain's various experiments with constitutional governance between 1812 and 1876 all contributed to Cuba's early development of associational life relative to most Latin American republics.[24] These associations ran the gamut from literary and scientific organizations populated generally by white elites, to Afro-Cuban *Cabildos de Nación* and other black mutual aid societies. This strong history of associational culture combined with exile traditions of association that were knitted to separatist politics.[25] Labor-based associations and Masonic lodges were also tied to separatism at critical moments throughout the nineteenth century. Cubans who left Cuba to resettle abroad during the nineteenth century drew from a history of association that owed its origins to both island and exile traditions.

Cuban political clubs in Mexico were also influenced by Mexico's vibrant associational culture. As Carlos Forment argues in his pioneering study of democracy in Latin America, "Latin Americans fashioned themselves into democratic citizens in voluntary associations." They "invested their sense of sovereignty horizontally in each other rather than vertically in government institutions."[26] Across the nineteenth century, associations of all kinds, including literary, scientific, philanthropic, educational, religious, artistic, and mutualist groups, proliferated as individuals subject to authoritarian governments sought ways to practice democracy. In Mexico, Mexicans organized 1,526 civic groups and 309 voting clubs between 1856 and 1881 alone. These associations where spread across the country with Mexico City and the state of Veracruz standing out as areas of greatest concentration.

Mexico City and Veracruz were both locations where Cubans established vibrant émigré communities. Many Cuban migrants of the older, established generation who lived in these cities became members of some of Mexico's most prominent intellectual, literary, and scientific associations. The Cuban clubs that were formed and that multiplied exponentially in Mexico during the mid to late 1890s comprised both Cuban and Mexican members and thus became reflections of both Mexican and Cuban traditions of associational culture.[27] The connection between the different traditions of association was further supported by the founding of cross-national clubs, which were co-created by Cubans and Mexicans. Clubs with cross-national memberships were far more common in Mexico than in the United States. Nearly one-third of Cuban clubs in Mexico reflected cross-national membership in their names alone. Clubs like Mexico y Cuba, Yucatán y Cuba, Juárez y Martí, and Club Cubano-Mexicano Poesia had Cuban and Mexican members, but so did clubs like Máximo Gómez and Nada con España, whose names did not reflect transnational solidarities.

Founding and Creation

Cubans arriving at the port city of Veracruz would have found it hard to avoid being swept up in the fervor around Cuban independence, especially if, like Dominga Valdes Corvalles de Muniz, they had come from another migrant community. However, those migrants who came directly from Cuba unsure what to expect would have found Cuban revolutionary politics unavoidable as well. In his memoir, Leandro Cañizares Gómez recalled how Cubans arriving in or passing through the town of Orizaba congregated at the Cuban-owned grocery store, El Brazo Fuerte, where they would bring news from Cuba and share impressions about the war. "Pristine and romantic was the patriotism that joined us in that tiny and distant corner of the world," Cañizares Gómez remembered. "We rejoiced in each and every triumph of the insurgents, which our patriotism magnified, and we suffered the military setbacks, which threatened to attenuate our patriotic faith." The revolution in Cuba was the obligatory topic of discussion at all the reunions that took place at El Brazo Fuerte.[28] Spaces like El Brazo Fuerte had existed for decades as centers of collaboration, conspiracy, and mutual support. However, after 1892 when the PRC was founded, and especially after the outbreak of war in 1895, these spaces became home to Cuban clubs newly galvanized by the call to all migrants to support the revolutionary movement.

The original inspiration for these clubs emerged out of the casual gathering of a few migrants who had the custom of meeting informally to discuss Cuban affairs like those at El Brazo Fuerte. Caridad Leon de San German of Mérida reported in 1897 that she invited a group of ladies to a special meeting at her home, where she proposed the formation of a club to reinforce and support the efforts of existing clubs in Mérida. Her proposal was accepted, and the new members proceeded immediately to the very important task of naming the club. In this case, they chose the name Cuba Libre in honor of the struggle. The final step, usually taken the same day of the founding, was to elect a directorate and announce the constitution of the club and its elected representatives to local sister organizations and to the party leadership in New York City.[29] One glance at the regular and detailed correspondence and diligent reports of club secretaries collected in the archives of the Cuban Revolutionary Party provides evidence of just how seriously individual clubs took their missions and their responsibilities.

Some clubs, like Cuba Libre, were composed of women, while others were cross-gender, like Club Cubano-Mexicano Poesia, of which ten of the fifteen founding members were women. Calling themselves a "gathering of liberals," they announced their formation to the flagship club in Veracruz, Máximo Gómez, as well as to the PRC leadership in New York in June of 1896.

Despite their being in the minority, the men of Poesia dominated the directorate of the club, a practice that was common in cross-gender clubs. The notice of the constitution of Poesia was published in *Patria*, the newspaper of the Cuban diaspora, which was edited and printed in New York City. Upon their constitution, Cuban clubs always insisted on being recognized in *Patria*, because that newspaper reached the Cuban migrations throughout the Americas and Europe. Also notable about Poesia is that it identified itself as "Cubano-Mexicano," which reflected its cross-national group of founding members. Similarly, the president of Cuba Libre noted in her letter that the club's members included "a majority of Cuban women," from which we can infer that the balance of members were Mexicans or possibly other foreigners.

Naming a club was nearly as important as founding one. Often Cuban clubs would take names that had already been used by Cubans elsewhere in and beyond Mexico. Such was the case with Club Máximo Gómez in Mexico City, which was established after the club of the same name in Veracruz. This was typically a way of establishing cross-regional connections within Mexico, but it could also be used to create linkages with Cubans in migrant centers in New York and Florida, among other places. Many clubs chose to venerate military and political heroes like Martí or Maceo, or revolutionary events like the Protesta de Baraguá, Grito de Yara, or Grito de Baire. Names of living revolutionary figures might be used to connect a club with the existing revolutionary leadership. The club Bartolomé Masó of Veracruz, which decided to take the name of the vice president of the Cuban "nation in arms," wrote Bartolomé Masó directly to inform him of the honor conferred in the naming. They received a reply, which indicated that the effort to establish a link to a powerful revolutionary figure was successful.[30] There were clubs dedicated to collecting medical and military supplies, like Compañeros del Doctor Zayas, and clubs that specialized in gathering weapons, like Metralla. By far the most common naming practice, however, was the use of club names to reflect Cuban-Mexican solidarities. Cuban clubs like Cuauhtemoc y Hatuey, Dolores y Yara México y Cuba, Yucatán y Cuba, Bravo y Maceo, Juárez y Martí, and Cepeda y Maceo took names of Mexican independence heroes, or juxtaposed Mexican and Cuban revolutionary figures and sites of revolutionary proclamations.

When the members of Bravo y Maceo came together to elect their directorship, the president of the organization reported to the director of *Patria*, the newspaper of the Cuban diaspora, that "a great number of citizens gathered together to elect the leadership of the club." According to the report, all those in attendance were "liberals at heart without any distinction of social class."³¹ This point is important as it reflects a commitment to inclusivity and a claim to citizenship. This statement of inclusivity may have been more rhetorical than real for many of the more elite clubs, but it was necessary to signal publicly that the club welcomed all Cubans and offered them an equal opportunity to participate in its democratic internal elections. As with the club Cuba Libre of Mérida, Bravo y Maceo's determination to have the narrative of their founding published in *Patria* speaks to their diasporic consciousness. The pairing in the club's name of Nicolás Bravo—a Mexican independence fighter who battled the Spanish alongside Guadalupe Victoria and José María Morelos, challenged the first Mexican emperor, and also fought against the United States in the Mexican-American War—and Antonio Maceo—the intransigent Cuban revolutionary general—says much about the politics of the club's members. Both men shared a total and uncompromising commitment to independence from Spain and the United States.

Bravo y Maceo was not the only club to venerate the great insurgent general Antonio Maceo. The clubs Antonio Maceo of Veracruz, Cepeda y Maceo of Saltillo, Morelos y Maceo of Mexico City, Hidalgo y Maceo of Tampico, and Vengadores de Maceo of Progreso were all named to honor the general. His death had inspired the formation of the club Vengadores de Maceo, and the name reflected the anger of its members at how Spaniards across Mexico celebrated Maceo's death with singing, dancing, and drinking. A cartoon published in the Mexican newspaper *El Hijo del Ahuizote* compared Spanish reactions to Maceo's death and Cuban reactions to the assassination of Spain's prime minister, Antonio Canovas del Castillo. One image depicts the Spaniards marking Maceo's death with revelry, drinking, and laughing. The other image depicts Cubans somberly paying their respects to Canovas del Castillo in a formal wake. Together, the images convey the idea that Cubans were more cultured than Spaniards, an argument often used to counter Spanish propaganda that depicted Cubans as uncivilized.³²

In late January 1898, the members of Vengadores de Maceo consented to change their name under pressure exerted by local Spaniards. They defiantly chose the name Maceo y Miró. The club's new name celebrated José Miró Argenter, a Catalán independence fighter in Cuba. Given Spain's struggle with anarchist challenges to state power in Catalonia, the choice to honor a Catalán insurgent was arguably as provocative as pledging vengeance for the fallen Cuban military general.³³ Of course, the gesture also celebrated a transatlantic solidarity in opposition to Spanish dominance. As the example of this club makes clear, naming a club was always an act of patriotism, but it was also a revolutionary gesture in and of itself, and often an act of defiance as well.

Once a club was formally constituted, its primary goal was to raise money to support the revolutionary cause. The PRC was permanently in need of funds to support various projects, including outfitting filibustering expeditions and supporting its various diplomatic campaigns. Thus, clubs aggressively recruited members, with the goal of leaving no new migrant unaffiliated. The meeting minutes of the club Bartolomé Masó of Veracruz give us a clue as to how recruitment took place. One of the first actions of the club's elected leadership was to assign a committee to recruit recently arrived Cubans in Veracruz. The secretary dutifully recorded the following: "It was proposed by one of those in attendance that a commission should be named to approach all of the newly arrived Cubans with the intention of procuring financial contributions from them, and enlisting their support for the cause."[34] On another occasion, Bartolomé Masó's members asked the president of Máximo Gómez, the oldest and most prominent Cuban club in Veracruz, for a membership list so that they could target new migrants who did not belong to that club. The move demonstrates how clubs collaborated to ensure that between them no Cuban was left unaffiliated. Bartolomé Masó members kept close tabs on new arrivals. At another meeting of the club, one member repeated a rumor that a wealthy Cuban by the name of Jacobo Mújica was not contributing to the cause, nor were his workers. A commission was immediately assembled and charged with investigating the matter. The members of the commission planned to visit Mújica personally and pressure him to donate 10 percent of his workers' salaries and a similar portion of his earnings to sustain the war effort.[35] Mújica's case reveals the paternalism of elite migrants, who saw the workers not as independent political actors but rather as wards of their employers. While workers certainly did create their own clubs in Mexico—the Obreros de Progreso is one example—it was also common for Cuban elites to coerce the participation of their employees. This kind of coercion existed in Cuban migrant communities elsewhere as well, although in places like Tampa and Key West workers' clubs far outnumbered any exclusively elite associations, and so this particular dynamic was not as common.

Effective recruitment was seen as the key to filling the coffers of the Revolutionary Party, because club members were expected to contribute monthly quotas and to work raising money for the cause. The most daunting challenge to the clubs' efforts to raise money was not recruitment, but the relative poverty of most migrants. This problem was exacerbated by the fact that financial contributions collected in Mexico had to be converted into U.S. dollars because the PRC, headquartered in New York City, operated in U.S. currency. Thus, even when substantial donations were collected in Mexico, they lost a considerable amount of their value due to a poor exchange rate. This devaluation led José Miguel Macías, president of Máximo Gómez in Veracruz, to recommend to Estrada Palma that clubs be permitted to send goods that would benefit the soldiers—like tobacco and coffee—instead of money.[36] On another occasion, the treasurer of Salvador Cisneros complained that the depreciation of the peso, coupled with the poverty of Cuban migrants, seriously hindered the club's ability to offer more significant contributions. A collection taken up among ninety-nine individuals had resulted in only $134.[37] Despite their modest contributions, the president of Yucatán y Cuba observed humbly that "although the colony here is small and poor and has few financial resources, it is rich in noble sentiments and is ready to make sacrifices and respond to the call of the nation."[38]

It is hard to say how much Cubans in Mexico actually contributed to the PRC between 1895 and 1898 because the remission of funds was not fully systematized. The PRC received contributions from the Agency, the CDC, PRC clubs and unaffiliated organizations, as well as individuals. It is clear that the migrants in the United States sustained the movement. The treasury notes published in *Patria* for the month of January 1898 demonstrate that, of the $23,158.04 collected that month, $18,444 was collected in the United States. Of the remaining contributors, clubs in South America provided slightly more than $1,000, $600 came from Cubans in Central America, $390 from those in Europe, and $100 from the Dominican Republic. In Mexico $2,622 was generated for the cause—more than the amount collected in Europe and the rest of Latin America combined. These proportions were consistent in reports submitted throughout the year, indicating that, toward the end of the war, Mexico led the migrant communities outside of the United States in financial contributions. This had to do with the relatively large number of migrants in Mexico, but it is also evidence of their level of organization. According to the treasury books of the PRC agency run by the revolutionary representative Nicolás Domínguez Cowan in Mexico City, the equivalent of $15,722 had been remitted to the party headquarters by the agency between 1895 and 1898. That was a contribution of more than $100,000 in today's currency.[39] However, in September of 1898, the flagship Cuban club in Veracruz, Máximo Gómez, reported that it alone had submitted $24,771.92 to the Revolutionary Party to date and had distributed another $995 to insurgent generals and their families.[40] The sum is impressive for one club, although Máximo Gómez had been founded in 1892 and had approximately 200 members at the start of the war.

Cuban clubs existed to channel material support to the insurgents on the ground, and their activities were largely geared toward this purpose. In addition to a weekly or monthly quota to be paid by club members, they staged events including auctions, raffles, bazaars, lotteries, and cultural celebrations in order to fill the party's treasury.[41] On 8 September 1896, Carlos Revilla stood before his fellow members of Bartolomé Masó and read a communiqué from Estrada Palma. Estrada Palma's letter concerned the need to "reinforce the reserves of the delegation at a time when the party was in dire financial straits." The PRC was often in need of money. Launching, outfitting, and manning filibustering expeditions to Cuba was a costly business, as was advancing diplomatic initiatives in several countries. Several gentlemen in the club responded immediately to Estrada Palma's request: one called for a raffle to be held, while another called for an urgent collection to be taken up.[42]

From the moment a migrant stepped off of a ship at the port of Veracruz, the pressure to affiliate himself or herself with the movement would be keenly felt. Cuban politics was an important part of everyday life in migrant communities. Cuban migrants would feel pressure to join clubs and pressure to sustain the cause financially. These pressures could at times be coercive, but in exchange the clubs provided social networks that were important for displaced migrants and refugees looking for a temporary home abroad.

The Public Face of Cuban Politics

The staging of public rituals and celebrations including parades, banquets, *veladas*, auctions, conferences, and other meetings were some of the many ways in which Cuban migrants laid the basis for national citizenship in exile. Daily life was punctuated by a succession of public patriotic events celebrating and commemorating key moments in the revolutionary struggle, for example, the *Grito de Yara* (the inauguration of the Ten Years' War), the *Grito de Baire* (the inauguration of the 1895 War), or the births and deaths of major revolutionary figures from current and past revolutionary conflicts. Class lines were drawn particularly clearly at such events. High profile, sumptuous, upper-class affairs existed alongside humble public meetings. The differences among these public celebrations and the greater importance placed on high profile events made clear the priorities of Cuban migrant communities: elite and professional members were eager to convey to Mexican and international audiences (including Spanish and U.S. immigrants) an image of Cuban respectability.

The patriotic events, ceremonies, and traditions observed abroad shaped nationalist practice at home. The marking of the birth and death of Martí and other revolutionary figures who had died in battle and the celebration of the initiation of the Ten Years' War and the 1895 War were standard observances in early republican Cuba. The ANERC, the organization recognized as carrying forth the legacy of the PRC, played a central role in these national celebrations after its founding in 1909. The decision to emphasize the importance of Martí's birth rather than his death was a deliberate attempt by Cuban political elites to reclaim Martí from those more radical working-class Cubans who preferred to commemorate his martyrdom, and the ANERC played a role in that decision. The inclusion of Martí's birthday in what the ANERC termed its *culto patriórico*, appears in the statutes of the organization at its founding in 1909. The first large-scale ANERC-sponsored celebration of Martí's birth took place in 1913, years before the passing of the Law of the Apostle, which made Martí's birth a national holiday in 1921.[43] If the state hoped to take control of the meaning of Martí, the ANERC aimed to claim Martí for the exiles by drawing public attention to his life abroad rather than his experience as a revolutionary who died in battle. In a formal invitation sent to the governor of Havana in advance of the 1913 celebration of Martí's birth, the ANERC as an organization recognized Martí as a man whose "doctrines proclaimed incessantly in and outside of the republic, culminated in the triumph of the independence of the fatherland." The ANERC directly attributed the success of the revolution not to the insurgents but to Martí's doctrines. It was through such statements and the accompanying celebrations that revolutionary émigrés sought to carve out a place and a role for themselves in republican Cuba.

Elite social gatherings in exile during the war years—and afterward in the Cuban republic—were events intended to display Cuban citizenship and Cuban nationalism. While in exile, Cubans wished to convey an image to international audiences of a Cuba that was unified, civilized, and modern. Larger gatherings called *veladas* were often sponsored by a number of clubs working together. These were usually upscale affairs meant to convey a sense of refinement and culture. Event programs included the performance of classical music compositions and poetry recitals as well as patriotic speeches. *Veladas* were attended by elegantly attired guests who sat and listened to lectures interspersed with piano recitals and other performances. Often held in theaters or meeting halls that were lavishly decorated, these events were fundamentally exclusive. Indeed, one Cuban émigré originally a native of Jamaica, remembers being able to attend the *veladas* only when he had enough money to pay the quota. Fernando Echermendia Flores was a member of México y Cuba and a committed patriot, but he did not have the same insertion as wealthier members of the club.[44] One *velada Artístico-Literaria* sponsored by the Mexico City–based clubs Hijas de Baire and México y Cuba to commemorate the anniversary of Martí's death was a gala affair held in the old skating rink on San Juan de Letrán. The space was decorated with an abundance of fresh flowers, some woven into the form of white stars, the emblem of the Cuban flag. The banisters of the central staircase were "adorned with Cuban and Mexican flags and trophies from which hung star-shaped pendants." Those in attendance were "a distinguished group of Cuban and Mexican young ladies and elegant gentlemen."[45] A journalist from Veracruz described another *velada* commemorating Martí that took place in that city the same year as having a "numerous and select" audience.[46] Larger community-wide events might also include parades to the houses of prominent community members or welcoming committees that would escort arriving revolutionary celebrities from docks or train stations to meeting halls with significant fanfare. For example, when the secretary and treasurer from the Cuban Revolutionary Party visited Veracruz, thousands of people converged to great them. A local newspaper reported that "many older people in this locale told us that they had never seen a reception of this size, nor one so enthusiastic in the city."[47]

Celebrations honoring Martí sponsored by the ANERC in the years after the war were no less lavish and often consumed 30 to 50 percent of the organization's budget in a given semester. For example, in 1928 the ANERC spent $500 on one event in honor of Martí, out of a total semester budget of $1,225.[48] In 1958, the amount allotted for national celebrations had risen to $1,000 and was the single largest expenditure between December and June of that year.[49] In both cases, the funds for the patriotic festivals were given to the association by the city of Havana and the Cuban state, demonstrating how the ANERC was seen as an integral national institution charged with preserving the legacy of the émigré contribution to the independence struggle. Judging from menus and programs, the patriotic festivals sponsored by the ANERC were nearly carbon copies of the events organized during the war in Mexico, the United States, and elsewhere. Elite venues, lavish banquettes, ornate decorations, high culture performances, and elegant attire were the norm.

The physical design of the ANERC's meeting space in central Havana is a window into its exclusivity as well. Inventories of the associations' belongings ordered by Fulgencio Batista in the early 1950s (and later by the Revolutionary government after 1959) indicate that the space occupied by the ANERC was sumptuous. The society collected numerous valuable artifacts that adorned its walls; tables in its meeting rooms were made of luxurious *caoba* (mahogany) wood, and seating took the form of expensive "living room" sets and high-end armchairs. Its library consisted of materials relating to the independence struggle housed in remarkably expensive bookshelves, which were often more valuable than the objects they contained.[50] Significant amounts of money were spent maintaining the property, and expenses included painting, repairs, and upkeep of a grand piano. The building, which still stands today, features a grand staircase, which leads to a landing adorned with a fabulous custom-made stained-glass window that depicts the famous landing of the Three Friends filibustering expedition and the insignia of the institution.

In addition to elaborate patriotic festivals, Cubans in exile staged academic and political conferences, which were also elite events. Like the *veladas*, conferences catered to wealthy, educated, often international audiences. Presentations usually featured highly academic, detail-driven presentations of issues such as Spain's financial mismanagement of Cuba or the history of Cuba's independence struggle. According to one reporter, the objective of these conferences was to "make propaganda to sustain the interests of Cuba."[51] The exclusivity of such gatherings was evident not only in the kinds of people who attended and in the topics that were covered but also in the fact that attendance was often by invitation only. Invitations may have been freely extended to anyone interested—as was reported in one local newspaper—but one still had to know how and where to procure them.

As spaces of debate, conferences enabled participants to discuss, challenge, and debunk rumors or claims made by those who doubted the strength of the insurgency and the viability of an independent Cuban republic. The presence of a diverse audience that included Mexicans and other immigrants as well as members of the press afforded Cubans the opportunity to explain and justify revolution while calling for international solidarity. On 9 June 1896, a member of Bartolomé Masó proposed that the club hold regular weekly conferences "regarding the Cuban Question with the intentions of creating propaganda."⁵² Like Bartolomé Masó, the club México y Cuba in Mexico City held regular weekly conferences on Sundays to debate Cuba's independence and create propaganda for the cause.⁵³ An article describing a conference hosted by the club Morelos y Maceo of Mexico City in January 1897 reported that the room where the event was held was filled to capacity with Cuban men and women as well as Mexican writers and journalists and several foreigners eager to participate.⁵⁴

In stark contrast to the conferences and lavish *veladas* staged by the wealthy members of prominent Cuban clubs in exile in Mexico—and later by the members of the ANERC in Havana—stand the small, humble, and regular gatherings of less prominent and less wealthy migrants. The Spanish consul in Veracruz recorded the following observations about a public gathering in the city of Veracruz:

> Inside the city walls, on Patrona street, Cuban insurgents celebrate daily meetings that can be easily observed from the street. I went to that street around 8:30 and approached the sixth or seventh door. At the right there was a group of people. I ascended the three stairs, and from there could see all that transpired in the room. There were many men and women. In front, there was a portrait of the president of the republic, Don Porfirio Diaz. To his right, there was a Mexican flag, to his left, the flag that the insurgents call their own. The other walls in the room were covered with portraits of Cuban leaders.
>
> They spent much of the meeting singing praises to the insurrection, accompanied by guitars. When they are not singing, they are giving patriotic speeches in which they yell *"vivas"* to free Cuba and death to Spain. These songs, speeches and cries can be heard in the middle of the street. After three quarters of an hour had passed, the meeting hall was more full and the subversive cries were repeated more frequently.⁵⁵

The consul's intention had been to spy on the Cuban club, but he found little need to employ stealth in the execution of his mission. The Cuban meeting was audible far beyond the walls of the meeting hall. Indeed, his experience differed considerably from that of the Spanish consul in Key West, who complained that the Cuban community there was impenetrable; he scrambled to hire detectives in order keep tabs on their activities. The consul in Veracruz, by contrast, was annoyed by the lack of discretion evidenced by the Cuban patriots. He chafed at the tone of the singing, poetry recitals, and motivational speeches he overheard. Cuban migrant Leandro Cañizares Gómez fondly remembered how the patriotic meetings at El Brazo Fuerte in Orizaba were equally audible and public. "The potent and sonorous voice of the owner of the store and that of some of the members who expressed themselves in vehement tones, could be heard two blocks away, which greatly surprised Mexicans who generally speak in low and measured tones," Cañizares Gómez wrote.[56] The Spanish consul and Cañizares Gómez's observations highlight the vibrancy and the patriotic spirit of more popular local events and gatherings. Unlike the elite *veladas*, where measured tones and piano recitals were the standard, the celebration on Patrona Street featured guitars, boisterous song, and loud hispaniphobic pronouncements.

In Veracruz, the Spanish consul also noted the presence of women in the audience of the meeting on Patrona Street. As we have seen, women formed and ran their own clubs and also held membership in cross-gender clubs, but they also participated in both elite and popular public events. Women rarely headlined the *veladas* with fiery political speeches, but they frequently participated by reciting poetry, singing, and playing instruments. Of course, there were always exceptions. A Mexican newspaper, *El Continente Americano*, reported that a young woman named Paulina Sotres was scheduled to give a conference in the Mexico City club Morelos y Maceo in April of 1897.[57] A Mexican woman named Emigida Limón was a featured speaker at a public meeting of the club Bravo y Maceo in Puebla in 1897.[58] Despite their omnipresence in migrant communities and in public spaces where they engaged actively in revolutionary politics, extraordinarily few women appear in the rolls of the ANERC as members.

Networks and Connections

In addition to serving in elected positions within two Cuban political clubs, Dominga Valdes Corovalles de Muniz embodied the kinds of networks and connections that existed between Cuban organizations and Cuban migrant centers in the Gulf World. Indeed, Cuban patriotic clubs in Mexico were intimately aware of what parallel organizations in New York, Florida, and elsewhere were accomplishing for the independence cause and, whenever possible, they forged links to other organizations within cities and states and across national borders. In a fashion similar to the clubs in Veracruz, the club Yucatán y Cuba from Mérida referred to its "brothers in Tampa and Key West," citing them as inspiration for a special collection the club had organized to raise money for weapons and ammunition in 1896. As we saw in chapter 2, there were significant links between Mexico-based and

Florida-based Cuban communities, who were knitted together by the travels of insurgents traveling between Gulf ports. Sometimes these links were visible in how Cuban clubs in the United States and Mexico adopted the same names. For example, a club by the name Vengadores de Macco existed in Tampa and also in Progreso.[59]

Much like the travelers who brought news from city to city, the party's official newspaper, *Patria*, served to connect migrant communities. The PRC published and circulated *Patria* throughout the Americas and Europe. Each issue of *Patria* included the statutes of the PRC, information about the progress of the war in Cuba, and news about activities of Cuban migrants. The regular correspondence from Veracruz published in Patria underscores that city's importance in networks that linked Cuba's principal port cities to others in the Gulf world. By reading *Patria*, Cubans could become aware of the events, contributions, celebrations, and speeches given for the cause and more. The newspaper contributed to the creation of a diasporic nationalist consciousness among Cuban migrants.[60]

When the members of Yucatán y Cuba referenced their "brothers in Tampa and Key West," they likely had learned about the actions of the Florida migrants through *Patria*, which reported extensively on the activities of United States–based Cuban communities. The connection went both ways, however. The newspaper *La Estrella Solitaria* from Matamorros reprinted an article covering a speech given by a prominent Mexican deputy supporting Cuban independence. The article had first been printed in a local newspaper called *Cuba* in Tampa, Florida.[61] Another example of how clubs influenced and inspired each other through Patria is when, addressing themselves to Estrada Palma in early September 1896, the members of Juárez y Martí from Tlacotalpam wrote, "This Cuban colony, which has with such enthusiasm decided to create a Cuban club, requests that you be so kind as to insert the attached announcement in *Patria*, which here enjoys many subscribers."[62] Some three weeks later, the notice appeared in the newspaper. Perhaps thinking about the readership of the paper, the club members made a point of mentioning that before coming to Mexico, the secretary of their club had been a resident of Key West, where he worked actively to support the revolutionary cause, for twenty-three years.

In asking to have their notice printed in *Patria*, the members of Juárez y Martí claimed membership in a broader Cuban diaspora joined by the party and the newspaper. *Patria* was sent across the Atlantic to Cuban communities in France, and disseminated throughout the Americas, reaching remote areas as well as capital cities. *Patria* was mostly dedicated to publishing communiqués from the party leadership and reports about events occurring in Cuba; however, the paper often published information about different migrant communities, including the formation of political clubs, the staging of patriotic events, and lists of financial contributions. These reports constituted a conscious and careful effort to encourage a sense of shared identity and common purpose among the migrants. A survey of the letters written to Estrada Palma from Cubans in Mexico demonstrates that several migrants, especially those in more remote areas, were concerned about receiving the newspaper and complained when it was not regularly delivered.

Patria was not the only vehicle for the circulation and recirculation of news. Mexican newspapers reprinted articles from United States–based Cuban newspapers, and these newspapers themselves circulated in Mexico. The Spanish consul at Campeche complained in the summer of 1895 that of the fifteen or twenty Cubans in that port, four were "dignified white workers" and the rest were "excitable blacks and mulattos who, due to some U.S. newspaper reports, figure they have the bunny by the ears."[63] Whether news was circulating through travelers, Cuban newspapers, Mexican newspapers, U.S. newspapers, or Cuban newspapers published in the United States, Cubans in Mexico's port cities, in the cities along the Veracruz-Mexico City corridor, and in its capital were abreast not only of the state of the insurrection in Cuba but of the details of the diverse labors of migrants across the diaspora in benefit of the cause.

Individual Cuban clubs in Mexico were also connected, both within and across regions. In the letter reporting their act of constitution, the club Dolores y Yara located in Gutierrez Zamora, Veracruz, noted that it had forged links to a couple of long-standing clubs in the state so that they may "guide our steps."[64] Multi-club membership and the conferral of honorary memberships was another way to establish interstate connections. Of twenty-two ANERC applicants who reported traveling to multiple cities within Mexico, nineteen belonged to clubs in more than one of the different cities and towns they inhabited. Cubans like Rafael Rodríguez Acosta, a member of twenty-two separate clubs, were human bridges between Cuban organizations, sharing news and information about community events and political practices.[65]

Often, a club would confer honorary membership on individuals associated with different clubs as a way of networking. When Bartolomé Masó was founded, the members immediately named José Miguel Macías as its honorary president. Macías was the president of Máximo Gómez, the largest and most established Cuban club in Veracruz. The honorary title was meant to demonstrate respect and cultivate good relations with an important local association. A few months later, the club created an entire honorary directorate composed exclusively of Cuban women, some of whom were the wives and daughters of male members, and others who belonged to different clubs. In 1896, Bartolomé Masó granted Dr. Joaquin Carvajal, one of the more influential Cubans residing in the nearby city of Tlacotalpam, honorary membership. Similar memberships were extended to several Mexican journalists as well.[66] Finally, the club's networks extended as far as New York City, where it conferred honorary membership on Afro-Cuban journalist Rafael Serra.

Democracy and Power

Connections between clubs in Mexico and the United States extended beyond the informal exchanges that took place through traveling Cubans, newspapers, or migrants who belonged to multiple clubs. They also included the adoption and emulation of political practices. For example, a handful of Cuban clubs in Veracruz took the statutes of the New York CDC as their own, as they looked to challenge what seemed to be corrupt and antidemocratic practices by the local counsel's leadership.

In the fall of 1897, the CDC in Veracruz authorized a handful of newly formed clubs to vote in the organization's internal elections. A number of migrants questioned whether the internal CDC elections were valid, since the newly constituted associations were given full voting power. Using the New York CDC's statutes as a reference point, they insisted that newly constituted clubs had to wait for the second session of the CDC to become voting members. Ultimately, the dissenters were concerned about corruption within the CDC, and they suspected that the quick inclusion of new clubs was a ploy to ensure that the existing leadership would remain in a position of power. This conflict was mapped onto the generational divide, with older migrants representing the CDC leadership and newer migrants making up the majority of the dissenters. Undeniably, there was jockeying for power between younger and older migrants in Mexico-based Cuban communities, but there was also a sincere concern on the part of the dissenting clubs that the democratic process was being violated. The conflict was mediated with the help of the party agent in Mexico City, who traveled to Veracruz in order to help resolve the dispute. Much to the chagrin of the dissenting clubs, the conflict was resolved in favor of the established authorities in the CDC.[67]

The outcome of the conflict illustrates the party's commitment to uphold the authority of established local leaders, many of whom were veterans of the Ten Years' War, even when it was possible they had become corrupt and were violating democratic principles. The reactions of the dissidents to the perceived violations, and the ensuing conflict, which was serious enough to require external mediation, demonstrate just how determined Cubans in Veracruz were to safeguard their political participation in the movement. Indeed, the formal structures and procedures that governed the inner workings of the clubs, as well as members' willingness to defend democratic practices against corruption, suggest that migrant communities were aware of their role not only as remote supports of the insurgents, but also as citizens of an emerging nation they expected to be democratic. The victory of the leaders of the Veracruz CDC, on the other hand, and the fact that they enjoyed the unwavering support of both the Mexico City–based and New York City–based leaders, is proof that democratic ideals were secondary to both the maintenance of stability and the personal reputations of the vetted leaders who were at the helm of the migrant communities. In the end, as a result of this conflict, the leader of the CDC expelled a total of nine clubs and two individual Cuban migrants from the organization. The expelled clubs were composed of new generation migrants whom Macías referred to as "antipatriotic."[68] Macías echoes the complaints of Rodrigo Menendez Peña from Mérida, who had called the younger generation of migrants by the derogatory term *guatíbaros*. Both men cast new migrants as poor opportunists whose loyalty could not be trusted. Their views were strongly classed, but the banishment of Hijas de America, the only Cuban club presided over by a Black female president, suggests the possibility of race and gender-biased discrimination.

Cuban clubs jealously protected their rights. A review of the letters written by club secretaries to the party between 1895 and 1898 demonstrates that most clubs dutifully reported the results of their internal club elections to the party leadership each year, often noting that the elections were performed in accordance with the statutes of the party. Rarely is there mention of corrupt or non-democratic practices within individual local clubs. A handful of club reports do reveal, however, that some clubs were so eager to participate actively in PRC-wide elections that they circumvented the established rules and practices in favor of a spontaneous expression of direct democracy. In 1898, the PRC offices in New York received letters from four Mexico-based clubs pertaining to the election of the treasurer of the party. Technically, the CDC was responsible for conveying the vote of individual clubs to the party, but these clubs chose to report the results of club-level elections directly to Estrada Palma.[69] Two of the three clubs indicate in their letters that they discovered elections would be held in April through a circular published in the party newspaper, *Patria*. The decision to send in election results and circumvent the CDC says much about the determination of clubs to have their votes counted, and about the failure of the CDC to represent all of the clubs in Veracruz. One other possible explanation is that these particular clubs did not meet the minimum requirement of active members to be eligible to vote according to party statute, but were determined to participate anyway.

As with the dispute between dissident clubs and the CDC leadership, the possibility that the aforementioned four clubs' actions were motivated by distrust of the CDC suggests the existence of corruption. Yet, these conflicts and struggles over proper democratic procedure, the drive to participate in party-wide elections, and concerns about being overlooked and left out of democratic processes, also indicate a sincere engagement with democratic practices on the part of Cuban migrants affiliated to the party who imagined themselves as rights-bearing citizens.

Curiously, very similar conflicts around democratic practices and procedures nearly caused the collapse of the ANERC decades later, and some of the same dissidents were major figures in the disputes. These later conflicts in the ANERC began in 1927 when Luis Lagomasino y Alvarez, a Cuban and former resident of Veracruz, was dismissed from the organization on the spurious charge that he had defamed the organization's president—Juan Ramón O'Farrill—and the president of the republic—the infamous dictator Gerardo Machado. Lagomasino had begun to investigate the misuse of the ANERC's funds by O'Farrill, who was spending large sums of the organization's money to bankroll his visits to Florida to reconnect with old friends, with expenditures that topped $300–$400 per trip. Lagomasino denounced O'Farrill abuses of power in a letter to the governor of Havana and called on him to remove the president.[70] Lagomasino's attack on O'Farrill sparked a conflict that eventually pitted Florida-based and Mexico-based migrants against each other and resulted in Lagomasino's expulsion. Preferential treatment for U.S.-based émigrés from Tomás Estrada Palma, who would become Cuba's first president, to O'Farrill, who served as mayor of Havana indicates that some migrants benefitted from patronage networks and favoritism after the war leading to resentment from those who didn't. As we have seen, O'Farrill himself valued the revolutionary contributions of Key West and Tampa migrants as if they were the only ones that mattered.

Another conflict involving Florida-based and Mexico-based migrants erupted a few years later in 1933. Like Lagomasino, two other Mexico-based migrants, Pascual Hernández y Fernandez and Ignacio Pinar y Pérez, pleaded for the governor of Havana's help to remove O'Farrill from power on account of his "Machado-style" leadership.[71] Given that a revolution had ousted Machado in 1933, appealing to the governor by likening O'Farrill to Machado was savvy on the part of the dissidents. However, the governor refused to become involved and urged the members of the ANERC to resolve their disputes internally. Hernández and Pinar then devised a brilliant strategy for removing the president. First, they locked him out of the building. Then, they granted a general amnesty to all members of the organization whose memberships had expired, thus securing enough loyalty votes to unseat O'Farrill through a democratic process. This was nearly the same move that the leadership of the Veracruz CDC had made in 1897 ostensibly to secure their own power. However, the crucial difference here is that the dissidents used the maneuver to depose a president who was abusing his power. Furthermore, the move attacked a policy of exclusion masterminded by O'Farrill and his supporters by which poor ANERC members were ritually disenfranchised through unfair quota hikes and the draconian laws that made the reactivation of lapsed memberships impossible. Following the removal of O'Farrill, a new administration presided over the rewriting of the ANERC's statutes. The revised statutes of 1935 and 1939 restored membership quotas to 20 cents, allocated more spending to poor émigrés and the sick, re-established the clause granting women participation and equal rights, and restored the Monte Christi citations in the *Bases*.[72]

The prominence of Mexico-based migrants in these conflicts is remarkable. By the 1920s, Cubans from Mexico had come to constitute a bloc within the organization. A close look at the applications of the two hundred ANERC members from Mexico indicates that the majority were vetted by a handful of established ANERC members. More than 25 percent of the applicants were vetted by some combination of just four individuals: Luis Lagomasino y Alvarez, Ignacio Pérez Gil, Pascual Hernández y Fernández, and Ignacio Pinar y Pérez. Pinar and Hernández, two of the prime conspirators against O'Farrill during the late 1920s and early 1930s, stand out as signing off on the most applications over the course of the second decade of the century. Luis Lagomasino y Alvarez was also a frequent witness. Lagomasino, Pérez Gil, Pinar, Hernández, and another Mexico-based migrant who was identified by O'Farrill as a conspirator, Juan Puig y Chappotín, were all admitted to the ANERC just after its founding and thus participated in the organization's early development. As residents of Old Havana and Centro Havana, they lived in close proximity to each other and to the ANERC's main offices. Over the course of the first three decades of the century, each of these men held elected positions that extended from *vocal* to vice-president, and they exercised considerable influence within the organization. But their connection predates their time together in the ANERC.

Lagomasino, Pérez Gil, Pinar, Hernández, and Puig all departed from Havana and established themselves in Veracruz, three of them in 1896. Two of the five men belonged to the same political clubs, although all five were members of closely linked clubs in that city. These clubs—Bartolomé Masó, Máximo Gómez, José de la Luz Caballero, Protesta de Baraguá, Calixto García, Poesía and Nada con España—were some of the most prominent in Veracruz, and each was to a greater or lesser extent involved in the scandals that rocked the Cuban community there in 1897 and 1898. Three of these clubs, Bartolomé Masó, Protesta de Baragúa, and José de la Luz Caballero, were among the Cuban organizations expelled from the CDC in 1898. The conflicts, which involved the misuse of revolutionary monies and the abuse of democratic protocols, would have had a significant impact on all of the members of these clubs and likely shaped the opposition of the dissidents to O'Farrill's abuses of power at the head of the ANERC years later.

The connections between the Mexico-based migrants, the way in which they vetted each other's applications, and their collaboration to unseat O'Farrill indicate that they operated as a group and that they harbored significant resentment toward U.S.-based, migrants who were more often favored in Cuba during the intervention and the first Republic. O'Farrill offers a case in point. His high profile career included becoming mayor of Havana and later president of the ANERC.[73] The existence of a Mexico faction underscores the fact that Cubans in Mexico, despite their small numbers relative to Cubans in the United States, wielded disproportionate influence in the association. That the Mexico-based migrants were the group sufficiently organized to take on O'Farrill reflects the tight connections forged between migrants in Veracruz during the war. Finally, the fact that the Mexican group challenged O'Farrill's abuses suggests that they were particularly attuned to abuses of democratic protocol at the hands of a despotic authoritarian figure. This, of course, is not surprising given their participation in the conflicts over democratic processes in Veracruz during the war. Furthermore, as we will see, debates over the idea and practice of democracy were lively in Mexico, a nation struggling with the increasing abuse of a dictatorial regime. In Mexico during the war, Cubans' struggles over power and the abuse of it had generational dimensions. In Havana after the war, the conflicts were mapped onto regional divisions; Mexico-based migrants competed with Florida-based ones for influence within the organization. Thus, while we see collaboration and cooperation between migrant communities in the Gulf during the war, we see conflict based on regional differences between migrants in early republican Cuba.

Cuban political clubs were the bedrock of migrant life and of the PRC. They ensured a steady stream of financial and other contributions destined to aid the revolution northward to the coffers of the Revolutionary Party, but they also did much more. As the clubs integrated newcomers and folded them into the struggle for independence, they offered new migrants the opportunity to exercise rights, practice rituals, debate national questions, and make solidarities—all building blocks of citizenship. But such benefits were unevenly distributed. For some, the freedom with which they constituted political clubs, the goals and statutes of the party to which they swore loyalty, and the democratic practices which they defended, gave them a sense of purpose, importance, and place in a future Cuba they could only have imagined. For others, the gradual erosion of democratic structures and the parallel rise of a marked hierarchy among migrants led to their disempowerment and marginalization. White, elite males with solid revolutionary credentials were the favored émigrés, the ones that best fit the image of Cuban civility and respectability that the PRC leadership wished to convey across the Americas. Strong evidence of this trend can be seen in the composition of the ANERC membership. Among two hundred members from Mexico, the majority of those who listed occupations were professionals, and many more show clear signs of privilege, either in their mobility, financial contributions, or multiple club memberships. Indeed, the practices of exclusion, which continued even as the PRC was disbanded, are evident in the privileges that elite, white males enjoyed in government appointments in Cuba upon their return after the war, and in the administration and functioning of the ANERC, where elites regularly marginalized poor members.[74]

Cuban Politics and Cuban Émigré Self-Fashioning

A close examination of the migrants' self-fashioning as they became émigrés reveals the processes of exclusion at work. According to the ANERC's definition of the revolutionary émigré, an individual claiming the status did not need to have been a political exile or a revolutionary collaborator before his or her departure. In other words, the émigré could be any individual who had felt compelled to leave Cuba during the war for any reason, and who then contributed to the revolutionary cause in a substantial way while abroad. As we have seen, the role of the émigré in the revolutionary struggle was twofold. On the one hand, émigrés were expected to be effective auxiliaries, financing and provisioning the soldiers in the fields through their fundraising and filibustering activities. On the other hand, émigrés were to be the face of a new Cuba in their host countries. As representatives of Cuba, the émigrés were expected to remain unified, to act honorably, and to convey the sense that the future republic would be civilized and modern. Both roles were significant, and the ways in which the migrants defined and redefined themselves reveal much about how the PRC determined the definition of the "ideal" émigré and how migrants embraced, engaged, and shaped that definition. In their correspondence and in their ANERC applications, Cuban migrants residing in Mexico did their best to cast themselves as ideal revolutionary émigrés by detailing their various services to the revolution, making themselves useful in myriad ways, and, in some cases, carefully dispelling suspicions about the circumstances of their emigration which might tarnish their reputations. The differing experience of wealthier and poorer migrants lays bare the preferences of the Revolutionary Party during the war years.

Compelling evidence of the ways that migrants sought to rehabilitate or build up their revolutionary profiles can be found in the personal correspondence directed to Tomás Estrada Palma from Cubans in Mexico during the four years of war. Implicit in the act of writing to party leaders was the assumption that the writer was important enough to be heard by the highest authority within the PRC. The majority of the migrants who wrote letters to the party leadership were confident about the importance of their contributions to the struggle and eager to forge or reinforce their connections to powerful individuals who were influencing the course of the war and would more than likely determine the future course of the nation. Migrant letter writers went to great lengths to demonstrate that they had fulfilled their revolutionary mission, showing how they had promoted the unity of the Cuban community, made important financial contributions to the war effort, and faithfully represented Cuba abroad. While much can be read into the letters themselves, whether or not these migrants' letters were answered—and if so, how quickly—provides important clues about the success or failure of their efforts to prove their value.

ANERC applicants tried to present themselves as revolutionaries as they prepared their applications to the association. In order to gain admission, they had to provide proof of their participation in the movement. The very process of completing the application was an exercise in self-fashioning. Like the letter writers, ANERC applicants also took care to emphasize the ways they went above and beyond the expectations delineated in the party statutes. The narrative that dominates both the letters and ANERC applications is one of continuous self-sacrifice in the name of the nation. If soldiers sacrificed life and limb, migrants sacrificed quality of life to provision the army. If soldiers demonstrated their valor and value through heroic acts, migrants demonstrated theirs through the myriad ways they worked selflessly to advance the cause of independence from afar.

As the migrants defended their claims to be revolutionary émigrés, they also emphasized their access to money, their possession of strategic knowledge/intelligence, and their role as representatives of the nation, all of which reflected the aspirations of the party as far as the émigrés' role in the struggle was concerned. As noted previously, Martí considered the emigrants the "wings of the army." But they were also Cuba's future citizens, trained abroad in the proper exercise of civic habits. Still, not all migrants had equal access to the ANERC or the ear of the party leadership. As we saw in chapter 2, letter writers and ANERC applicants represented an elite fraction of the entire population of Cuban migrants. They fashioned themselves to fit one of four models of revolutionary patriot: the self-sacrificing and patriotic mother, the émigré insurgent, the exceptional auxiliary, or the defender of Cuban civility.

The Long-Suffering Mother as Revolutionary Patriot

As we have seen, women were omnipresent throughout the Cuban migrant communities, and many women participated actively in Cuban revolutionary politics. Nevertheless, revolutionary exile politics was gendered, as was participation on the battlefields in Cuba; both were dominated by men and were seen as parts of a masculine enterprise.[75] As Ada Ferrera has observed, the discourse of racial unity wrote women out of the birth of the nation by celebrating the union of black and white male Cubans forged on the battlefield, instead of celebrating *mestizaje* through miscegenation.[76]

In spite of this, the extent of women's involvement in the revolution is actually quite striking. Cuban women in exile participated both in politics and as auxiliaries, and in Cuba, in rare cases, women even served as soldiers during the war. Although the Cuban Revolutionary Party was not radical in terms of women's rights, a broad space of action and participation was allowed for women, and they took advantage of these openings.

That only 19 of 298 Cuban migrants in our sample of letter writers and ANERC applicants were women says much more about the source material than about women's actual participation. With regard to the ANERC, struggles over the place of women in the organization punctuated the early twentieth century. At the society's founding in Havana in 1909, a parallel organization was established for women. By the early 1920s, women were integrated into the ANERC and offered equal rights. In the mid- to late 1920s, just as the Machado dictatorship was gaining ground, this policy was reversed, and women were stripped of their rights as members. In the 1940s, equal rights were restored once more, probably a reflection of the gains of the feminist movement enshrined in Cuba's progressive 1940 constitution. Over the course of its history, the ANERC's exclusively male leaders were ambivalent about how and to what extent the organization should recognize women's patriotic labors. In terms of hard numbers and despite its periods of greater openness to women, the ANERC was a male-dominated institution. Few women found a place in the ANERC as members, and no women held elected positions in it in the first decades of the twentieth century.[77]

Yet, women were ubiquitous among the revolutionary émigrés in Mexico. A close reading of club lists, including the correspondence of Cuban club secretaries who wrote to the party leadership in New York and lists of contributions made by women, reveal that women held directive roles within numerous clubs. For example, Rosa Gómez Viuda de Guerol was the secretary of Club Cubano Hatuey in Monterrey. Antonia Casanova de García Garófalo appeared as the vice president of Juárez y Martí. Emma Findlay was listed as the same club's treasurer. Three additional women appeared in elected positions in Juárez y Martí. The fact that Antonia de García Garófalo's husband, Ricardo García Garófalo, was listed as the secretary of the club clearly indicates that the membership was cross-gender. Women are listed among the founding members of Club Cubano Poesia, the same club that Mercedes Perlamo Viuda de Chirino claimed to have presided over in her ANERC file. In addition to cross-gender clubs, there were a number of clubs that were exclusive to women, wherein all the elected positions were held by women. Among them were Hijas de América; Club Fraternidad and Protectoras de la Patria (later Protectoras del Ejercito) in Veracruz; Hijas de Baire, Protectoras de la Patria, and La Cadena in Mexico City; the Grupo Reformista de Señoras de Puebla; Cuba Libre in Mérida; and Mujeres de Saltillo in Coahuila. Hijas de América, the only club with a black female president, was also the only club composed of women that the CDC expelled from the organization in 1898. Its president Julia Alvarez de Xiques took a strong stance against Macias and the CDC when she decided that the club would submit its financial contributions directly to the PRC in New York.

The true number of female migrants who participated in the revolutionary struggle is difficult to ascertain, because clubs rarely recorded a total number of members. Many simply referred to their membership as both male and female. Lists of financial contributions were often recorded in Mexican and Cuban newspapers, however, and these showed the contributions made by both elite and working class women. For instance, the workers' club Obreros de Progreso published the results of a collection in which twenty-four women and twenty-six men listed their names as participants and contributors.

If club correspondence, membership lists, and published records of financial contributions reveal the extensive presence of women in the movement, the reports of public events also demonstrate women's active participation in the revolutionary cause. Women were important organizers, participants, and audience members of the many meetings, bazaars, commemorations, and *veladas* that punctuated the daily life of Cuban migrant communities. In these settings, women usually played a supplementary role to men. They were celebrated for their recitations of poetry, renditions of songs, or simply the elegance of their presence in the room.

While some women fit well within prescribed limits, others exceeded them. In March of 1896, Josefina A. de Betancourt, a Cuban living in Monterrey, Mexico, wrote to the head of the PRC asking if he knew the whereabouts of her brother. Upon learning that he had been drowned at sea during a botched filibustering expedition, she wrote, "Oh! my friend, how many tears has this war for Cuban independence cost us, how can Spain contemplate the loss of so many lives with such indifference."[78] On 2 October 1897, Magdalena Cabrera of Veracruz wrote a similar letter asking Estrada Palma to forward a message to her son, a soldier in the insurgent army. "You must understand the pain that I feel as a mother, a Cuban mother who cannot communicate with him."[79] Both women bore the patriotic sacrifice of their brothers and sons with the kind of fortitude expected of

Cuban women during the revolution. In these letters, each woman articulated her emotions with temperance, flanking expressions of sadness with patriotic statements about the nobility of the cause that had shattered their personal lives.

The acceptable image of the female Cuban patriot was that of the stoic and patriotic suffering mother, wife, sister, or daughter who watched the men in her life assume the patriotic sacrifices necessary to bring about the independence of Cuba. Letters written by women like Betancourt and Cabrera reinforce this trope again and again. Regardless of their actual level of participation, male migrants generally felt entitled to claim a publicly lauded revolutionary identity, but women, even those who were highly active in Cuban exile politics, neither sought nor received much public recognition. After all, the ideal émigré, like the ideal insurgent, was normatively male.

Louis Pérez Jr., Maria Prados-Torreira, and Lillian Guerra have all noted how Cuban revolutionary woman both embraced, exceeded, and at times challenged the expectations of their male compatriots during the wars.[80] While Josefina de Betancourt appears to operate firmly within convention, a closer look at her letters reveals an interesting twist. She did not write Estrada Palma merely to express a sister's grief; she also recorded her opinion on the climate of support in Mexico for the Cuban struggle and offered to send copies of a newspaper published in Mexico City by a group of Mexican students that was at the forefront of the movement to support Cuban independence in that city.[81] Betancourt was abreast of revolutionary developments and she followed the Mexican press, perhaps as a subscriber to the *Continente Americano*, the newspaper she offered to send to Estrada Palma. Betancourt understood the importance of public opinion, solidarity, and the international reputation of the movement and she offered her services to the leader of the Revolutionary Party not as a grieving sister, but as a revolutionary patriot.

Women like Caridad de Leon y de Quesada, a founding member of the two most important clubs in Yucatán, had an even more active role in the movement. She offered her home as a meeting space for both of the clubs she was affiliated with, Yucatán y Cuba and Salvador Cisneros. Another woman, Candida del Rio y Rosas, one of only four female applicants to the ANERC from Mexico, reported providing countless services to the revolution over the years, including hosting revolutionary figures such as Martí, PRC secretary Gonzalo de Quesada, and PRC treasurer Benjamín Guerra during their trips to Mexico.[82] These three men were some of the most important figures in the Cuban emigrations and occupied the highest positions in the PRC. The contributions of the women who served as club presidents, vice presidents, secretaries, and treasurers are equally as impressive.

Given that so few women applied to the ANERC compared to the number of women who rendered services to the revolution abroad, the applications of the four women who did apply offer intriguing clues about their lives and revolutionary identities. The marital status of the four female ANERC applicants from Mexico sheds much light on their decision to apply to the ANERC. Three of four of these women identified themselves as widows. As such, these women may have felt a greater freedom to apply on their own behalf. It is easy to imagine that many married female former migrants declined to apply or were dissuaded from applying to the ANERC by their husbands. The three widowed female ANERC applicants proudly list their accomplishments and contributions without mentioning their husbands or crediting them with any participation. Dominga Valdes Corvalles de Muniz stands out as the only married woman in the group. She was forty-nine years old at the time of her application, the youngest applicant. However, like the other three female applicants, Corovalles de Muniz does not mention her husband's participation in the war effort, nor does she suggest that her entry into politics took place through collaboration with a male relative. In fact, she reports having worked for the revolution in exile first as a young unmarried woman in Key West, Florida, serving as a secretary of a club there, and, later in Veracruz. The only time she mentions her marriage is to alert the committee to her name change so that they may be able to locate her by her maiden name to corroborate her early participation in the movement. In all four cases, these women were determined to take full credit for their own participation.[83] The fact that all four women served in elected positions within the PRC club structure also indicates that they took advantage of the political openings that the PRC provided for women in exile and suggests that they wished to be recognized for that service. Their active and high-profile revolutionary careers help us understand their decision to apply to the ANERC. Like their male counterparts, these women were proud of their accomplishments and sacrifices, and they wanted to leave a record of their participation in the struggle.

Even if women's roles in these gatherings were restricted and conventional, their actions leading clubs, gathering funds, staging events, corresponding with leadership, and offering opinions and information about the situation of the migrants and the movement in Mexico make it clear that women were omnipresent and had multiple roles within the Cuban migrant community. Women were a fundamental part of Cuban revolutionary organizing in Mexico: from those who applied to ANERC boldly claiming the right to be publicly recognized as revolutionaries, to those who occupied positions in the directories of various co-ed and female clubs and appeared as contributors on the lists of various financial collections, to those who recited poetry at Cuban public and private celebrations. The fact that so few female members and participants can be identified through the ANERC files and letters tells us more about the marginalization of women within the historical memory of the struggle and within the archive than it does about their actual revolutionary participation.

Risking Life and Limb: The Émigré Insurgent as Revolutionary Patriot

Some other migrants sought to fashion themselves as revolutionary patriots by adhering to an ideal we might call that of the émigré insurgent. Typically, these were men who had formed part of the insurgency either in the 1860s or in the 1890s, but who were deported, or who sought refuge in exile voluntarily. In his very first letter, Fernando Cisneros, a veteran of the Ten Years' War, informed Estrada Palma of the services he had rendered to the revolutionary cause and the persecution he had suffered at the hands of the Spanish after four years in prison in Cueta. Cisneros explained at great length the ways in which he continued to support the cause as one of a tiny handful of migrants living in Túxpam. Cisneros was the nephew of Salvador Cisneros Betancourt, the famous insurgent general and president of the Cuban republic in arms. Cisneros was able to use his revolutionary parentage, his past patriotism, and his continued labor for the cause in order to command the attention of the party leadership in New York.

Gabriel López García's experience was palpably different from that of Fernando Cisneros. First, he was not related to the great military heroes of the revolution, although he was, himself, a second lieutenant in the Liberation Army. López García owned nothing but the clothing he wore on his back, but, despite his poverty, he made financial contributions to the revolutionary cause as an exile. Yet, whereas Cisneros demonstrated his continuing support for the cause by offering Estrada Palma a variety of services and asking nothing in return, López García was forced by the poverty of his circumstances to leverage his patriotic sacrifice for financial support to alleviate his desperate situation. Languishing in Tampa and unable to find work or make ends meet, he wrote to the party asking for financial support and defending his request by arguing that, "when I was here for three months as an expeditionary, the party did not waste a penny on me because I worked and gave 10% of my salary to the cause."[84] The difference between the two was a matter of class and revolutionary pedigree. López García wrote of his poverty and of his inability to find work in "innumerable factories" despite his best efforts.[85] His last communications indicate that he had made it from Veracruz to Tampa—where he had left his family years earlier—without any financial support from the party, although he believed he was entitled to such support. While Cisneros's letters were answered quickly and he sustained a meaningful correspondence with party leaders, López García was clearly deemed less of a priority. It took party leaders two months to answer López García's first letter, whereas they responded to Cisneros's in ten days. López García's subsequent letters met a similar fate. At one point he complained to Tomás Estrada Palma that he had been waiting two months and seven days for a response to another letter. López García's treatment was typical of poorer migrants with fewer connections and resources. Despite the party's rhetoric of inclusion and the prominent role that working-class migrants played in the founding of the party, in practice, migrants who fit into a particular image—one embodied by Cisneros rather than by López García—were favored.

Poor émigré insurgents like López Garcia often found it necessary to try leveraging their sacrifices, for little or no gain. Even elites and professionals, though, could receive a cold shoulder for various reasons. José Antonio Caiñas sent six letters at regular intervals to the party leadership over the course of the three years he lived in Veracruz, most of which were ignored. His main preoccupation in his early letters was to explain how he was able to escape Cuba in 1896. He was honest about the fact that he did so with the support of family friends who were Spanish loyalists. His candor on this point seems to suggest that the truth around the circumstances of his exile would soon be, or was already, widely known. The subsequent letters were focused on one singular aim: convincing Estrada Palma to help him launch a filibustering expedition to return to Cuba and to the war. It seems relevant here to indicate that there was no greater glory for an émigré than to outfit a filibustering expedition, and few greater glories for an insurgent than manning such an expedition and arriving in Cuba with resources to bolster the insurgency. But Caiñas's requests met with a persistent and frustrating silence. As he speculated about the possible causes of this silence in yet another letter to Estrada Palma, Caiñas began to fear that Estrada Palma questioned his loyalty. As if to preempt concerns of treason,

Caiñas quickly reminded the delegate that although he accepted Spanish aid, he did not remain with the Spanish forces where he would have found safety and "convenience."[86] Caiñas was desperate to clear his name and restore his reputation, which explains the urgency with which he describes his patriotic labors in exile and his plans to return to Cuba. The silence in the records indicates, however, that Caiñas was denied his much-longed-for absolution. Given his prominent place as an active member of the Veracruz Cuban community, we might expect that he would have applied to the ANERC. Evidence in his letters does suggest that he returned to Cuba after the war, but his absence from the ANERC leaves us wondering whether he was ever able to live down the dubious circumstances of his emigration.[87]

The ANERC applicant Ignacio Martín Arbona y Domínguez's story resembles Caiñas's in that he also escaped Cuba due to the intervention of a Spanish official who was a family acquaintance. However, Arbona did apply to the ANERC. Where Caiñas was deeply concerned about his reputation in his letters to Estrada Palma in the 1890s, Arbona seemed uninterested in defending his record of loyalty when he filed an application with the ANERC thirty years after the war. He focused instead on crafting a coherent narrative of continual sacrifice. Arbona's petition spans ten pages and reads like the recollections of an aging patriot nostalgic for his youth and eager to leave behind some tangible evidence of his participation in the struggle.

Cisneros's, López García's, Caiñas's, and Arbona's different stories offer a range of examples of how insurgents in exile refashioned themselves as émigré insurgents. At the core of each narrative was a story of continuous self-sacrifice and unbroken loyalty to the revolution. Caiñas perhaps best embodies the dilemma of being both an insurgent and an émigré. His time abroad was marked by his singular determination to return to the war, a passion that became an obsession. As he laid the intricate plans for his expedition, and pled with the PRC leadership to support him, he knew that launching an expedition was a consummate example of émigré patriotism and revolutionary action, and he hoped that it would be the vehicle through which he could return to the war a hero and restore his tarnished reputation. In the end, however, he would have to make peace with the life of a migrant. Of all four individuals, Cisneros is the only one whose correspondence is answered expediently and regularly and whose gestures and efforts are applauded by party leadership. Cisneros's success has much to do with his revolutionary credentials as a member of the 1868 generation. Neither López García, Caiñas, nor Arbona possessed this advantage, and in fact Caiñas's and Arbona's royalist connections may have harmed them. In the eyes of an older generation, the revolutionary sentiments of these younger men were not as "pure" as their own, which had driven them to leave Cuba so as not to live under the Spanish regime after the defeat of the revolutionaries in the Ten Years' War.

The Wings of the Army: The Exceptional Auxiliary as Revolutionary Patriot

Fernando Cisneros had another strategic advantage over his compatriots: his financial capital. After Estrada Palma rejected Cisneros's offer to bankroll the voyages of several aspiring insurgents to New York City, Cisneros changed course, seeking money and representation instead of recruits. Estrada Palma consistently refused to support the many filibustering expedition plots that were organized by Cuban émigrés in Mexico (like José Antonio Caiñas) and elsewhere outside of the U.S., arguing that the migrants needed to focus on financial contributions that could be used to buy arms and supplies rather than on sending men to Cuba who might not have had substantial military experience, and who might not succeed in the wartime environment of the *manigua*. As a result, poorer men who had been insurgents and who wanted to return to the war found it increasingly difficult to do so. Those within the emigration who had the most financial resources and flexibility, as well as the most important political connections, could fund their own travel to Cuba or to a point in the United States where an expedition to Cuba was being organized. Furthermore, Estrada Palma ignored many letters offering a myriad of services to benefit the war effort. Some of the more outrageous letters included intricate plans, schemes, and inventions such as a hydrogen-powered air balloon and a "*bomba de terror*," which came with a detailed diagram.[88] While these schemes went unappreciated, Estrada Palma regularly answered letters of those who offered sustained financial contributions or substantial sums of money.

It was standard in the correspondence of young men or veterans for one to mention one's willingness and desire to fight and die in the war, but the majority of the émigrés in Mexico were not, and had not been, insurgents. They had fled the war as refugees and became revolutionaries only later. Although they often mentioned the desire to take up arms, these Cubans generally fashioned themselves as exemplary auxiliaries. Some emphasized their financial and other contributions, while others remade themselves as representatives of the Cuban people, liaisons between the independence struggle and the Mexican people, both of which fit well within the image of the ideal émigré envisioned by Martí and perpetuated by his successors.

About one-quarter of the revolutionary émigrés staked their patriotism on their financial sacrifices made for the war. These émigrés, ranging from the very wealthy to the working poor, understood the power of framing themselves as the financial backbone of the movement. As a mark of his revolutionary patriotism, Manuel Ruano of Mexico City committed himself to a monthly quota, which he sent directly to the party headquarters. Over the course of thirteen months, he sent $250. This was a significant amount for one individual and would have been worth approximately $2,000 today.[89] As we might expect, Estrada Palma promptly responded and encouraged Ruano's gestures of support. Even more spectacular gestures were made by men like Agustín Meulener, a commissions agent with his own business and resident of Orizaba, who reported sending nearly $3,000 over a two-year span.[90] The choice that wealthier members made to send their contributions straight to the party rather than have them bundled in with other financial contributions made to local Cuban clubs is a clear statement of their desire to be recognized personally for their service to the revolution.

There were also more humble émigrés who pledged money to the cause. For example, Francisco Gargallo Cáceres, who lived a modest life as a *lector* in a tobacco factory in Cuba, pledged 20 percent of his earnings (even though only 10 percent donation was customary and expected). To forfeit a percentage of one's salary was to identify with early emigrations to Florida, where the practice of salary donation had been initiated among tobacco workers. Ten out of the eleven ANERC applicants who reported residing on farms and working as farmers upon their return to Cuba list contributing 10 percent of their salaries while in exile; again, this was consistent with the accepted practice among workers in the emigrations. Yet neither Cáceres nor any of the farmers in the number above appear in positions as elected members of the ANERC during the lifetime of the association. Given how many elected positions there were and the prominence of Mexico-based Cubans in such positions within the association, the absence of any poor or working-class émigrés in elected positions strongly suggests their marginalization.[91]

Other contributions to the cause highlighted by letter writers and ANERC members alike included exceptional services to the party through active membership in its structures. As a member of twenty-two different clubs in four Mexican cities, Rafael Rodriguez Acosta stands out for his record of exemplary service, as does Rafael Cuevas y Oliva, who belonged to distinct clubs in Mexico City, Veracruz, and Puebla. Many subagents, club leaders, founders, and active members of these associations placed the independence struggle at the center of their lives and hoped to be recognized for that choice. They busied themselves recruiting new members and unaffiliated Cubans, organizing and carrying out fundraising schemes, and staging innumerable patriotic celebrations, conferences and other events, all while dutifully reporting these activities to party leaders. That so many ANERC applicants belonged to more than one political club indicates meaningful involvement with Cuban politics and highlights the interconnection of club life and club activities. Nearly all of the 110 letter writers understood themselves as revolutionary émigrés for whom support of the Cuban independence cause was a central and pressing concern.

Bearers of Civilization: The Defender of Cuban Civility as Revolutionary Patriot

Safeguarding the name of the revolution in exile and projecting an image of civility to foreign observers became two of the central preoccupations of Cuban revolutionary émigrés. Defending the reputation of *Cuba Libre* was of paramount importance, especially in light of persistent efforts made by Spanish immigrants to discredit the movement by casting Cuban immigrants as largely black, poor, unsophisticated, and aimless men whose only talents involved singing and dancing. One Spanish journalist caricatured Cuban émigrés in the following fashion: "Cuban youth, without occupation, looking to marry wealthy Mexican woman. Has previously worn shoes to present himself with. Dances *danzón* admirably and sings *guajiras* with style. Can be found on any street corner."[92] The references to *danzón*, an Afro-Cuban art form, and the *guajira*, a rural musical tradition, highlight how these stereotypical portrayals were raced and classed. The journalist's inclusion of them, along with references to the émigré's just barely acceptable appearance and his desire to entrap a wealthy Mexican woman, are meant to leave the reader with the impression that Cuban revolutionary émigrés were poor, black, idle adventurers not qualified to lead an independent republic. As we saw in chapter 2, Cuban émigré Leandro Cañizares Gómez worked hard to counter the depiction of the insurgent army as a mass of vengeful black men and the image of *Cuba Libre* as a second Haiti. His fundamentally racist rhetoric emphasized the fact that blacks in Cuba were destined for extinction through immigration and miscegenation.

Fernando Cisneros went out of his way to describe to Estrada Palma the responsibility he felt in representing Cuba as one of a small handful of Cubans in Tabasco. Referring to the invitation extended to him by local Spaniards to attend a funeral service for the recently assassinated Spanish prime minister Antonio Canovas del Castillo, Cisneros writes, "With your approval I will attend with my family because this way we can make them understand the difference between the innately generous Cuban and the carnivalesque Spaniard."[93] Cisneros compared the way in which the Spaniards "drank and danced with glee when our unforgettable Maceo died," with the respect Cubans expressed at the death of Canovas del Castillo.

Cisneros's complaint was one of dozens from Mexico received by the party leadership during the war years regarding the Spanish immigrant community. Cuban revolutionary émigrés regularly complained that the greatest obstacle to their organizing efforts was the presence of a wealthy and well-connected Spanish immigrant community in Mexico that was bent on obstructing their patriotic labors. Cisneros's decision to attend Canovas del Castillo's funeral services in Mexico in order to make a statement about Cuban civility and the "barbarism" Spaniards displayed in the wake of Maceo's death was a reflection of the constant need to bolster the image of the insurgency as a movement led by civilized elites.

In a conscious reversal of the rhetoric often employed by Spaniards to denigrate Cubans as poor vagrants, one Cuban journalist writing in Mexico City for a short-lived independent newspaper called *La Libertad* insisted that Cuban émigrés were political exiles who intended to return to Cuba once their nation was free and independent, while Spanish immigrants were poor, destitute, uncultured individuals who came to Mexico with empty pockets looking for the means to survive.[94] Both Spaniards' efforts to cast Cubans as vagrants and Cubans' insistence on doing the same to Spaniards demonstrate how class and civility had become central to arguments over Cuba's right to independence and its viability as an independent republic.

Among the fiercest defenders of *Cuba Libre* was Cuban journalist Manuel Márquez Sterling. Journalism and travel to and from Mexico had been mainstays of Márquez Sterling's life since he was a boy. A passion for writing and for revolutionary ideas drew him to the pen, and a love for Mexico born out of a constant engagement with the country drew him consistently back to its shores. During the 1890s, Márquez Sterling served as a staff writer for the Mexican newspaper *el Diario del Hogar* and also as director of his own newspaper, *La Libertad*. A firm defender of Cuba's independence, he worked over the course of the war to dispel the idea that Cubans were not prepared to govern themselves and that the cause of independence was ill-conceived or premature. On 31 July 1898, Márquez Sterling defended the viability of an independent Cuba vigorously, writing that "even being enslaved Cuba has shone like no other American nation for her advancements in the arts and sciences. Cuba has had publicists and orators that have surpassed all those of the Americas; Cuba has sustained political parties more disciplined than any across the Americas one century after independence. Cuba has taken its contributions in philosophy and the natural sciences to Europe one thousand times over . . . Cuba can and knows how to govern herself."[95]

Manuel Márquez Sterling's intended audience was composed of Mexicans who in 1898 had begun to express doubt about Cuba's ability to stand on its own. With the Spanish-American War looming, many Latin Americans worried that the United States would defeat Spain and then invade and annex Cuba. After all, the United States had long coveted the Pearl of the Antilles. Referring to and simultaneously dismissing fears about the annexation of Cuba by the United States and taking a jab at Spain in the process, Márquez Sterling went on to say that if "the nations who are so expert in the art of self-governance have the right to annex those who are deficient in this respect, then the government of Porfirio Díaz should send an army to occupy the Spanish throne." The émigrés and their supporters commonly repeated the argument that Spain was less capable of self-governance than either its current or former colonies. A statement like this was meant to goad and irritate Spanish immigrants, yet it points to something more. Márquez Sterling's comment is a reflection of what James E. Sanders has dubbed "American Republican Modernity," the idea that the Americas rather than Europe were the vanguard of modernity in the Atlantic world and that old world monarchies had much to learn from new world republics about governance.[96] Although Sanders argues that American Republican Modernity had largely been supplanted by Western industrial modernity by the late nineteenth century, he recognizes the Cuban independence movement as a possible exception. Indeed, Cuban revolutionaries revived American Republican Modernity, positioning Cuba at the center of a movement for the reform of Spain—and more immediately, Mexico. As we will see in subsequent chapters, the Cuban insurgency was seen as heir to Mexico's own struggles for independence, while the future Cuban republic was imagined as a beacon of republicanism and democracy that could help guide Mexico, a nation that Cuban revolutionaries and their Mexican supporters believed was drifting dangerously toward authoritarianism and conservatism.

Conclusion

The Cuban independence struggle inserted itself into the daily lives of Cuban migrants, whether they liked it or not. It might come as the unwanted pressure to forfeit 10 percent of one's earnings to the revolutionary cause, or it might take the form of a welcome invitation to belong to a new social network. For those who were already committed revolutionaries, Cuban migrant communities became a home away from home where they could continue revolutionary labors and realize new projects. For those who welcomed Cuban revolutionary politics into their lives, the institutions of the nation in exile must have seemed open and inviting. The Revolutionary Party found a place for those individuals, regardless of class, race, or gender, who wanted to dedicate themselves to the struggle, and in exchange it offered membership in a national community. That national community was, in part, being formed in exile. Indeed, the leaders of the Revolutionary Party had a vision of the role that the migrant would play in the stabilization of the new republic. The migrant would be a salutary force. Migrants had lived at the "crossroads of the world," had "gone out to prepare," and had engaged in "creative and sustaining work in the more capable nations of the world," and so they were "bringing their own efforts on behalf of the country's misery."[97] If they were lucky enough to be among "thousands of white persons" to have "completed their education in foreign countries . . . where they have become accustomed to republican practices and to the exercise of their rights as free men," their place in Republican Cuba would be assured. During the war they may have been merely auxiliaries, but after the war, they would become leaders. The work and life experiences of the émigrés would prepare them and their "children for the exercise of those same rights in their native land when it shall be emancipated from Spanish domination."[98]

The National Association of Cuban Revolutionary Émigrés was established in Havana after the war with precisely this vision in mind: to concretize the important role that the former migrants would play in the new republic. Its own charter made clear that the goal of ANERC members was to show, through "stimulus and example, experience and lesson . . . the exercise and practice of civic responsibilities" that were indispensable for the maintenance of a stable, prosperous, and democratic state. Yet, despite the inclusive vision and extensive reach of the PRC, and despite the ANERC's assertion in its statutes that Cubans might belong to the association without "regard to class," both institutions proved exclusive.[99] In the end, only certain Cubans—those who were positioned to convey the image of respectability that proved so crucial to Cuban insurgent diplomacy in Latin America and in the United States—were allowed full access to the ANERC and its resources.

Cuban political elites worried that the Cuban insurgent army looked far too black to many skeptical onlookers in the Americas, and the poor Cuban migrants of the kind who attended public meetings on Patrona Street in Veracruz singing, dancing, and strumming guitars were not the men and women that they wanted to put forward as representatives of the nation. Far better suited were the white, well-dressed, and well-educated men and women attending conferences and high-class fundraisers in Mexico City, where they toasted to *Cuba Libre* with glasses of champagne and listened to classical music recitals and poetry reading. In these elite gatherings, women might find a place if they were the wives, sisters, or daughters of well-to-do Cuban men, but poor, non-white Cubans were not welcome and, generally, not present. The ANERC, which similarly focused on exalting the labors and contributions of those Cubans whom the party deemed the best representatives of the nation, also found little space for poor migrants, Afro-Cubans, and women.

Among those who lost the most, we find Cubans like the indentured worker Juan Ortega Manzano, who escaped servitude in Yucatán, but who could not save his family. The U.S. and Cuban governments managed to repatriate some migrants from Florida, but migrants in Mexico were left to their own devices. Eventually, even the ANERC gave up the cause. What became of those migrants is material for another study, but they were victims of the pernicious politics of exclusion. His sacrifices as a second lieutenant in the insurgent army forgotten, Gabriel López García complained bitterly of the need to debase himself working as a sailor in order to pay his passage to Tampa to find the family he had left there. Forced to walk from where the ship docked, a location along the Florida coast he failed to name, he arrived at Tampa with his clothes in tatters from having slept on the road. To his family, Gabriel must have seemed a shadow of the man who had left them a year before as a proud insurgent.

4 Internationalizing *Cuba Libre*
Cuban Insurgent Diplomacy and the Building of Transnational Solidarities

• •

Although he would become the founder of the Cuban Revolutionary Party and the mastermind of Cuba's final struggle for independence, José Martí started out much like other Cuban migrants and exiles. Like the lives of Gabriel, Ignacio, and Dominga, José's early life as a revolutionary was marked by persecution, dislocation, and exile. While his travels would take him beyond the Gulf World, Martí spent time living in exile in both Mexico and the United States.[1] Mexico, a nation with an international reputation for prosperity in the late nineteenth century, attracted Dominga and her family, who migrated to Veracruz seeking new opportunities and horizons. José Martí's family left Cuba for Mexico for similar reasons. As the first Cuban independence conflict moved into its sixth year, and with their son exiled to Spain, the Martís decided to establish themselves in Mexico, hoping to secure a better future for their daughters. Once he was sure of their departure, José finalized his plans to travel to Mexico via Paris and New York. He arrived in Mexico in 1875.[2]

While we can trace the ways that the Gulf world shaped the travels of migrants like Gabriel, Ignacio, and Dominga, it is more difficult to glean the impact of the Gulf on their thinking. In Martí's case, however, numerous letters and essays published in exile speak to the importance of the Gulf in his thought, and especially of the relationship between Mexico, Cuba, and the United States. From the first moment that he set foot in Mexico, Martí imagined himself as the nation's adopted son. En route between Veracruz and Mexico City, he wrote "Oh, beloved Mexico! . . . . Hear the call of a son of yours who was not born unto you." Indeed, in many of the articles he published during his two-year stay in Mexico, Martí would speak for the Mexican people as one of them, blurring the distinction between Latin Americans. For example, when Porfirio Díaz came to power via a coup in 1876, Martí, incensed, wrote, "So then is it true? That Mexicans are once again killing each other? That a tradition has been violated, a government overthrown . . . to further discredit ourselves . . . and make the self-respect we were starting to earn even more impossible."³

Martí's outrage and the profundity of his despair reflects his deep love for Mexico and the important place that the nation held in his imagination. He was taken by the nation's glorious history of struggle against foreign invasion, as well as by its spectacular modernization, already visible in the locomotive he rode along the Mexican Railway when he traveled from coast to capital in 1875. One scholar described the rail line as "an engineer's miracle" that wound its way around mountains, through tunnels, and over perilous bridges as it ascended from the Gulf Coast to Mexico City.⁴ Martí also described the trip from Veracruz to Mexico City, making reference to the two impressive locomotives dragging numerous train cars in a serpentine fashion up and into the valley of Mexico as if in a procession.⁵ Martí's description imagines the railroad as powerful and modern, yet ominous; this ambivalence also characterized his later writings on other technological feats like the Brooklyn Bridge in New York City.⁶ Mexico's modernization, its heroic struggles against imperialists, and its unique geographical positioning (vis-à-vis the United States and Latin America) placed the nation in the role of guide and protector of Latin America. Martí wrote,

> Oh, beloved Mexico! . . . see the dangers that surround you! Hear the call of a son of yours who was not born unto you. In the North an evil neighbor is gaining strength. You will put your affairs in order. You will guide yourself; I will have died, oh Mexico, defending and loving you, but if your hands weaken, if you were not worthy of your continental duty, I would cry under the earth—with tears that would later become iron for lances—like a son nailed to his coffin that sees how a worm eats the entrails of its mother.⁷

The imagery is dark, and the words convey hope, dread, and doubt all at once.

In 1875, Liberal forces in Mexico had recently beaten back a European invasion, and the nation, while basking in the glories of that triumph, was struggling to "come together" and find its footing. The French intervention was the fourth foreign attack or invasion that Mexico had faced in its first six decades of independent life. But despite Mexico's heroism, Martí's faith in his new country was laced with doubt: "if your hands weaken, if you were not worthy." By the end of the passage, Martí lays out the dreaded consequences of failure by invoking the specter of an adopted son—Martí himself—forced to witness the gruesome decomposition of his mother from within his own coffin. The only possibility for redemption is found in the potential of his "tears" to "become iron for lances." Mexico was not alone in carrying the weight of the continent on its shoulders. We might read Martí's mention of lances as confirmation of his own determination to forestall the advance of U.S. imperialism, even as Mexico falters.

Two decades later, Martí had achieved the impossible. He had founded a new political party, the Cuban Revolutionary Party; he had healed debilitating divisions between and among Cuban migrants and civilian and military revolutionaries in Cuba; and he had helped organize a new war for Cuban independence. Not content to be a poet and an intellectual, he was determined to be a man of action, an insurgent. Martí traveled alongside the insurgent general Máximo Gómez to Cuba and arrived in mid-April with the intention of fighting in the war effort. In May of 1895, he was in Cuba preparing for battle. As he set down his final reflections in a letter to his friend Manuel Mercado, Martí's thoughts turned to Mexico. They were reminiscent of his musings twenty years earlier: "I have lived inside the monster and I know its entrails. My struggle is akin to that of David. . . . Over here I have done my duty. The Cuban war . . . has come at the right time in America to avoid . . . annexation to the United States . . . And Mexico? Is there not an immediate, effective and sagacious way for her to aid, in a timely manner, her defenders?"[8]

Martí's thoughts on Mexico's role in the hemisphere in the mid-1870s and his thoughts in 1895 bear a close resemblance. In both cases, he assigned Mexico great responsibility in hemispheric affairs, while also expressing doubt about its readiness to assume that responsibility. An important distinction, however, is that in 1875 Martí imagines Mexico as Cuba's defender. In 1895, the roles have reversed. It is Cuba that will now save Mexico. Martí's tears have been converted into lances, and with them he takes up the fight that Mexico has abandoned. As Martí makes clear, the fight for *Cuba Libre* is a fight for more than the liberation of a colony: it is a struggle to secure the freedom of all Latin America. Cuba and Mexico were seen as the front line of that defense.

This chapter explores how the Cuban independence struggle and the idea of *Cuba Libre* became bound up with the fate of the continent. More specifically, it examines Mexico's particular place in the history of Cuba writ large across the Americas. Over the course of the nineteenth century almost every country in the Americas was preoccupied at one point or another with the struggle for *Cuba Libre*, but Cuba's nearest neighbors, the United States and Mexico, were undoubtedly the most affected by, and the most engaged in the island's struggles. From as early as the 1820s, Cubans, U.S. Americans, and Mexicans imagined Cuba as central to the future of their own nations and of the Americas in general. For Cubans like Tomás Estrada Palma, the unique links between the United States and Cuba were evident, and it was hard to imagine an independent Cuba that would not be guided by the United States. Similarly, Cuban Mexicans like Carlos Americo Lera, who served as secretary to the Mexican minister of foreign relations, advocated for a strong relationship between Mexico and Cuba, even proposing the annexation of Cuba to Mexico in 1896. From the early patriots who looked to Mexico to help liberate the colony from Spain in the 1820s, to those who saw their independence war and Mexico's war of restoration in the 1860s as twin struggles, Cubans turned to Mexico for support consistently throughout the nineteenth century. The evolution of U.S. interest in Cuba over the course of the nineteenth century is well documented, but less known is how Mexican interest in Cuba developed over time and was affected by the nation's relations with the United States and Spain. As the threat posed by Spain receded mid-century, and the dangers posed by imperialism dawned, Mexican statesmen's interest in Cuba increased. They looked for the most advantageous position on the Cuban Question, which would safeguard Mexico's national interests.

This chapter enriches the history of the international dimensions of Cuban independence by situating Cuban insurgent diplomacy in the larger context of the Gulf World. Cuban exiles in the United States worked assiduously between 1868 and 1898 to conquer U.S. public opinion and convince the U.S. government to take a position in favor of Cuban independence, and their story is familiar because their efforts were in many ways successful. However, as this chapter demonstrates, the full complexity of Cuban insurgent diplomacy from the 1820s forward was as robust, if not more so, in Latin America than it was in the United States.[9] It was not, however, competitive; Cuban insurgent diplomacy, which evolved dynamically over the last three decades of the nineteenth century, was collaborative. Efforts to advance diplomatic projects in the United States were related to those being pursued in Mexico and elsewhere.

The first section of the chapter examines how Cuban migrants purposefully internationalized the Cuban struggle throughout the nineteenth century by framing the Cuban Question as a matter of continental relevance. Long before Martí evoked the connection between Mexico and Cuba, Cuban revolutionaries scoured Latin America, forging solidarities in the name of a shared struggle for self-determination and against colonialism. They worked to invest the Cuban independence struggle with a significance that extended far beyond the imagined future nation.

The second section examines the PRC's diplomatic efforts to gain Mexican support, including Martí's 1894 visit to Mexico and his interview with Porfirio Díaz, as well as two diplomatic missions sent to Mexico in 1896 and 1897. Martí's last words to Manuel Mercado, in which he expressed vain hopes for Mexico's support, seem almost anguished; Martí knew by then that Cubans could expect little from Porfirio Díaz. Yet, despite dim prospects and discouraging signs, the PRC sent top officials to meet with the Mexican president on two more occasions during the War of 1895.[10] No other Latin American country received that kind of attention from the Cuban revolutionary leadership. Cubans' focus on Mexico can be explained by the role that Mexico had historically played in Cuban revolutionary struggles, the international reputation of the country under the Díaz dictatorship, and the strategic position of Mexico in relation to both Cuba and the United States. However, much to the dismay of the revolutionaries, Mexico proved stubbornly cold and elusive. Yet, even as the prospect of official government recognition in Mexico and elsewhere in Latin America waned, the Cuban Revolutionary Party continued to encourage transnational solidarities between Cubans and Latin Americans. Building on nearly a century of tradition, the PRC urged Latin Americans to view the Cuban cause as their own. In particular, the party leaders valued unofficial solidarities, because they exerted effective pressure on governments and their policies. The correspondence between Estrada Palma and his agents and envoys is replete with references to the importance of generating solidarities and influencing public opinion on behalf of the Cuban cause across Latin America.

The third section of the chapter explores the transnational solidarities forged between Mexicans and Cubans in the space of the Cuban and Mexican pro-Cuban independence clubs, and in newspapers and press houses, all of which were critical to the Cuban solidarity movement in Mexico. If the official attitude toward the Cuban cause in Mexico was cold, the popular sentiment was favorable toward solidarities with *Cuba Libre*. The fight for Cuban independence resonated with Mexican liberals who saw in the movement and its guiding documents a reflection of their own liberal and democratic ideals.

Internationalizing the Cuban Question

The argument that Cuban independence was indispensable to Latin America's security was not new in the 1890s. Mexican and Columbian statesmen, as well as early Cuban dissidents, arrived at a similar conclusion as early as the 1820s. With the threat of renewed conquest looming, and Spain intention to use Cuba as a base of operations, the mission to liberate Spain's remaining colonies in the Americas became a matter of survival for the young nations that surrounded it. In Mexico, the Spanish occupation of the military fort of San Juan de Ulúa off the coast of Veracruz, which they held until 1825, was an especially vivid reminder of the nation's vulnerability to a Spanish-controlled Cuba.

As they conspired to liberate Cuba in the early 1820s, Cuban and Spanish- American patriots wove the struggle for Cuban independence into the fabric of a discourse of continental solidarity. The idea of unity was rooted in an older sense of continentalism inherited from the colonial period, and its foundational moment was the rising up of Spanish Americans against Spanish colonial rule in the early nineteenth century. Simón Bolívar's Congress of Panama in 1826 was the first concerted effort to shape the idea of continental unity. The call for unity reflected Bolívar's conviction that Spanish Americans stood the best chance to protect their independence if they banded together. Bolivar himself raised an army for the invasion and liberation of Cuba, although he abandoned the project due to U.S. opposition and the pressing needs of his own Gran Colombia, which was threatening to fall apart.

Simón Bolivar was a direct inspiration for another plot that originated in Cuba but was supported by a diverse array of Latin Americans living on the island, at least one of whom was a colonel in Bolivar's army. Called the Soles y Rayos de Bolivar, the conspiracy was organized and concealed by freemasons in Cuba. When the plot was uncovered by Captain General Dionisio Vives in 1824, over six hundred conspirators were incarcerated or exiled.[11]

A year later, the Gran Legión del Aguila Negra (1824–1829) was established in Mexico by the president of the Republic, Guadalupe Victoria.[12] Victoria, known for inviting the famous Cuban exiled patriot and poet José María Heredia to live in Mexico, worked closely with Cuban patriots to develop a plan for the liberation of the island. The Gran Legión set in motion an intricate plan that grew and spread between 1824 and 1829. Like the Soles y Rayos de Bolivar, it involved Cuban and Latin American collaborators conspiring throughout the Gulf in U.S., Mexican, and Cuban port cities. The organization was discovered in 1829 and disbanded.

A third plot coordinated in Mexico in the early decades of the nineteenth century involved the York Rite masons who concocted a plan to recruit black soldiers in Haiti and along with them raise a slave insurrection in Cuba that would lead to independence. This plot was met with the vigorous opposition of conservative Mexican statesman Lucas Alamán, who crushed the initiative. Called to defend his position, Alamán argued that the existence of another Haiti in the Caribbean was not only undesirable in and of itself, he worried that such an insurrection would not be tolerated by the Spanish, the British, or especially the United States.[13] This last nation, he insisted, would use the insurrection as an excuse to occupy Cuba. Although these early conspiracies failed, the fate of the Spanish Antilles would concern most Latin Americans who articulated projects for continental unity throughout the century.

In the 1820s, the idea of continental unity in Latin America was defined by the drive to protect newly independent states from foreign, especially Spanish, aggression.[14] But as the United States gained power over the century, it became the principle threat to Latin American sovereignty. As Louis Pérez has argued, Cuba in particular had become an obsession for U.S. American statesmen. Since Cuba was an island within sight but out of reach, control of Cuba was seen as essential to the United States' security and well-being.[15] U.S. statesmen were concerned about the possibility that sovereignty over Cuba might change hands, and they worked energetically to avoid a British takeover of Cuba in particular. The United States favored the perpetuation of Spanish rule, which it did not perceive as a threat. Aware of the keen interest of the United States, Mexican statesmen considered collaborating with the British to aid in the liberation of Cuba, and they even considered the possible annexation of Cuba to Mexico as early as 1823. While the United States imagined Cuba as a natural extension of the Florida peninsula, Mexicans argued that Cuba had once formed part of the Spanish viceroyalty of New Spain and therefore might naturally be reunited with the landmass that was now Mexico. At least, this was the logic for possession that undergirded Carlos Americo Lera's annexation project. Indeed, both Mexico and the United States saw the benefit of a close relationship with Cuba.[16]

Spain renewed its efforts to reestablish control over her former colonies in the middle of the nineteenth century. During the 1860s, Spain reincorporated the Dominican Republic, backed the French intervention in Mexico, occupied the Chincha islands off of Peru, and bombed the Chilean port of Valparaiso. In 1865, in response to Spain's aggression, the Chilean government, with the Peruvian government's support, sent a representative to the United States to organize a plot to liberate Spain's Caribbean colonies. Benjamín Vicuña Mackenna recognized as a confidential agent of the Chilean government, slipped by the Spanish blockade at Valparaiso in the hold of a packetboat called *Chile*. Arriving at the Chincha islands in Peru, Vicuña met with Peruvian general Mariano Ignacio Prado. The two men sealed an alliance in defense of the Americas, which included the liberation of Cuba. Vicuña then went on to the United States, where he established himself in New York City. His mission was to solicit U.S. support for the liberation of Cuba. In New York he met and collaborated with numerous exiled Cubans, including Pedro Santacilia, the future son-in-law of the Mexican president Benito Juárez. Despite his vigorous efforts, however, Vicuña failed in his mission and the Chilean-Peruvian effort to decolonize Cuba floundered.[17]

In Latin America at the middle of the nineteenth century, aiding in the liberation of Cuba and sympathizing with the insurgents who rose up in arms against Spain in the Ten Years' War came to be seen as a sacred duty. Within one year of the outbreak of the Ten Years' War, motions for the recognition of Cuban belligerency rights were passed by representative bodies in Bolivia, Brazil, Chile, Colombia, Mexico, Peru, and Venezuela. Indeed, the climate of support for Cuban independence among political elites in Latin America during the 1860s and 1870s was remarkably strong.[18] General Mariano Ignacio Prado, the same man who had met with Benjamín Vicuña Mackenna years earlier in the Chincha islands, who heroically defended Peru from Spain in the Battle of Callao, and who was also elected president, delivered a speech in 1874 pledging his support for the Cuban insurgents: "The oppression of Cuba is the dagger of tyrannous monarchy lodged the heart of republican America. The indolence of her brothers is a crime that will be condemned by history . . . Peru, a country of free men, cannot, without tarnishing her glories . . . be indifferent to a people who fight to win their rights."[19] Prado articulated the ideological assumptions that underlay widespread support for Cuban independence in Latin America at the time. Especially noteworthy is his definition of the Americas as a constellation of republics with certain rights and responsibilities, including the right to be free from colonial and monarchical rule and the responsibility to support anti-colonial movements in the Americas. Similar sentiments about the unique nature of Latin America's liberal traditions were articulated by other prominent Latin American statesmen who had shown sympathy for Cuban independence, including the president of Mexico, Benito Juárez, and the president of Ecuador, Eloy Alfaro.[20]

The expressions of Latin American solidarity with *Cuba Libre* in the 1860s and 1870s as well as in the 1880s and 1890s cannot be understood without considering the activities of Cuban migrants throughout the region.[21] Those Cubans played a central role in interpreting and fomenting that solidarity. Although there were isolated groups of Cubans in Latin America before the 1860s, migrant communities grew significantly during the Ten Years' War. Many of these early exiles and migrants, which included middle-class intellectuals and professionals as well as less affluent members of the insurgent army, enjoyed access to Latin American elite political circles. Pedro Santacilia, the Cuban private secretary and son-in-law of Benito Juárez, influenced Juárez's decision to support the insurgents in 1869 by allowing boats flying the Cuban flag to enter Mexican ports. Cubans José Joaquín Palma and Rafael María Merchán became the private secretaries of Marco Aurelio Soto, president of Honduras, and Rafael Nuñez Moledo, president of Colombia, and used their connections to aid the insurgent movement. Palma was instrumental in convincing Soto to provide aid to Máximo Gómez and Antonio Maceo during their exile in Central America after the Ten Years' War.

In the 1880s and 1890s, Cubans abroad continued to lobby Latin American political elites for their support. Just as they had from the 1820s forward, Cubans continued to see Cuban independence as an issue of continental relevance. Convinced that no Latin American or Caribbean should be indifferent to their cause, they constantly created propaganda for the movement. As a new war dawned in 1895, Cuban revolutionaries energetically and optimistically sought support in Latin America. With that support not forthcoming, Cubans worked even harder to move Latin American statesmen to embrace multilateral collaboration on behalf of *Cuba Libre*. In 1895, with public opinion in Latin America hostile and uninformed, Enrique José Varona published and widely circulated an essay addressed to the Spanish American republics designed to reveal the truth about Spain's exploitation of Cuba.[22] The Cuban government in arms circulated a manifesto to "the republics of Latin America" in 1896, which laid bare Cubans' expectation of solidarity based on historic precedent:

> The government of the republic of Cuba believes it has a duty to address the other American states that share the same origin in order to explain the grave motivations that have led it to take up arms in order to constitute itself, and to express to them its sincere

hope that it will find in them a great moral force that will help it to put an end to the bloody conflict it is involved in. From the wisdom of the free nations of Latin America, it expects the recognition that, above and beyond national frontiers, there exist linkages older and more permanent than political structures constituted by a community of origin, history, language, the similarity of customs and beliefs.

It is in the supreme interest of America, Luso-hispanic America, that Cuba cease to be a bloody battlefield where, periodically, American freedom and European despotism are at odds . . . Cuba bled and ruined can be an easy victim for races that, if not antagonistic, are different. It is clear that it is in the interest of the nations of Latin America to intervene, with their council and influence . . . so that Spain recognize the independence of Cuba . . . [and] affirm one more time their adhesion to the principals to which they owe their existence . . . and their right to be heard in an international matter. . . . The independence of Cuba, cemented with the blood and the efforts of the Cubans [should] be crowned by the intervention of all the states of our own race.[23]

The manifesto contains several critical elements that demonstrate the expectations and concerns of the provisional government. First, the Cubans expected the support of Latin America because they believed that Cuba and Latin America shared a tradition of American solidarity that was fundamentally supranational and rooted not only in anti-colonial struggle, but also in shared "principles." In addition to asking Latin American republics to put aside national differences and allow themselves to be guided by American solidarity—something older and more enduring than nations and frontiers— the Cubans asked their fellow republics to recognize that the liberation of Cuba carried a significance far beyond the island itself. Echoing Martí and countless Cubans before him, the members of the provisional government argued that in supporting and defending Cuba, Latin America could forestall the occupation of the island by the Anglo race, a race that was "different" and, ultimately "antagonistic" to the Latin race. Finally, the manifesto makes clear that the republics of Latin America had a unique opportunity to demonstrate their own strength by demanding that Spain grant Cuba independence, thereby challenging Spain in the realm of international affairs. The implication is that if the republics failed to make this effort, they would reveal their own weakness as states while knowingly compromising the future of a continent increasingly menaced by the United

States. In this manifesto there are echoes of the words of Mariano Ignacio Prado from when he spoke of the defense of "republican America" and of the crime of "indifference."

The manifesto also includes another intriguing element: the breadth of its call. It includes within its "community of origin" and its "own race," republics that are Luso-American (Brazil) and Latin (including Francophone America). Indeed, the government and its secretary of foreign relations and minister plenipotentiary in the United States had specifically identified Brazil and Haiti as countries in which to seek support. Thus, a broad diplomacy was supported by an inclusive list of countries that by race and origin were seen as connected to Cuba.

The inclusion of Haiti in Cuban insurgent diplomacy in the 1890s is particularly surprising, given how skillfully Spanish royalists in the nineteenth century had manipulated the fear that Cuba would become another Haiti, especially during the Ten Years' War. Still, the Cuban Revolutionary Party and Cuban Legation established official representatives in Haiti. Ulpiano Dellundé, a medical doctor of Afro-Cuban descent who owned a pharmacy in Cap Haitien and who had been a close friend and collaborator of José Martí, became an agent of the Cuban Legation after 1895. Dellundé worked hard to organize Cuban migrants in Haiti and build profitable solidarities among Haitians for the Cuban cause. His efforts to secure support from the Haitian president reveal Cuban revolutionaries' complex views about Haiti's place and role in the Americas. Dellundé began his letter to President Florvil Hyppolite by indicating that the same institution of slavery had oppressed Cubans and Haitians alike. He went on to celebrate Haiti as a beacon of freedom: "great was that day on which, for humanity, our ancestors, in an act of desperation, broke their chains and with their irons formed knives and machetes to shake off the yoke that converted them into beasts of burden . . . and thus the republic of Haiti was born!" By referring to "our ancestors," he claims African slaves in Haiti as the forefathers of Cuba's emancipatory struggle, a claim that would have troubled many white Cuban elites. Dellundé continued by evoking Haiti's long-standing commitment to freedom in the Americas. As Ada Ferrer has noted, Haiti was active in an Atlantic struggle against slavery and colonialism. It established free soil policies and offered critical aid to Latin American independence fighter Simón Bolivar in exchange for a commitment on his part to abolish slavery in lands wrested from Spain, both of which made the nation a beacon of freedom in a world of slavery.[24] On this precedent alone, Dellundé argued, Haiti should embrace and support Cuba as the insurgents struggled to break free from Spanish colonialism and the racism that he attributed to the Spanish colonial legacy.

Dellundé's own private correspondence with Estrada Palma presents a slightly different pircture. In fact, he would admit to Estrada Palma in private correspondence that he was deeply disappointed with Haitians, whom he criticized for their obsession with "racial prejudice." Dellundé had faith that Cuba would be grander than Haiti, that it would be a republic where black and white men could live side by side as equals and where "only two kinds of men are recognized: those who are honorable and those who are not." He also explained his views on race: "I do not believe there are superior races—as many insist—but superior men—for example, Confusius, Juárez, Touissant Louverture."

Dellundé's celebration of Toussaint Louverture, the hero of the Haitian Revolution, in his letter to Estrada Palma confirms that the significance he gave the event in his letter to the president of Haiti was earnest. His disappointment in post-revolutionary Haiti does not render his positive statements about the revolution false. Nor does it invalidate the fact that the Cuban Revolutionary Party appealed for support to the president of Haiti and in so doing accorded that nation a prominent place at a time when Haiti was routinely denied recognition either for the accomplishments of its revolution or its efforts to support anti-colonial and anti-slavery movements in the Americas.

Cubans' efforts to cull support in Haiti are perhaps even more striking if we consider the force of the Spanish anti-independence propaganda, which rested nearly exclusively on the conviction that *Cuba Libre* would become a second Haiti. Despite this powerful and pervasive anti-Haitian discourse, or perhaps because of it, Cubans pursued the support of Haitian citizens and the Haitian state for their movement, just as they did elsewhere in the Americas. The inclusion of Haiti in a broader conception of the Americas was apparent among Mexican supporters of the Cuban independence movement as well. In 1896, Mexican student journalists celebrated the Haitian Republic's strong stance against the machinations of the Spanish minister in Haiti and his active attempts to expel Cubans from Haiti.[25] Cubans cast a wide net as they developed their insurgent diplomacy in the late nineteenth century. Cuba's late independence struggle was seen as being of a piece with the U.S. Revolution, the Haitian Revolution, Latin American Independence Wars, and Mexico's War with the French—each of them critical moments in the continental struggle for independence, republicanism, democracy and, in some cases, emancipation. An expansive rhetoric was accompanied by a multifocal diplomacy.

Cuban revolutionaries in the PRC and affiliated to the Cuban Legation envisioned Cuban insurgent diplomacy as dynamically evolving on many fronts at once. In fact, the intensification of Cuban insurgent diplomacy in the United States after 1896 is directly related to the failure of Cuban efforts in Latin America. Latin America and the United States traded places in the 1890s, and, as one early twentieth-century Cuban diplomat argued, we must see the U.S. Congress's recognition of Cuban belligerency rights in 1896 as an echo of the proclamations made by numerous Latin American republics in the late 1860s and early 1870s.[26] In a letter to Arístides Agüero y Betancourt, a PRC special envoy in South America, Estrada Palma made plain his commitment to diplomacy in both the United States and Latin America, rejecting the idea that one should be privileged above the other: "I do not doubt that the recognition of belligerency rights by the United States would be fortuitous; however, I do not believe that the initiative [in Latin America] should be subordinated to this circumstance." A little later he added, "It would be pleasing and opportune to hear the voices of the states of South America resonate now that we have such an advantageous [military] position."[27] Indeed, in March 1896, spirits were running high as news spread of the insurgent invasion of western Cuba.[28] Estrada Palma hoped that the military successes of Máximo Gómez and Antonio Maceo would dispel concerns that Cubans were incapable of defeating the Spanish. A show of Latin American solidarity could be potentially important, especially if diplomatic efforts in the United States stalled. When Estrada Palma wrote the letter to Agüero in March, the U.S. Senate and House of Representatives had already passed a resolution supporting Cuban belligerency rights, but President Grover Cleveland did not acknowledge the measure. "Cleveland's sentiments are unknown," Estrada Palma wrote despairingly in March of 1896.[29] Indeed, Cleveland was deeply committed to maintaining the United States' formal neutrality in relation to the Cuban conflict, even in the face of mounting pressure from Congress, and he remained so committed throughout his presidency.

Cuban insurgent diplomacy in Latin America in the 1890s depended on Cuban migrants just as it had in the 1860s and 1870s. The primary mission entrusted to these representatives was the recognition of Cuban insurgents as belligerents. They argued that, due to the size and organization of the insurgent army and the existence of a provisional government, the revolutionaries were qualified to be considered belligerents rather than rebels and therefore were entitled to the rights and protections that the status would afford them. Requesting belligerency rights instead of formal recognition of the insurgent government had two benefits. First, Latin American countries had already granted the insurgents the status of belligerents in the 1860s and 1870s, and Cubans hoped they might do so again in the 1890s. Second, while it signaled support for the Cuban cause, the recognition of these rights did not technically constitute a violation of these nations' neutrality agreements with Spain. While there were some concrete benefits that might come from the conferral of belligerency rights, such as the ability of Cuban ships to dock and provision themselves at Caribbean and circum-Caribbean ports, the PRC leadership was most interested in the demonstration of moral solidarity that the act of granting them would signify. As is evident in the manifesto to the republics of Latin America, Cubans believed that if they could marshal the widespread moral solidarity of Latin American states (something that did not seem inconceivable in 1895), it might be possible to pressure Spain to negotiate an end to the war. Mexico had been the first country in the Americas to pass a congressional resolution recognizing Cuban insurgents as belligerents in 1869, and it was one of the most powerful and modern countries in Latin America, so it was fitting that Mexico became the most important site of Cuban insurgent diplomacy in Latin America.

Cuban Insurgent Diplomacy and the Mexican State

In 1894, as he was gathering funds and support for the war in preparation, José Martí took a trip to Mexico. The purpose was to meet the president of Mexico, Porfirio Díaz, face-to-face and ask him to support the Cuban independence movement, of which Martí was now the leader. A few years before this visit, Martí had made the acquaintance of the anti-Díaz revolutionary, Catarino Garza, while the two men were in Florida. Garza was eager to join Martí's movement, but the Cuban leader dithered.[30] Elliott Young surmises that despite Martí's deep skepticism about the Mexican president, he still saw the value of currying favor with the dictator. Martí was significantly more successful than his compatriot Antonio Maceo, who had also tried to meet with Díaz only a few years earlier and was rejected. Unlike Maceo, Martí was a white intellectual who had lived in Mexico and had important contacts among Mexico's elite and political class. Mexican statesmen like Justo Sierra who held important positions in the Díaz administration were incredibly fond of Martí. And, even though he had not returned to Mexico since 1875, Martí's articles, including his famous essay *Nuestra America* (1891), had been published in Mexican newspapers.

In advance of his 1894 trip, Martí published an article in the Cuban newspaper, *Patria*, which he intended to circulate among Mexico's political elite to prepare the way for his arrival. In the article, written in commemoration of Benito Juárez, Martí figured Mexico as the savior of Latin America, as he had done in earlier writing. Celebrating the triumphalist spirit of Mexico's Reform, and signaling how the great achievements of the past had the power to shape the future of Mexico and Latin America, he wrote: "Mexico grows stronger and comes together while the neighbor to the north decomposes. And it is because a mestizo land announces to the avaricious world that the Indian who saved liberty and perhaps saved America, has now become a nation; because a just principle, emanating from the depths of a cave, can achieve more than an army. Mexico proves to the world with each year its determination to be free. And it will remain free because it has dominated arrogant men. Juarez dominated them without anger."[31] In an earlier reflection written two decades before, Martí had imagined Mexico as still coming together and somewhat vulnerable as compared to the United States. This articulation in 1894 portrayed Mexico as a strong modern nation, but the United States as a country that was weakening. After fourteen years in the United States, Martí had developed a strong critique of the country and its culture.

The key to Mexico's strength was its faith in what he called "just" principles, something the "avaricious world" (i.e., the United States) did not understand. Moreover, Mexico, which was clearly superior in Martí's mind, had been made great by an "Indian," Benito Júarez. Like Dellundé, the Cuban agent in Haiti, Martí saw Juárez as an exemplary "Indian." The idea that "the Indian . . . had now become a 'nation' " that was announcing itself to the world demonstrated pride in what was autochthonous to Mexico, its Indian heritage. Of course, in the Mexico of the mid-1890s, reverence for principles had been replaced with respect for the science of politics, and elites customarily lamented the existence of Indians who did little in their minds but hold the nation back. A new class of politicians in Mexico, the *científicos*, had come to dominate the Porfirian regime with their positivist doctrines and their faith in the science of race. These new liberals placed economic progress ahead of political ideals. Still, Martí, like the provisional government in the manifesto of 1896, emphasized political ideals and solidarity, hoping that celebrating Júarez as a liberator might remind Díaz that Cuba's fight for independence mirrored Mexico's fight against the French. The "just" principles of independence and self-determination, for which Juárez and Díaz had both fought, were the very same principles that motivated the Cuban struggle.

Although there is no transcript of Martí's visit with Porfirio Díaz in 1894, his correspondence about the meeting suggests that he worked to obtain the president's promise that Mexico would intervene to protect Cuba from the possibility of U.S. occupation or annexation. He also reported having received a financial contribution from the president in the order of $20,000.[32] Shortly after his return from Mexico, Martí threw himself into the final preparations for the insurgency. Martí's correspondence with Cuban migrants in Mexico—like Nicolás Domínguez Cowan and Rodolfo Menéndez Peña—shows that he urged them to operate with caution. Martí was aware that the Díaz government might have offered him financial support and perhaps the vague promise to protect Cuba, but he was also aware of what it would mean for Mexico to take an official stand in favor of Cuban independence given its allegiance to Spain and its many ties to the United States. Thus, Martí urged his compatriots in Mexico to operate carefully and to take care not to create a situation that might be perceived as aggressive by the Mexican government. For example, in 1893, Martí wrote to Nicolás Domínguez Cowan urging him to be patient, for he had a plan: "My inattention to our compatriots in Mexico has been intentional and for a greater cause, which you will approve of. . . . Now I just need you to be good and counter to the degree possible the Spanish effrontery that is increasingly prevalent in the [Mexican] press."[33] Carlos Bojórquez Urzaiz speculates that the plan to which Martí alluded here and which he would share with Domínguez Cowan at a later date was the request for formal recognition from the Mexican government, which may have been a subject of his private interview with the president.[34] It is possible that Martí in 1893 believed official recognition from Mexico could happen. Judging by his correspondence, the 1894 visit with Porfirio Díaz left him in a positive frame of mind. Even days before his death, Martí clung to the hope that Mexico would assume its continental duty, a key part of which was to promote and protect Cuban independence.

When Tomás Estrada Palma began to appoint official representatives of the Cuban Legation in key countries in Latin America in September of 1895, Mexico was an obvious first choice. The Mexican state had not only been friendly historically to the movement, but Díaz had given Martí considerable financial support. Mexico was also one of the most politically stable, prosperous, and influential countries in the region. Like his predecessor, Tomás Estrada Palma was convinced that gaining the support of Mexico was the key to wooing rest of Latin America, and thus he appointed Nicolás Domínguez Cowan as his first agent in Latin America.

Domínguez Cowan was an astute choice given his participation in the first Cuban independence struggle, his position as an established and respected member of the Cuban community in Mexico City, and his connections to some of the city's most important elite political circles. It is this last point that likely explains why José Miguel Macías was not offered the position, although he was the leader of the Veracruz-based Cuban community.

In early September 1895 Domínguez Cowan sent Estrada Palma a detailed report that explained the Mexican government's attitude regarding the independence struggle. Estrada Palma had solicited this information in a letter to Domínguez Cowan in the hope of assessing whether Mexico would be amenable to recognizing Cuban belligerency rights. Domínguez Cowan responded by stating that many Mexican citizens supported the cause, but that they were disheartened by the fact that the Díaz government refused to recognize the Cuban insurgency officially, opting instead to honor a treaty with Spain that prohibited Mexico from intervening in Cuban affairs. Furthermore, the Spanish community, which Domínguez Cowan described as "influential, numerous and wealthy," posed a threat to Cubans in Mexico. "Mexico has shaken off the yoke of the oppressive metropolis," he continued, "but the pressure of the Spanish element here is still palpable."[35] Given these difficult circumstances, Domínguez Cowan informed Estrada Palma that he had a plan to obtain official recognition for the Cuban cause by subtly pressuring Mexicans in the capital to petition the congress on behalf of Cuba. He begged Estrada Palma to consider the fact that he had been living in Mexico for some time and knew how to navigate the political situation. Domínguez Cowan was convinced that a Cuban petition for recognition would surely fail, but that if Cubans in Mexico could persuade Mexican citizens to launch a petition, it might succeed. Echoing José Martí's belief in Mexico's ability to lead the hemisphere, Domínguez Cowan insisted that "the moral effect" of his plan to have Mexicans pressure the Mexican congress to authorize the recognition of Cuban belligerency rights "would resonate all over the Americas."[36]

Sometime later, Domínguez Cowan wrote again to Estrada Palma, informing him that he had met with several prominent Mexicans and had gone to great lengths to convince them to pressure the Mexican congress to authorize the president to recognize Cuban belligerency rights. Disheartened, Domínguez Cowan observed that "sympathies for Cuba abound, but when it comes to petitioning congress, some stall and others lose their nerve."[37] It would not be until May of 1896 that Domínguez Cowan would have positive news regarding this matter. On 29 May he described a public event hosted by Cubans commemorating Martí's death. "I can promise you that we have gained important ground among Mexicans who until now have been indifferent," he wrote. "The poet and federal deputy Juan A. Mateos spoke in favor of Cuba. . . . He was the first Mexican of political importance who has dared to come forth."[38] Domínguez Cowan believed that others would follow suit, and he expressed hopes that Mateos's actions heralded a change of attitude in official circles. A significant number of Mexican journalists and students came out in favor of Cuban independence, but there were few vocal supporters among the political elite. Estrada Palma responded enthusiastically to Domínguez Cowan's report. Having a federal deputy like Mateos, a man who was well respected in Mexico's political circles and who was a veteran of Mexico's war against the French, was a victory indeed.

Nicolás Domínguez Cowan did not limit his activities to Mexico's City's elite political circles. By 1897, he had established twenty-two subagencies staffed by subagents throughout the republic. The reach of the party through these organizations was impressive and encompassed numerous points up and down the Gulf Coast and also places in the interior such as Guadalajara, Penjamo, Irapuato, Oaxaca, Queretaro, and Pachuca.[39]

While Domínguez Cowan's initial reports were filled with enthusiasm and hope for the fate of the Cuban cause in Mexico, neither he nor *Cuba Libre*'s Mexican sympathizers were able to influence the Mexican congress to officially recognize the Cuban insurgents' belligerency rights. This was an upset that Estrada Palma initially refused to accept. Following Martí's example, Estrada Palma sent the PRC secretary Gonzalo de Quesada to Mexico in May of 1896 with explicit orders to deliver a message directly to the president. In the message, Estrada Palma addressed Porfirio Díaz as "the chief of the most powerful Latin American nation in the new world" and asked him directly to use his "influence with the other governments of free America, so that all or some of them take collective action to convince Spain to grant Cuba her independence." Like Domínguez Cowan, Estrada Palma also recognized the power that Mexico's endorsement of the insurgents could have. Perhaps aware that talk of "just principles" would fall on deaf ears, Estrada Palma appealed to an issue near and dear to Porfirio Díaz's heart: economic progress. A long war fought with no quarter had made the destruction of property by the insurgents a necessity. By intervening, Díaz might be able to forestall the "total ruin" of the island.[40] On this point, Estrada Palma's appeal to Díaz was structured similarly to his appeal to U.S. statesmen and congressmen, who he also hoped would advocate for U.S. intervention to save Cuba from financial disaster.[41] Even though Estrada

Palma did not directly reference Mexico's past commitment to Cuban independence under Juárez, the existence of that critical precedent was known to both men. Mexico had led Latin America in recognizing the belligerency rights of Cuban insurgents in the 1860s; perhaps Díaz would lead Latin American republics in a movement to pressure Spain to desist and to grant Cuban independence.

Gonzalo de Quesada was denied an audience with Díaz in 1896, but the party refused to accept the message, sending both the secretary and treasurer to Mexico in 1897 with the intention of convincing Díaz to change his policies once again. According to Matías Romero, Mexico's ambassador to the United States, Quesada had made the intentions of his 1897 visit to Mexico explicit. "Gonzalo de Quesada . . . came to see me and told me that he is convinced through his conversations with high functionaries of the government of the United States that if the war in Cuba continues, the result will be the annexation of the island to the United States, a solution that the Cubans would like to avoid at all costs."[42] The representatives were denied access to the president a second time and were forced to limit their activities to touring different Cuban communities and taking up collections for the cause.[43]

Romero reported to his superiors again in March of 1898, after the explosion of the *USS Maine* when the United States was on a war path. Gonzalo de Quesada had approached him again, insisting that the United States would intervene militarily in Cuba and that that intervention would "result in the loss for Spain of Cuba and Puerto Rico and their annexation to the United States." Quesada then insisted that Mexico recommend that Spain recognize the independence of the colonies in the interest of avoiding such a fate.[44] The Mexican state had made clear its willingness to cooperate with the United States in such a mediation, and it had also offered its good offices directly to Spain earlier in the conflict, in the hope that it might play a role in the resolution of the war in Cuba. In neither case were Mexico's overtures accepted.[45] But Quesada—like Estrada Palma—was asking for something else. Both men encouraged Díaz to create a multilateral alliance in Latin America capable of pressuring Spain. In any case, in response to Romero's report in 1898 recalling Quesada's visit and request, Ignacio Mariscal, Mexico's secretary of foreign relations, stated that "to recommend to Spain the recognition of the independence of Cuba would be counterproductive, for such a proposition would be considered offensive and would not cause any other result other than a major irritation to the government and the people of Spain."[46]

Struggling to understand Díaz's position, Tomás Estrada Palma wrote to Nicolás Domínguez Cowan, saying "the conduct of the Hispano-American republics is strange and we are ashamed to see them always prepared to sacrifice our rights, which are also their rights at the behest of the Spanish. It affects us not because we lack in material support, but because it is sad to see nations commit acts against liberty when they should worship it, and in favor of the same tyranny that mistreated them and which led to the conquest of the same independence that in Cuba they see as a nefarious crime."[47] Here Estrada Palma's evocation of rights and responsibilities recalls Martí's references to just principles in his article honoring Juárez in 1894, and the Cuban provisional government's message dedicated to the Latin American republics in 1896. Curiously, all three are also reminiscent of Mariano Ignacio Prado's calls for solidarity with Cuba in 1874. Ignacio also emphasized the role of principles in governance.

In the 1890s, Cubans held firmly, even stubbornly, to a tradition of Latin American solidarity, that was quickly disappearing from elite political circles across the region. Political elites were far more interested in order, progress, and technological modernity than they were in rights, constitutions, popular sovereignty, and inter-American solidarity.

The Conquest of "Public Spirit": Cubans and the Crisis of Diplomacy in Latin America and Mexico

Latin American solidarity founded on anti-colonialism and "just principles" may no longer have held sway among political elites, but outside of official politics support for *Cuba Libre* was still strong across Latin America during the 1890s. Cubans' commitment to building solidarity with grass-roots organizations even as they courted political elites is reflected in a letter José Martí sent to a liaison in the Dominican Republic in 1895: "Call at every door and then call again," he wrote. "Every city in America should be treasure chest of liberty for Cuba . . . demand of every Cuban the quota expected of a son; and, when it is necessary, that of a brother of every son of America."[48]

After Martí's death and with the transition in the PRC to Estrada Palma's leadership, the latter continued to emphasize solidarity-building efforts. There was both a historical and an institutional framework for these efforts. The PRC drew on existing traditions of Latin American solidarity with Cuban independence while formalizing the practice of building solidarity and converting it into a pillar of the party. As revolutionary émigrés, guided by the PRC, assumed the responsibility of representing the nation in exile, they forged a close relationship between citizenship and solidarity.

Even though it did not offer guidelines about the inclusion of foreigners in the struggle, the Cuban Revolutionary Party's statutes encouraged relations with "friendly nations" and placed significant emphasis on the power of public opinion, especially across the Americas. While he did not share Martí's deep suspicion and concern about the United States, Estrada Palma's hope was that if Cubans could win U.S. public opinion, the insurgents could convince U.S. statesmen to recognize Cubans as belligerents. As belligerents, Cubans would be seen as legitimate revolutionaries rather than mere rebels, which would lend a measure of legitimacy to the struggle in the eyes of the international community. When initial appeals to statesmen failed, Estrada Palma instructed his agents to galvanize not just political elites but also students, journalists, artisans, and workers, hopeful that winning the hearts and minds of the people would cause a shift in public opinion significant enough to influence diplomatic policy. Writing to one of his agents, Aristides Agüero y Betancourt, Estrada Palma urged him to intensify his efforts to influence public opinion in South America, arguing that "the truth will shine through, and the attitude of the popular masses, who have been moved and influenced through healthy agitation, will have an effect on those in power."[49] He wrote a similar message to his contact in Peru, insisting that the indifference of Latin American governments made it all the more important to "work near them and in the sphere that surrounds them in order to conquer the forces that are contrary to us. This way, the Latin American governments, inspired by public sentiment, will unite and defend the Cuban cause."[50] A week later, Estrada Palma sent a similar note to Joaquín Alsina, the PRC representative in Costa Rica. "We are interested in forming opinions and influencing public spirit so that in a given moment our influence will be felt in official spheres."[51] Between 1895 and 1898, reports detailing the success of grassroots solidarity-building efforts poured into the PRC offices in New York City from North America, South America, Central America, and the Caribbean.[52]

Cuban-Mexican Solidarities

When José Martí wrote to Domínguez Cowan in 1893, he encouraged the veteran migrant to push back hard against the Spanish immigrants who endeavored to control public opinion in Mexico. In the years before the formal Cuban uprising, Martí hoped to generate as much positive press as he could for the revolutionary movement. Similarly, when writing to his agents throughout Latin America between 1895 and 1898, Estrada Palma urged them to conquer public opinion. The Spanish had mounted an aggressive campaign to discredit the Cuban independence movement throughout Latin America. In Mexico, as in other parts of Latin America, the space of the political club and the press became crucial vehicles for the building of transnational solidarities around *Cuba Libre*. In addition to lobbying Mexican congressmen and political elites, Cubans focused on building grassroots solidarities and on the press, propaganda, and public opinion. They worked as staff writers for sympathetic Mexican newspapers, and they created and directed their own newspapers. Mexicans belonged to Cuban clubs, but they also attended and supported Cuban public events and conferences and were often featured speakers at both. In fact, Cuban migrant communities were so open to Mexicans and the Cuban question was framed so broadly that Mexicans also founded their own clubs dedicated to the Cuban cause, which sometimes had no Cuban members at all. Mexican club leaders dutifully reported to the PRC and sent their financial and other contributions to the Revolutionary Party headquarters in New York City like their Cuban counterparts.

The press was a key site of Cuban-Mexican collaboration in the 1890s. Newspapers served to disseminate news and opinions, but newspapers and press houses also served as physical spaces of collaboration for Cubans and Mexicans in solidarity. This was especially true of the pro-Cuban independence newspaper *El Continente Americano*. *El Continente Americano* commenced publication in Mexico City in 1895, the same year as the outbreak of the Cuba's final bid for independence. In the paper's very first issue, the staff announced that it would dedicate a third of the paper's profits to the cause, remitting those funds directly to the Cuban Revolutionary Party in New York City. Much like a political club, then, the journalists understood the collection of funds to support the war effort in Cuba as being central to the paper's mission. The student journalists also envisioned other ways that the newspaper and press offices could serve the Cuban cause. Indeed, Cubans used *El Continente Americano* and its offices for mundane purposes like advertising events, meetings, and conferences, publicizing the formation of new clubs, and changes in club leadership. In this way, *El Continente Americano* effectively supplemented the Cuban Revolutionary Party's main publication, *Patria*. As we saw in chapter 3, the Cuban newspaper *Patria* published information about the founding of new clubs and sums of money party members collected for the cause. By publishing similar information, *El Continente Americano* helped Cubans stay abreast of how

Cuban organizing and the solidarity movement were developing in Mexico. But with correspondents in New York City and Santiago, Chile, *El Contintente Americano* also kept tabs on pro-Cuban independence sympathies across the continent.

Notices in the pages of the press relating to Cuban club business were accompanied by invitations and announcements about Cuban public celebrations, meetings, and conferences. Some of these notices came from within Mexico City and some from Puebla and Veracruz. On 5 March 1897, the members of Hijas de Baire of Mexico City asked the director of the paper, Remigio Mateos, to announce the bazaar that they were organizing for the cause. The conferences organized by Morelos y Maceo and México y Cuba were regularly advertised in the paper and included the day, time, address, and speaker, as well as any changes in times or locations. For example, *El Continente Americano* reported that the Morelos y Maceo conference that was scheduled for 10 January had been postponed, and was being held instead on 14 January at 11 A.M. That the newspaper published information as specific as schedule changes indicates that Cuban and Mexican members of clubs were interacting with the paper regularly and not only to keep abreast of political debates but also as a means of communication. On Sunday, 11 July 1897, the club Hijas de Baire posted a notice in the paper informing their associates that a meeting was to be held the next day at 4 P.M. Such an announcement presumes that the intended community of readers were subscribing to the newspaper, or otherwise receiving it on a regular basis.

Cubans also relied on the paper and the press offices for other purposes, like distributing pamphlets, circulating petitions, and staging demonstrations. For example, *El Continente Americano* sold the books of many Cuban authors. On 6 May 1897, a notice appeared in the paper announcing that a text by the Cuban José María García Montes dedicated to the Cuban Question was being sold for 25 cs. *El Continente Americano* also became a common place for Cubans to handle official business. On 11 November 1897, México y Cuba called an urgent meeting to discuss the recent reforms that Spain had offered as a last-ditch effort to bring an end to the independence war. Cubans in the United States had signed multiple petitions rejecting the reforms, and Cubans in Mexico City were eager to do the same. At the meeting members decided that a protest against the reforms would be drafted and signed. The document was subsequently made available at the offices of the student newspaper between 11 November and 18 November from 4 to 7 P.M. so that Cubans could sign it.

During Mexican Independence Day celebrations, the press offices themselves became a site for the celebration of conjoined struggles. In 1897 the students hoisted the Cuban flag from the building and publicly sang the Cuban Revolutionary anthem, the *Himno de Bayamo*. Local residents and an enthusiastic group of citizens from Puebla filled the street in front of the press house and cheered.[53] Once the official festivities were over, a group of nearly two thousand Mexicans and Cubans marched to *El Continente Americano*'s office, which had become the symbolic center of the Cuban solidarity movement. There, in front of the press house, "before the flag of our sister republic and to the great satisfaction of the crowd, speeches were pronounced. The names of Hidalgo, Céspedes, Martí, Morelos, Gómez and Maceo inspired demonstrations of true patriotic fervor."[54]

If in its day-to-day engagements with Mexico City's Cuban migrant community *El Continente Americano* resembled a political club, it may have been, in part, because many of its staff members belonged to Cuban political clubs as well. Journalists of *El Continente Americano* and many at the offices of the two other Mexico City–based newspapers that were strong supporters of the Cuban cause, *Diario del Hogar* and *El Hijo del Ahuizote*, belonged to Cuban clubs in Mexico City and Veracruz as both active and honorary members.

As we have seen, PRC agents were instructed to support Cuban efforts to influence "public opinion" in their host countries, but they also welcomed the extensive participation of foreign supporters in the Cuban movement, inviting Mexicans to become members of Cuban clubs and found their own independent solidarity associations. Thus, Mexicans participated alongside their Cuban counterparts in educational conferences, while also giving motivational speeches and holding public events, raising money for the cause, collecting arms, and assembling mixed groups of volunteer soldiers. The exact number of Mexican participants in Cuban clubs is unknown, but letters written by club secretaries and sent to the PRC headquarters suggest that Mexican membership was substantial and widespread. The members of Dolores y Yara wrote to Estrada Palma, stating that their name was chosen to represent the "Mexicans and Cubans united here and the principles of liberty proclaimed in each place."[55] The president of Morelos y Maceo of Mexico City reported that the club had been founded with fifty male members who were Mexican and Cuban.[56] Remigio Mateos and José P. Rivera, directors of two Mexico City–based newspapers, were members of the Cuban club Cuauhtemoc y Hatuey and honorary members of Morelos y Maceo, and in 1898 José P. Rivera appeared as the president of the Mexico

City-based club Juárez y Martí. Daniel Cabrera, director of the Mexican newspaper *El Hijo del Ahuizote*, was also an honorary member of Morelos y Maceo. Mateos and Rivera participated actively in Cuban public events, while Cabrera's newspaper regularly defended the Cuban cause. On 10 October 1897, Rivera and Mateos figured as guests of honor at a special meeting to commemorate the second anniversary of the third war for Cuban independence.[57] On 21 May 1896, a year earlier, José P. Rivera was a featured speaker at a *velada* honoring Martí's memory.[58] Remigio Mateos traveled to Puebla on 17 February 1897, as an invited speaker for the club Bravo y Maceo. Both men were also offered honorary membership by the Veracruz-based club Bartolomé Masó.[59] Honorary memberships were conferred to Mexican journalists in recognition of their newspapers' commitment to the Cuban cause, but they also served to extend linkages between Cubans and sympathetic Mexicans.

Some clubs were comprised exclusively of Mexican members. On 25 November 1897, Amado Escobar of Saltillo, Coahuila, wrote to Estrada Palma regarding the climate of support for the independence movement that existed there: "I am proud to report to you that here there are many Mexicans who support the Cuban republic, are enthusiastic admirers of its great men and heroes, and contribute with their grain of sand to the cause."[60] By December of 1897, Escobar and his associates were determined to found their own club. Escobar communicated with Nicolás Domínguez Cowan, the PRC agent in Mexico City, stating his intention to create a club and, presumably, received the regional leader's blessing. A few months later Escobar wrote Estrada Palma again, this time notifying him that the club Cepeda y Maceo had celebrated its inaugural meeting. The name Cepeda y Maceo, like that of so many Cuban clubs in Mexico, was meant to evoke the historic brotherhood shared by Mexico and Cuba, since Maceo was a well-known hero of the Cuban insurgent army and Victoriano Cepeda was a local Coahuilense hero of the Mexican independence war. This type of club activity in a city with few, if any, Cuban residents confirms that news and information about the Cuban movement reached far beyond the centers of Cuban activity in Mexico.

While some Mexicans made their contributions through direct participation in clubs, others offered financial contributions to signal their support. Charting these gives us a sense of the geography of participation and the diverse class background of Mexicans in support of *Cuba Libre*. Mexican citizens from many Mexican states made financial contributions to the Cuban cause, including groups of students, workers, women, and men who submitted donations from places as diverse as Veracruz, San Luis Potosí, Sonora, Puebla, Yucatán, Michoacán, Chalco, Campeche, Guanajuato, Tamaulipas, Hidalgo, Guerrero, and México.[61] That Mexican contributors who sent their donations to *El Continente Americano* came from places far beyond the centers of Cuban emigration in Veracruz, Merida, and Mexico City is intriguing, because it illuminates the spread of information via newspapers, letters, or other means of communication. There is a temporal correlation between Mexican and Cuban contributions: both peaked during the years 1896 and 1897. Although they were generally modest, donations from Mexicans ranged from 10 Mexican pesos to more than 100 U.S. dollars. The collections were taken up by both small groups of ten to twenty friends and family members and by large groups of workers and associates that could include between seventy and one hundred individuals. The contributors were mostly male, but every list of contributors also includes the names of several women.

While most contributors seem to be middle class or elite, there were a number of reported contributions from workers. The notes accompanying these donations provide specific information about donors' social class and occupation. On 28 June 1896, *El Continente Americano* printed the headline "Hooray for the Workers." The short article that followed acknowledged the interest in and contributions to the Cuban cause made by laborers and artisans from different industries including bakers, cantina workers, carpenters, and stonemasons. Journalists made special mention of the fact that by contributing even a modest amount, these workers were depriving themselves of the very money they used for subsistence. On several occasions workers from the textile and the railroad industry spontaneously took up collections and sent money to *El Continente Americano*. On 20 December 1896, eighty-eight textile workers from the factories Barron and La Colmena signed their names to a contribution of 33.25 pesos, an average of 38 cents each, which was about one day's wage for many workers.[62] A month later, on 4 January 1897, ninety-two workers associated with the Ferrocarril Hidalgo collected 45.87 pesos among themselves and proudly signed their names to a short statement of support for the Cuban cause, which was subsequently published in *El Continente Americano*. The paper referred to the workers as "poor Mexicans but generous of heart." On 25 July 1897, student journalist Juan Tizoc recorded being "moved as I have rarely been moved in my life" by a group of fifteen working-class children who came to the press house, bringing with them two coins that they had collected for the Cuban cause. Tizoc offered the "commission" a seat, but the children refused and insisted on standing as they delivered their speech: "Sir, we are insurgents and we want to help the Cubans. . . . Long live free Cuba!"[63] A month later, on 29 August 1897, a group of workers from a cigar factory in El Valle Nacional, Xalapa, sent a contribution of twenty pesos collected from eighty-seven laborers. Given the fact that Cuban planters moved themselves and transported workers to the Valle, some of the contributors must have been Cuban. Approximately a week after that, a contribution of 11.80 pesos was submitted to the journalists from thirty-four self-described "poor" citizens from El Puente de Ixtla de Hidalgo, Morelos. In December of 1897, the journalists acknowledged receipt of a contribution of 25 pesos from "people pertaining to the proletarian class" in Irapuato, Guanajuato.[64]

In studying the relationship between students at the professional and preparatory schools and the "*populacho*" in the late nineteenth-century Mexican public sphere, Pablo Piccato argues that due to their unique position between workers and elites, students were able to "expand political participation beyond class divides and spaces of elite sociability."[65] Students took politics to the streets, holding meetings, marches, and street battles and engaging in street oratory, riots, and combat journalism. According to Piccato, this kind of student activism in Mexico in the 1880s irreversibly opened up the public political sphere. As Claudio Lomnitz observes in his study of the anarchist and revolutionary, Ricardo Flores Magón, student activists from the same schools openly protested Porfirio Díaz's third reelection in 1892.[66] These students launched public protests and clashed with police on the streets of the capital. In 1892, as in the 1880s protests that Piccato explores, students were flanked by workers in rallies and marches. By the time the Cuban question exploded on the Mexican scene in 1895, Mexican students had a decades-long tradition of anti-government, cross-class mobilization.

Students' support for the workers and their commitment to highlighting worker investment in the Cuban cause came out of a longer tradition of cross-class action. But that support does not tell us much about the workers' motivations for allying themselves with Cuban cause. Different groups of workers offered financial contributions to the Cuban cause for different reasons, and it is hard to know with any certainty what those reasons might have been. Certainly, many workers found the Cuban cause a convenient way to frustrate Spanish bosses whom they found abusive. The number of times Spaniards complained that workers cried out "*Viva Cuba Libre*" and "*Muera España*" to goad them testifies to this. At times, these very words led to physical confrontations between workers and their bosses. Conflicts attributable to anti-hispanist sentiment will be further explored in chapter 5, but there are a number of possible explanations beyond anti-Hispanism. For instance, Mexican workers expressing solidarity with *Cuba Libre* were aware of, and likely inspired by the working-class radicalism of cigar workers in Florida and of the important role they played in the founding of the Cuban Revolutionary Party. One way this information was transmitted was through the reprinting of articles from *El Continente Americano* in Mexican working-class newspapers. For example, the workers' newspaper *El Fandango* of Pachuca regularly reprinted articles from *El Continente Americano*, which in turn carried news from Tampa and Key West. The fact that Veracruz was commonly thought of as the Key West of Mexico is evidence of the fact that Cubans in Veracruz were not only intimately aware of Cuban politics in Florida, but also identified closely with the communities there. Connections between Florida and Veracruz were forged by Cuban migrants like Dominga Valdes Corovalles de Muniz and others who spent time organizing in Tampa or Key West before arriving in Mexico. One of the three Cubans living in Mexico who had served as tailors for insurgents, mending and sowing clothes for filibustering expeditions in Florida, also collected financial contributions from workers in a tobacco factory in Tampa. All three tailors, Florencio Casals y Echarte, Armando Pérez de la Osa, and Simón Váldez y Laza, would certainly have transmitted information about Florida's Cuban communities.[67] Cuban migrants who connected multiple centers of Cuban revolutionary activity were not limited to workers, tailors, and insurgents. Elite Cuban migrants like Luis Lagomasino y Alvarez, who was an agent of the *comité directiva* of Key West, traveled to Veracruz from Florida expressly to energize the emigrations there.[68] He had intimate knowledge of the workings of the party and its working-class base in Florida. As the editor of a local newspaper in Veracruz, *El Grito de Baire*, and as a member of the prominent Cuban club Bartolomé Masó, Lagomasino Alvarez was an important figure in the Veracruz community. Similarly, both the treasurer and the secretary of the club Cubano-Mexicano Poesia had lived in Key West for about twenty years before migrating to Mexico.

The somewhat nefarious recruitment efforts of the club Bartolomé Masó provide another possible link between Cuban and Mexican workers. The documents of the club indicate that Cuban elites drew directly on practices pioneered in Florida when it came to coaxing or coercing the participation of Cuban workers. Cuban clubs like Bartolomé Masó recruited Cuban workers and solicited financial contributions in factories where Mexicans also labored, and thus Mexicans would have likely come to know about the Cuban question through their Cuban coworkers.

Although financial contributions by workers were common, these were often submitted without an explanatory text. In the few instances in which Mexican workers' contributions were accompanied by short written statements explaining the offering, the statements highlighted the importance of solidarity and emphasized the historical continuity between Mexico's independence struggle and Cuba's fight against Spanish colonialism. For example, the workers of the tobacco factory *El Valle Nacional* wrote, "Unfortunately . . . we belong to the eternally subjugated class of people who must constantly fight for survival. This is why our donation is so meager. But we are satisfied knowing that with the donation we will have contributed by revealing to the public light that anguish that throbs in the countries of the free America for those fallen Cuban soldiers who we recognize as our brothers in a struggle identical to the one that our fathers waged in 1810."[69] The language used by Mexican workers here is reminiscent of the militancy of Cuban workers in Florida, who advocated aggressively for their rights as workers even as they prioritized the national struggle. Given the circulation of news and newspapers throughout the Gulf World and the presence of the lector, who read newspapers out loud to cigar rollers as they worked, it is possible to imagine that these workers were aware of the activities of their fellow workers in Florida.

Middle-class Mexicans were drawn to the cause for similar reasons, although the oppression they felt did not emanate directly from Spanish bosses, and the liberty they sought did not depend on the amelioration of their poverty. Rather, middle-class Mexican liberals took up the cause of *Cuba Libre* because they felt that the Cubans' fight to bring about a liberal and democratic republic mirrored their own efforts to preserve, protect, and, at times, resuscitate Mexico's liberal and democratic traditions. Such was the case of Catarino Garza, the anti-Díaz revolutionary who conspired for a short time with Cuban exiles in Key West to aid them in the overthrow of the Spanish colonial regime in Cuba. Like those Mexicans back home who were critical of the Díaz regime, Garza saw himself as part of a continent-wide, if not Atlantic-wide, movement for the triumph of republicanism and democracy against tyranny.[70]

The discourse of fraternity forged in common experience and the idea that fraternity mandated solidarity is visible in the comment by the cigar workers at El Valle Nacional who recognized Cubans as "our brothers in a struggle." Similar language permeated the opinion pieces of numerous contributors who voiced their views in the pages of *El Continente Americano*. Indeed, allusions to the idea that it was the duty of Mexico and is citizens to support the Cuban struggle were pervasive.

The solidarity with *Cuba Libre* expressed by middle-class Mexicans rested on a number of ideological pillars: independence, republicanism and democracy, anti-colonialism/anti-imperialism, and *americanismo*, or hemispheric American solidarity. *El Continente Americano*'s inaugural issue announced that the paper had been founded by "a group of Mexican students" who, "inspired by the conduct of our neighboring republic [the United States] and that of the nations of Central and South America, came together and agreed to defend the cause of Cuban independence."[71] Inspired by reports they had read about the demonstrations of solidarity the Cuban cause had generated across the hemisphere, the students felt that they could not stand idly by. Modeling the position they felt the Mexican government should take, the students made a firm public stand in solidarity with *Cuba Libre*.

In 1895, *El Continente Americano* focused much of its energy on the search for belligerency recognition. In fact, Tomás Estrada Palma's decision to revive and revitalize Cuban insurgent diplomacy in the mid-1890s gave Mexican and other Latin American champions of Cuban independence the opportunity to do more than engage in clandestine activities like gathering arms and making financial contributions to the Cuban Revolutionary Party. Now Mexicans could advance a public, political campaign for solidarity with *Cuba Libre*. The appearance of opinion pieces calling on Mexican congressmen to pass a measure granting belligerency rights coincided with Domínguez Cowan's plan to prompt Mexicans to mount a campaign for recognition on their own. Given the close links between Domínguez Cowan and the Mexico City–based pro-Cuba press, the timing can hardly be a coincidence.

In addition to its own campaign, which largely consisted of front-page, large-print calls for the measure, *El Continente Americano* also published several petitions to the government authored by groups of Mexicans and Cubans from Mexico City, Ozoluama in Veracruz, Guadalajara, and Pachuca. The petitions were addressed to President Díaz, and they insisted that he grant the Cuban insurgents' belligerency rights. The petition from Ozoluama was signed by 89 individuals, while the Pachuca petition boasted five hundred signatures. Those who signed their names to the Guadalajara petitions numbered 1,830.[72] The petitioners argued passionately that to refuse to lend support to the Cuban insurgents was to betray the core values enshrined in Mexico's 1857 constitution.[73] They also urged Mexico to take the lead in the recognition of Cuban independence. In the United States, they argued Americans "rush to protect the cause with their manifestations in Chicago and all their grand cities: but before them, let us of the Latin race, brothers of those who suffer . . . let us recognize their status as belligerents."[74]

El Continente Americano's own demand for the recognition of the Cuban insurgents was reprinted eight times in one month. The notice was meant to raise consciousness and incite action. The call for the recognition of belligerency rights was a call for Mexicans to re-embrace the politics of the late 1860s. The journalists, like the students from Guadalajara, emphasized that it was Mexico's duty to support the insurgents. They also urged their readers to pay attention to the press because all "the republics of the continent" were on the side of the independence fighters. The students called on their readers to recognize Mexico's responsibility to form part of, and even lead, the continent-wide movement in favor of the insurgency.

El Continente Americano's announcement regarding belligerency rights stood out for its location on the front page of the newspaper and for its bold print and large size. The student journalists specialized in provocative visual propaganda. *El Continente Americano* was the only newspaper in Mexico to print full-page images of Cuban insurgents with accompanying biographies. These illustrations, like the belligerency notice, have a striking visual effect. By catching the eye of the reader, the journalists hoped to incite passions and animate debate.

The Cuban biographical sketches included an image of the individual that was life-size or very nearly so, with an accompanying text describing the life of each revolutionary figure located on the back of the image page. The image and text could be conveniently detached from the rest of the paper and perhaps used in a variety of ways—passed around for educational purposes, or perhaps hung on a wall as a point of pride. As Carlos Forment reminds us, "in Mexico, Puebla and Veracruz, newspaper vendors turned street corners into centers of public discussion."[75] Street corners and taverns were places where Mexicans of all classes whether literate or not could become informed. It is no surprise then that streets and bars were the most common cites of confrontation between Mexicans, Cubans and Spaniards clashing over the Cuban Question in the 1890s. It is clear that the life size images of Maceo and other Cuban revolutionaries were used for more than

FIGURE 4.1 Image of Antonio Maceo, *El Continente Americano*, 21 June 1896. Political cartoon.

private reading. The public burning of the issue of the newspaper that contained the portrait of Maceo (fig. 4.1.) by Spanish immigrants in Puebla suggests as much and is evidence that the students' campaign was provocative enough.[76] The journalists pointed out that Spaniards were driven to distraction by the image of the revolutionary hero and that their reactions ultimately served to reaffirm the power of Maceo, adding to his glory. In another case, a group of Spaniards publicly shredded an issue of the paper that featured a Cuban flag superimposed on its text.[77] Again, the presence of an image deemed subversive made *El Continente Americano* a target of Spanish ire.

The representation of the Cuban national flag was a powerful affirmation of Cuba's nationhood, even if independence was not yet won. Figures like Maceo and Martí who represented values like national self-determination, republicanism, democracy, and equality provided Mexican journalists with an endless fount of inspiration to press their political leaders to respect these same principles, "[L]ike an aroma in the forest that is inevitably carried forth," the student journalists observed, "the ideas of liberty and equality, proclaimed by the vigorous cry of Martí, were disseminated throughout the American continent, reverberating in the hearts of noble and generous men."[78] The student journalists considered themselves "noble and generous men" and believed that to turn their backs on the Cuban revolutionary struggle would be shameful. It would be tantamount to forsaking the Mexican Constitution. "Were we to be indifferent or hostile towards the Cuban revolutionary movement," they wrote, "this would constitute a grave sin . . . [we would be] divorcing ourselves from our liberal principles, set down with blood and tears in our sacred Constitution, and would be betraying . . . our heroic ancestors. The ashes of Hidalgo, Morelos and Allende would tremble in their graves."

A group of students from the Instituto del Estado de Guerrero sent in an article also expressing the hope that Mexico, in keeping with her values and ideals, would be the first nation to formally recognize the belligerents. Echoing the student journalists of *El Continente Americano*, they insisted that were they to remain silent on the Cuban Question, they would not be worthy of having been born "on the sacred ground of the Patria of Cuauhtemoc, Hidalgo and Juárez." The obvious connection between the three great men was their anti-colonialism. However, it would not escape the reader that the lives and struggles of these three anti-colonial figures spanned the late fifteenth through the mid to late nineteenth centuries. The effect was to implant the notion that Mexico's struggle against European tyranny spanned the centuries from the resistance of one of Mexico's most famed indigenous leaders to the original Spanish conquistadores through to a creole priest's call for independence from the Spanish colonial state, to the heroic defense of a nation and a republic from the pretentions of the French colonial state. Mexico's struggles for independence and against conservatism were part of a movement that shared fundamental similarities with the Cuban independence cause.[79] Cubans were seen as picking up the mantle of Juárez and all those who came before him in the defense of America. In line with the students of Mexico City and Guerrero, the authors of the Guadalajara belligerency petition called on President Díaz to change his policy, referring to Cubans as "our emulators by struggle and our brothers by blood" and insisting that "the best demonstration of how we Mexicans esteem our autonomy has been our [disposition] to sympathize with the cause of liberty." Like the students from Guerrero, who referred to "values and ideals," the Guadalajara petitioners argued that "the time has come for Mexicans to make a gesture consonant with our principles . . . as a sovereign nation jealous of the cause of liberty."[80]

In 1896, the Mexican members of the Cuban political club Mexico y Cuba wrote the following statement clarifying their objectives in a short-run newspaper also called *Mexico y Cuba*:

> We are Mexicans and with true pride we defend our nationality. We are liberals and what is done in support of the political advancement of peoples inspires and moves us. We are democrats and republicans and the sovereignty of the people . . . the election of its leaders, limits placed on executive power . . . equality that does not recognize any differences but those based on the moral and intellectual capabilities of an individual by comparison with others . . . constitute our desires. . . . We are, in the end, also Americans and we desire the independence of all of the European colonies that exist in this continent, which is the envy of the democrats of the world despite its defects. . . . This is why we proclaim, "Cuba for the Cubans."[81]

For the members of Mexico y Cuba, anyone self-describing as Mexican, liberal, republican, a democrat, or American was duty-bound to support the Cuban struggle. Their insistence that the American republics are the envy of the democrats of the world places not just the United States, but Mexico, Cuba and Latin America at the forefront of the development of democracy on a global scale challenging the notion that Latin American republics were chronically war torn and backward.

Southeast of Mexico City in Puebla, in 1897, a young Mexican woman by the name of Emigida Limón electrified an audience at a meeting of the Cuban club Bravo y Maceo when she referred to Cuba as a sister nation who had risen up against her oppressors in search of liberty, progress, and democracy.[82] In that same year, Roberto Embleton and a handful of co-conspirators from Coatepec, Veracruz sent the PRC leadership a sample of the notice they had publicly disseminated to convince Mexican residents of Coatepec to donate money for the Cuban cause. The notice read: "You cannot forget the bloody sacrifices and sublime heroism that our national heroes exhibited in order to conquer the liberty of the 'Patria' freeing her of Spanish tyranny. Today, in Cuba, the same scenes are being reproduced, and in the fields as sons of America, our brothers, fight for the right to be citizens of a democratic republic." Like Limón and the members of Mexico y Cuba, the citizens of Coatepec also spoke of Cuba's right to constitute a democratic republic.[83] The repeated references to liberty, democracy, and rights and the evocation of a fraternal bond between nations across all the letters and speeches demonstrate that average citizens understood Cubans and Mexicans to be engaged in parallel struggles.

Conclusion

Looking back over the nineteenth century from the 1820s forward, it is clear that Latin Americans understood the fate of the island of Cuba as being deeply connected to the future of Latin America. Broadly speaking, Latin American elites supported the Cuban independence struggle in the first two-thirds of the nineteenth century because of their distrust of Spain, their modest concern about the role that the United States might come to play in Latin America, and the revolutionary ethos of the time, which cast Cuban independence as one in a long line of legitimate anti-colonial struggles in the Americas. However, the fundamental changes in hemispheric politics that occurred in the last third of the nineteenth century conspired to doom Cubans' diplomatic initiatives in Latin America. The recession of *americanismo* paralleled the rise of a nationalism in late nineteenth-century Latin America that privileged technological modernization above political ideals. Nowhere was this more apparent than in Mexico, the nation that seemed to exercise a magnetic hold on the Cuban revolutionary José Martí and the nation to which so many other Cuban patriots both before and after Martí affixed their hopes for a Latin American solidarity that could aid Cuba's liberation from Spain.

The shift from a mid-nineteenth century dominated by political liberalism to a late-nineteenth century driven by economic liberalism created the context in which empowered elites in Latin America came to see the Cuban movement as a relic that perhaps belonged to a glorious shared past, but had become incongruent with the Latin American present and future. With their eyes fixed on "order and progress," modernization, and economic advancement, Latin American elites were skeptical of social justice and democracy and deeply disapproving of revolution as a means to achieving them.

A history of diplomacy in relation to the Cuban independence movement, however, does not capture the wide and deep transnational solidarities that Cubans forged together with their Latin American counterparts. These were solidarities that drew legitimacy from nearly a century of efforts to frame Cuba's independence as a question of continental relevance and a matter of continental responsibility. The capaciousness of Cuban revolutionary politics made it easy for Mexicans attuned to Cuban discourses of anticolonialism, democracy, and republicanism to relate to the Cuban cause and to make it their own.

The potential cost of encouraging foreigners to adopt the Cuban cause was felt most acutely in the United States, where Cuban efforts to make the independence war relatable ultimately served a broader imperialist project. In Mexico, though, the building of solidarity backfired in a concrete sense as well. Those Mexicans most moved by the Cuban cause were not the powerful Porfirian elites that Domínguez Cowan and Estrada Palma had thought might influence Díaz to shift his policies. On the contrary, *Cuba Libre* supporters came from among the people most ill at ease with the calculations of the Porfirian regime and its modernization project. While they celebrated Mexico's economic progress, these liberals lamented the sacrifice of constitutional rights and political democracy, which political elites under Díaz deemed necessary for Mexico's advancement. Before exploring the connection between an emerging opposition to the Díaz regime and the Cuban movement, we must explore the Mexican state's rationale for its refusal to take a stance in support of the Cuban insurgency.

5 Spanish Immigrants, the Mexican State, and the Fight for *Cuba Española*

On 9 March 1870, Andrés Clemente Vázquez departed Havana for Veracruz on the French steamship, *Panama*. Like José Martí, who would arrive in the port two years later, Andrés was an outspoken revolutionary sympathizer, and persecution was the cause of his departure. Andrés made his way to Mexico City and found a supportive, if small, community of Cuban exiles already established there. Nicolás Domínguez Cowan, the future regional head of the Cuban Revolutionary Party, had migrated there in 1868. When José Martí arrived in Mexico City in 1875, Andrés befriended him, and the two men found themselves moving in the same circles. Each made ends meet by working as a journalist for Mexican newspapers in the capital. But here their stories diverged. While José Martí figured himself as an adopted son of Mexico in his writings, Andrés Clemente Vázquez officially adopted the nation as his own and became a Mexican citizen in the early 1870s.

For many migrants and exiles from the decade of the Ten Years' War, substituting foreign citizenship for Spanish subjecthood was hardly a weighty decision and was often used as a strategy to better pursue revolutionary activities in exile. Thus, we find a disproportionate number of naturalized citizens among the older generation of Cuban migrants in the United States, Mexico, and elsewhere.[1] For men like Andrés, loyalty to two *patrias* was a fact of life, and it gave a particular shape to his experience. In the early 1880s, Andrés had gained a position in Mexico's legation in Central America. From there he went on to become Mexico's consul in Cuba for eighteen years. As consul, Vázquez struggled to reconcile his unfaltering loyalty to Mexico and his deep empathy for the land of his birth. The recommendations he made to the Mexican minister of foreign relations—urging him toward a more active stance on Cuba after 1895—emanated from Andrés's sincere care and concern for both of the nations he claimed as his own.

Andrés Clemente Vázquez was caught in an impossible bind. As Mexico's official representative in Cuba, he dined with and courted Spanish officials. For some Cubans, Andrés's friendliness with Cuba's colonial administrators constituted a serious betrayal. One journalist who knew of

Andrés's publications in defense of Cuban independence (penned before he became a member of Mexico's foreign service) reprinted and circulated those materials in the 1890s in an effort to embarrass Andrés and depict him as a Cuban traitor.[2] Just as Andrés was critiqued by Cubans, he was also attacked by Spaniards. The Spanish foreign minister in Mexico tried to pressure the Mexican government to replace Andrés because of his historic sympathies for the insurgents. The Díaz administration refused to acquiesce to this request and assured the Spanish minister of their faith in Andrés's neutrality. Ignacio Mariscal, Andrés's superior, defended his consul from Spanish attacks, while also refusing to heed his advice, consistently resisting the opportunity to take a leading role in relation to the Cuban Question. Mariscal's determination to deny the Spanish one moment and acquiesce to Spanish demands the next perfectly exemplified the push-pull relationship the Mexican government retained with Spain throughout the 1890s. Seeking always to remain in control of the relationship, the regime collaborated with Spain when it deemed such collaboration beneficial. For example, the administration aided the Spanish foreign minister in tracking and at times thwarting activities in support of *Cuba Libre*, especially when the activists in the crosshairs happened to be Mexican citizens who were critics of the Díaz regime, as often was the case.

The Mexican state's shift from a pro-Cuban independence position in the late 1860s to a pro-Spanish position in the 1890s was felt most acutely by Cuban migrants like Andrés who had become Mexican citizens during a time when popular and elite opinion was favorable toward *Cuba Libre*. By the 1890s, though, everything had changed. Being a loyal Mexican citizen working for the state required a man like Andrés to conceal his sympathies for the Cuban insurgents as well as any antipathy he might harbor for the Spanish colonial state, while also cautiously suggesting that Mexico's national interests might be best served by a policy other than the one that the Díaz regime had committed itself to. Even though Andrés had accepted Mexican citizenship in the early 1870s, it did not seem then that he belonged to two antagonistic *patrias*. In the 1890s, however, Mexico and *Cuba Libre* seemed worlds apart. This chapter explores the Mexican state's ideological and tactical alliance with Spain during the Hispano-Cuban conflict. Setting the relationship between Spain and Mexico in context allows us to understand Andrés Clemente Vázquez's difficult position as he tried to reconcile what had become a seemingly unbridgeable gulf between his adopted and native lands.

If *Cuba Libre* and Mexico were distant in the 1890s, *Cuba Española* and Mexico were close. To fully understand the Díaz regime's rejection of Cuban independence in the 1890s, we must explore Mexico's relationship to Spain in that period. Two intertwined processes paved the way for the warming of relations between Mexican and Spanish elites half a century after Mexican independence: the renovation of Mexican-Spanish relations after the defeat of the French in 1867, and the transformations in Mexican liberalism in the late nineteenth century. The two processes were intimately connected. Mexican and Spanish political elites traveled parallel roads from the late 1860s forward. The disillusionment resulting from the failure of the first Spanish republic led to a rejection of political liberalism and embrace of authoritarianism during and after the restoration of the monarchy in 1874. Similarly, the Díaz regime, which had come to power on the promise to defend democracy, had by the 1890s decided to subordinate its ideals to the pragmatic search for political order and material progress. A similar distancing from political ideals and an embrace of positivist doctrines and scientific politics occurred in both countries.

The first section lays out the policy of the Díaz regime on Cuban independence in the 1890s. The regime's policy can be described as a distinctly pro-Spanish neutrality. The renovation of Mexican-Spanish relations in the late 1860s and the related rise of *hispanismo*, or Hispanism, anchors the second section and offers a first explanation for the regime's pro-Spanish position. Close attention is paid to the ideological orientation and the patriotic activities of the Spanish immigrant community in Mexico during the 1895 War. An examination of the explicit links between the Spanish foreign minister and the Mexican government during the war is at the heart of this section. The foreign minister's documents reveal the existence of covert arrangements between the Spanish representative and members of the Díaz administration for the purpose of repressing Cuban political activities. Using his network of consuls as well as Mexican policemen and detectives, the Spanish minister José Brunetti y Gayoso kept close tabs on Cuban migrants. Yet, Cuban migrants were not the only dissidents in his sights. Brunetti also received Mexican government support to target and repress Mexican citizens who were supporters of the Cuban independence cause. Despite the minister's efforts to deter manifestations of sympathy for *Cuba Libre*, the streets of Mexico erupted with conflicts between Cubans, Mexicans, and Spaniards who exchanged words and came to blows over the Cuban Question. The single most common cause of conflict was the shouting of the words "*Viva Cuba Libre*" and "*Muera España*." The minister redoubled his efforts to neutralize Cuban revolutionaries in Mexico in response to these escalating conflicts.

Meanwhile, one Mexican federal deputy by the name of Carlos Olaguíbel y Arista initiated a "scientific" debate on the issue, publishing several articles dissecting the Cuban Question from the vantage point of Mexico's national interests. The third section examines the ideological position that undergirded Carlos Olaguíbel y Arista's defense of Mexico's position of neutrality. Olaguíbel's arguments constitute a uniquely clear example of the way Mexico's new political elites who were far more conservative than their predecessors rationalized the nation's rejection of a fundamentally liberal cause, one that Mexican elites had resoundingly supported just a few decades earlier. Olaguíbel's articles lay bare the deep connection between the rise of *hispanismo* and the consolidation of the conservative liberalism that marked the later Porfiriato.

The Gulf framed the thinking of Spanish royalists in Mexico and Mexican Hispanists just as it did that of Cuban revolutionaries like José Martí and Tomás Estrada Palma. Dismissing Cubans' claims to the island known as the *llave del golfo*, or key of the Gulf, Spaniards and their Mexican sympathizers saw the Gulf as a contested space in which Spain, Mexico, and the United States sought to project their power. While the United States coveted Cuba, and Spain defended the last remnants of its empire, Mexico was caught in the middle. With modest imperial ambitions of their own in the Gulf, Porfirian statesmen made the best calculation they could as they crafted their Cuba policy. Confident in Mexico's close and reciprocal relations with Spain, and equally clear that its relations with the United States, fraught as they were, were indispensable, Mexicans preferred a Spanish Cuba. Unable to compete for control of the Gulf, Mexican statesmen saw a pro-Spanish position as one that would help contain the United States' influence by creating a buffer between Mexico and the United States. As we saw in the previous chapter, José Martí had also envisioned the Gulf as buffer zone, but his visions rested on the collaboration of Mexico with a free and independent Cuba, two states that together would insulate Latin America from the United States.

The Mexican State and the Cuban Cause

Years after the independence war in Cuba, Manuel Márquez Sterling, a Cuban journalist and former Cuban migrant in Mexico, traveled to Mexico City to interview Porfirio Díaz. The year was 1904. The Hispano-Cuban conflict had ended in the Spanish-American War, and the United States, which had established a military protectorate in Cuba between 1898 and 1902, had nominally left Cubans in charge of their own nation. Elsewhere in the greater Caribbean, the United States was making a habit of intervening in the affairs of other nations, with a military presence in places like Haiti, the Dominican Republic, Puerto Rico, Panama, and Nicaragua, to name a few. It was in this year that Theodore Roosevelt proclaimed what is famously known as the Roosevelt Corollary to the Monroe Doctrine, thereby legitimizing his government's overseas aggression. Thus, when Díaz and Márquez Sterling came together to talk, both men had the United States very much on their minds. The United States may not have invaded Mexico's territory in the early years of the twentieth century (although it would in 1914 and again in 1916), but Mexico had grown economically dependent on the United States during the Porfiriato. At the very beginning of the interview, Márquez Sterling asked Díaz for his frank opinion of Cuba's future. The aging dictator drew a parallel between Cuba and Mexico as he answered. After insisting that the most significant danger Cuba faced was the steady acquisition of Cuban lands by U.S. citizens, he qualified the statement by saying, "something similar is happening to us here in Mexico. But there is no resisting progress, and to be strong is to accept those who come with their money and their initiatives to better your country."[3] Díaz drew a firm distinction between the U.S. government and U.S. businessmen. Indeed, he called the president of the United States, Theodore Roosevelt, an "imperialist" and "little democratic," while in the same breath defending his decision to allow U.S. investment to transform Mexico.[4]

Díaz recognized the risks and dangers of his economic policy, and he maneuvered in numerous ways to create a counterbalance to U.S. influence. One way the Díaz regime sought to resist the U.S. culturally was through its embrace of Hispanism. The interview with Márquez Sterling turned to the topic of immigration, and particularly that of the Spanish, a group with a significant presence in both Mexico and Cuba. Díaz insisted that his favorite immigrants were Spaniards "because they had done wonders for Mexico." He further explained that while the benefits brought by U.S. American immigrants were undeniable, the perfect cultural affinity between Spaniards and Mexicans ensured that they would assimilate fully, while U.S. Americans remained alien. U.S. capital and immigration might be a necessary evil, but Spanish immigration was an unquestionable boon to the nation.

What is most fascinating about Márquez Sterling's interview with Díaz is the direct parallel the latter drew between Mexico and Cuba. In fact, as Cuban foreign minister in Mexico Carlos García Vélez remembered it, Díaz made the comparison between Mexico and Cuba in the first place "as if to console us." The minister suggested that Díaz may have recognized that his assessment of Cuba's destiny—the idea that the island would soon be entirely bought up by U.S. investors—would be deeply distressing to his guests. Thus, Díaz offered consolation in the form of empathy: Mexico was suffering the same opportunity. Indeed, by 1911, 100–120 million acres of land in Mexico would be U.S.-owned.[5]

The parallel drawn by Díaz reveals his own perspective on the Gulf. Both Mexico and Cuba, by virtue of their geographical proximity to a United States that was expanding rapidly in the nineteenth century, represented the first line of defense against U.S. imperial conquest. To strike a balance between the potential and the threat, both of which were inherent in close relations with the northern colossus, was a deep and enduring challenge. In his interview with Márquez Sterling, Díaz seemed to position himself and Mexico as a guide for the fledging Cuba as it navigated the unique politics of the Gulf World. As we will see in chapter 6, it was common within the pro-Cuban solidarity movement in Mexico to figure Mexico as Cuba's tutor rather than the United States, even as the United States intervened in the Cuban war and established a protectorate in the island. If Díaz could impart one lesson to Cuba, it would be a lesson in how to balance national and foreign interests. Díaz's answer to the promise and the danger represented by the United States was to embrace "defensive modernization." William Schell Jr. argues that through defensive modernization Díaz exerted considerable control over Mexico's economic relationship with the United States. He goes as far as to see Porfirian economic policy as a kind of "Porfirian dollar diplomacy."[6] While seeking to retain a degree of control over its economic relationship to the United States, the regime resisted U.S. cultural imperialism through a kind of defensive hispanization.

While Manuel Márquez Sterling's interview with Porfirio Díaz reveals Díaz's sense that Mexico and Cuba shared a precarious position, it also sheds light on the regime's complete rejection of Cuban independence during the 1890s. The Mexican state would do everything it could to avoid a U.S. annexation of Cuba without compromising its own national interests. Bearing in mind that Díaz likely saw U.S. economic control in Cuba in the mid-1890s with the same wary optimism that he did in 1904, he would have likely assumed that Cuba's dependence on the United States would only grow, as had Mexico's. Only, Mexico was not nearly as vulnerable as Cuba, which might easily be annexed in its entirety by the United States. Thus, while embracing Spanish culture would provide some insulation from U.S. influence in Mexico, in Cuba preserving Spanish control of the island was essential for safeguarding the island from a complete U.S. takeover.

At its core then, Mexico's pro-Spain policy was rooted in the belief that a Cuban republic independent of the United States was unsustainable. In this, Mexico and Cuba differed fundamentally. The difference, in the minds of Mexicans opposed to Cuban independence, had to do with time, circumstance, and geography. In the particular geopolitical context of the 1890s, Mexican skeptics concurred with their Spanish counterparts that if Cuba became independent from Spain, the island, incapable of governing itself, would be taken over by the United States. This was the argument that Manuel Márquez Sterling worked so hard to refute as a young journalist in Mexico City between 1896 and 1898. When faced with the argument that Cuba could never stand on its own, he defiantly insisted that if the Latin American republics that constituted themselves at the beginning of the nineteenth century were not made to demonstrate their capacity for self-governance, neither should Cuba be forced to do so.[7] Even so, the Díaz regime based its Cuba policy on three factors: concern about U.S. expansionism, the shoring up of the "Latin race" as a potential bulwark to the same, and the idea that a Cuban republic was inherently unviable.

The Díaz regime's action on Cuban independence fell far short of the expectations of Cubans like Márquez Sterling and their Mexican supporters, but to suggest that the Mexican states' position was an incomprehensible betrayal (as many dedicated supporters of Cuban independence did) obscures the complexity of Mexican politics and diplomacy in the late nineteenth century. Cubans and their counterparts generally expressed outrage and shock at Latin American states' abandonment of Cuba. But Porfirian foreign policy on the Cuban independence wars was not seen in romantic terms as a question of loyalty or betrayal to a cause. To be sure, Porfirians liked to speak of Mexico as a bastion of liberalism and a nation of principles and struggles for justice, but this rhetoric was removed from policy.

As we have seen, Porfirian foreign policy on Cuba in the 1890s was a pragmatic balancing act. After sustaining a neutral position in the Hispano-Cuban conflict for three years, the Mexican state proclaimed in 1898 that it would also remain neutral in the Spanish-American War. A political cartoon in *El Hijo del Ahuizote* satirized Díaz's acrobatics. The cartoonist depicted Porfirio Díaz walking a tightrope labeled "neutrality" and using an acrobat's pole to retain his balance. On one end, the rope was fastened to a base labeled "American colony" and on the other end to a base labeled "Spanish colony." The "loose rope" offers little stability for the shaky-legged dictator, who concentrates as he fixes his stare on the U.S. Capitol in the background. The loose rope suggested that the policy of neutrality was seen by the cartoonist as representative of Mexico's weakness, a view that the liberal opposition to the dictator held firmly. However, in the background of the image is a crowd of "*agachupinados*," a derogatory term for hispanized Mexicans, who are wearing stereotypical native dress (a marker of their perceived barbarism) and shooting arrows at the president in an attempt to destabilize him. The cartoon highlighted public recognition of the regime's delicate and precarious position as it sought firm footing in a very complicated diplomatic and political terrain in the years leading up to the war of 1898. Balancing U.S. and Spanish interests was difficult enough, but the cartoonist here saw Mexico's conservative and pro-Spanish minority as an especially disruptive element that was likely to make the dictator lose his balance. The culprits in the scene are the Spanish and their allies in Mexico who are seen dragging Díaz down.

The journalists' caricature might have been a joke and a subtle jab, but Porfirio Díaz was, in fact, a very skilled political acrobat. As PRC agent in Mexico City Nicolás Domínguez Cowan observed in 1895, Díaz's policy of neutrality responded to the "pressure of the Spanish element" in Mexico. At the same time, though, Díaz "turn[ed] his gaze to Washington" and would not make a move on the granting of Cuban belligerency rights unless it was sanctioned by the United States.[8] Seeking to balance Spanish and U.S. interests, Díaz also paid attention to Mexico's own international reputation. Mexico could not afford to be publicly pro–United States, pro-Spain, or pro-Cuba.[9]

If a public pro-Cuban position would alienate the Spanish and potentially risk obstructing United States designs on Cuba, a pro-Spanish position proved problematic for Mexico's international image. After all, propagandists worked hard to depict Mexico as a liberal, democratic republic, proud of its revolutionary tradition. As we have seen, Mexico had a long tradition of supporting Cuban independence, one that stretched back to the 1820s. To publicly disavow the Cuban insurgents' aspirations for independence in the 1890s would undermine Mexico's public image. Key to Díaz's own cult of personality was his status as a revolutionary hero in the independence war against the French. In the article that anticipated his arrival in Mexico in 1894, José Martí intentionally depicted Mexico as a Liberal republic that Juárez had inaugurated and Díaz had nurtured to greatness in order to curry favor with the dictator. Architects of the Porfirian regime had made an art of figuring Díaz as heir to Juárez and to Mexico's founding fathers in the many state-sponsored celebrations held each year. This cult was satirized in the newspaper *El Hijo del Ahuizote*, where Díaz was figured toppling a statue of the icon of Mexican independence and father of the nation, Miguel Hidalgo, and taking his place on the vacant podium. The Díaz regime could not possibly support Spanish colonialism in Cuba without seeming to be out of step with a national culture founded on the consecration of its own anti-colonial independence struggles against both the Spanish and the French. Furthermore, Díaz's contribution of $20,000 to Martí and his cause suggests that, at least in 1894, he privately identified with the insurgents.

In sum, Mexican political elites were oddly for and against all parties involved, a contradiction that left neutrality the only option. Renewed relations with Spain bolstered pro-Hispanist solidarities, but, Mexico's own history of anti-colonial war formed a potential basis of solidarity with Cuban insurgents, but suspicions about the viability of the future Cuban state and concerns about U.S. imperialism made a pro-Cuba position untenable. Economic and security interests bound Mexico to the United States, but Mexicans worried about the costs of growing dependency on their northern neighbor.[10] Between 1895 and 1898, neutrality in Mexico served as a veneer for a set of contradictory but meaningful actions and inactions vis-à-vis Cuba.

Publicly, the Díaz regime offered to mediate the dispute between Spain and Cuba during the 1895 War, and again between Spain and the United States in 1898. Both offers were rejected. In relation to Cuban migrants, Díaz permitted them to settle in Mexico and did little to outwardly obstruct their political organizing, which included the raising of money and gathering of arms for the revolution. The Spanish perceived this stance as frustrating inaction on the part of a state they felt should be more aggressively pro-Spain. Years later Cuban diplomats would lavish praise on Díaz for opening Mexico's arms to Cuban migrants during the war and allowing Mexico to be a safe haven for them. But just as the regime was providing a safe shore for Cubans, it was covertly undermining Cuban revolutionary efforts in Mexico by providing the Spanish foreign minister in Mexico with intelligence about Cuban clandestine activities. The records of the Spanish minister in Mexico make repeated references to the explicit collaboration of everyone from Ignacio Mariscal, Mexico's minister of foreign relations, to local policemen and undercover detectives. Far from the shaky-legged figure of the cartoon, Díaz and his ministers proved to be rather skillful acrobats. The strategic combination of action, inaction, and covert action allowed the regime to preserve Mexico's international image, safeguard the nation's profitable relationship with the United States, and at the same time attempt to mitigate the penetration of U.S. American cultural imperialism through a celebration of Mexico's Hispanic heritage.

A brief and unsuccessful project for the annexation of Cuba to Mexico is worth mentioning here because it reveals both Mexico's imperial aspirations and U.S. opposition to them. The project's leader was the Cuban Carlos Americo Lera, who, like Andrés Clemente Vázquez, was a naturalized Mexican citizen. Lera had begun developing the idea of annexing Cuba to Mexico in the 1880s. However, the opportunity to push forward with the project came in the 1890s, when he worked for Ignacio Mariscal. Over the course of one year, 1896, the idea caught fire and went as far as spawning a short-lived political party with numerous members attached and a multi-point platform. Lera's defense of the natural fit between Cuba and Mexico is revealing because it rests on a vision of the geography of the Gulf of Mexico that challenged other visions, especially those that U.S. imperialists took for granted. Lera wrote the following in defense of the project: "The union of Cuba and the Mexican federation, far from presenting the inconveniences that the acquisition of new territories often brings, must be seen as the reincorporation of a region that has been as Mexican as Chiapas, Oaxaca or Veracruz and that is much closer to the capital of the republic than any of its frontier states . . . the island of Cuba until 1820 was a dependency of New Spain . . . linked by the most extensive connections . . . today the two countries are estranged only by the vicissitudes of politics."[11] In Lera's vision, Cuba is not a natural appendage of the United States (as John Quincy Adams famously imagined it in the 1820s), but rather a territory that had been part of Mexico for hundreds of years and should be reunited with it. History was the cornerstone of his argument, but geography mattered as well. That Cuba was nearer to the capital of Mexico than some of Mexico's own northern states seemed to provide clear evidence that Cuba had perhaps even more reason to be part of the Mexican federation than did, for example, Sonora.

The project for *Cuba Mexicana* made headlines in Mexico and was covered in the press for a year. The proposal rocked the Cuban migrant community in Mexico. Cuban migrants from Veracruz traveled to the capital outraged that a number of traditional supporters of Cuban independence had expressed approval of the project and had even signed on as members of a Cuba-Mexicana party, which was constituted in the capital. At the same time, the annexation project caused some consternation among the Cuban

Revolutionary Party's leaders in New York City. Ironically, Carlos Americo Lera shared much with figures like Estrada Palma and his more conservative counterparts in New York City who wished to see a very close relationship between Cuba and the United States after independence. Indeed, *Cuba Mexicana* was a project dreamed up by a Cuban Mexican who earnestly desired the union between his adopted and native lands, as did his counterparts who had lived decades in exile in the United States.

It was always clear that Cuba's annexation to Mexico would be accepted by neither the Cuban insurgents nor the Spanish state. However, in an interesting twist, the project was supported by John Sherman, the prominent U.S. senator who opposed a U.S. annexation of Cuba and saw Cuba's unification with Mexico as a perfect solution for an island he thought was unlikely to fare well as an independent nation. The *Cuba Mexicana* project also had backing among the U.S. immigrant community in Mexico, likely for economic reasons. The director of the U.S. colony's newspaper, the *Mexican Herald*, was a member of the Cuba-Mexicana party. The support of some U.S. statesmen and immigrants for Mexico's annexation of Cuba seems counterintuitive given the United States' long-term interest in controlling Cuba. However, ten years later, after the Spanish-American War and in the wake of the pronouncement of the Roosevelt Corollary to the Monroe Doctrine, Theodore Roosevelt himself would work to fan the flames of Mexico's imperial ambition while enlisting Mexico's support in the subjugation of the hemisphere by recommending that Mexico colonize all of central America and take over Cuba, Puerto Rico, and the Dominican Republic. As the Mexican ambassador suspected, this was a trick. The United States would only give Cuba to Mexico because it knew that, in doing so, it would retain control of both. Resolving to maintain its distance from the United States' imperial projects, the regime respectfully declined the offer.[12] While Roosevelt's actions in 1904 had a precedent in the 1896 project to annex Cuba to Mexico, the United States government ultimately disapproved of the project in that year. This was much to the relief of Cuban revolutionaries in New York City, who found the project troubling. While those Cubans most open to U.S. involvement in Cuban affairs were favorable toward some form of U.S. intervention, the idea of being annexed to Mexico seemed as outlandish to them as it seemed natural to a Cuban-Mexican like Carlos Americo Lera.

The project for *Cuba Mexicana* was seriously considered by the Díaz regime, especially Díaz's foreign minister Ignacio Mariscal, who was a close friend of Lera. Margarita Espinosa Blas has argued that the project served as a barometer by which Mexico gauged Spain's and the United States' reactions to the possibility of Mexico's direct involvement in the Cuban Question. Their negative reactions reaffirmed the Díaz regime's commitment to official neutrality.¹³ Indeed, a precondition of moving forward on the project was that Cubans, Spaniards, and the U.S. government be on board; it would never come to pass. The project met an abrupt end as soon as Díaz got wind that the propaganda was not sitting well with Washington.¹⁴ Despite its timidity, the fact that the regime considered the *Cuba Mexicana* project at all points to Mexico's own imperialist ambitions, ambitions that would not be realized in the Caribbean, but instead vis-à-vis Central America in the early twentieth century.¹⁵ All told, Díaz's Cuba policy aimed to protect the nation's profitable relationship with the United States, while also nurturing its relations with Spain to create a cultural counterweight (if not physical buffer) to U.S. influence. At the same time, the *Cuba Mexicana* project shows how the regime contemplated its own independent challenge to the United States by vying, however timidly and briefly, for influence in the Gulf and the Caribbean.

After returning to Cuba in 1904, interview notes in hand, Márquez Sterling published an extremely unflattering article about Porfirio Díaz in the Cuban newspaper, *El Mundo*. According to Carlos García Velez, the piece was all that the members of the Jockey Club in Mexico City could talk about. So damning was the portrayal of Díaz that the dictator promptly censored the article and pronounced Márquez Sterling persona non grata in Mexico.¹⁶ Deeply offended, Márquez Sterling insisted that his article on Díaz was not defamatory at all. It was simply true, he argued. Working for *El Diario del Hogar*, a newspaper known for its criticism of the Díaz regime, Márquez Sterling had been exposed to the oppositional stance of the Mexican liberals he worked with, and he had learned well the skill of masking critique. Reflecting on the art of disguise that his Mexican journalist friends had perfected, he wrote "with all the trappings of an article in pro, their 'editorials' were, nonetheless, in contra."¹⁷ However, since his return to independent Cuba, Márquez Sterling no longer had to hide and could express his honest views on Mexico and its leaders. Thinking back on the article and responses to it, Márquez Sterling went on to state that "every autocratic government is . . . suspicious: it fears the air, sound, and, more than anything, it fears the truth."¹⁸ Blunt and unforgiving, Márquez Sterling aimed to tell the "truth" and he took Díaz to task, recognizing his greatness, while also laying bare his faults. In contrast, the journalists Márquez Sterling worked with regularly spared Díaz and displaced their critique onto the hispanized Mexicans, who were seen as the true force of regression in the nation.

Hispanism and Anti-Hispanism in Late Nineteenth-Century Mexico

The journalists of *El Hijo del Ahuizote* were heirs to a nearly century-long tradition of anti-Hispanism that had been born in the Age of Revolution. The first half century of Spanish-Mexican relations after Mexico's independence was rocky. The Mexican independence war unleashed a torrent of anger against Spain, which culminated in the expulsion of Spaniards from the new republic in the mid to late 1820s. Meanwhile, in Europe, Spain refused to recognize the Mexican republic until 1836 and attempted to reconquer Mexico in the 1820s and 1830s.

Dreams of regaining its vast empire were definitively laid to rest in the early 1870s when Spain realized that healing relations with the republics of Latin America might be the key to holding onto its last few colonies. The late 1860s marked a major turning point in Spanish-Mexican relations. In 1868, the September Revolution in Spain brought the first Spanish Republic into being, but the new government was faced with an economic crisis and wars at home and abroad. The fledgling republican government sorely needed to cultivate friendly relations with former colonies.[19] By the same token, Mexico emerged in a weak state from the wars to oust the French, who had launched an invasion in 1861 that lasted until 1867. The French Intervention followed a decade of brutal civil war brought about by the conservative opposition to the mid-century liberal reform movement. With a dire economic situation on his hands in the late 1860s, the president of Mexico, Benito Juárez, saw concrete benefits to resolving Mexico's disputes with Spain and to beginning an era of mutually beneficial relations. The ideological alignment between Spain's republican revolution and Juárez's own republican movement—and the economic benefits deemed mutually advantageous—paved the way for the renewal of relations at the end of the 1860s. The price of the decision, however, was that Mexico, a nation whose elite and popular classes strongly favored Cuban independence, had to commit itself to a strict neutrality in relation to the conflict between Cuba and Spain. Díaz chose to continue the policy of pursuing a closer relationship to Spain while gradually and delicately distancing Mexico from Cuban independence during the 1870s and again in the 1890s.

The shift that Benito Juárez set in motion gave Spain the opportunity to fundamentally transform its relationship to Mexico. During the last decades of the nineteenth century, better relations led to a rise in Spanish immigration. Spanish immigration to Mexico grew significantly from the late nineteenth century through the early twentieth. In 1877 there were 6,400 Spaniards in Mexico; in 1895 there were 13,000; and by 1911 that number had increased to 29,500. The majority of these immigrants settled in Mexico City and Veracruz.[20] Though the immigrant population was small relative to the larger Mexican population, the Spanish immigrant community had a significant impact on Mexico due to its concentration in important economic sectors like banking, transportation, industry, mining, and commerce.[21] In addition, many Spanish immigrants married into wealthy Mexican families and thus tied themselves to the Porfirian elite.

The story of Telesforo García, a Spanish immigrant who became an important Porfirian statesman, offers a case in point. García migrated to Cuba as a young man in 1865 and started out with a humble job in a general store in Mexico City. He eventually married into a well-to-do Mexican family and had four children. Gradually, he became a successful journalist and then a businessman. During the 1860s, he was among the journalists who worked for *La Libertad*, a newspaper in which many of the ideas inherited by the famous Porfirian *científicos* were first articulated. In addition to securing a place in Mexican politics, García also became a prominent and powerful figure within the Spanish community.[22] His influential position in this community resulted from his involvement with the *Casino Español* in Mexico City. As vice-president and then president of this organization in the 1890s, García became one of the most outspoken defenders of the Spanish colonial cause. Perhaps the most important intellectual connection between men like Garcia and the Mexicans who were their intellectual compatriots was the firm belief that they were living a race war between Anglos and Latins. The shared concern over how best to counter the spread of Anglo-Saxon cultural imperialism formed the bedrock of an emerging *hispanismo*, or Hispanism, an ideology that advocated racial solidarity between members of a besieged Hispanic race. At times, this conception was expanded to include Portuguese America as well, and then it was termed *iberoamericanismo*, or Ibero-Americanism.

The roots of *hispanismo* can be found in Spain's nineteenth-century quest to recover its lost imperial glories. This quest became the cornerstone of Spanish nationalism.[23] Nineteenth-century Spanish elites understood Spain's overseas territories, or *La Espana Ultramarina*, as integral parts of the nation. Spanish historians argued that the Spanish conquest had either erased and replaced native populations—as in Cuba—or integrated those that survived into the Spanish nationality—as in Mexico.[24] As a result, Mexicans were fundamentally Hispanic, while Cubans were Spaniards.

Spain's rhetorical absorption of its former colonies into a greater Hispanic race and its existing colonies into the Spanish nation was driven by the desire to resist the depiction of Spain as an archaic imperial power. As historian Aimer Granados writes, "in the process of the construction of a Spanish national identity during the nineteenth century, the idea of the nation's imperial character appears as one of the most determining elements. . . . Spain wanted to be considered part of the group of nations belonging to the white 'race' that at the turn of the nineteenth century began to dominate the world."[25] If Spain was preoccupied with belonging to the "white race," it was also concerned with defining the differences between the Latin and Anglo races. Mexico, in particular, was seen as the optimum place to build pan-Hispanic solidarity in Latin America due to its geographical position in the Gulf World between Spain's last stronghold in the Americas and its archnemesis. Romana Falcón writes that "Mexico became somewhat symbolic for Spain. The country was seen as a possible bulwark against the advance of the Anglo Saxon race and the Protestant religion, which sought to displace the Latin Race and Catholicism. . . . The vestiges of imperial glory and the desire to recuperate past honors were also important for Spain."[26] Spaniards worked to reinterpret both Spanish colonialism in the Americas and the early nineteenth century independence wars, which eventually came to be seen as the natural rebellion of restless nations that had come of age. The new discourse, meant to draw Latin Americans and Spaniards together, was based on racial, religious, cultural, and linguistic similarities. Spain was to be honored as the bearer of civilization, not the root of Spanish America's postcolonial problems.[27]

The idea that the Spanish "nation" was a transnational, multiracial entity whose essence or spirit was unalterable was equally popular among liberals and conservatives in Spain during the 1880s and 1890s. The idea of the Spanish nation as a deterritorialized entity can be dated to the last third of the nineteenth century. Though several earlier histories of empire were published in Spain, the 1870s marked a shift in the attention paid to representing Spain's past. During the early years of the conservative restoration (1875–1923), Antonio Cánovas del Castillo spearheaded a search for the "true self of the nation."[28] Thus, well before the crisis of 1898, Spain had been constructing a master narrative of empire to serve the needs of nation building.

At the center of efforts to build Latin race consciousness was La Unión Iberoamericana, established in Madrid in the 1880s. La Unión quickly created sister organizations throughout Latin America and set about fostering Ibero-American solidarity. In Mexico, La Unión and the Casino Español, a social club dedicated to protecting the interests of the Spanish immigrant community, both worked to foment stronger connections between Mexicans and Spaniards. As soon as a new insurrection broke out in Cuba, a patriotic junta with branches in several smaller cities throughout the republic was organized within the Casino Español. The activities of the *juntas patrióticas* were similar to those of the Cuban political clubs in that they sent food and supplies to Spanish soldiers in Cuba and organized the Spanish community in Mexico around their cause. Between 1895 and 1898, it was virtually impossible for Spaniards to be unaware of or disinvested in the Cuban Question. Not only did the Spanish press report on Cuban affairs on a daily basis, but Cuba was a popular topic of conversation on the streets, in bars, and in places of work. Indeed, non-elite Spaniards became embroiled in the Cuban Question as it penetrated their daily lives. Between 1895 and 1898 the Cuban and Spanish migrant communities in Mexico battled each other for the attention and the sympathies of the Mexican people. The existence of two militantly active foreign communities in Mexico warring over an issue of such deep and enduring significance to Mexico and to Mexicans created endless conflicts in public and private spaces.

Understanding the development of Spanish-Mexican relations after 1872 and the rise of *hispanismo* is important to making sense of the profound and destructive psychic impact of the Cuban independence struggle on elite Spanish immigrants in Mexico in 1895, but it alone cannot explain why Mexicans and Spaniards came into constant conflict between 1895 and 1898 over the Cuban Question. Equally important is the way in which the Cuban Question exacerbated longstanding tensions and conflicts between Spaniards and Mexicans, especially between workers and bosses. For Spanish immigrants the cries of "long live Cuba" and the accompanying "death to Spain" challenged the fiction of unity and confraternity that Spaniards had begun to take for granted. But, for Mexican workers, these cries could represent an affirmation of their anger at exploitation suffered at the hands of Spanish bosses. The cries were heard in public venues from street corners to theaters and cafés and in places of work.

Scholars identify three distinct historical periods in the nineteenth and twentieth centuries in which postcolonial tensions between Spaniards and Mexicans reached critical levels. The immediate post-independence period (1821–1834) was a particularly important one as far as hispanophobia is concerned. Spain's reluctance to recognize Mexican independence and its repeated attempts to reconquer the island did little to repair relations between the two countries in the 1820s, and this period culminated in demands that Spaniards be expelled.[29] The second period in which anti-Spanish sentiment is considered to have been serious was the late 1860s, immediately after the defeat of Maximilian and the ousting of the French. Mexicans were not eager to cultivate relations with Spain or any European power that had recognized the ill-fated emperor. The third period marked by hispanophobia was the Mexican Revolution. Of the foreigners targeted during the Revolution, the Spanish constituted the majority (32 percent) of those expelled. Revolutionary leaders were quick to utilize anti-colonial discourse and invoke the rebellion of 1810 as a justification for the persecution of Spaniards in positions of power.[30] But Spanish-Mexican tensions also existed during the Porfiriato, despite the fact that this period is seen as one of amicability between Mexico and Spain.

Tensions between Spanish immigrants and Mexican citizens around questions of labor and exploitation were discernible in the 1840s and 1850s, as well as during the Porfiriato. Tracking the conflicts between Spanish proprietors and Mexican workers in the mid-nineteenth century, Romana Falcón analyzes violent altercations between these groups in Yucatán, Guerrero, and Morelos. She specifically notes the role that the modernization of agriculture played as workers and proprietors came into head-on conflict for land and water.[31] Other scholars have similarly explored the conflicts around labor between Spaniards and Mexicans in the Porfiriato. For example, conflicts erupted regularly between Mexican textile workers and Spanish bosses in Puebla during the later decades of the nineteenth century.[32] If Mexican workers suffering discrimination and unfair treatment at the hands of Spanish bosses expressed their anger through anti-Hispanism, it was because anti-Hispanist discourses were part of Mexican national culture. Despite the healing of relations between Mexico and Spain and the notable rise of Hispanism in the later nineteenth century, patriotic speeches delivered before large crowds on the yearly celebration of Mexican independence were ritually anti-Spanish in tenor.[33]

The outbreak of war in Cuba resulted in the exodus of revolutionaries and royalists from Cuba, many of whom arrived in Mexico. They brought with them their experiences and their resentments. Cubans and Spaniards on both sides of the independence question were constantly at odds, but as Mexicans found themselves drawn to one side or the other, the Hispano-

Cuban conflict became a vehicle for the expression of existing and historic tensions around the presence of Spanish immigrants in Mexico.

Mexican and Spanish newspapers meticulously tracked and commented on everyday conflicts that occurred in theaters, plazas, bars, and the workplace between supporters and opponents of Cuban independence. Although the majority of the encounters recorded in Mexican and Spanish newspapers occurred in Mexico City, Veracruz, and Puebla, Cuban letters and Spanish consular records indicate that alterations were commonplace in every Mexican city where Cubans and Spanish communities existed. Curiously, both Mexican and immigrant newspapers agreed that while Mexicans tended to incite conflict, it was Spaniards who were usually guilty of escalating confrontations. Spaniards most often justified their reactions as a defense of personal or national honor.[34] As Pablo Piccato has argued, Mexico in the late nineteenth century was in a moment of peace, so masculine honor was not being measured through military service; instead, it was made and defended in the public sphere. Mexican elites imagined themselves as fighting for the nation by giving it shape and direction, so they drew a close relationship between honor and patriotism.[35] So, too, did the Spanish in Mexico, who saw the defense of their personal honor as synonymous with the defense of the nation and attacks on the nation as a personal affront.

On 29 January 1897, a poor Mexican entered a Spanish-owned bar and, intending to goad the barman, asked for a "glass of free Cuba with Spanish tears." In a fit of rage, the owner leapt over the counter with his cheese knife and cut the Mexican across the ribs and face. A crowd immediately gathered outside the bar, and the police conducted both men to the local police station.[36] Conflicts in bars were exceedingly common. In two other instances, Mexicans who in casual and private conversation lauded Antonio Maceo were unexpectedly attacked by Spanish patrons in bars. Antonio Maceo's success as an insurgent general and his widespread popularity outside of Cuba made him an icon that Spaniards in Mexico targeted.

Mexicans knew that the best way to irritate Spaniards during the Cuban independence wars—besides celebrating the Afro-Cuban general Antonio Maceo—was to call out "Long live free Cuba!" This particular cry had a longer history in Mexico: it was uttered and printed often during the Ten Years' War (1868–1878) and can also be traced to the original early efforts toward Cuban independence in the 1820s. When a drunk Mexican yelled "Long live Cuba" to a group of Spaniards on the street in the summer of 1896, the Spaniards pursued him with the intention of attacking him. They were turned back by a group of local stonemasons who defended their compatriot. The Spaniards were forced to take refuge in a cigarette factory while the masons threw rocks at them. The *Diario del Hogar* reported this incident under the headline, "As in a conquered land." Referring to the incident, journalist José P. Rivera wrote that if the government didn't act quickly, tensions were running so high that a riot between Spaniards, Mexicans, and Cubans would surely erupt. Rivera blamed the Spaniards for exacerbating the situation and warned them to alter their conduct. "It is indispensable that Spaniards understand that patriotism cannot be expressed through brutality. . . . The Spanish colony like all other colonies here has both educated people and yokels. It falls upon the former to instruct the latter and make them understand that this is not a colonized country, but a nation that can and will exercise its rights."[37] Nevertheless, only two months later a fight broke out between two men drinking at the bar Doce de la Noche after one proclaimed a toast to *"Cuba Libre."* The Spanish owner of the bar was offended and proceeded to physically attack both men.[38] During the independence day celebrations in Mexico City in 1896, several Cubans called out "Long live free Cuba!" in a parade along with Mexicans who were calling "Long live Mexico!" Aimer Granados makes the point that it was common to hear *"Vivas!"* to Mexico as well as "death to Spain" on Independence Day. Spaniards particularly feared these celebrations, as often these cries were accompanied by a temporary resurrection of anti-Spanish feeling and at times resulted in vandalism.[39] Spaniards ritually boarded their windows on 15 and 16 September.

The Spanish paper *El Correo Español* also occasionally reported altercations around the Cuban Question. Curiously enough, they are not very different from those found in the Mexican pro-Cuban independence press. Spaniards usually complained that they had been verbally insulted by Mexicans and cited this as the prime reason for conflicts. On 8 April 1896, in an article entitled "Dangerous Intemperances," *El Correo Español* reported that "the *'Viva Cuba Libre'* that was emitted from the gallery at the Abreu theater, and that deserved the public protests of the Mexicans and Spaniards in attendance, was an attempt not only against the public order that all foreigners should respect, but also against a country that is a friend and ally of Mexico, a country that is currently fighting and making heroic sacrifices to maintain the integrity of its national territory and conserve a small part of the immense continent that it discovered and civilized."[40] Spanish journalists often emphasized the unique and privileged position that Spain enjoyed with regard to the Mexican government. They insisted that, due to their special status and to the fact that they brought civilization to Mexico, Spaniards should be protected from verbal assaults such as the one described above. By framing the Cuban independence struggle as a secessionist rebellion rather than as an anti-colonial movement, the journalists hoped to coax empathy from their readers for Spain's struggle to maintain national integrity.

There were other instances. On 15 September 1896, several Spaniards gathered in the Casino Español of Puebla to discuss and formulate a protest against the Mexicans and Cubans who had tried to raise the Cuban flag during an independence day parade and who had called out "*Muera España.*"[41] A few months earlier, on 29 May, a Spaniard reported overhearing a group of twenty-two Mexicans who worked for the Ferrocarril Mexicano, a Mexican railway company, lauding the Cuban insurgents and saying terrible things about Spain. The Spaniard who complained was told not to worry about these "scandalous drunks," but a Spanish journalist suggested that the man's concern was motivated by the fact that these individuals did not form part of the ignorant masses but were distinguished people. In chapter 4, we saw how a group of Mexican workers affiliated to the Ferrocarril Hidalgo made and publicized their financial donation to the Cuban cause. Clearly, not only railroad workers but even some of their bosses maintained a distinctly pro-Cuban and anti-Spanish stance.

Casting Spaniards as ideal, respectful immigrants and contrasting them with Cuban migrants in Mexico, another *El Correo Español* journalist described a scandal that occurred on the street in Mexico City in the following terms: "a group of Cuban separatists, the kind who come here to fight for Cuban independence in the bars and theaters of Mexico, started to publicly insult Spain and the Spanish while also praising free Cuba." A Spaniard who was offended by this spectacle reacted, and the police were forced to intervene.[42] On 26 May 1896, a few Spaniards in Querétaro threatened to take matters into their own hands if the foreign minister did not take seriously their complaint about an offensive article published in a local paper. In a letter they wrote, "If this incident were ignored, we would be forced to resort to actions that, up until now, we have avoided."[43] On another occasion, Spaniards in Progreso overheard that a newly formed Cuban political club had convened for the express purpose of insulting Spain. The Spanish consul hurriedly reported that "they had agreed to go to Progreso that day so that if the Cubans did something to offend Spain . . . they could take justice into their own hands and dissolve the meeting."[44] The consul's reports to the minister reveal his concern about the escalation of violence and about the aggressiveness of their own citizens.

The reports of the Spanish foreign minister betray a similar concern. He worked to contain these passions and to preserve the image of Spanish immigrants as hard- working and law-abiding. The Spaniards causing trouble were not the wealthy Spanish members of the Casino Español who formed part of the Porfirian elite, but middle-class journalists, small-business owners, and workers. Local Spanish immigrants were demanding that the minister, José Brunetti y Gayoso, intervene to defend their honor, and the Spanish secretary of state and the Unión Iberoamericana also pressured the minister to be more aggressive in his efforts to defend Spain's national interests in Mexico.

On 6 November 1895, Brunetti received a circular from the Unión Ibero-americana urging him to demand that Mexican authorities demonstrate their support for the Spanish cause: "The time has come for the expressions of mutual sympathy between Spain and the Latin nations to move beyond publications and speeches, and include pressuring governments to curb certain kinds of demonstrations. [We hope that we can] cooperate so that the [Cuban] ingrates become disillusioned, and to avoid the possibility that foreign elements try to ruin us in order to take over countries that they will never be able to dominate."[45] The Cuban independence war marked a shift in the kind of commitment the Unión Ibero-americana expected from its sister organizations in Latin America. It was time to move from discursive support to more tangible and concrete expressions of solidarity. In the minds of Spaniards, the Cuban conflict offered Latin Americans with whom they had cultivated strong ties an opportunity to demonstrate their loyalty to Spain. Furthermore, at a moment when "foreign elements" like the United States threatened to establish dominance over the hemisphere, it was imperative that the Latin American republics join with Spain to help crush Cuban independence. The key role of Spanish immigrants throughout the Americas was to reinforce the bonds between Spain and Latin American republics by stopping insurgents from gaining any support from surrounding nations.

Only a few months before Brunetti received the circular from the Unión Ibero-americana, the minister of state in Spain had written to him ordering that he practice strict vigilance over Cubans and try to encourage the Mexican government to restrict Cuban activities. The minister was skeptical that Mexican laws, which he thought were excessively liberal, would permit the federal government to repress these public expressions of solidarity with Cuba, but he still recommended that Brunetti try to work within the Mexican penal code to deter Cubans from collecting funds for the movement. The foreign minister promptly organized a meeting with Ignacio Mariscal, the Mexican secretary of foreign relations, and obtained from him total assurance that Mexican authorities would do what they could to cooperate with him. Both the President and his ministers supported and were willing to aid Brunetti—so long as the efforts remained unofficial.

During the course of the 1895 War, Brunetti used Mexican policemen to surveil Cuban activities in various areas of the Republic. Where possible, he assigned spies to infiltrate Cuban organizations. On at least three occasions, first in Mexico City and then in Puebla and Mérida, he used his connections to stop Cubans from celebrating public events commemorating their struggle. The foreign minister's letters to his superior also reveal his concern that Cubans might launch filibustering expeditions to Cuba or aid expeditions coming from the United States that passed along the Mexican Gulf Coast. Brunetti was constantly in communication with his consuls in Progreso, Mérida, and Veracruz in an effort to make sure that any such attempts were thwarted. In a report to the governor of Cuba just two months after the outbreak of the war, Brunetti expressed his concern about Yucatan: "the great distance that separates it from this capital and the few lines of communication between them make it very difficult to be informed about what goes on there. On the other hand, its proximity to the island of Cuba and the fact that among the Cuban residents are veterans from the past war makes me think that they may be planning to join this one."[46] The minister assured the governor of Cuba that he was working closely with the governor of the state to impede Cuban activities.

The foreign minister's crusade against the Cuban solidarity movement was focused on the Cuban and Mexican press. On 9 January 1896 he wrote to the minister in Spain expressing his concern about the circulation of false information: "You will have noticed that since last Christmas, there has been a notable increase in the transmission of false news referring to Cuba fabricated in the Cuban revolutionary juntas. The falseness of this information is obvious to the sensible reader, but not to the common man, who takes to it eagerly the more exaggerated it is. This constant propagation of myths does us harm. Even if this news is immediately repudiated, it still has an effect and leaves traces."[47] The minister recognized the importance of public opinion and was deeply concerned about the "myths that do hurt us." Sensationalist news was the culprit, leading the "common man" to engage in violent confrontations on the streets of Mexico. These altercations drew negative attention to the Spanish community. Indeed, during 1896 and 1897, Mexican and Spanish newspapers reported dozens of aggressive confrontations between Mexicans, Spaniards, and Cubans in public spaces, many of which ended in violence. Altercations ranged from the shouting of obscenities to the destruction of property to defamation in the press and physical assaults on persons. In 1897, one observer noted that "conflicts on the streets and in theaters and cafes" over the Cuban Question had become commonplace.[48] The minister was sensitive to the fact that the Cuban cause was resurrecting old animosities and anti-colonial sentiments that had been put to rest. Eager to preserve the goodwill that had been painstakingly constructed during the 1880s and 1890s, Brunetti dug in his heels and looked for any opportunity to discredit and silence those propagating a negative image of Spain.

On 4 February 1897, Brunetti noted the following in a letter to the Spanish minister of state: "As I have reported to you on other occasions, a certain part of the press of this capital, Cuban papers and those who sympathize with the cause, have repeatedly published articles harmful to Spain and her government. It has not been possible to charge and punish them in the courts. Until now, I had not deemed it necessary or prudent to file an official complaint because the intentions of the publications were not entirely clear and I wanted to avoid being rebuffed."[49] The pro-Cuba newspaper that most irritated and preoccupied the Spanish minister was *El Continente Americano*, a student paper published in Mexico City. Curiously, the newspaper itself had been the cause of numerous physical confrontations between Mexicans, Cubans, and Spaniards. For example, on 7 March and 11 November 1897, two vendors of the paper *El Continente Americano*, one in Veracruz and one in Guanajuato, were attacked by Spaniards. In both cases the attacks were motivated by the visual representation of the Cuban insurgent flag. The vendor in Veracruz was selling an issue of *El Continente Americano* that bore colorful painted images of the Cuban and Puerto Rican flags. The vendor in Guanajuato proudly wore a button with the Cuban flag on his lapel.

In two other instances copies of the newspaper were confiscated and torn apart by Spaniards. On 18 March 1897, a man in Chihuahua left an issue of the paper on his desk only to find upon his return that a Spaniard who worked in the same store had torn it to shreds. In Zacatelco, Tlaxcala, a group of workers were left to face an even more disturbing scene. Their issue of *El Continente Americano* was torn up and symbolically placed underneath a plate of beans and a wooden spoon. In a letter to a local authority, which was subsequently published in *El Continente Americano*, the workers speculated as to the meaning of this gesture:

> We do not understand what they mean to convey with this gesture. . . . Do they do it to throw our misery in our faces, the misery that through the education we received from them in the disgraceful colonial period and that now we suffer in the form of their systems of usury and their *tiendas de raya*? Or, perhaps they are trying to tell us that the sons of the nascent Cuban republic are hungry. In that case, Cubans could say the same as us and with more reason, considering that they have suffered under the corrupt and opprobrious tutelage of the Spanish throne longer than we did. Have they done this with the intension of offending the editors of *El Continente Americano*?[50]

In two of the explanations they offer, the workers blamed the Spaniards for their misery and for that of the Cubans, connecting the two anti-colonial struggles and collapsing historical time. Their poverty, they reasoned, could be traced back to the Spanish colonial period, just as the current colonial regime was to blame for the Cubans' suffering.

However, the workers were motivated by current as well as historical factors. Not only were the Spanish responsible for the historical circumstances that resulted in the workers' state, but their systems of usury and "*tiendas de raya*" also oppressed the workers. While elite Mexicans and Spaniards had found common ideological ground in *hispanismo* in the later nineteenth century, poor migrants and the Mexicans they came into contact with did not share that sentiment. Solidarity with *Cuba Libre* proved to be a way for working-class Mexicans to express resentments against Spanish immigrants. The fact that one of the signatures on the above-quoted letter was that of a worker assigned to take up collections for Bravo y Maceo, the principal Cuban club in Puebla, is evidence of the connections between Cuban and Mexican workers who were making common cause against different scales of oppression.

Some issues of *El Continente Americano* were stolen or shredded, and some were symbolically burned. On 7 January 1897, in Puebla, a group of Spaniards publicly burned the issue of the paper that featured a life-size portrait of the Cuban insurgent general Antonio Maceo. Under the title "Hazaña Quijotesca," *El Continente Americano* reproduced a scathing report from *La Revista de Puebla* describing the incident:

> At about 9:20 P.M. on Wednesday night, the honorable Spaniards Ricardo Landa, Matías Barrios and Félix Martínez, inflamed with the fire of . . . patriotism, committed an enormous act, worthy only of

very courageous *PELAYOS* . . . that night these young men burned an image of Maceo published by *El Continente Americano* in the central plaza! . . . While Maceo was alive they trembled at the mention of his name, and now that he is dead . . . those who would say nothing when he lived, insult his memory . . . let those three know that they have not succeeded in offending this venerable soldier, because even as his image was being burned, it emitted brilliant flashes of light that blinded them.[51]

In this report, the Spaniards are referred to as *"pelayos,"* a term which, like *gachupín*, suggests that they are crazed imperialists. Don Pelayo was an eighth-century nobleman who is seen as the initiator of the reconquest of Spain. The act of tearing up Maceo's image here is presented as a cowardly act by crazed and irrational men.

El Continente Americano became a focal point of Spanish attacks because it was the most visible symbol of Mexican solidarity with *Cuba Libre*. While Spanish immigrants burned, shredded, and stole copies of the newspaper, the Spanish foreign minister was determined to persecute and punish the student journalists. Following the advice of the Spanish minister of state, the foreign minister looked for any legal infraction he might use to denounce the student journalists. On 4 February 1897, Brunetti wrote to his superior stating that he had found the perfect opportunity to denounce the newspaper. On two occasions, *El Continente Americano* reported that it had gathered funds to "aid and foment the Cuban revolution." According to the minister, this was a clear infraction of international law, and he was determined to capitalize on this journalist's carelessness.[52] Brunetti immediately reported this blatant violation of the neutrality agreement to the Mexican minister of foreign relations, Ignacio Mariscal. After he was shown the evidence in the newspaper, Mariscal agreed that, indeed, a violation had been committed. He took it upon himself to present the minister of justice with the case. Frustrated, the Spanish minister wrote to his superior on 7 May, noting that his denunciation "has remained suspended." This was not surprising given that the Díaz administration resisted directly harassing Cuban migrants or intervening with their activities, as long as they maintained a low profile. But Brunetti was so concerned about the delay that he called for a meeting with Porfirio Díaz on the matter. Par for the course, Díaz made his usual "friendly declarations and offerings," but did not give the minister any real assurance that his denunciation would come to anything. Unsatisfied, Brunetti immediately called on Mariscal again. The minister of foreign relations broke the dispiriting news that not one clause could be found in the penal code that could be applied to the director of *El Continente Americano*. But Mariscal assured the minister that "it was not over." He told Brunetti that he was sure that there was some lawful way these journalists could be punished and that if the Spanish minister so much as heard rumor of another infraction, he should bring it to Mariscal's attention right away.[53]

A perfect opportunity to attack *El Continente Americano* presented itself sooner than the minister could have expected. In late April, the newspaper's director Daniel M. Islas published an article in which he allegedly insulted none other than Don Telesforo García, the Spanish immigrant and longtime close collaborator of the Díaz regime. García, no doubt in consultation with the Spanish foreign minister, lost no time in denouncing Islas for defamation. The director of the paper was charged with the crime and confined in the prison of Belem in Mexico City, a common destination for journalists who ran afoul of the regime. The key to the successful attack on the student newspaper was a change in the procedure for prosecution of crimes against honor, such as defamation and calumny. Before 1883, crimes committed in the press were tried by popular jury but, afterward they were transferred to the tribunal of public rights.[54] As a result, journalists were more effectively prosecuted and more severely punished. This legal change paved the way for the persecution of the opposition press during the later Porfiriato. As the Díaz regime became more entrenched, the government increasingly repressed the independent press and financed publications dedicated to reporting "objective" news. Government-subsidized newspapers like *El Imparcial* were able to print thousands of daily issues, while smaller papers were squeezed out. Daniel Cosío Villegas argues that though there is not much evidence that Porfirio Díaz was directly responsible for the campaign against the independent opposition press at the turn of the century, it is clear that his ministers were and that they did not act without his consent.[55] The collaboration between Brunetti and Mariscal is just one example of the way in which the Díaz administration's repressive practices could be exploited by Spanish representatives in Mexico for mutual gain. The Spanish curbed the Cuban movement and the Mexican state's critics were simultaneously discouraged and suppressed.

The staff of *El Continente Americano* were not the only Mexican journalists persecuted at the behest of Spanish immigrants. Samuel G. Avila, of San Luis Potosí, recounted how in February of 1897 three policemen on the night shift came to his home and hauled him off to prison, where he was held for four days without knowing the charges brought against him. Later he discovered that several Spaniards had denounced him for being the author of a pamphlet calling for an attack on Spanish business, which he insisted he did not author.

In November of that same year, José Agustín Escudero of Ciudad Lerdo, Durango, a Mexican journalist and Cuban independence sympathizer, wrote a letter to Tomás Estrada Palma complaining that the "powerful Spanish community . . . dominates everything and takes every opportunity to make life difficult for me." The local Spaniards shut down the only printing press in the city, making it impossible for him to publish his articles in support of Cuban independence. The day before Escudero wrote his letter to Estrada Palma, the *Jefe Político* of Ciudad Lerdo came to his house demanding that he stop printing a small local newspaper in which he publicized his views on Cuba, because the governor, presumably in league with local Spaniards, opposed it. In his letter to Estrada Palma, however, Escudero was defiant: "the people are with me. No one can challenge the influence that I have here. Every time an issue of my paper is printed, it is sold out immediately and this infuriates the *gachupines*."[56]

On 19 May 1897, *El Correo Español* republished a letter from local Spaniards in Matamoros. "Mr. Director of the Correo Español. The courts have processed your denunciation. The *Estrella Solitaria* has ceased publication. The press has been decommissioned due to the crime. The publishers are now fugitives. The law pursues them."[57] This must have been music to the ears of *El Correo Español*'s directorship, since the paper was involved in the formal denunciation of the pro-Cuban independence newspaper, the *Estrella Solitaria de Matamoros*. In an urgent letter, the founders of the *Estrella Solitaria*, Ireneo H. Rodríguez and José A. Demastini, wrote to Tomás Estrada Palma in New York, informing him of their predicament. Referring to local Spaniards, they stated that "the Spaniards who reside in this port . . . did their best to persecute us, going as far as bribing a judge to apprehend us, incarcerate us and decommission the press where we published *La Estrella Solitaria*. Once in jail, they tried to offer us money if we discontinued our activities. All of this made us more angry. As a result, we were tried for slander and we stayed in jail suffering the fury of that evil race that achieves everything through money."[58]

These cases of repression and intimidation all reflect similar dynamics and follow an almost identical pattern. Several journalists, all fervent supporters of Cuban independence, were persecuted for publishing articles critical of the Spanish cause or the Spanish immigrant community in

Mexico. In each case, it was prominent Spanish immigrants who had pro-Cuban journalists in Mexico City, Matamorros, and San Luis Potosó jailed, and who harassed José Agustín Escudero, costing him his job and livelihood. What is clear in all cases, however, is that there was close collaboration between Mexican and Spanish authorities in the repression of Mexican journalists.

Despite the minister's tireless efforts to discourage Cubans determined to support and supply the war effort, expeditions still weighed anchor and refueled at remote ports along the Yucatán peninsula, arms were still gathered, volunteers were still recruited, and financial contributions were still made. And, despite persecutions and denunciations aimed at quelling the Cuban solidarity movement, tensions between Mexicans, Cubans, and Spaniards continued to escalate as the Hispano-Cuban conflict wore on. It was precisely this escalation that motivated one Mexican conservative intellectual call for a public debate about the Cuban Question in the summer of 1897.

Mexican Conservative Liberals and Cuban Independence

The rise of *hispanismo* in Mexico during the later nineteenth century was the result of the growing alignment between Mexico and Spain, but Mexican conservatives had long been proponents of Mexico's Hispanic heritage and defenders of colonialism as a civilizing force that was at the root of Mexican culture. They had also long been enemies of the United States and its seemingly insatiable imperialist appetite. However, after the liberal restoration in Mexico in 1867, traditional conservative politics was fundamentally discredited. The politics of reconciliation, begun under Juárez and perfected under Díaz, which aimed at bringing political extremes together, gave the conservatives some room to reenter politics. Reconciliation politics is one factor that contributed to the attenuation of radical liberalism and the emergence of conservative liberalism in late nineteenth-century Mexico. Indeed, the conservative ideological alignment between Spaniards and Mexicans of the late nineteenth century was not an alignment between traditional conservatives in both countries, but between self-proclaimed liberals on both sides of the Atlantic. The intimate friendship between the liberal Spanish immigrant Telesforo Garcia and the Spanish statesmen Emilio Castelar is a case in point.[59] Garcia and his Mexican *cientifico* collaborators admired Castelar, who, although he began his political career as a staunch republican, became disillusioned with the fate of the republic in

Spain after the 1868 liberal Revolution. By the early 1870s, Castelar's politics had shifted, and he became a supporter of the restored monarchy who condoned strong, centralized, authoritarian government. Like Porfirian political elites, Castelar believed that the key to modernization in Spain and Latin America was political stability at any costs. As under the Porfiriato, the restored monarchy in Spain mercilessly repressed dissidents and workers in the interest of maintaining order.

While José Brunetti y Gayoso was busy persecuting pro-independence journalists with the tacit support of Mexican state, a prominent Mexican hispanist took on the Cuban solidarity movement from another angle. During the summer of 1897, Carlos Olaguíbel y Arista, Mexican Federal Deputy and longtime collaborator with the Díaz government, decided that something had to be done to quell the Cuban solidarity movement in Mexico. He agreed with the Spanish foreign minister that support for *Cuba Libre* had heightened tensions between Mexicans and Spaniards to unacceptable levels. These tensions did not only play themselves out in the streets, they also affected Mexican intellectuals and statesmen who came into conflict over the issue, and that threatened a central tenant of the Porfirian program: reconciliation politics itself. Olaguíbel decided that the only way to resolve these disputes was to subject the Cuban independence struggle to rigorous scientific study. He hoped that elevating the Cuban Question to the level of scientific inquiry might help quell the passions that were provoking such disorder on the streets of Mexico and igniting similarly passionate and emotional debates in its newspapers.[60]

During the 1890s, Carlos Olaguíbel y Arista wrote extensively on the Cuban Question, and his published articles illuminate the ways that Porfirian statesmen justified the decision to uphold a neutrality that was de facto pro-Spanish. Olaguíbel stood apart from most other Porfirian elites, who were uncomfortable expressing outright opposition to Cuba's struggle even if they believed Cuban independence to be antithetical to Mexico's national interests. Even Mexican statesmen who sympathized with the Cuban cause, like the influential politician Justo Sierra, were cautious in their speech. For example, at an event commemorating the recently assassinated Spanish prime minister in 1897, Sierra stated that "without any possible hatred for Spain, our [sentiments] are on the side of those who fight as we fought, and suffer as we suffered."[61] Although the statement conveys support for the insurgents, Sierra offered nothing more concrete than sentiments, and his sentiments are qualified by the insistence that he bore "no possible hatred for Spain." The responses to Sierra's comment varied widely. Traditional liberals and Cuban independence supporters were incensed that he articulated such benign feelings about Spain, while Spaniards were horrified that such a prominent politician had expressed solidarity with the insurgents. Sierra's attempts to express both affinity for Spain and solidarity with Cuba reflected the kind of balancing act the Díaz regime was also attempting in its Cuba policy. Unlike Sierra's, Olaguíbel's writings constitute an unusually clear and analytical study of the Cuban Question.

Carlos Olaguíbel y Arista's intellectual trajectory reflects the growing conservatism of the Díaz regime at the end of the century. He formed part of the *La Libertad* group, alongside Telesforo García and Justo Sierra. The government-subsidized *La Libertad* newspaper, which ran from 1878 to 1884, was their platform. Olaguíbel was responsible for introducing some of the more important themes taken up by *La Libertad*. Among them were the reconciliation of conservatives and liberals, the idea that social problems should be met with practical solutions, and the primacy of order, peace, and economic advancement.[62]

Olaguíbel worked for the government in some capacity for over twenty years. Between 1886 and 1907, he served as a federal deputy for the states of Guanajuato, Guerrero, and Hidalgo.[63] In 1893, Olaguíbel, who had already begun to gravitate toward more politically conservative positions, came out strongly in opposition to a reform bill proposed by his colleague and fellow *La Libertad* journalist Justo Sierra. The bill, which called for life tenure for federal judges, was aimed at curbing the power of the executive. Olaguíbel rejected Sierra's attempts to limit executive authority on the grounds that a strong state was the only answer to a number of social problems in Mexico.

Olaguíbel's position on the Cuban Question was intimately connected to his more conservative criticisms of the 1893 reform proposal. For example, Olaguíbel believed in strong, centralized executive authority, regardless of the form of government. In fact, he argued that a good constitutional monarchy was as capable of offering stability and guaranteeing rights as any republic. "In our times, the word monarchy is no longer a synonym of despotism," he argued. "Today's constitutional monarchies . . . guarantee as many liberties . . . as the best democratic republics can assure."[64] The Spanish constitutional monarchy was a perfect example in his opinion. Spaniards enjoyed the rights to freedom of press and association, as well as the right to universal suffrage. He argued that the Spanish parliament accommodated all political parties, which were invited to express their ideas freely even if they were not in accordance with the monarchy. The Spanish constitution of 1876 was widely considered one of the most liberal constitutions in Europe at the time, he insisted. What was most important, Olaguíbel contended, was not the form of government so much as the efficiency of institutions and their ability to ensure political rights and promote progress.⁶⁵

Eager to test his ideas about Cuba against those of a fellow intellectual who had professed open support for the Cuban insurgency, Carlos Olaguíbel y Arista challenged Francisco Bulnes, a politician, journalist, and orator who was a known Cuban independence sympathizer, to a debate on the Cuban Question. In late April of 1897, the two men met in the offices of their mutual friend and respected colleague Telesforo García to discuss the logistics of the debate. Incidentally, García was at that very moment embroiled in the denunciation of the student journalists of *El Continente Americano*. The debate would take the form of a series of articles that were to be published in the *Correo Español*, the Spanish community's leading paper. Four debate questions were drafted, all geared to examining the Cuban independence movement with a special focus on what the debaters referred to as the "American political criteria" and Mexico's interests therein.⁶⁶ Much of the debate about the Cuban insurrection up until 1897 had centered on the interests and rights of Spain or the United States, but the central purpose of this debate was to explore how the Cuban independence struggle would affect Mexico. The four questions that the debaters and moderators agreed on were the following:

1. Are there any real similarities between the emancipation of Mexico and the Cuban independence project?
2. If Cuba were to obtain its independence, would it have the elements necessary to constitute a nation worthy of figuring among the other Hispanic-American nations?
3. Can Mexico, given its patriotic determination to conserve its own territory, sympathize with revolutions whose objectives are to dismember national territories?
4. Would it benefit Mexico for Cuba to gain its independence from Spain? The framing of the questions show clearly that regardless of which side they were on, pro-Cuban and pro-Spanish Mexicans agreed that the outcome of the Cuban independence war would be consequential for Mexico.

Shortly before the debate was to have occurred, Francisco Bulnes decided that, since the war seemed to be coming to a close—the insurgents enjoyed an advantageous position in the late spring and early summer of 1897—a debate was no longer very useful. Olaguíbel accepted Bulnes's decision, but he disagreed that the debate was no longer relevant. In fact, he believed that the Cuban conflict contained critical lessons for Mexico's future. So, he went ahead and published his opinions on the four questions in four short articles. Once Olaguíbel's articles appeared, Bulnes felt obliged to respond. He wrote a response, which *El Correo Español* refused to publish, but which *El Continente Americano* printed. The article departed radically from the debate format and was a vituperative, passionate, and unrestrained critique of Spain. During the summer of 1897, the debate became a singular obsession of many Mexico City journalists and statesmen, who argued over the core issues brought up by the debaters in numerous articles.

While Bulnes's response and the exchanges that ensued are fascinating, Olaguíbel's original engagement with the debate questions provides great insight into the ideological underpinnings of Porfirian neutrality. We can see a Porfirian imprint in everything, from the desire to subject the question to scientific study, to the interest in wresting the issue from the liberal and conservative parties driven by passions and ideologies, to the actual substance of the arguments, which apply a uniquely conservative/liberal logic to the analysis of the Cuban struggle.

In the first of four articles, Olaguíbel struck at the heart of solidarity with *Cuba Libre* by criticizing the idea that the Cuban and Mexican independence struggles were connected struggles, a fundamental assumption of the Cuban solidarity movement. There were only three instances in which a nation could legitimately fight for its independence, he argued. In the first case, a conquering civilization takes control of a foreign society, but does not exterminate the existing indigenous population, which then claims its right to throw off its foreign colonizers. In the second, the conquering society intermarries with the conquered people and produces a new social organism that is assimilated totally or partially by the conquerors, but then eventually desires independence. In the third case, the conquerors take control of an unpopulated land or a land where the native population dies out, settles the land with its own kind, and then subjects them to unfair and unequal laws, which stokes the flames of independence among the creoles.

In the case of the Mexican independence struggle (1810–1822), the Spanish *conquistadores* intermarried with an existing indigenous civilization in Mexico. The product of these unions, the *mestizo*, carried both Spanish and indigenous blood, and constituted a new social organism. "The conquest . . .

gave birth to a new ethnic and social entity that was the product of the union between the *conquistadores* and the women of the conquered people . . . with time [the offspring] would aspire to dominate . . . arguing that their rights were based on the ancient rights of the race of their mothers."[67] This new social group retained the originary rights of the native inhabitants but also possessed the virility and drive of the Spanish race, a drive that would inspire them to claim their independence.

The Cuban case, however, presented an entirely different situation. All the native population in Cuba was killed off or wiped out by disease, leaving the island populated only by Spaniards and the slaves they brought with them. According to Olaguíbel, no intermarriage took place, and therefore no "new ethnic product who in the political realm can claim the rights of the ancient inhabitants" was created. "The group . . . of the Iberian family that occupies the island of Cuba is the product of Spain . . . [and] has never been subjected to foreign domination," he insisted. Olaguíbel saw no legitimate group in Cuba that could claim autochthonous rights to the land, a fact that rendered any parallel between Cuban independence and Mexican independence false and unfounded. Lastly, Olaguíbel argued that Cuba could not claim to be held as a colony of Spain but was rather an integral part of the nation—and its inhabitants Spanish citizens.

Olaguíbel found further evidence of the illegitimacy of the Cuban's claims in his contention that they would be fundamentally unfit to govern and sustain an independent state. In his second article, Carlos Olaguíbel y Arista argued that the conflict was the result of a series of mistakes made by the Spanish. He identified three key mistakes. The first occurred at the level of the most intimate family dynamics and was common to all Hispanic American republics. Olaguíbel believed that Spaniards who came to the Americas and worked hard to amass their fortunes generally made the fatal mistake of not requiring their sons to follow in their footsteps. Spanish fathers wanted their sons to enjoy the advantages of their class position, encouraging them to pursue literary careers, which they seldom finished, as they did not feel the slightest bit of urgency. Ironically, Spanish fathers alienated their sons from power by not helping them to acquire the skills and knowledge necessary to maintain it. These sons then swelled the ranks of a disgruntled middle class, which Olaguíbel felt was the single greatest threat to the state. The middle class bore the dubious privilege of being intellectually savvy enough to fuel its ambitions to power, while also lacking the skills necessary to realize its desires. This paradoxical situation led the middle class to express its frustration in the political arena, inspiring revolutionary plots and rebellious movements like the revolutionary insurrection in the case of Cuba.

The problem of estranged and wayward youth was one that Mexican intellectuals and educators were concerned with in the later nineteenth century as well. Both the Juárez and the Porfirian administrations dedicated significant attention to education. Charles Hale has observed that positivism made its first appearances in Mexico around the founding of the National Preparatory school in 1869. The school's founder, Gabino Barreda, sought to institute a universal curriculum geared to the sciences. The five-year program introduced students to mathematics, astronomy, physics, chemistry, natural history, and logic. Barreda was interested, above all, in developing the students' capacities for observation and experimentation. He was convinced that this sort of education would create a new elite fit to modernize the nation. Barreda and other positivists believed that the greatest threat to social order was anarchy. Intellectual anarchy, he reasoned, could be controlled by a carefully crafted education system which would be the key to fomenting social reconstruction in Mexico.[68]

Although Olaguíbel believed that Mexico suffered from the Spanish misguidance of its youth under colonialism, but the consequences of this error were being borne out in Cuba with particular vengeance. Olaguíbel believed that the Cuban middle class's desire for power outweighed its ability to maintain it. Therefore, if it succeeded in unseating the colonial elite, the nation would be plummeted into disarray. The ultimate nightmare of the Porfirian elite was that Mexico might succumb once again to the cycles of revolution and instability that marked the first two-thirds of the century. Olaguíbel believed that Mexican supporters of Cuban independence were a perfect example of the sort of middle-class element that worked against the state. Rather than see middle-class Mexican supporters of *Cuba Libre* as ill-intentioned revolutionaries, however, he depicted them as misguided liberals. Mexican advocates of Cuban independence shared an affinity for metaphysical politics and abstract ideals with their Cuban counterparts. It was not the threat of revolution that Olaguíbel feared, but the Cubans' impractical visions of republicanism, egalitarianism, and democracy, which he believed were anathema to modernity and progress in Cuba as well as Mexico and therefore could threaten stability. A weak nation would be vulnerable to external threats. Paramount among them were the misguided Mexican supporters of *Cuba Libre*, whom he avidly criticized.

The second of the three mistakes that Spanish elites in Cuba made, according to Olaguíbel, was even greater than the first. Having already alienated their sons from power, Spaniards encouraged them to stray from their race by regularly sending them to be educated in the United States. Somewhat similar to his discussion of race in the first article, here Olaguíbel focused on the largely cultural differences between the Anglo and Latin races. Olaguíbel argued that U.S. influence was damaging to members of the Latin race. In particular, he fastened on the idea that North American political institutions were not applicable in Latin America. Cuban youths who returned from the north filled with an admiration of U.S.-style republicanism, or what he terms "the most delirious Jacobinism," were a grave danger to the island.[69] Modern day "Jacobins," like their French counterparts, were understood to be individuals who couldn't conceive of social change without a state of chronic upheaval. According to Olaguíbel, their motto was "save the principles and let the world go to waste."[70] While adherence to abstract principles may have worked to create a modern democratic society in the United States, Olaguíbel believed, as did many Porfirians, that similar attempts in Latin America would fail.

The concerted efforts on the part of Cuban insurgents to obtain official recognition from the United States did not come as a surprise to supporters of the Spanish cause like Olaguíbel. After all, the independence movement itself was organized in the north by the Cuban Revolutionary Party in exile. Furthermore, the strength of the annexationist platform during and before the Ten Years' War gave Spaniards and their supporters every reason to fear that Cuban insurgents had annexationist intentions. After dividing the insurgents into two camps—the *independentistas* and the annexationists—Olaguíbel argued that the former were the least fit to govern, given their lofty and impractical ideas, whereas the latter were more shrewd and less idealistic. He surmised that, so divided, Cuba's political elite would have little chance of maintaining control of the country after independence. The ensuing anarchy would give North Americans the perfect opportunity to increase their influence in Cuba. Just as the island had been a strategic point from which the Spanish had extended their influence in the Americas earlier in the century, he argued, so might Cuba serve the same purpose for the United States.

The third grave mistake that the Spanish made in Cuba was the recognition of Afro-Cubans as citizens with rights. Though laudable for its humanism, Olaguíbel argued that emancipation and the granting of rights to liberated slaves was an act of purely "metaphysical" politics. The freeing of the slaves had not only fed the insurrection, but the allocation of rights had emboldened black Cubans, adding a third element to the contest for power. If Spain were defeated, Cuban blacks, who he argued were less civilized due to the fact that many were recently arrived from Africa, would also enter the struggle for power along with whites. Divided, white Cubans would not be able to defeat the ex-slaves and would have to appeal to international support to maintain their position. This would offer the United States the perfect excuse to intervene. In this argument, Olaguíbel sounds remarkably similar to the early nineteenth-century Mexican conservative statesman Lucas Alamán, who stymied the efforts of Mexico's York Rite masons when they attempted to incite slave insurrection in Cuba to foment independence. Alamán argued that a black uprising in Cuba would bring about U.S. intervention. Olaguíbel's discussion also reflects debates surrounding abolition in Spain and the colonies earlier in the century. Spanish and Antillean conservatives held up the specter of anarchy and black rebellion in order to make a case against abolition. They were convinced that, in addition to race conflict, abolition would cause a decline in Spain's prosperity. On the other side, liberal abolitionists in Spain and in the colonies used antislavery to undermine conservatives on both sides of the Atlantic. They asserted that abolition would strengthen rather than debilitate Spain's hold on the colonies by gaining the loyalties of disgruntled sectors and "undercutting the appeal" of the independence movement. As it turned out, both were wrong. Abolition neither reduced Spain's prosperity nor did it secure its colonies.[71]

As we have seen, the idea that newly-freed Afro-Cubans would try to wrest power from white Cubans and bring about another "Haiti" was an idea that had been mobilized by the Spanish to frighten white Cubans into supporting Spanish colonial rule since the beginning of the century. Unlike many Spaniards, however, Olaguíbel was not afraid that Afro-Cubans would take over the nation, but that such instability would play into the hands of the United States. He saw a parallel problem in Mexico's endemic native uprisings. Between the 1840s and 1880s, there were a number of significant rebellions by indigenous groups, including the caste wars in Yucatán (which were not put down until 1905), Indian raids on the northern frontier, and Manuel Lozada's guerrilla movement in Jalisco. The rebellions themselves were put down forcefully, but the fear of indigenous uprising lingered. Hale notes that a member of the *La Libertad* newspaper's staff, writing in 1878, expressed his concern that Indians ultimately strove to destroy the white race.[72] Olaguíbel was not so concerned that native rebellions in Mexico or

Afro-Cuban ambitions in Cuba would challenge the power of governing elites, but he felt that the threat these kinds of rebellions made to political stability was worrisome.

Olaguíbel argued that Spain had dug its own grave in Cuba by disempowering its own sons, allowing U.S. models of republicanism to influence the island's youth, and by granting rights to former slaves. These three errors had two distinct, paradoxical consequences. First, they created optimum conditions for the insurrection, and second, they made Cuba unfit to sustain an independent existence. Though critical of Spain, Olaguíbel clearly sympathized with the Spanish in Cuba, since he saw their position as analogous to that of Latin American elites throughout the continent who needed to repress any elements standing in the way of political stability and material progress. Carlos Olaguíbel y Arista hoped that Mexicans would learn from Spain's failure and acquire a deeper understanding of what it took to maintain order and perpetuate elite rule in a republic such as Mexico, which had a history of endemic anarchy and revolution, and in a continent threatened by a new and powerful imperialist adversary.

The third and fourth articles Olaguíbel published on the Cuban question concerned the position that Mexico ought to assume in the conflict. The driving questions were: *Can Mexico, given its patriotic determination to conserve its own territory, sympathize with revolutions whose objectives are to dismember national territories? Would it benefit Mexico for Cuba to gain its independence from Spain?* The first of these two questions depended on Olaguíbel's ability to demonstrate that the Cuban independence movement was nothing more than a rebellion that threatened to dismember Spain. Olaguíbel answered his question succinctly: "Hispanic-American nations cannot afford to help establish a precedent where a province or a state that is not under the rule of a foreign government, nor under a regime of conquest, be permitted to separate itself from the nation it belongs to. Such a precedent would tend to authorize, at any given moment, a rebellion on its own soil and would also make the nation vulnerable to the machinations of its enemies."[73] Mexico, a nation that had already suffered "the machinations" of its enemy when it lost half of its territory to the United States in the Mexican American War, could not possibly condone Cuba's separation from Spain. Olaguíbel skillfully created an alignment between Mexico and Spain by arguing that the Cuban independence movement was more similar to the Texas rebellion of 1835–1836 than it was to the Mexican independence movement. Cubans and Mexicans did not share a common struggle against imperialism; it was Mexicans and Spaniards who shared an identical struggle for the defense of national integrity in the face of U.S. expansionism.

Although recent historical studies of northern Mexico before the war with the United States in 1848 suggest that the Mexican government had tried to establish effective government, settlement, religious institutions, and economic systems there, there is no question that this was a difficult task in light of U.S. interest in the region.[74] By the 1830s, California and Texas had grown dependent on North American manufactured goods. After the war, Mexican conservatives and liberals became increasingly polarized in their responses to Mexico's vulnerability. While liberals favored thoroughgoing social and economic reforms to strengthen the nation, conservatives believed that only a strong constitutional monarchy could restore stability to Mexico and ensure that the nation was protected from further U.S. expansion. The new liberals of the Porfirian era inherited the fears of their conservative antecedents; in light of the discrediting of conservatism after the defeat of the French, they could hardly argue in favor of monarchy, but they continued to believe in strong, centralized government. Olaguíbel's opposition to the reform bill that would have placed checks on Díaz's power is an example of this insistence on strengthening executive authority.

Like conservatives more hard-line than he was, Olaguíbel believed that federalism, which liberals had embraced believing it was the United States' secret to success, made Hispanic-American nations more vulnerable to separatism and foreign encroachment. Federalism tended to encourage resistance, rather than unification, in regions that were not well integrated into a Mexican nation or the national market. To dramatize the dangers of federalism, Olaguíbel pointed to the civil war in the United States. The conclusion of that war confirmed the importance of a strong centralist and unified state. On these grounds, Olaguíbel defended Díaz's authoritarian and centralist administration as the perfect solution to the problems inherent in the federal system.

Mexico knew all too well what it was like to lose a piece of its national territory to the United States, and for that reason should be in solidarity with Spain, but, more importantly, Olaguíbel argued that allowing the United States to occupy Cuba and surround Mexico was adverse to the nation's geopolitical and economic interests. This was a concern that was broadly shared within the Díaz administration and even more widely within Mexican political circles, especially in and after the summer of 1897, when U.S. intervention of some kind seemed increasingly likely.

In Olaguíbel's opinion, the aggressive attitude toward Spanish immigrants that the pro-Cuba element spearheaded was inappropriate. Mexicans in favor of Cuban independence had resurrected dormant anti-Hispanism and continually harassed Mexico's Spanish immigrant community, a community that Olaguíbel argued (as Díaz would later in his interview with Márquez Sterling) was one of the more productive and beneficial to the nation. Like many elite Porfirians, Olaguíbel believed that Mexico's potential greatness rested on its ability to attract and retain European immigrants. He described the Spanish immigrant as "the only foreigner to come here who rejuvenates the national organism with his blood . . . he is the only one that the nation assimilates, the only one who identifies with us."[75]

The pro-Cuban independence solidarity movement threatened Mexico's economic interests by agitating the Spanish community and ignored the nation's geostrategic interests by blindly supporting a movement that would result in a U.S. annexation near Mexico's shores. The debates over Cuba had also polarized the Mexican political sphere, pitting traditional liberals against conservatives. This ran against the ethos of the regime, which, guided by reconciliation politics, drew political opposites to the center and into a party of the government engineered by *científicos* to maximize political stability. Reflecting on the disturbances caused by the cause of *Cuba Libre*, Olaguíbel wrote: "Some people, taking advantage of the ultra-Jacobin element that seems not to comprehend the idea that progress can be achieved without a chronic state of social upheaval . . . succeeded in creating significant agitation in favor of the Cuban insurrection, agitation that was not limited to manifesting sympathies, but more specifically was expressed in demonstrations of hatred for Spain."[76] Olaguíbel was troubled both by the anti-Hispanism of Cuban independence advocates and by the ideological and political orientation of the Mexicans who were aligned with the movement, individuals whom he described as *"ultra-jacobino."* These misguided and overly passionate individuals, whose mantra was "save the principles and let the world perish," were deeply threatening to Mexico's future. Taken as a whole, Olaguíbel's four articles constitute a coherent critique of Jacobinism. In his opinion, Jacobin liberals had been the downfall of Mexico in the past and threatened the nation's stability in the present. Olaguíbel used a synonym for Jacobin politics when he described Spain's humanism as "metaphysical politics." It was the humanist impulse that had led Spain to grant rights to the formerly enslaved in Cuba, a move that enabled those former slaves to enter the contest for power on the island. Jacobinism also drove the Cuban insurgency itself, for the movement was guided by abstract principles without a care for cold, hard facts and scientific assessments of the kind Olaguíbel prided himself on using. Carlos Olaguíbel y Arista was not a raving Hispanist *agachupinado*, as traditional Mexican liberals were fond of calling him. In fact, he was deeply critical of Spain's colonial mismanagement of Cuba. Olaguíbel valued Mexico's Spanish heritage, admired Spain's constitutional monarchy, and felt a kinship with Spaniards as members of a broader Latin race. But, at his core, he was a Mexican nationalist who had Mexican national interests at heart.

Mexicans who favored Cuban independence would challenge Olaguíbel's fundamental assumptions as well as the categories that he took for granted. For *Cuba Libre* supporters in Mexico, as we will see in the next chapter, the ultimate struggle was not between the Anglo and Latin races or between metaphysical and scientific politics, but between the forces of tyranny and colonialism on the one hand and republicanism and democracy on the other. In this context, *Cuba Libre* represented an inspiration and potential model for Mexico, a republic that some Mexican liberals felt had deviated from the course set by its own liberators and its great liberal statesmen. Just as a fundamental dislike and distrust of traditional liberalism undergirded Olaguíbel rejection of Cuban independence, a deep suspicion of rising conservatism was at the root of Mexican traditional liberalism's embrace of a sister republic's struggle for independence and sovereignty.

Conclusion

After they were thrown in jail for dishonoring a Spanish immigrant, the student journalists of *El Continente Americano* could not but be bitter. They had dedicated themselves to sustaining a cause that they believed they were duty-bound to support as liberals, as Mexicans, and as Americans. Not only had their pleas and petitions on behalf of *Cuba Libre* been ignored, but they were persecuted for their beliefs. The success of Brunetti's efforts to target the students was even more disheartening because it demonstrated how the Díaz regime, rather than protect its own citizens, would allow their rights to be violated at the behest of a foreigner—and, worse, a representative of the Spanish colonial state. The involvement of Telesforo García, a Spanish immigrant, underscored the close collaboration between the Mexican establishment, Spaniards, and former Spaniards that so troubled Cubans and their supporters.

The Díaz regime had definitively shown its cards, and Mexican liberal supporters of Cuban independence could draw only one conclusion: beneath the regime's jealously guarded neutrality there lay a firm commitment to supporting the Spanish cause. What Mexican advocates of Cuban independence may not have seen, because the dealings between the Spanish minister and the Mexican state were purposely concealed, was that the attack on them was intentional and calculated. The foreign minister's desire to teach the student upstarts a lesson blended perfectly with the Díaz regime's policy of periodically attacking an emerging opposition, some of whose most vocal representatives were journalists.[77] The shift in the laws and procedures for prosecuting crimes of defamation made it seem as if Telesforo García was simply defending his tarnished honor against the disrespectful student journalists who attacked him, when, in fact, the Spanish minister was behind the denunciation.

In his dissection of the Cuban Question, Olaguíbel clearly identified two dangers for Mexico. One was internal: the resurrection of metaphysical or Jacobin politics threatened Mexico's political stability by resurrecting tensions between liberals and conservatives and between Mexicans and Spaniards, tensions that had lain dormant. Indeed, on the home front, pro-Cuba madness was causing all kinds of trouble. There were violent altercations on the streets, in bars, theaters, cafés, and other spaces. Combat journalism had descended to new lows as journalists on both sides of the question traded insults and offences, and at others led to violent confrontations between the parties involved. The other danger was external: the feared U.S. occupation of Cuba would allow that nation to dominate the Gulf and effectively encircle Mexico. Supporting a movement that would, it was believed, inevitably result in Cuba's annexation was tantamount to historical amnesia, for Mexico had lost a territory in this same way to the same usurper only decades before. The support that the Díaz regime lent to Spain in the repression of Cuban activities and those of the Mexicans in solidarity with them was aimed at forestalling both negative outcomes. Ultimately more damning than the covert aid for the Spanish cause, though, was Mexico's complete disavowal of the Cuban one. *Cuba Libre* was simply deemed impossible, and, being that it was impossible, to pursue Cuban independence was reckless and dangerous for Cuba, for Mexico, and for Latin America.

Cuban revolutionaries and their supporters in Mexico were alarmed by the climate of official hostility toward Cuba and by the Díaz regime's alliance with Spain. It took little to put two and two together. The regime's rejection of a cause that reflected the political ideals enshrined in its own constitution—political ideals which mid-century Mexican statesmen and revolutionaries, including Porfirio Díaz, had fought for—and its embrace of a cause that represented the continuation of European colonialism in the Americas and that celebrated monarchism could only mean one thing. Mexico and Mexicans were being led astray. However, rather than attack the regime directly, emerging dissidents did so obliquely.

Months after the Spanish persecutions of *El Continente Americano* and after Olaguíbel's articles and the public debate they sparked about the Cuban cause, an article appeared in *El Continente Americano* that might have even confounded Carlos Olaguíbel y Arista. The article, written by a Spaniard, went far beyond calling for the victory of the insurgents or advocating for Mexican solidarity. Rather, it called for the de-hispanization of Spain itself.

6 Affirming Americanismo

Desespañolización and the Defense of America

Leandro González Alcorta first came to Cuba the way that many young Spanish men did in the late nineteenth century, through obligatory military service. Arriving to Havana in 1880, Leandro, who had little interest in the military, enrolled as a student in the University of Havana. During the 1880s and 1890s, he completed his service and his studies and was offered a position as a professor in the premier secondary school in the province of Pinar del Rio. In 1896, Leandro's revolutionary sympathies cost him his job and he was deported to Spain. Leandro refused to be silenced. He worked as a journalist writing for the Madrid-based newspaper *La Paz*. This time his pro-independence position cost him his freedom. If exile did not persuade him to desist, neither would prison. While incarcerated, Leandro served as a remote correspondent for the Mexico City–based newspaper, *El Continente Americano*. Upon his release, he traveled to Mexico, where his family, having fled the war, awaited him. In Mexico City and later in Campeche, Leandro worked tirelessly to promote the Cuban cause in the press and as a member of multiple political clubs. He was known for his scathing critiques of Spain. In a gesture that shocked many fellow Spanish immigrants, he called for the de-hispanicization of Spain, arguing that only by liberating its colonies, shedding its imperial aspirations, and embracing republicanism would Spain be able to progress and join the modern nations of the world.

Leandro's call for dehispanicization reflected a fundamental pillar of Cuban-Mexican and (in rare cases Spanish) solidarities. As we saw in chapter 4, *Cuba Libre* meant much more to Mexicans than the elimination of Spanish colonial rule in Cuba. Mexican supporters of Cuban independence identified with the movement because they saw in it an affirmation of their own faith in political liberalism currently under attack in Mexico. These Mexicans pronounced their adherence to principles, values, and ideals over the "science" that Carlos Olaguíbel y Arista Olaguíbel and his conservative-liberal counterparts advocated for. In fact, they often made fun of the so-called "científicos," calling them base political opportunists who masqueraded as illustrious individuals. However, as they came to terms with the Porfirian regime's refusal to support the Cuban movement and its tacit backing of Spain, Mexican traditional liberals, those Olaguíbel would pejoratively call Jacobins, became increasingly convinced that Mexico and Cuba were not only similar in terms of the origins and aims of their respective struggles for independence and self-determination, they also faced the same obstacles in pursuit of them. As they reflected on the ideological alliances between Porfirian and Spanish elites, Mexican traditional liberals and men like Leandro González Alcorta insisted that Mexico and Cuba must be de-hispanicized and decolonized.

Rather than an expression of anti-Hispanism, dehispanicization was a call for the decolonization of Spain, Cuba and Mexico. In Cuba, decolonization meant independence. In Mexico it meant the eradication of pernicious colonial legacies. In Spain, decolonization would open the way for modernization and progress. In lieu of the *hispanismo* advocated by their opponents, Mexican "Jacobin" liberals advocated for *americanismo*, a form of continental solidarity based on politics and geography rather than race and that imagined an America composed of mutually respecting republican and democratic states united in the defense of their principles and their sovereignty. *Americanismo* is an ideology whose nuances have been overshadowed by the Anglo/Latin binary which structures conventional understandings of U.S.–Latin American relations after 1898. Once Spain was definitively no longer a colonial power after its demise in the Spanish-American War, *hispanismo* became the main ideology standing in opposition to U.S.-directed Pan-Americanism. Literary greats such as Rubén Darío and José Enrique Rodó were among the most prominent Hispanist poets and writers at the turn of the century. Yet, before 1898, alongside the elite, conservative ideology of *hispanismo* and the U.S. Pan-Americanism there existed *americanismo*, a vision of the Americas not reducible to either, but which contained elements of both.

This chapter seeks to contextualize Cuban and Mexican responses to the war between Spain and Cuban insurgents and to the events of 1898. Looking beyond the binary that pits Spain against the United States in a conflict imagined as race war reveals the deep significance of the Cuban question for Mexico and opens the way for future explorations of its significance for Latin America. Before the U.S. military intervention, Cubans, Mexicans, and Spaniards speculated about what the outcome of the war would be, but after the U.S. declaration of war it seemed a foregone conclusion. Spaniards and their Mexican allies felt at once vindicated and terrified at the likelihood of a U.S. victory, while Cubans and their supporters almost reflexively supported the United States, arguing that when all other American republics had abandoned Cuba, the United States alone had upheld the sister republic ideal. This pro-U.S. position was sustained to a greater or lesser degree throughout the first U.S. intervention in Cuba.[1] But a pro-U.S. position must not be construed as the open and unproblematic acceptance of U.S. imperialism. Beleaguered by Spanish anti-Cuban propaganda and disillusioned with Latin American official hostility, Cubans and their supporters felt they had little choice as the events of 1898 unfolded. They had been left alone with "America." Their embrace of the United States was never seamless: it was sometimes earnest and hopeful and other times reluctant and cautious. While Cubans generally turned their backs to Latin America out of resentment, for Mexicans the U.S. intervention highlighted Mexico's own weakness on the international stage and its internal decomposition. As a stable and prospering nation, they believed that Mexico should have a more robust international personality in the hemisphere than it did. But even more troubling was what the nation's rejection of Cuban independence indicated about the less than subtle shifts in its national political culture. Ever vigilant, traditional Mexican liberals cried out against the rising conservatism, which was the root cause of the Díaz administration's rejection of Cuban independence.

Cuban reactions to the Mexican state's neutrality form the basis of the first section of the chapter. The migrants expressed disappointment, outrage and disbelief at the inaction of the Mexican state. Cubans were so convinced of the place that Cuba held in an anti-colonial movement envisioned as hemispheric and century-long that they could hardly comprehend the rejection of their cause by their sister republics. By 1898, feelings of outrage and betrayal were displaced by the need to concentrate on creating lives anew after the war. For some returnees, their time in Mexico was easily overshadowed by the imperative to move on and not look back. But for others it remained a persistent and bittersweet memory. A decade after the war, Leandro Cañizares Gómez remembered his time in Mexico as a life-defining and overwhelmingly positive experience with one exception. Cañizares Gómez lamented the "hostile passivity" of the Díaz government with respect to Cuban independence.[2] While returnees carried conflicted feelings home with them, many thousands of others would not return at all. These Cubans watched helplessly as the nation they had fought for from exile failed to recognize and repay their sacrifices. Bitterness was not a sentiment unique to Cubans in Mexico but was detectable in Cuban migrants across Latin America during and after the war. Cubans in Mexico, Costa

Rica, Colombia and other places embraced the United States almost defensively with a zeal tinged with regret. Thus, rather than dismiss pro-U.S. sentiments as naïve, or as proof of secret desires for annexation, support for the United States must be placed in the proper historical context. So profound was the impact of Latin American official neglect that, years after the conclusion of the war, a former Cuban migrant from Mexico observed that early twentieth-century Cuban historians consistently wrote the history of Cuba's independence struggle as if it were profoundly disconnected from Latin America. This is remarkable given a century-long effort to argue the opposite. The idea that Cuba was but a continuation of Latin America's long independence struggle was the bedrock of transnational Latin American solidarities surrounding Cuban independence from the 1820s forward.

The second section of the chapter shifts to consider Mexican supporters of Cuban independence and their reactions to the regime's indifference. They saw Cuban independence and the ongoing efforts of Mexico's staunchest liberals to preserve and protect Mexico's liberal tradition as conjoined struggles. Mexican Liberals and Cubans *independentistas* saw themselves at the forefront of a universal struggle between the forces of republicanism and democracy and those of monarchism and conservatism. Between 1895 and 1898, Mexican traditional liberals came to understand the Díaz regime's rejection of Cuba as a symptom of rising conservatism, which was itself the result of persistent colonial legacies given new life by flesh-and-blood Spanish immigrants who brought a haughty, entitled, and imperialistic attitude to Mexico and who monopolized certain industries. Ultimately, Díaz's Cuba policy gave an emerging opposition in Mexico another reason to criticize the regime and its stewardship of the nation. But in a climate of increasing repression, targeting the regime directly could be costly. The journalists affiliated with *El Hijo del Ahuizote*, *El Diario del Hogar*, and of course, *El Contintente Americano*, knew this all too well. Hence Mexican traditional liberals called for the dehispanicization of Mexico instead. They rejected *hispanismo* not because they refused to recognize Mexico's Spanish heritage, but because it was an elite, conservative and, pro-imperialist ideology. They also rejected any interpretation of Pan-Americanism as a veneer for U.S. imperialist expansion, opting instead for *americanismo*. I contend that the enthusiasm Mexican traditional liberals displayed for the United States in and after 1898 was a reflection of their stubborn refusal to accept the demise of *americanismo* and the consolidation of *hispanismo* as the ideology of solidarity in Latin America rather than an indication of their acceptance of U.S imperialism.

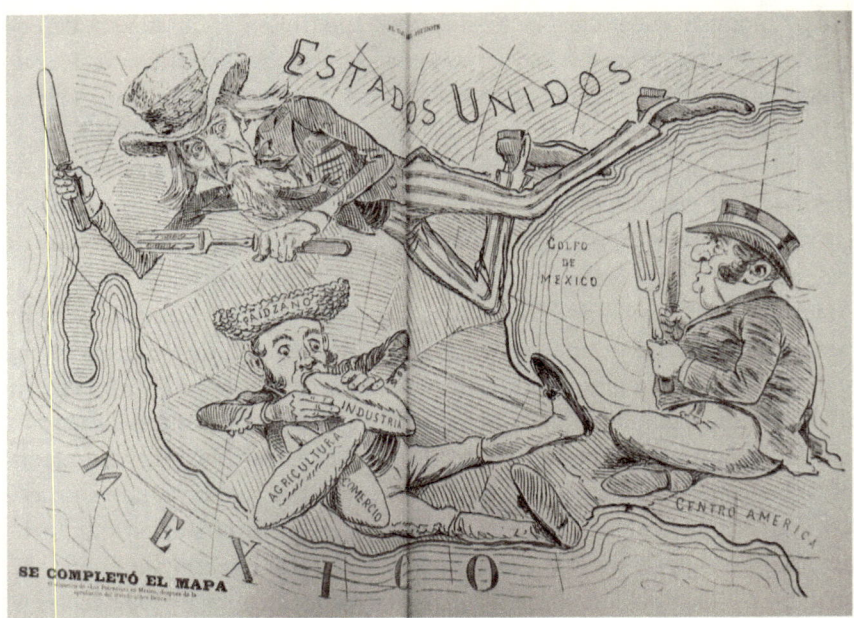

FIGURE 6.1 "Se Completó el Mapa," *El Hijo del Ahuizote*, 2 May 1897. Political cartoon.

The map in fig. 6.1 reflects the concerns of the Mexican liberal opposition in the 1890s. Mexico is figured here as a land to be carved up by foreigners, be they the avaricious U.S. Americans north of the border, the British menacing Mexico from the south, or the Spanish who literally consume Mexico from within. Entitled "The Map Is Now Complete," this image, published by *El Hijo del Ahuizote* in 1897—shortly after the treaty between Mexico and Britain to fix the limits of Belize was settled—is a representation of the way the journalists viewed the Gulf and the dangers Mexico faced. Tellingly, Cuba is not represented on the map. The danger that a U.S. takeover of Cuba might represent for Mexico is seen as remote when compared to the more direct threat on the border. Also more significant than Cuba were the dangers of European encroaches, both from Belize and from a powerful Spanish immigrant community determined to secure and defend its economic and political interests from within Mexico. This map is an answer to the arguments of the likes of Olaguíbel, whose own depiction of the Gulf World would have likely reflected the vision prevalent in U.S. political cartoons of the day. These often included an outsized figure of Uncle Sam menacing Mexico on the border and straddling the Gulf with one foot

214 Chapter Six

securely on Cuba. The absence of Cuba from the *Hijo* journalists' depiction discredits the idea that Cuba is a danger to Mexico, refocusing the viewer on the United States, Britain, and especially on Spain eating the nation from within.

The figure of the *"paidzano"* in the image consumes Mexican "agriculture," "commerce," and "industry" in the shape of breads. Spanish immigrants were often depicted as bakers and were accused of coming to Mexico as poor men looking to amass a fortune and return to Spain with their profits instead of remaining in Mexico and contributing to the nation's advancement. In the minds of the journalists, there was only a short distance between Spain's consuming Mexico and its controlling Mexico. In sum, Cuban independence advocates in Mexico were not as concerned with how U.S. power and influence in Cuba might affect Mexico. By disavowing the very basis of Carlos Olaguíbel y Arista's argument in support of Mexico's neutrality, they insisted that Mexico had a responsibility to support Cuba's independence struggle and that such a move was in Mexico's best interest. Taking up Olaguibel's challenge to prove the benefits of Cuban independence for Mexico, they argued that the gains were not economic necessarily, but political and geostrategic.

The Unthinkable: Cubans Respond to Latin America's Official Rejection of Cuban Independence

Cuban migrants' efforts to influence Mexico's foreign policy toward Cuba between 1895 and 1898 were an utter failure, as were PRC efforts to do the same across Latin America. For much of the war, the party was unsuccessful at influencing U.S. policy as well, since their efforts were met with cold indifference there. Cubans reacted to their failure in Latin America with disbelief and a sense of profound betrayal. Their visceral and powerful reaction is laid bare in the language Cubans used to express their frustration, language which reveals that certain fundamental assumptions anchored Cubans' expectation of Latin American support. After all, Cuban migrants and exiles had painstakingly built an understanding of *Cuba Libre* that was predicated on the idea that Cuban independence was indispensable to the protection of Latin American sovereignty. From the earliest days of the conspiracy of the Soles y Rayos de Bolivar and the Gran Conspiración del Aguila Negra, the idea that Cuban independence would secure the independence of surrounding Latin American republics had formed the basis of solidarity between Cubans and their Latin American co-conspirators. In José Martí's last letter written to Manuel Mercado, we detect an expression of hope laced with doubt about whether Mexico would fulfill the continental duty Martí had ascribed to it. Indeed, during the 1895 War, doubt would give way to disappointment for Cubans in Mexico and those elsewhere in the Americas.

The rejection of support for Cuban independence was also a gesture of support for Spain, and this did not escape Cuban migrants and their Latin American supporters. The fact that American republics, which had broken free from Spain would align themselves with their former colonizer rather than another victimized colony was incomprehensible. According to Cubans, there were only two possible explanations: that colonial legacies persisted in Spanish America; or that narrowly defined national interests of the kind that Carlos Olaguíbel y Arista had articulated were being given priority.

As he searched for an explanation for Mexico's lack of support for Cuba in September of 1895, Nicolás Domínguez Cowan blamed the "Spanish element" which weighed so heavily on the Mexican government.[3] Responding to Domínguez Cowan, Tomás Estrada Palma echoed his concern about the influence exerted by Spain in Latin America. Estrada Palma was puzzled, "sad," and "ashamed" by the willingness of Latin Americans to sacrifice their principles under pressure from a former colonizer.[4] Finally, he observed correctly that Latin Americans saw Cubans' insistence on pursuing independence as criminal. The insurgents' struggle for independence was seen as a criminal act that constituted a betrayal of Latin race solidarity. In other words, Cubans were expected to subordinate their desire for independence to the greater needs and interests of a Latin race that was locked in mortal combat with the Anglos to the north. Cubans fought hard against this reframing, which subsumed their struggle in a larger race war and utterly changed its meaning.

On 23 October 1895, Enrique José Varona, the well-known Cuban writer and founder of the Cuban exile newspaper, *La Patria*, addressed the Hispanic-American nations in an essay explaining and justifying the Cuban revolutionary struggle in order to counter the view that the Cuban movement was illegitimate or unjustified. His essay was translated into several languages and circulated widely within the Americas and in Europe. It constituted a call for solidarity. After several pages of detailed analysis regarding Spain's mismanagement of the colony and abuse of its colonists, Varona ended by insinuating that Latin America's rejection of the Cuban cause was both immoral and unfair: "if the world turns its back on us, it will be worse for everyone. A new iniquity will have been consummated. The principle of human solidarity will have suffered another defeat. . . . Cuba is a nation that only requires liberty and independence to become a factor of prosperity and progress in the world in the concert of civilized nations. Today it is a factor of . . . disorder and ruin. . . . Cuba does not offend, it defends itself. Look America, look world, [see] on whose side is reason and right."[5] Varona's message, while intending to attract Latin American supporters, is much more defensive than it is seductive. The tone of the piece indicates that Cubans' disillusionment with Latin America's failure to immediately support the revolutionary cause was expressed early on in the struggle. That bitterness would fester in the following years and reach a climax in 1898.

A Cuban migrant in Mexico, identified only as *"Un Cubano,"* published a letter in a Mexican newspaper a month after Varona's essay circulated. The writer insisted that if Mexico were to recognize the legitimacy of the insurgency it would set off a domino effect in Latin America. "Unfortunately," he wrote, "Mexico has decided to stay in the rearguard behind all the Latin American nations."[6] Although he made these observations in 1895, months before the Cuban Question began to gain ground in Mexico, *Un Cubano*'s pessimism, like Varona's, would prove prophetic.

During the fall of 1896, Constantino R. Villaverde, nephew of the Cuban writer Cirilio Villaverde, who served as the New York City correspondent for *El Continente Americano*, published an opinion piece in the paper echoing *Un Cubano*'s and Estrada Palma's concerns about Latin America's cold reception of the independence cause. Villaverde had originally written the article for the Cuban exile newspaper *La Patria*, but the editor rejected his submission, arguing that it might offend Hispanic-American sensibilities. Villaverde then submitted the article to a Mexican newspaper, and it was published on 29 October 1896. In the article, Villaverde wondered how it was possible that so many Latin American nations had forgotten the offenses they had been subjected to by Spain in recent history. In Chile, "the bombardment of Valparaiso should still fill the hearts of all Chilenos with wrath," he wrote. Spain had also tried to take the Chinchas islands from Peru and had invaded the Dominican Republic. Not twenty years earlier, the Spanish had collaborated with the French, who invaded Mexico and established a monarchy there. "That all of America, forgetting what it does not have the right to forget, should be on the side of Spain . . . that has no valid explanation. . . . What explains the attitude of Latin America toward the Cuban question?" he asked desperately. Villaverde threw up his hands, "No one knows!"[7] Villaverde harshly criticized fellow Latin Americans by evoking the language of rights, which was also present in Estrada Palma's critique. While Villaverde insisted that Latin Americans did not have the "right" to forget the past, Estrada Palma chided them for their willingness to "sacrifice" Cubans' "rights." If Latin Americans saw Cuban revolutionaries as criminals, Cubans believed that Latin Americans indifferent to the Cuban cause were equally guilty.

Decades after the war, Leandro Cañizares Gómez, a former Cuban migrant in Mexico, admitted that the official rejection of Cuban independence "was the only painful memory of my unforgettable time in that hospitable land . . . how we Cubans lamented that almost hostile passivity, that coldness in official spheres . . . *Cuba Libre* owes nothing to the government of Porfirio Díaz."[8] This observation is all the more strange because Cañizares Gómez's book was otherwise one long celebration of Porfirio Díaz, a man he described as having a "lucid mind, heart of a patriot and iron fist." Like Domínguez Cowan, Cañizares Gómez tried to explain a rejection that seemed to him counterintuitive. "On many occasions I tried to study the phenomenon . . . and it was not really incomprehension or lack of sympathy, but rather a latent fear that Cuba could become a possession of the United States." It wasn't that Mexicans didn't understand Cubans' struggle or even that they lacked sympathy for the Cubans, Cañizares Gómez argued. The rejection of Cuban independence came down to a complete disavowal of it: Cuba could not stand on its own as a republic.

As we saw in previous chapters, Cubans worked hard to challenge this idea by marshaling statistics to demonstrate Spain's mismanagement of the colony, debunking the idea that racial tensions threatened the stability of the nation, and defending Cuba's right to make mistakes as a fledgling nation. Arguing against the idea that fitness was a basis for freedom, Manuel Márquez Sterling wrote that "when the Latin American republics were constituted by the hands of their liberators, no one made them prove they were capable of self-governance. . . . They were nations that deserved to govern themselves and deserved to control their own destinies. . . . If they didn't know how to govern themselves, the school of their own errors would give them the necessary lessons. . . . Even if she didn't have the conditions for self-government today, [Cuba] would still deserve her independence just as the rest of America did without knowing how to govern itself."[9] Why should Cuba be treated any differently from any other European colony aspiring to achieve its freedom? Why should Cuba be held to a higher standard than her sister republics who achieved independence early in the century?

Cuban revolutionaries customarily argued that Cuba was, in fact, more prepared for independence than its fellow Latin American republics had been when they broke their chains. The Manifesto of Montecristi, the guiding document of the revolution, is a perfect example. In the manifesto the revolutionaries argued that, "Unlike the rest of Latin America which emerged from colonialism to suffer the rule of *caudillos*, the slavish imitation of foreign ideas and doctrines, the perpetuation of feudal customs, and short sighted reliance on single industries . . . these factors are by no means the problems of Cuban society."[10] Thus, for Latin Americans to question the viability of the republic was not only unfair, as Márquez Sterling argued, it was short-sighted and simply incorrect. The gap that separated Cubans' own understanding of the Cuban struggle and the promise and potential of the Cuban republic from that of their Latin American opponents was unbridgeable.

The Cuban Independence War ended in 1898, and not as most Cubans had anticipated. The brutal struggle between Spanish royalists and Cuban insurgents that had ravaged Cuba for three years was not resolved by the undisputed victory of one adversary over the other, but through the military intervention of a foreign government. As we have seen, Cuban migrants in Mexico and in Latin America were varied in their response to the war. Some were more wary of U.S. involvement than others. Those who took the U.S. intervention in stride were often subject to criticism by Mexican citizens for whom the U.S. entry into the war was a game changer. In the summer of 1898, Mario L. de la Mola, a resident of Mérida, wrote, "Since the United States' intervention, which marks a new phase in our revolution, public spirit here has changed radically." De la Mola was concerned about his property—he owned a printing press—and his personal safety. He worried about what would happen if "hostile sentiments are made public."[11] In addition to expressing concern for his safety, de la Mola described the U.S. intervention as "a new phase in our revolution." For him, the U.S. declaration of war did not nullify the Cuban struggle (as it did for Spain's supporters); it simply represented a "new phase." Given the broad-based efforts of the PRC to generate diplomatic support for mediation or intervention, it makes sense that Cubans like de la Mola residing in exile would welcome the news of the U.S. declaration of war and see it as the natural extension of a diplomatic project designed to encourage American republics to play a role in determining Cuba's future.

Probing some of the articulations of support for U.S. involvement in the war reveals that Cubans often defensively embraced the United States. Such was the case with Rafael Maria Merchán, PRC agent in Columbia. In 1898, Merchán issued a strident critique of Latin Americans and defensively embraced the United States. "Members of the Union [the United States]," he wrote, "we would be proud to join our forces with yours and help you defend the rights of the American republics so their independence will not be seized from them by Europe. We relish the opportunity to be guarantors of the liberty of our sister nations." Although in the first sentence Merchán does imagine Cuba joining a fight directed by the United States, he insists that the two nations will join forces and work together. U.S. American statesmen and military figures generally believed Cubans to be incapable of self-government and would likely have laughed at the idea that Cuba might become an equal partner in the defense of the hemisphere. Merchán's statement reveals his firm faith in Cuba's potential to be independent of, yet work alongside, the United States. The second sentence is an even bolder statement of Cuba's role as guarantor of Latin American liberty, one that is strikingly reminiscent of a similar claim made often by José Martí. Manuel Márquez Sterling, too, had faith in Cuba, and in 1897 he vigorously defended the island, arguing that it was deserving of its independence. He predicted that Cuba would prove its critics wrong by quickly becoming a strong, unified and modern republic. Yet, after the Cuban constitutional convention accepted the Platt Amendment, which constituted a clear affront to Cuba's sovereignty, Márquez Sterling's faith in Cuba's leaders waned. Indeed, while he was a staunch opponent of the amendment, he was far more critical of the Cuban political elites who passed the amendment than of the U.S. for proposing it. In fact, he expressed broadly positive views of the first U.S. intervention in which "the flower of our ideals was converted from blood to clean pastures." Of course, Márquez Sterling was anti-imperialist, but he consistently placed the burden of responsibility on Cubans themselves to resist that U.S. pressures. As we sill see, Mexican opposition journalists who were critical of Díaz's neutrality vis-à-vis the Cuban movement also placed the onus on Mexico to resist the United States.

Despite their pro-U.S. sentiments in 1898 and after, neither Merchán nor Márquez Sterling had hoped for a U.S. military intervention. In fact, Merchán had favored autonomy for Cuba under Spanish rule before he became an advocate for independence. For both men it was not lack of faith in Cuba that influenced their defense of the United States, but lack of faith in Latin America that led them to support the United States, which seemed to be their only option. Merchán Márquez Sterling and Borrero's statements must be understood in relation to the history of Cuban migrants' frustrated efforts to revive *Americanismo* in the service of Cuban independence during the 1890s.

Return

Recovering the perceptions that migrants had of Mexico at the end of the war is difficult, but the evidence that is available suggests that those who returned found it difficult to forget the pernicious neglect of the Mexican state. Men like Merchán and Márquez Sterling would make their views plain in letters and published articles. As for those who remained behind in Mexico, any resentment of Mexico after 1898 was quickly subsumed by the migrants' frustration with the U.S. and the Cuban government's lack of responsiveness to their needs during a time when the future of the republic was still uncertain. Indeed, when Mario de la Mola wrote to Tomás Estrada Palma in 1898 asking that U.S. consuls be instructed to offer support to Cuban migrants, he expected the PRC to take an active stance in the defense of migrant interests. De la Mola may have taken the U.S. intervention in stride because he believed it represented just "another phase" rather than a radical break in the movement, but he also may have taken the intervention in stride because of his faith in the PRC and its ability to stand strong in defense of the Revolution it had begun and the revolutionaries who had carried forth the struggle. Unfortunately for de la Mola and many other migrants, the Cuban Revolutionary Party was dissolved by its leaders in 1898, leaving thousands of Cubans abroad stranded. The wealthiest used their resources to return home. Many more remained in exile.

In the years after the war, Cubans from all over the Americas sent requests to Cuban authorities asking for either repatriation or representation. The vast majority of Cuban migrants were too poor to fund their return to Cuba. Having made financial sacrifices for the revolution, they expected first the Revolutionary Party and later the Cuban government to help them return to Cuba. Their pleas would fall on deaf ears, and most migrants would become immigrants against their will. In Veracruz, over one hundred working families came together to submit a request for repatriation. The request was supported by a number of well established and well-to-do Cubans in the city, who wrote the Cuban government representatives on the workers' behalf. Even so, the request would not be granted.[12]

For those who chose to stay—and for those who didn't—the challenges were significant. As we saw, Cubans in certain Mexican cities began to feel unwelcome after 1898, as public opinion shifted from pro-Cuban to pro-Spanish in the wake of the Spanish-American War. Some, like Juan Ortega Manzano, continued to suffer oppression and semi-enslavement and were unable to inspire sympathy in Spanish, U.S., or Mexican authorities. Manzano's wife would die waiting to be rescued from the misery of her abuse, and it is unclear if Manzano ever saw his children again. Across the Gulf in Tampa, a city that was home to thousands of migrants active in the revolution, Cubans suffered kidnapping, abuse, and forced deportation at the hands of white vigilante groups who tolerated the foreigners during the war, but turned on them afterward.[13] Cubans from Venezuela, Puerto Rico, the Dominican Republic, and Columbia all wrote to Cuba seeking aid and expecting a return on their revolutionary sacrifices. None was forthcoming.

Dehispanicization and Americanization: Mexican Traditional Liberals Respond to Mexico's Indifference

Like Cubans, Mexicans affiliated with the Cuban revolutionary cause also became increasingly disillusioned between 1895 and 1898. Just as Cubans had used the solidarities they forged with Mexicans to bolster their nationalist cause, Mexicans used the Cuban movement to support their own quest for reformation in Mexico. Thus, the Mexican state's rejection of Cuban independence disappointed Mexican *Cuba Libre* supporters not only because they championed Cuban independence, but also because it signaled a regression for Mexico as a nation. The rejection of Cuban independence and the rise of Spanish influence in Mexico became inseparable in the minds of Mexican supporters of *Cuba Libre*, from the Porfirian regime's shift toward conservatism and authoritarianism in the 1890s. More specifically, Mexican pro-independence advocates saw Mexico's failure to support Cubans' anti-colonial struggle to found a liberal and democratic republic was a symptom of its failure to prize and protect the nation's liberal values. They saw the regime's rejection of Cuban independence as symptomatic of a deeper problem. For *El Continente Americano* journalist Juan Tizoc, that problem was the "petrification of *americanismo*," while for journalists at *El Hijo del Ahuizote*, the problem was the breakdown of liberalism and the rise of conservatism. The two were related; as political liberalism was displaced by economic liberalism, *hispanismo* gained ground against *americanismo*. While outright criticism of the Díaz regime could be dangerous, scapegoating Spanish immigrants was, generally speaking, safer. Thus, Cuban independence advocates freely blamed the Spanish for the rise of conservatism in Mexico and called for the *desespañolización*, or dehispanicization, of Mexico. However, even anti-Hispanism—which was nearly a national sport, especially during independence day celebrations—became perilous after 1897, as the persecution of *El Continente Americano* journalists made clear.

While the late nineteenth century is not generally seen as a period of rising anti-Hispanism, it is productive to see Spanish-Mexican relations across the entire nineteenth century not as a series of clearly discernible moments of reconciliation and reaction, but instead as a continuum marked by frequent eruptions. The Cuban independence war was one such eruption, because it reawakened anti-colonial sentiments for those Mexicans who identified with the Cuban cause. The close alignment between the Mexican government and Spanish representatives in Mexico developed in a political context in which conservatism was reemerging due to reconciliation politics. The parallel rise of *hispanismo* and conservatism greatly concerned Mexican liberals, who concealed their criticism of the regime behind anti-clericalism and anti-gachupinismo.

On the day of the newspaper's sixteenth anniversary, the staff of *El Diario del Hogar* drew a clear connection between the Cuban cause and the fight against rising conservatism—especially the renewed power of the clergy—in an article entitled "Our Labors." "The same liberal principles that have inspired us to defend Cuban independence have guided us in our attacks on the clergy," the journalists wrote; "it has pained us to see the friendly relations that the regime sustains with the church."[14] Ultimately, it was their commitment to liberalism that drew together the struggle for Cuban independence and the fight against the Mexican church. The quotation also reveals the journalists' disillusionment with the regime's conciliatory attitude toward the clergy.

The "friendly" relations between the Díaz regime and the clergy was an issue that appeared repeatedly in *El Diario del Hogar* in the fall of 1896 and spring of 1897. A journalist from *El Diario del Hogar* vehemently criticized the regime in 1896: "Lately the press has been debating the potential benefits of this pernicious politics of reconciliation that would be better described as a politics of weakness. Not only has this politics given our enemies public positions, but it has also closed our eyes to the abuses and flagrant transgressions that these individuals have committed against our institutions . . . where will this regressive march that is erasing the epic pages of our history of progress end?"[15] The "pernicious politics of reconciliation" was the policy begun under Juárez and continued under Díaz whereby Liberals, triumphant after 1867, pardoned conservatives and invited them into government positions while also attenuating the attack on the clergy. Mexico's renewed relations with Spain are another example of reconciliation after the Liberal restoration. The "enemy" referred to the clergy, who this writer saw as violating the nation's constitutional laws and rolling back the progress made by the Liberals of the Reform era. The accusation that the clergy had violated the nation's laws, however, echoes the criticisms made by these same journalists against Spanish immigrants, whom they accused of trying to censor their manifestations of support for *Cuba Libre* and of persecuting them outright under false pretenses. While taking stock of the ills suffered by Latin American nations, the student journalists often blamed those "political groups wedded to the traditions of a shameful past."[16]

The politics of reconciliation had begun to heal the divide between the Liberals of the Reform and the church. Since Mexican traditional liberals identified Spaniards with the church, they believed that the regime was too close to both.[17] In October of 1896, Juan Tizoc commented on an article he read in *El Correo Español*, from which he learned that a priest in Mérida had proposed a project to create a statue of Hernán Cortés in the main plaza. The priest, Pedro Peréz de Elizagaray, sent a circular to the Spanish immigrant community asking for its support. Incensed, Tizoc wrote, "we want to believe that this is all a bad joke." He reiterated that if any statue were to be erected, it ought to be of the "immortal" Hidalgo. Spanish immigrants like Elizagaray would surely chip away at the foundations of liberalism in Mexico if they were permitted to do so. Others, like the Mexican statesmen Francisco G. Cosmes, would argue that the Spanish conqueror of Mexico Hernán Cortés should be considered the father of the nation. Cosmes's assertions led to widespread and heated debate in Mexico in 1890.[18]

Mexicans who allied with Spain, like the local priest Elizagaray, were dubbed *agachupinados*. During the Spanish-American war, Juan Tizoc took stock of Mexican public opinion. "There exist three classes of people who hope for a Spanish victory," he argued. "A small part of the pueblo, the clergy and a group of people who are difficult to pin down (or perhaps it would mortify us to do so). About half of these are free thinkers, part liberal and part absolutist, somewhat French by arrogance and at the core *gachupines* by education and ancestry."[19] These were the *agachupinados*. Among the *agachupinados* we find Carlos Olaguíbel y Arista and his close collaborator, Francisco Cosmes, whom the journalists described as the "new, hackneyed champion of *agachupinamiento*" for his position on the Cuban movement.[20]

Olaguíbel was described as "Alfonsista, like any *gachupin*," likely for his comments defending the Spanish monarchy.[21] Like the *científico*, the *agachupinado* (which were often one and the same) threatened Mexican liberalism by empowering reactionary forces. The *agachupinado* was identified by the liberal opposition as a dangerous figure in Mexican politics because of their shifting political loyalties and their claims to be both Catholics and liberals at the same time. Pamela Voekel argues that at mid-century, liberalism and Catholicism were not perceived by all as incompatible. Ignacio Altamirano's novela *Christmas in the Mountains* is often cited as an example of how liberals could admire the "right" kind of priest, in a context in which the church was not seen as a threat. By the 1890s, though, the church was again seen as a threat, so the incompatibility between liberalism and Catholicism resurfaced.[22]

Dozens of political cartoons satirized the relationship between Spaniards, conservatives, *agachupinados*, and the regime during the 1890s. An image that appeared in *El Hijo del Ahuizote* illustrates these connections well. Archbishop Nicolas Averardi, a special envoy from the pope sent to Mexico to seek closer ties with Díaz regime, was depicted pulling a reluctant Porfirio Díaz toward the edge of a precipice labeled "The Republic." Below the cliff, a mixed group of clerics and *agachupinados* (including the directors of conservative Mexico City–based newspapers *La Voz de México* and *El Tiempo*) weaken the nation by chipping away at its bedrock with pickaxes labeled "fanaticism," "ignorance," "stupidity," and "bad faith." The rocks represent the constitution and the Reform laws. In the background, a group of clergymen look on, grinning. The cartoon is titled "The Rock and the Abyss," and the descriptive caption reads, "A Tuxtepecan landscape in the *sierra* of reconciliation."[23] The message is unequivocally clear. While the president is naive and his reconciliation politics misguided, those who are truly responsible for destabilizing the nation are the clerics, the Mexican conservatives, and the *agachupinados*. The consequences of their actions will amount to nothing less than the destruction (collapse) of the republic. Direct attacks on Porfirio Díaz were rare because of the potential cost to life and limb. Opposition journalists were generally more tactful, depicting the dictator as a dupe and those around him as criminals. It was not a flattering portrayal, but it laid blame not on the dictator himself but on his ministers and other statesmen.

As a remedy for the ills of conservatism, authoritarianism, and *hispanismo*, liberal opposition journalists repeatedly called for the dehispanicization of

Mexico. The move reflected Cubans' own desire to distance themselves not only from the Spanish state but also from the Spanish colonial legacies they felt had hobbled their sister republics in the Americas. The observations of men like Domínguez Cowan, whose efforts to foment the cause of Cuban belligerency rights were frustrated due to the pervasive influence of the "Spanish element" in Mexico, demonstrate Cubans' growing sense that while Spain was fighting a war against the insurgents, it was winning a war against the migrants in Latin America, where colonial legacies continued to plague republics eighty years out from independence. Cubans became convinced that Latin America must be saved from Spain. Constantino Villaverde reflected bitterly in his critique of Latin America, which was published in *El Continente Americano* and rejected by the Cuban newspaper *Patria*, that Latin America might fail Cuba today, leaving her to fight her titanic battle alone, but tomorrow "[Latin Americans] would have in Cubans and in their sons good brothers prepared to help them with their modest efforts to . . . dehispanize themselves!"[24]

In 1897, an article entitled "La Desespañolización" appeared in *El Continente Americano*. Two years later, the same piece was reproduced in *El Hijo del Ahuizote*. Penned by the famous traditional liberal Ignacio Ramírez in 1865, the essay was a meditation on the rejection of Spanish influence in Mexico. Ramírez had written the piece in response to an article by the prominent Spaniard Emilio Castelar, at the time a republican, who wanted to understand why Latin America had forsaken Spain. In both cases, the journalists of the above-mentioned newspapers reprinted this piece as a reflection of their own desire to dehispanize Mexico. Reprinting an article from 1865 demonstrated that the work to eradicate colonial legacies in Mexico continued to be urgent thirty years after Ramírez's call.

A careful reading of Ramírez's letter reveals that his call for dehispanicization is not Hispanophobic. Writing in 1865, before the Spanish republican revolution in 1868, Ramírez acknowledged a difference between Castelar, a republican, and the monarchy ruling Spain. When Castelar asked Ramírez why the Americas had rejected Spain, the latter replied, "we Mexicans renounce your nation, Mr. Castelar, and we do so for the same reasons that you should renounce her as well." Drawing attention to the grave ills—including corruption, fanaticism, and inequality—that Spain suffered under the monarchy, Ramírez urged Castelar to dehispanize himself. Ramírez wrote that "the Spain you describe does not exist and has never existed. It is a figment engendered by your democratic soul. It exists in the future."[25] The Mexican author complained that men like Castelar, with democratic souls and republican aspirations, did not come to the Americas. Those who did come to Mexico had only "left us temples that it took a revolution to destroy." Like traditional liberals thirty years later, Ramírez believed that the church was one of the most detrimental and backward institutions that Mexico inherited from Spain. Toward the end of the article, the author drew a series of parallels between Castelar's republican ideals and those of the Americas. With deep pride in Mexico's political modernity and in the lessons about republicanism and democracy that Mexico could impart to Spain, he called on Castelar to become more American. "*Americanícese*, [Americanize yourself] Mr. Castelar," he wrote. "Come to America," he urged. "All that awaits you in Spain is the parochial priest who will deny you proper burial. . . . In Mexico you have long been one of our brothers."[26]

By the 1890s, Emilio Castelar had fallen in the eyes of many traditional liberals, who saw him as a traitor to the very republican and democratic ideals he had espoused. The director of the *El Diario del Hogar* described him in 1896 as "the famous republican who today lives as a parasite on the rotten trunk of the monarchy."[27] Emilio Castelar was hated by the *puros* for the same reason that he was praised by *científicos* and conservative liberals like Olaguíbel. During his brief time as president of the Spanish republic in 1873, Castelar used socio-scientific reasoning to defend his decision to implement several conservative measures. Castelar's example greatly inspired the architects of the Díaz regime, who also sought to modernize Mexico through conservative means. Where *puros* lost respect for Castelar, however, they continued to revere Ignacio Ramírez for his dedication to Reform-era liberalism and *desespañolización*.

Like Ramírez, traditional liberals of the 1890s were not necessarily Hispanophobes. Too often scholars who study anti-Hispanism in nineteenth-century Mexico look for the roots of anti-Hispanism either in a learned cultural rejection connected to the Black legend, or in a resentment of Spanish immigrants for social and economic reasons. In the case of the Cuban Question, the anti-Hispanism of liberal opposition journalists is very specifically targeted against *gachupines* rather than Spaniards globally. In its first issue, *El Continente Americano* journalists stated that, despite their criticism of Europe, they valued Mexico's commercial relations with the old world and they opened their doors to respectful and hardworking immigrants. "Let the immigrant come, let him come from where he will so long as he comes to work . . . but let him abstain from trying to govern us, or to exert influence in our political matters."[28] The description of immigrants who overstepped the boundaries of acceptable behavior was a direct reference to the Spanish immigrants in Mexico who attacked, abused, insulted, and persecuted *Cuba Libre* supporters in Mexico because they felt a certain sense of entitlement. A far cry from these *gachupines* were the valiant republicans of the kind Castelar used to be—Spaniards like Leandro González Alcorta—who believed in universal republicanism and who drew connections between the independence war in Cuba, the beleaguered republican movement in Spain, and Mexican liberals' struggle against conservatism. One political cartoon that perfectly depicted the connection between Cuban independence and Spanish republicanism was called "Forjando El Porvenir," or forging the future. The image depicted three insurgent generals (Máximo Gómez, Calixto García, and Antonio Maceo) working in a forge to create the new nation. The three men have melted the Spanish crown and are seen hammering it into a new shape. Uncle Sam stands in the background fanning the fire with a bellow that reads "Monroe Doctrine." In the foreground are two signs that read "model": one sign depicts the "Cuban Republic" and the other reads "Spanish Republic." The caption on the image reads, "The blacksmiths Máximo Gómez, Antonio Maceo, and Calixto García in the forge of the Manigua."[29]

When Ramírez called for Castelar to de-hispanicize himself, he was not insisting that Castelar reject Spain wholesale, only that he purge from himself all that Ramírez perceived as retrograde in Spanish culture. Three decades after the publication of Ramírez's letter, traditional liberals associated with the opposition press in Mexico would similarly criticize monarchical Spain and lament the demise of the republican movement there. According to them, Spaniards either supported the government of the 1874 restored monarchy that had crushed the Spanish republican movement, or like González Alcorta counted themselves among the persecuted republicans. The latter were usually avid proponents of Cuban independence and devout liberals in the traditional sense.

Leandro González Alcorta was a fierce republican of the kind that Emilio Castelar had been in the 1860s and 1870s. On 24 October 1897, González Alcorta submitted an article to *El Continente Americano* in which he railed against the Spanish monarchy and its war in Cuba. The arguments he put forth in the article are reminiscent of those that Ramírez had hoped Castelar would make in the 1860s. Addressing himself to all Spaniards, González Alcorta wrote the following:

> Do not be fooled: the origin of all of your ills is in the system of government you have been tolerating, and in the patience with which you have borne those traitors who have formed alliances with all the dynasties to treat you like beasts of burden, whether you are called Spain, the Antilles or the Philippines. . . . The cure for those ills is in a change in the system of government. . . . What has the monarchy given you after so many centuries? She and her ministers and their families have . . . devoured the lives and treasury of the people . . . the friar and the military . . . and the bureaucracy . . . they have pushed [the people] to emigrate and enrich other countries . . . [p]roclaim there the republic and reintegrate each region with its own sovereignty.³⁰

Like Ramírez and the Mexican traditional liberals, González Alcorta identified both the monarchy and the church as institutions that were weakening Spain. According to him, the Spanish system had pushed the colonies to rebel, and justifiably so. Urging Spaniards to recognize that the monarchy was destroying not only the colonies but also the metropolis, he pushed his compatriots to recognize the colonies' right to independence, to learn from them, and to proclaim a republic in Spain as well. Or, he added angrily, "if you are unable to understand that which dignifies free nations, and you insist on continuing to be slaves of foreign families and subjects of the old white-haired man in Rome that so fascinates you . . . continue your suffering." Between 1895 and 1898, like Ramírez decades before, González Alcorta thought it was possible and desirable for Spain to dehispanize and Americanize itself, and so he called for a *desespañolización* rooted not in a rejection of Spanish culture but in a fundamental repudiation of monarchism and conservatism.

If *desespañolización* was seen as analogous to the fight for republicanism and liberalism, it was also seen as an important step in protecting the hemisphere from the very real dangers posed by the Old World. Where Mexican *agachupinados* like Olaguíbel saw the United States as a looming threat, advocates of Cuban independence saw Europe as the greatest danger to Latin America. Not only did Europe have a long history of intervening in Latin American affairs, but its current colonial ventures in Africa and its more recent attempts to exert its influence in the Americas, including in Brazil, Venezuela, Cuba, and Belize, were evidence of Europe's ill intentions toward the American continent. Referring to Europe's colonizing impulse, *El Continente Americano* wrote that "it is not difficult to imagine where this ambitious spirit will lead given the fact that [Europeans] perceive no difference between America and Africa."[31] Three months later, Tizoc observed that "there is no difference between the conquerors that were sent to us three centuries ago and those they now send to Africa." While this was not an expression of global south solidarity, it was nevertheless an intriguing statement that demonstrates the journalists' recognition of the global reach and voracious appetite of European colonialism in the nineteenth century. As evidence of European interest in America, Tizoc highlights English machinations in Belize and Venezuela, French incursions into Amapá in Brazil and, of course, the Spanish effort to annihilate the Cuban insurgents.

Conservative liberal like Olaguíbel knew that they could do little to change Mexican foreign policy. The real battle was at home. The Cuban Question had resurrected partisan struggles over the meaning of liberalism and Mexico's future, challenging the reconciliation politics that the Mexican state worked hard to advance. The traditional liberals' call for *desespañolización* was a call for the rolling back of the political gains made by Mexico's traditional conservative sectors, most notably the church and the clergy, but also those made by the Spanish element and its allies, the Mexican conservatives. This fight created the basis for a natural alliance with the Cuban insurgents, who were fighting the same forces in Cuba.

In January of 1898, Cerefino Sifuentes, a Mexican citizen from the city of Matehuala in San Luis Potosí, wrote a letter to Tomás Estrada Palma in which he asked for Cuba's help. "We are antagonized in our country and we would like your hand, the hand of our sister [Cuba], so that we may follow in her footsteps and, united, move forward toward that future [which holds] our liberty and our rights. Each day our guarantees are [less] . . . it is sad when we forget the open path that our ancestors entrusted to us in 1810." Throughout the letter, Sifuentes referred to Cuba as "our sister," and to Cubans as "our brothers in political ideas."[32] Like so many Cubans and Mexicans united behind the fight for *Cuba Libre*, Sifuentes evoked shared rights and a common struggle. He also made clear allusions to repression and the violation of constitutional guarantees in Mexico, which intensified in the mid to late Porfiriato.

Mexico, 1898, and the Liberal Opposition Press

The U.S. intervention of 1898 was not unexpected, but it was still shocking. Spaniards and Mexican Hispanists sounded the alarm. Those who had opposed Cuban independence from the start believed that they had been correct in their predictions, and they spoke out with even more confidence about the need to rally behind Spain in the oncoming war that would pit the Anglo and Latin races against each other in a struggle for supremacy. Now convinced by the kinds of arguments that Olaguíbel advanced, a number of former advocates of Cuban independence switched sides and championed the Spanish cause.

Cubans like Mario de la Mola of Mérida prepared for the storm, as they anticipated the anti-Yankee hostility to come from Mexicans who changed sides, while other Mexicans remained steadfast supporters of Cuban independence, U.S. intervention and all. The journalists from *El Continente Americano, El Diario del Hogar,* and *El Hijo del Ahuizote* saw the actions of the United States during the spring and summer of 1898 as honorable and as an affirmation of the sister republic ideal that Latin American republics had failed to honor. Whereas the "petrification of Americanism" had led Mexico "to ally with the enemy of liberty," the United States had allied with the soldiers of liberty, the Cubans.[33] Liberal opposition journalists cried out against Mexico's decision to remain neutral in the Spanish-American War. "We will soon suffer the consequences of this inexplicable and lamentable behavior," Tizoc wrote on 30 January 1898. "The American republics have knowingly opted to help Spain in her savage effort to kill and exterminate [the insurgents] . . . they have been accomplices and are responsible for the events that tomorrow will horrify humanity."[34]

Tizoc warned his readers of the potential moral consequences of the regime's actions, while the journalists of *El Hijo del Ahuizote* warned of the political ones. After criticizing the Díaz government for its neutral stance, one article stated that "the nation, weak today, is poised in the not so distant future to become either a respectable and strong country, or a tributary of a much more powerful nation. *Tuxtepecanos*, clerics, and liberals are all aware of this, but none of them are willing to do what is necessary to promote the first and avoid the second." It separated "*Tuxtepecanos*" and "liberals," rejecting the potential conflation of the two. The *Tuxtepecanos* were Díaz's old cronies, men who had been with him since he rode into power with the Plan of Tuxtepec in hand, a plan that had as its slogan effective suffrage and no strategy for reelection. Twenty-two years later, Díaz was still in power and had never truly given up control of Mexico. Calling on the true liberals to take action, the journalists urged them to allow themselves to be influenced by the phrase "Mexico for the Mexicans" in international matters and "Neither friars, nor soldiers!" regarding national affairs. The first phrase refers to the importance of protecting the nation's interests against any pernicious foreign elements. We can assume that the "much stronger nation" of which Mexico might become a tributary was the United States.[35] The article argued that, to remain strong and avoid a shameful future, Mexicans also needed to be wary of those pernicious forces that were weakening the nation from within. The phrase "no friars, nor soldiers" referred to the rise of the church and the increasing militarization of the nation. In national matters, traditional liberals believed that statesmen ought to be concerned about the rebirth of conservatism and the tendency to rule through force rather than by example.

These comments clearly indicate that by 1898 liberal opposition journalists were beside themselves fighting a losing battle. Although the maneuvering of Díaz and his ministers was intentionally vague and deflecting, the inaction of the government was clear as day. While it had long been apparent to the opposition that the Díaz regime supported the Spanish minister, it was now evident that it was utterly subservient to the United States as well. The 1,800 individuals from Guadalajara who petitioned the government for the recognition of Cuban belligerency rights urged their lawmakers in 1895 to "anticipate the *pueblos* of the Saxon race who are moving quickly to protect the blessed cause of the independent Cubans, with their demonstrations in Chicago and other big cities." Mexicans, they argued, "of the Latin race, brothers of those who suffer, you should have been the first to recognize the belligerency rights of the independent Cubans."[36] These young students were not just concerned that Mexico would not honor its duty to support the struggle of an aspiring democratic American republic; they feared that the United States would determine the course of Cuban independence if Mexico and other Latin American nations did not act quickly. This, of course, was exactly what came to pass when the battleship *Maine* exploded in Havana's harbor on 15 February 1898.

Ironically, while visibly concerned about Mexico's sovereignty and the dangers posed by the "much stronger nation" to the north, the liberal opposition journalists praised the United States for its decision to go to war with Spain in the name of the Cuban insurgents. They argued that, although Latin American republics had betrayed *americanismo*, the United

States had taken on the cause and defended the principles of American solidarity.

Despite their celebration of U.S. involvement in the Cuban struggle, the journalists did not espouse the idea that the United States should have complete influence over Cuba. The defense of the idea that all American republics should be equal and that no republic had the right to colonize another was enshrined in the statement made by the students of *El Continente Americano* in their inaugural issue: "All the nations of the new world have the absolute and perennial right to govern themselves with complete independence from any foreign power regardless of its provenance. . . . Americans should resolve their differences in a humane and peaceful way, always condemning any attempt at usurpation or domination of one American nation over another without any exception."[37] This statement echoed the ideas of the Monroe Doctrine, but the students flatly rejected any interpretation of the Doctrine that identified the defense of the hemisphere as the sole right or responsibility of the United States. Thus, they urged the Mexican government to assume its continental responsibility to aid the Cuban independence project, which was a movement understood to be weakening European control in the hemisphere. In 1896, when Porfirio Díaz proclaimed his own doctrine in response to Richard Olney's request that the republics of the hemisphere ratify the Monroe Doctrine, supporters of *Cuba Libre* rejoiced. Díaz's position lined up perfectly with their own stated views. However, Díaz would not uphold his doctrine in relation to Cuba. The wasted potential of Díaz's momentous claim would weigh heavily on them and add to their sense that the regime was bankrupt.

Journalists from *El Hijo del Ahuizote* shared *El Continente Americano* journalists' interpretation of the Monroe Doctrine and expressed their views in a series of political cartoons published in 1898 and 1899. These images were specifically directed to Mexican readers, whose fear of U.S. imperialism had driven them to abandon the Cuban cause. One cartoon that depicts the relationship between American republics in the wake of the Spanish-American War is called "Su Medio de Oro" (fig 6.2). The cartoon features the figure of Uncle Sam accompanied by three native Mexican heroes who pay him tribute for his victory over Spain. All the figures are of equal stature. Juárez praises Uncle Sam, saying, "What a fight, dear uncle! We haven't seen a fight like that since the Cerro de las Campanas. You have avenged the Indians!"[33] Uncle Sam bows slightly to the Mexican heroes as he accepts the tribute they offer. Cuba and Puerto Rico are both figured as children here, although

FIGURE 6.2 "Su Medio de Oro: Tres Americanos Ilustres Premian el Triunfo de Tio Samuel" (Juárez, Xicotencatl, y Cuauhtemoc), *El Hijo del Ahuizote*, 1898. Political Cartoon.

Cuba stands apart holding aloft its own national flag while Puerto Rico's arm is being held tightly by Uncle Sam. Read one way, this cartoon condones U.S. tutelage of the Antilles. Uncle Sam is poised symbolically at the center between the older Mexican heroes who represent the past, and the young representatives of the Spanish America, the Antilles. It was Uncle Sam who "avenged the Indians" rather than Mexico or Latin America. Another interpretation, however, might emphasize the fact that Uncle Sam bows to the great Mexican heroes, who are seen here as rewarding his actions in favor of Cuba.[39] There is no indication of a difference in rank between the Mexican heroes and Uncle Sam, who are of the same stature. When read alongside the caption, which acknowledges an equivalence between the U.S. victory over the Spanish in Cuba and the Mexican victory over the French at the Cerro de Las Campanas, it is clear that the cartoonist is suggesting that Mexico and the United States are equals in protecting the hemisphere from European encroachment.

FIGURE 6.3 "El A, B, C de la democracia," *El Hijo del Ahuizote*, 8 January 1899. Political cartoon.

In this cartoon, Uncle Sam shares the stage with other equally "illustrious Americans": Juárez, Cuauhtemoc, and Xicotencatl. The three men are important historical figures in the traditional pantheon of Mexican heroes, and here they stand in for the nation. Each of these three Mexican heroes protected the nation against colonial and monarchical forces at different points in time between the fifteenth and nineteenth centuries. Not only does Uncle Sam bow to Mexico, but he bows to Mexico represented in the figure of three indigenous leaders. The portrayal of the United States as seeking validation and accepting tribute from native figures is poignant, given the general tendency in the United States to dismiss Latin Americans as racially inferior. Furthermore, the journalists provocatively suggest that the United States is only joining a fight that Mexico has been carrying on for centuries in the defense of America.

Like their intellectual heirs depicted in the image, the liberal opposition journalists who created and published the illustration struggled to defend the continent from European expansion. While the press coverage of the Cuban Question in 1898 and 1899 demonstrates that Mexican liberal opposition journalists supported the U.S. intervention, they clearly did not believe that the United States had the right to stand alone as the protector of the continent.

In an image from 1899 titled "El A, B, C de la democracia" (fig. 6.3), a generic figure of America beckons to Cubans, Puerto Ricans, and Filipinos, inviting them to learn about democracy. The figure of America holds a tablet, which reads "The Spelling Book of the Free America, A.B.C. of Democracy." The caption reaffirmed the message in the image. "Come here, little ones," the teacher says, "free America will show you the doctrine of sovereign nations." In the image, "free America" is represented in the form of a woman with no national markers. The land she stands on is as much, if not more so Mexican than it is emblematic of the United States. For example, the tropical and desert flora and fauna depicted in the landscape were common to both, as was the transcontinental railroad.

The images in *El Hijo del Ahuizote* and the many letters and articles written by Mexican citizens demonstrate the deep pride that Mexicans felt in their own liberal and democratic traditions and in the role Mexico had played defending the hemisphere from European encroach. In hindsight, the journalists' insistence that the United States was just one of many equal nations in the Americas and that the intervention in Cuba was a confirmation of the sister republic ideal seems to be incomprehensibly naïve, but we must understand their reasoning in context. Mexican liberals who favored Cuban independence rejected the conservative call to support Spain on ideological grounds, but they also rejected the idea that siding with Spain somehow promised to insulate Mexico from U.S. imperialism. While Spaniards and Mexican conservatives argued passionately that the best way to safeguard Mexico's sovereignty was to keep Spain in Cuba and to build close bonds between Latin countries.

Other, pro-U.S. figures argued that the spread of U.S. influence could have a salutary effect on "backward" Latin nations. Among the later we find Francisco Bulnes, Olaguíbel's erstwhile debate partner in 1897. In response to Olaguíbel's articles, Bulnes published an incendiary piece that virulently attacked Spain and defended Cuban independence. However, for Bulnes, the key to Cuba's potential success as a republic rested on its close relationship with the United States, a nation he described as so dynamic it was the "son not of its day, nor of the hour, but of each minute in which through its prodigious activity it reconciles incommensurable interests."[40] Bulnes began by rejecting Olaguíbel's insistence that Cubans were simply Spaniards, and he defended the idea that a people could rid themselves of undesirable cultural characteristics, or so-called superorganic characteristics. Thus, Bulnes believed that Cubans had become less Hispanic and more like U.S. Americans because of the close links established with that country. In Bulnes's mind, Cubans were especially fit for self-governance because they had absorbed the superior habits and culture of their Anglo Saxon neighbors. In a strange way, then, Bulnes, like his opponents, also disavowed the viability of a future Cuban Republic, intimating that Cuba's future was dependent on that of the United States.

While the journalists of *El Hijo del Ahuizote*, *El Diario del Hogar* and *El Continente Americano* and other Pro-Cuban independence newspapers celebrated Bulnes' defense of the insurgents, they were far less pro-U.S., less anti-Hispanist and more Latin Americanist than he was. In fact, they drew an equivalence between Cuban independence, the Mexican Reform movement, Spanish Republicanism and U.S. democracy, figuring each as critical in a shared struggle against tyranny. They concentrated on challenging the conservative viewpoint, which was singularly obsessed with the power of the United States, although from a different angle than Bulnes. On one hand, they argued that Mexico's relationship to the United States was independent of Spain's fate in Cuba. As the staff of *La Patria* joked, unless Spain could physically remove the United States from its present geographical location where it bore down on Mexico from the north, there was nothing Spain could do to shield Mexico from the northern giant.[41] In a letter addressed to Justo Sierra, the famous Porfirian statesman, Juan A. Mateos, the military veteran, federal deputy, and intransigent liberal, challenged the idea that U.S. intentions in Cuba should dictate Mexico's policy. He critiqued the idea that the U.S. occupation of Cuba would "close the Gulf." "[The United States] has already closed it with its navy, without any need for Cuba, and the flag of the Monroe Doctrine waves across the continent. As for us, we are not concerned with that entrance. The American union leans against our frontier with his feet in the sands of the Rio Bravo and his head resting on the gold rich mountains of California."[42] If there was a danger, Mateo argued, it emanated from the North and not from the Caribbean. This view is reflected in the map published by *El Hijo del Ahuizote* in 1897 (fig. 6.1), where Cuba does not appear at all.

Furthermore, the journalists in favor of Cuban independence were offended at the idea that Mexico should look to Spain, its former colonizer, to secure its own independence. "Mexico's independence depends on Mexicans themselves," *La Patria* insisted. "Mexico will be independent even through Spain's disaster and the United States' triumph because its independence does not depend on the luck of Spain or the whims of the United States. It depends on us the Mexicans, on our patriotism and our valor . . . only those who doubt this fear for Mexico's future."[43] These views bear a strong similarity to those of *El Hijo del Ahuizote* journalists who also refused to accept the idea that Mexico, a nation with such a glorious tradition of fighting to protect its independence, would need external support to defend itself, and from Spain, of all places. But the insistence on Mexico's ability to protect itself, or at least its commitment to die trying, reminds us, too, of the writing of Manuel Márquez Sterling. In response to those opponents both Mexican and Spanish who felt that Cuba would not be capable of self-governance, he defiantly proclaimed that Cuba was perfectly fit to stand on its own and that, even if it weren't, Cuba had a right to learn from its own mistakes just as every other American republic had. In these different iterations by Cubans and Mexicans, there is both an insistence on rights, an affirmation of patriotic pride, and an awareness of vulnerability. That vulnerability is evident in Márquez Sterling's statement defending Cuba's right to independence even if the nation was not able to conserve it. Similarly, the staff of *La Patria* oscillated between being secure about the ability of Mexicans to defend the nation and unsure that it could stand up to the United States. "Why should we fear the United States?" the journalists wrote. "Because they will grow in power? And so what? In terms of their superiority over us, what does it matter that they are twenty or twenty-one times more powerful? What matters in a situation like ours is that we are prepared to succumb with glory. Is there proof of our heroicism? That is all we need."[44]

After 1901, the perception of the Mexican pro-Cuba press shifted due to the imposition of the Platt amendment as a condition for U.S. withdrawal from Cuba. The amendment undercut Cuba's sovereignty by not allowing the nation to enter into foreign agreements without U.S. approval, while permitting U.S. military intervention at will to stabilize Cuba. That the Platt amendment was a pernicious move on the part of the United States was clear to Mexicans and Latin Americans across the continent. Although these shifting perspectives on the United States would not lead to an uncritical or unproblematic embrace of *hispanismo*, the Platt amendment certainly made clear that the U.S. intervention in Cuba was not, in fact, an expression of continental solidarity, but rather an example of imperialist greed. Many migrants who suffered callous neglect at the hands of a new imperial government unwilling to aid stranded Cubans abroad after 1898 learned this early on. Nevertheless, Mexicans celebrated Cuba's "independence" in 1902. One newspaper reported how in Mexico City more than

500 students "just as enthusiastic as they had been during the war for Cuban independence" came together on the Paseo de la Reforma and ran through the streets calling out "long live the Cuban republic!" We cannot dismiss Mexican advocates of Cuban independence who celebrated the inauguration of the Cuban republic in 1902 as naïve. They maintained their faith in the Cuban people and in the revolutionary émigrés they had come to know well. They also retained a vain hope that Mexico, having failed Cuba during the independence struggle and during the Spanish-American war, would find ways to guide and protect the fledgling republic into the future.

At the time of the celebration of Cuban independence in May of 1902, *El Hijo del Ahuizote* published a political cartoon celebrating the inauguration of the new Cuban republic.[45] In it, Cuba was figured as a young debutant presented to the world by an admiring figure Uncle Sam. In the background Máximo Gómez proudly waves the Cuban flag, while U.S. governor general Leonard Wood rolls up the U.S. flag, his back turned to the viewer. At the bottom left of the image, on the same panel as the figure of Cuba and of Gómez stands the figure of the Ahuizote, a mythical creature that symbolized Mexico. The Ahuizote draws roses from his hat, which he throws toward the figure of Cuba to *fete* her. The image portrays the U.S. intervention in a positive light: Uncle Sam helped Cuba grow in a short time from the child figured in the 1898 *Hijo* cartoon called "Su Medio de Oro" into the young woman now pictured.

The images that circulated in the U.S. press during 1899, 1901, and 1902 most often used racist characterizations to depict Cuba as an uneducated and rebellious child and Uncle Sam as a strict father/teacher. In the most positive representations, a young female Cuba is taught to ride a bicycle or a Cuban child is cast out to sea in a boat.[46] In none of these U.S. images do we see the insurgent general Máximo Gómez being revered. Indeed, in *El Hijo del Ahuizote*'s cartoon, the appearance of Gómez raising the flag at long last and the figure of the Ahuizote who celebrates the debutant strikes a very different tone from that of the cartoons that proliferated in the U.S. press in 1902. General Leonard Wood's insistence that Cubans were fundamentally unfit for self-governance indicates that these cartoons were not isolated images. They reflected an imperial ideology in the making as the United States built its overseas empire. The Mexican newspapers' depictions are consistent with the way Cuba was imagined throughout the 1890s in Mexico. They purposefully rejected racist and anti-black caricature, most often portraying Cuba as white in reaction to Spanish propaganda,

Affirming Americanismo 239

which sought to discredit the insurgency by depicting it as largely black. In Mexican cartoons throughout the war, Cuba was represented alternately by the figure of a delicate woman, by the figure of her male liberators, or by the figure of an independent child.

Over the course of the wars, both Cuban revolutionaries and Mexican liberals insisted that, even if their nations were weaker and more vulnerable than superpowers like the United States, they could turn to their own traditions of struggle—struggle for independence, struggle for rights, and struggle for just principles—to find strength and courage. They would also find strength in *americanismo*. Cerefino Sifuentes's image of Cuba and Mexico moving forward hand-in-hand in the defense of shared rights was a uniquely poignant articulation of the potential and the value that an average Mexican citizen from Matehuala, San Luis Potosí, saw in solidarity.

Like many Mexican traditional liberals and Cuban patriots, Manuel Márquez Sterling's reflections on the first U.S. invention were mixed. He was grateful to the United States for aiding in the liberation of Cuba from Spain and optimistic about the way the U.S. helped rebuild and modernize Cuba in the years after the war. Yet, he referred to the Platt amendment as "Cleopatra's asp." The asp, he wrote, referring to the second intervention of 1906–1909, "stung the naked arm of the Republic."[47] Márquez Sterling saw Cleopatra's suicide as a suitable metaphor for the political suicide committed by Cuban statesmen, who both accepted the terms of the amendment and invited the U.S. government to intervene in Cuban affairs in 1906. He would describe these men as "blind and inexperienced" and as the "new adversaries of our independence." Finally, he said in reference to the second intervention that "there is nothing more bitter for a nation that fought half a century to liberate itself from the yoke of a foreign power."[48] Just as Mexican liberals would blame their own statesmen for Mexico's failings, so too would Márquez Sterling blame Cuba's statesmen for Cuba's, without sparing the United States its due criticism. Both Mexicans and Cubans diagnosed national ills they felt were deeply embedded in their respective countries, but they saw those ills mirrored in each others societies. This identification became the basis of important transnational solidarities.

Conclusion

Cubans' inability to move the Mexican congress or the Díaz administration to change its position on Cuban independence was deeply frustrating, as the comments of *Un Cubano*, Cirilio Villaverde, Nicolás Domínguez Cowan, and Tomás Estrada Palma at the beginning of this chapter make clear. The unique connection between the increasingly conservative political ideas of many Porfirian elites and Spanish elites, as well as their shared concerns about the spread of U.S. influence, created an especially challenging environment for Cuban organizing. Diplomatic projects would be stillborn, while grassroots efforts would be hindered by Spanish spies working with local Mexican authorities. Cuban migrants did not hide their dismay and disappointment. Although shocked by the indifference of states that had once recognized Cuba's right to constitute an independent nation and had once supported the insurgent struggle, Cubans in Mexico and across Latin America did not give up. They worked continuously to support the war effort, while defending the Cuban cause in their diverse host lands.

As we have seen, forging transnational solidarities was a central platform of Cuban revolutionary politics. Cubans worked to convince Latin Americans that their fight for independence was inseparable from a larger continental and even transatlantic struggle for the affirmation of republicanism and democracy. Ironically, in Mexico this rhetoric drew to the Cuban cause those Mexicans who staunchly defended a liberal tradition that ruling political elites subscribed to only in name. As a result, the hope that popular solidarities would shift public opinion and possibly impact government policy remained illusory. As Cuban migrants watched their most committed defenders, the students of *El Continente Americano*, arrested and imprisoned for supporting their cause, they were forced to recognize that Mexico was not what it seemed—or, more accurately, what they imagined it to be.

In light of the events of 1898, Cubans in Mexico and elsewhere in Latin America had become accustomed to disappointment. Some revolutionary émigrés channeled disappointment into a fierce and forceful embrace of the United States. In his 1898 essay, "The Redemption of a World," Rafael María Merchán symbolically accepted an imaginary offer from the United States to defend the Americas together. "Members of the Union," he declares boldly, "We would be proud to join our forces with yours." Of course, the United States never offered to partner with Cuba in the defense of the hemisphere. Yet, like the cartoonist of *El Hijo del Ahuizote* who depicted Mexico as equal in stature with the United States, Merchán rhetorically defended the ideal of the sister republic by figuring Cuba as a partner of the United States. However, while *El Hijo del Ahuizote* drew the mature Mexico as an adult and the fledgling Cuba as a child after the war, Merchán rejected the infantilization of Cuba and argued that the nascent republic was equal to her sisters. As the twentieth century dawned and Cubans began to write their national history, they depicted Cuba as "apart" from Latin America in an effort to forget the disappointment and disillusionment of the 1890s.

Mexicans, too, were deeply disillusioned with the government rejection of Cuban independence between 1895 and 1898, a rejection which they saw as a symptom of the greater ills of the reconciliation politics that sought to heal divides between traditional liberals and conservatives while easing the traditional hard-line policy on the separation of church and state. Juan Tizoc of *El Continente Americano* offered an ominous prediction in the fall of 1896: "The republic has needed a period of rest, the duration of which no one dares calculate, in order to once again take up the painful march along the path that its heroes, martyrs, soldiers and philosophers paved toward the conquest of the nation's most prized liberties. We find ourselves now in a moment of transition. Distrust bubbles up within us and we anticipate the eruption of a catastrophe that will tear apart the harmony of our outwardly tranquil existence, an existence purchased at the expense of patriotism and progress and solely for the achievement of material gain."[49] The "period of rest" Tizoc alludes to is the Porfirian peace, the "painful march" is the struggle to constitute a truly democratic republic, and the "distrust" he experiences encapsulates his feelings about the regime. In his eyes, the catastrophe he anticipates will be brought about by a new clash between the forces of liberalism and conservatism.

Throughout the late 1890s, the journalists blamed the current regime for bringing about its own future demise. In the 1890s, liberal opposition journalists were by and large reformers rather than revolutionaries. They believed that it was their responsibility to push the Mexican government to reform in the interest of preserving peace, while moving steadily toward the realization of a liberal, democratic vision.[50] Rather than call for revolution, then, they warned of its coming. Something would tear asunder the "harmony of our outward tranquil existence" bought at the expense of Mexico's most sacred values, principles, and ideals. Tizoc's "progress" was not Díaz's progress. It was not the crude quest for "achievement of material gain" alone. Tizoc's vision for Mexico was a vision of a nation that would be capable of adding to its newfound economic progress the political glory it once possessed. As 1897 dawned, Juan Tizoc and his coworkers found themselves in the sights of the Spanish foreign minister, who was eager to persecute them. The minister may have succeeded in one sense, but the students of *El Continente Americano* would not be cowed. They wrote scathing articles from their prison cells and sneaked them out to be printed. The students decried Spanish influence in Mexico, and railed against the clergy and the politics of reconciliation that was allowing conservatism to rear its head once again.

As 1897 gave way to 1898, Mexican and Cuban advocates of Cuban independence were exhausted and frustrated. The spectacular explosion of the battleship *Maine*, the suspicion that it was Spaniards' handiwork, and the anti-Hispanist zeal it engendered, all combined with their own sentiments and frustrations to create a perfect storm. But in their enthusiasm for the United States' taking up the defense of Cuba, Cubans and Mexicans did not forget what they were fighting for. Their vision of the Americas was not one in which, as Porfirio Díaz had claimed to Márquez Sterling, "to be strong is to accept those who come with their money and their initiatives to better your country" regardless of the cost. In contrast to Porfirio Díaz in his interview with Márquez Sterling, Mexican supporters of *Cuba Libre* argued that to be strong was to recognize the value of your own traditions, to honor them and to seek a way forward through and with them.

Just before he died, José Martí described Cuba as Mexico's defender, even as he wondered whether or not Mexico could come to Cuba's defense in the time of need that was approaching. After the Spanish-American War, there was a perceptible shift in Mexican portrayals of Cuba. During the 1895 War, the insurgent republic was depicted either as a full-grown woman—the classic iconography of western nations—or in the persons of its military heroes and generals. After the Spanish-American war, however, that depiction changed. Alongside these more traditional images we see other examples in which Cuba is either seen as sick and frail or as a child. In the political cartoon "Su Medio de Oro" published by *El Hijo del Ahuizote*, Cuba is represented as a young child in need of guidance and tutelage, while in "El A, B, C de la democracia" an adult female figure of América beckons the newly liberated colonies, who are diminutive by comparison, to a land symbolically rendered as the Americas where they will learn about democracy. Cuba is figured as child vis-à-vis not only the United States but also Mexico in both images; both images also imply that the tutelage that Cuba needs to reach political maturity can be learned in Mexico as well as the United States. It is noteworthy that Cuba, once seen as a leader in her republic struggle is, after 1898, figured as a child in need of guidance. As revolutionaries, Cubans were at the vanguard, but as citizens of a fledgling nation, they are children, new to the problems and challenges of state building and nation formation. The depiction of Mexico's role vis-à-vis Cuba in these images may have been fanciful, but it reveals much about the journalists' resistance to the writing of Mexico and Latin America out of the history of Cuban independence and the future of the Cuban nation. When the conflict over Cuba was framed as one fought between the United States and Spain, or between the Anglo and Latin races, Latin America was relegated to the background. Mexicans protested Mexico's marginalization in American affairs by defiantly depicting Mexico as on par with the United States and poised to play an equal role as guide and teacher to a fledgling Cuba.

Epilogue

The Legacies of Cuban-Mexican Solidarities
....

"In my sentiments, I am almost Mexican."
—Manuel Márquez Sterling, 1905

Manuel Márquez Sterling had a longer history and a much older connection with Mexico than many of his fellow Cuban migrants, most of whom had found their way there during the 1895 War. His mother had sent him to Mérida as a boy from time to time to alleviate his debilitating asthma. In the 1880s, Manuel's uncle, Carlos de Varona, lived in Mérida and worked as the regional head of the Mexican National Bank, a prestigious and lucrative position. In 1892 a restless Manuel left Cuba looking for new horizons. By this time his uncle had moved to Mexico City to occupy an even more important post as the national bank's president. Mexico City looked promising for Manuel. Thanks to his uncle's contacts, he easily found work as a journalist in Mexico City upon his arrival. Due to his revolutionary pedigree—his uncle had been an important asset to the revolutionaries in the Ten Years' War, and his father had been a representative of the Cuban government in arms in Peru—Manuel also gained acceptance among the existing older generation Cuban exiles, who were established figures in the capital. He knew Nicolás Domínguez Cowan well, and he had the opportunity to meet José Martí in 1894, when the revolutionary leader came to Mexico to solicit the support of Porfirio Díaz and to hear something of his plans for revolution.

When the war broke out in 1895, inspired by Martí's own personal sacrifice, Manuel immediately traveled to Florida and placed himself at the service of General Enrique Collazo, hoping to travel with Collazo's expedition to Cuba. Collazo took one look at his old friend and laughed. Manuel blamed his "malicious asthma and the endemic fevers" for his feeble appearance. Adding insult to injury, one of Collazo's men came forward and said, "you, sir, are not even fit to wash or sweep."[1] Collazo did employ Manuel's services as an aide-de-camp in Camaguey, but persecution forced the aspiring young insurgent to return to Florida and to exile. His dreams of military glory dashed, Manuel relocated to New York. There he worked closely with the Cuban Revolutionary Party as a journalist and as an archivist cataloguing José Martí's papers after his death. Even though New York City was the nerve center of Cuban politics in the 1890s, Mexico had become his home. By 1896, he was back at his desk in Mexico City working as a journalist and participating actively in Cuban revolutionary politics as a member of the Cuban club Morelos y Maceo.

In Mexico City between 1896 and 1898, Manuel worked as a staff writer for *El Diario del Hogar*, one of Mexico's principal opposition newspapers. He also wrote for and collaborated with *El Continente Americano*. Juan Sánchez Azcona, the Porfirian statesman and, later, supporter of the revolutionary government that unseated Díaz, called Manuel Márquez Sterling "one of the most effective propagandists for the freedom of his fatherland among innumerable Mexican sympathizers." Sánchez Azcona fondly remembered how, along with Manuel and a handful of other Cubans, "together we formed a nucleus to raise funds for the Cuban insurrection and organized and celebrated literary and musical *veladas* that were very successful and that augmented Mexican sympathies for that grand cause."[2] During his time at *El Diario del Hogar*, working alongside opposition journalists in Mexico, Manuel came to see Cuba's struggle as related to the struggles of his coworkers as they, too, fought against anti-democratic forces. Both revolutionary Cubans and reformist Mexicans saw themselves as the frontline in a battle against resurgent conservatism and Hispanism. Their shield and weapon was *americanismo*. When Manuel returned to Cuba after the Spanish-American War, he carried with him seven years of experience in Mexico City. He had witnessed the virulent debates in the press, the conflicts in the streets. He had been buoyed by the unbreakable solidarity of the Mexicans who supported Cuba Libre and devastated by those who denied Cuba's independence by disavowing it.[3]

Like the more fortunate of his compatriots, Manuel returned to Cuba shortly after the war. He lived in Havana and worked as a journalist and writer, publishing a significant number of books between 1901 and 1909, when he began a diplomatic career. Among these publications, one in particular stands out for its unique vision of the history of Cuban independence. The text, titled *La diplomacia en nuestra historia*, was published in 1909. The work was conceived as a response to the idea that the Cuban independence struggle was fundamentally separate from the turn-of-the-century Latin American independence movements. This belief had come to hold sway in intellectual circles in Cuba in the early twentieth century, largely as a result of the failure of diplomacy by Cuban insurgents in Latin America during the 1895 war. Manuel found the absence of any mention of the "debt of gratitude that binds us to the other nations of our race and our continent" troubling. Accusing Cuban publicists and intellectuals of ignoring the important historical connections between Cuban independence and the independence of Latin America, he vowed to correct the omission. Manuel's observation that Cubans tended to depict Cuba as "a case . . . apart . . . disconnected from the common problem of Spanish America, with no discernable relationship to the nations of the south, fighting in the midst of the most horrifying snares and disloyalties" is indicative of how deeply Cubans felt Latin American states' indifference toward the Cuban independence struggle in the 1890s.[4]

Of course, the idea that Cuba was both part of and apart from Latin America was enshrined in the Manifesto de Montecristi, in which Cuba was depicted as more prepared for republican statehood than the Spanish American republics that made the transition to independence at the turn of the nineteenth century. Cuba, the revolutionaries imagined, would emerge from colonialism and begin independent life free of the colonial legacies that had handicapped their counterparts in Latin America. Yet even as they held themselves aloft in some ways, Cubans expected Latin America's recognition and support. They expected that their brothers throughout the continent would see the Cuban struggle as the culmination of a decolonization project that began in 1810. Hence, the "disloyalty" exhibited by Latin American states was received as "horrifying." So bitter was the memory of this betrayal that it affected the way that they remembered and represented Cuban history. Like many of his Mexican compatriots, Márquez Sterling embraced the United States in 1898 out of frustration with Mexico and Latin America, but by 1909 he was deeply disillusioned with the U.S. and with Cuban politicians. Searching for answers to Cuba's political woes, he turned his gaze toward Latin America.

Written and published in the same year that the United States occupying forces left Cuba for the second time, *La diplomacia en nuestra historia* is a product of Manuel Márquez Sterling's deep disillusionment with the United States' imperialist actions, but even more so it is a product of his conflicted view of Latin America. He was bitter about Latin America's abandonment of Cuba, but recognized the power of Latin American solidarity outside of official politics. Referring to the Cuban cause as "as aspiration of the

American race," he insisted that the solidarity with Cuba that "the press, intellectuals . . . and popular masses" expressed was unaffected by the actions of Latin American governments.[5] This unbroken record of solidarity, which united Cubans and Latin Americans from the time of the Ten Years' War forward, inspired Márquez Sterling to explore the connections between Cuban independence and Latin American independence that his fellow Cubans ignored. In so doing, Márquez Sterling hoped to reaffirm the faith in Latin American solidarity that his compatriots had lost.

His book begins with an exploration of Latin American politics and social relations in the late nineteenth century. Márquez Sterling argues that Cuba's sister republics in Latin America did not come to Cuba's aid in the 1890s because they were suffering a crisis as profound as Cuba's struggle for independence. "When we were breaking our colonial bonds, the majority of those nations had to destroy the dictatorships that emerged from the depths of their own lands. The torments that covered with disgrace those realities were barely less than ours. Whether or not it originates from a faraway metropolis, tyranny always yields the same results."[6] Márquez Sterling understood Cuban independence as a continuation of the process of decolonization begun in Spain's mainland colonies during the Age of Revolutions, but here the parallel he draws is between Cuba's struggle for independence and Spanish America's struggle with colonial legacies. The argument is a crystal clear reflection of the views that were sustained by the Mexican journalists and other traditional liberals who supported Cuban independence during the war. The fight against Spanish tyranny and against "dictatorships" across Latin America was one and the same. This ran contrary to the thinking of men like Tomás Estrada Palma and other Cuban revolutionary émigrés affiliated with the PRC, who had worked to court Díaz and who admired his leadership and the modernization of Mexico, over which he presided. One need only remember Estrada Palma's letter to Díaz and his plea that the president of Mexico intervene to stop the economic destruction of Cuba.

According to Márquez Sterling, Latin American statesmen lost their way between the 1860s and the 1890s when they chose to sacrifice "*americanismo*" to base material interests and narrowly nationalist concerns. Just as he had drawn a parallel between authoritarian governments in Latin America and Spain, Márquez Sterling implicitly compared their economic motivations, which he found similarly exploitative. For Márquez Sterling, economic concerns should not be elevated over political and ideological considerations, which he believed should drive the actions of states. His ideas were out of step with the Latin American political elites of his day who had staked their careers and the futures of their nations on the idea that in order to become modern they had to achieve economic progress, and that in order to attain economic progress they must sacrifice political ideals. In the end, the solidarity that mattered was not the solidarity between Cuban migrants and the Mexican state whose attention they desperately courted during the war, but rather between the migrants and those Mexicans who were bound together by a shared struggle against tyranny in both Mexico and in Cuba. The struggle for *Cuba Libre* was thus more than a nationalist struggle. It quickly assumed continent-wide significance as it became the banner behind which those opposing the rise of dictatorship and oligarchic rule in late nineteenth-century Latin America rallied.

The 1860s and 1870s represented the pinnacle of official Latin American solidarity with Cuban independence, but this solidarity had collapsed by the 1890s. For Márquez Sterling, the disjuncture between Latin American statesmens' views of Cuba in the middle of the nineteenth century and those at the turn of the twentieth is subsumed by the great continuity he sees in the preservation of *americanismo* among the people of Latin America from Chihuahua to Patagonia, all of whom eagerly awaited the end of the conflict and the establishment of the Cuban republic.[7] It was this spirit of *americanismo* that formed a bridge between the early nineteenth-century independence wars and Cuba's later struggle. According to Márquez Sterling, this pure and noble ideal remained constant, while the definition of national interests defended by political elites and statesmen was changing. For him, the Latin American statesmen of the mid-nineteenth century, who understood the value of *americanismo* and who knew how to interpret the will of the people of their nations, were the true heroes. *La diplomacia en nuestra historia* was meant to educate Cubans about Cuban revolutionary representatives who traversed the continent in the interests of the movement and about the Latin American statesmen whose actions in favor of *Cuba Libre* during the 1870s would forever change the course of Cuban history.

The core argument of the book is one that presents a revisionist view of the history of Cuban independence during the Ten Years' War. After several chapters dedicated to a critical diagnosis of the failure of *americanismo*, Márquez Sterling turns to a long exploration of Cuban diplomacy during the Ten Years' War, restoring agency to Latin America's historic role in the Cuban independence process. He argues that Latin American diplomatic action in favor of Cuba during the 1860s and 1870s was of critical importance to Cuba's independence process, because the recognition of Cuban belligerency rights by key Latin American states in the 1870s legitimized the insurgency. Explaining the connection between Latin American diplomacy in relation to the Ten Years' War and U.S. diplomacy in relation to the 1895 war, Márquez Sterling writes: "The diplomacy in one period gave the other consistency, strength and personality. The United States recognized us as a legitimate nation because that legitimacy was recognized as of 1870 by the principle nations of Latin America."[8] By arguing that Latin America's sanctioning of the Cuban cause in the 1860s and 1870s was a defining moment of the Cuban independence process, Márquez Sterling wrests the glory from the United States, which had been imagined as the sole liberator of Cuba, but he also challenges historians to recognize the importance of Latin American diplomacy in relation to the question of Cuban independence.

A year after the publication of *La diplomacia en nuestra historia*, the Mexican Revolution took the Americas by storm. Márquez Sterling watched anxiously from across the Gulf as the world he knew was turned upside down. His efforts to return to Mexico before 1910 had been rendered impossible by his status as persona non grata, imposed after he published an unflattering article about Porfirio Díaz in 1904. After 1910, however, the new political climate and his old contacts paved the way for his return, this time as Cuban ambassador to the government of Francisco Madero. Arriving to Veracruz on his way to Mexico City in 1912, Márquez Sterling was immediately transported back twenty years to when he arrived in the port as a migrant looking for a home. "It was a morning with a clear blue sky," he remembered. "From the deck of the ship, I delighted in contemplating in the faint distance the snow-capped peak of the Orizaba [volcano] . . . and the city that extended lazily from its soft pedestal of sand."[9] The future Cuban minister was quickly ushered to the railway station, where he continued on to Mexico City. When he set foot on the streets of Mexico City, the same streets that he had crossed so many times as a young revolutionary journalist at the height of the Porfirian regime, he noted sadly that now, two years into the Revolution, "the Capitol building which was meant to be a senate without senators contains within its foundations the exhausted democracy . . . over the marbled columns constructed by the fugitive dictator, new men fight with old structures." Márquez Sterling recognized that the weight of over thirty years would be hard to lift.

Although the dictator had fled, Márquez Sterling was still plagued by doubt as to whether Mexico would emerge victorious from its struggle against the legacy of the dictatorship. He wrote, "a third of a century of oppression still wanders this immense panorama, there is no greatness where it does not rest, there is no rubble where it has not lain."[10] But Márquez Sterling, having worked closely with the opposition journalists of *El Diario del Hogar*, had developed a critique of the Porfiriato long before he arrived in 1912 to contemplate the "rubble" of the old regime. Juan Sánchez Azcona remembered how, back in the 1890s "in addition to his patriotic activities, Márquez Sterling dedicated himself to the study and observation of the men that surrounded him, and in a sober critique of the imperial pomp of the Porfirian regime which appeared in one of his early publications, he predicted the coming of the Mexican Revolution with such confidence and clarity that he even identified some of us men who were little known then, but who were among those that initiated it."[11] Indeed, as we have seen, Mexican opposition journalists often figured the Díaz regime as teetering dangerously at the edge of a cliff, or otherwise predicted that some force would "tear apart"—in the words of Mexican journalist Juan Tizoc—the delicate Porfirian peace. Sánchez Azcona's observations simply demonstrate the degree to which Márquez Sterling was part of the intellectual world of the emerging opposition to the dictatorship coalescing in Mexico City in the 1890s. As we will see, that space served as a critical classroom for Márquez Sterling as he developed his ideas on Latin American politics and solidarities.

Márquez Sterling's life was changed by the *decena trágica*, the period of ten days during which counterrevolutionary forces successfully overthrew Francisco Madero's revolutionary government. He recounts the events of those days, including his vain efforts to save the lives of Francisco Madero and José María Pino Suárez, in his book *Los Últimos días del Presidente Madero*. After Madero's assassination, Márquez Sterling accompanied the former president's wife and remaining family to Cuba where they sought refuge for a short time. Horrified by the murders, and especially by the complicity of the U.S. ambassador Henry Lane Wilson in Victoriano Huerta's overthrow of Madero, Márquez Sterling abandoned his career as a diplomat and returned to his work as a journalist. As the director of two Cuban newspapers in the years after 1913, Márquez Sterling worked to counter negative propaganda emanating from the United States that vilified the Revolution. He was supported and encouraged in these efforts by revolutionary generals, such as Salvador Alvarado and Venustiano Carranza, who were both aware of his work as a journalist in Cuba. Márquez Sterling also offered employment and friendship to many Mexican revolutionaries who sought refuge in Cuba, among them the aforementioned *Maderista*

Juan Sánchez Azcona and the Mexican lawyer, diplomat, and politician Carlos Trejo Lerdo de Tejada. After Madero's assassination, Lerdo de Tejada fled the country to Cuba. In 1916, he published a book in Cuba about the Mexican Revolution, entitled *La revolución y el nacionalismo: todo para todos*. He asked Márquez Sterling to write a review for the book, and the Cuban journalist readily accepted.

In his review, Márquez Sterling drew attention to the author's scientific and sociological rigor and his insightfulness. But there is more than praise for Carlos Trejo Lerdo de Tejada in the piece. According to Márquez Sterling, the book contained an accurate analysis of the political ills of all Latin American countries:

> In this book, it is Mexico and all of our America that is, in her psychological and anatomical development, meticulously [depicted]. Equally infirm, with the same symptoms and ills emanating from identical infections, [our republics] require the same treatments to achieve a measure of common good and moral advancement. It is for this reason that we read Mr. Lerdo de Tejada with the interest that only a work of continental relevance can produce. . . . Any one of our democracies would suffice to characterize this work; it would be enough to substitute names, countries, and occasionally dates. Wherever [we look, we see] the mis-diagnosis of problems, the blindness of *caudillos*, the imbalance of the apostles, images of blood and death, in times of peace and civil war, the product of the sacrifice of some and the despotism of others.[12]

As he watched the Mexican Revolution unfold from Cuba, Márquez Sterling saw in Mexico a reflection of the challenges that faced Cuba and Latin America as a whole. He concurred with Lerdo de Tejada's call for social reform and believed it was the key to fundamental change for all of Latin America. Although it was omitted before publication, Márquez Sterling's first draft of the review included the following statement: "The flag of social reform raised by Lerdo de Tejada is the key . . . [to] the creation of a national spirit in the countries that don't yet have one, the reinvigoration and consolidation of [that spirit] in those that do, the redistribution of national wealth . . . [and] the true freedom of the peasantry and the proletariat from the claws of hypocritical bourgeois minorities that appropriate everything and who criminally subjugate [everyone] in the name of foolish prejudices."[13] After urging revolutionary soldiers, statesmen, and average citizens to read this book, Márquez Sterling ended the draft review by affirming that within the text's pages the reader would find "lessons for . . . the nations of Latin America, where sooner rather than later the hour of the demand for social equality will come."[14]

Pablo Yankelevich has argued that the revolution in Mexico alarmed but also inspired leaders in other Latin American countries. The possibility that a similar fate might befall their nations was frightening. However, during World War I, Latin Americans began to question their affinity for Europe, and as the Mexican Revolution evolved into more than just a rebellion, they increasingly saw Mexico as a "laboratory in which to realize national projects and materialize utopian dreams of regeneration and continental unity."[15] These words could easily describe how Latin Americans saw the Cuban Question during the 1890s as well. Manuel Márquez Sterling's life and work connects these two movements of continental significance.

By 1917, Márquez Sterling had become severely disillusioned with Cuban politics. He bemoaned the corruption that had become routine in all Cuban administrations, whether they were liberal or conservative. It may have been easy to govern the Cuban people, Márquez Sterling contended, but it was difficult to govern the governors. He insisted that the men who led society must be governed by their own sense of "duty, love of progress, strict interpretation of the law, and honest administrative measures."[16] The principal problem in Cuba was the immorality of the nation's leaders who were given to arbitrary actions, violations of the law, and corruption. In 1916 a friend of Márquez Sterling living in Mérida, Yucatán, wrote an impassioned critique of Cuban politics: "I am convinced that our sickness is in the very marrow of our being."[17] Márquez Sterling's review of Lerdo de Tejada's book reflected a growing trend in Latin America, a tendency to cast social and political problems in terms of physical illness and debilitation. Reinaldo Funes Monzote has argued that the application of medical language to describe Cuba, especially the language of disease and contagion, was not common in Cuba itself in the early twentieth century. In fact, from the first republic forward, Cubans touted their advances in health and hygiene.[18] The language of illness that Márquez Sterling appropriates in his discourse might have been a product of his deep engagement with political debates in late nineteenth-century Mexico. The call for reform that Márquez Sterling saw as critical to the healing of the republic would begin to be addressed in the Revolution of 1933. However, Márquez Sterling feared that the chronic instability of those years would lead to yet another U.S. intervention. In September of 1933, concerned that the United States might use the Platt Amendment to intervene and stabilize the government of Cuba and operating once again as Cuban ambassador in Mexico, Márquez Sterling made an appeal to the governments of Argentina, Chile, Brazil, and Mexico, asking them to submit formal statements preempting any attempt on the part of the U.S. government to invade Cuba.[19] A year later, as Cuban ambassador in the United States, he would work assiduously to abrogate the Platt Amendment, which was finally repealed on 29 May 1934. He died shortly thereafter.

Márquez Sterling had been a staunch critic of the Platt Amendment as early as 1901, but he made sense of the amendment and its passing by reflecting on Mexican history. In a conversation with his friend (later his biographer) René Lufríu, Márquez Sterling drew a parallel between the Platt Amendment and the Porfiriato. In his 1938 biography of Márquez Sterling, René Lufríu wrote, "I remember that once he [Márquez Sterling] told me that the two contemporary acts most harmful to America for having generated collective mental states of deep disturbance were the Porfiriato and the Platt Amendment."[20] The comparison is illuminating. In *La diplomacia en nuestra historia*, Márquez Sterling drew a connection between the Porfiriato and other late nineteenth-century dictatorships in Latin America on the one hand and the tyranny of the Spanish colonial state on the other. However, later in his conversations with Lufríu, he compared Porfirian elites, who had compromised Mexico's liberal and democratic traditions in the interest of economic progress and mortgaged Mexico to the United States in the process, to the Cuban elites, who essentially mirrored the actions of their Mexican counterparts by accepting the Platt Amendment.

Márquez Sterling's implicit juxtaposition of Cuban Republican elites, Porfirian elites, and Spanish colonial elites is telling for what it reveals about his sense of continuity. The same factors that undergirded the solidarity between Porfirian elites and Spanish colonists in Mexico during the Cuban independence war of 1895—especially the consolidation of conservative liberalism—also motivated men like Tomás Estrada Palma, who aspired to make Cuba a republic in the image not only of the United States, but also of Porfirian Mexico. Although he would not see it clearly until years after the war, Márquez Sterling's own affiliation with the anti-Díaz opposition in Mexico would drive a wedge between him and the Cuban Revolutionary Party's more conservative elites. Just as the Cuban Question served Mexican dissidents as a vehicle and platform to critique the Díaz regime, the program of the opposition changed the way that Márquez Sterling and others like him understood Cuban Revolutionary politics. Initially disillusioned with Latin American official neglect of Cuba during the 1895 War, Márquez Sterling shifted his disappointment onto Cuba's politicians after the war. Watching the machinations and mistakes of Mexico's and Cuba's political elites in the early twentieth century produced "collective mental states of deep disturbance." Never a complete pessimist, Márquez Sterling came to understand that if there was faith to be had, it was in the "American" people and in *americanismo*, the solidarity that could bind people across the continent outside of official politics.

Reflecting on his years spent living as an exile in Mexico, Manuel Márquez Sterling said, "in my sentiments, I am almost Mexican." A life lived between Cuba and Mexico deeply informed the way Márquez Sterling thought about Cuba and about Latin America more generally. Rather than see the region as a set of discreet republics, he saw Latin America as a region of states that had emerged from the same colonial history, had struggled after independence with the same colonial legacies, and whose similar problems required the same solutions. This conviction was at the core of his evolving *americanismo*. *La diplomacia en nuestra historia* is one if his earliest articulations of *americanismo*, which he saw as a force that propelled the Cuban struggle against Spain and Latin Americans' struggles against oligarchy and dictatorship. Unlike the many Cubans who refused to recognize the history of connections between Cuba's independence war and the Latin American struggles of the 1820s, or between ongoing struggles in Cuba and Latin America against bad governance, Márquez Sterling refused to lose faith in the possibility of Latin American solidarity. If the problems were held in common and common solutions were required, then Latin Americans would need to stand together in the struggle. His close affiliation with Mexican revolutionaries in the 1910s and 1920s, his commitment to defending the Mexican Revolution as a transformative movement that contained critical lessons for Latin America, and his marshaling of Latin American solidarities in the 1930s to secure Cuba's sovereignty from the United States are all evidence of the fact that Márquez Sterling's *americanismo* was closely associated with a life lived between Mexico and Cuba.

The Gulf World was a space of circulation and migration, although Cuban migrants experienced different degrees of mobility. From the time of José María Heredia to the time of Martí, elite political exiles and migrants found few obstacles that their ingenuity—traveling in disguise, or with false documents—could not overcome. Others, perhaps less privileged but also fortunate, like Ignacio Martín Arbona y Domínguez and Gabriel López

Garcia, were supported by the large, long-standing, organized, and politicized communities of Cuban migrants existing throughout the region. If they drew on the resources of these communities while abroad, as insurgents in Cuba during the war, they benefitted from their revolutionary, and in some cases royalist contacts, both of which proved critical for navigating Cuba. Finally, the most unfortunate, the poorest Cubans, when and if they made it back, found that little of the *Cuba Libre* they imagined had come to pass. Instead, they faced marginalization, unemployment, and a state that cared little about their revolutionary sacrifices. Even the ANERC, the association founded and built ostensibly to honor their work, raised barriers to their participation.

The Gulf was also a contested space, fought over by nations, empires, and revolutionaries. Cuban revolutionaries contended with Mexican, U.S., and Spanish statesmen for their place in the region, and each played the hand they thought best. Cubans mounted a multifocal campaign, working toward diplomatic solidarity and recognition while gathering funds and supplies to keep the war going. While the Spanish state dedicated every man and every peseta to the war effort, Spaniards abroad worked hard to counter Cubans' efforts to forge profitable solidarities. Jealously guarding the close connections they had with political elites throughout Latin America, Spaniards used these connections to ensure tacit cooperation with the mission to preserve *Cuba Española*. Mexico maintained a Spanish-friendly neutrality, the only option for a nation hemmed in by U.S. strategic and financial interests and by its own conviction that *Cuba Española*, or possibly *Cuba Mexicana*, were the only acceptable options for Cuba's future. The United States emerged victorious, wresting the fragments of Spain's empire from her firmly clenched fist and frustrating Cubans' efforts to found an independent republic. But, the ousting of Spain from Cuba also represented a gain for the United States in relation to Mexico, a republic that had lost and ceded much territory to the United States over the course of a century. What had once been the *"seno Mexicano"* was now, truly, an American Mediterranean.

Finally, the nineteenth-century Gulf World was a space of solidarities, and not just elite solidarities. Cuban and Mexican workers from the textile, tobacco, and railroad industries pronounced their support for the Cuban cause in their actions, in their contributions, and, occasionally, through their words. These solidarities, this spirit of *americanismo*, was precisely what Manuel Márquez Sterling drew his readers' attention to in *La diplomacia en nuestra historia*. The true legacy of the Cuban cause in Latin America was not the bitter rejection of Cuban independence by political elites and statesmen who, manipulating a discourse of national interests, worked to enrich and sustain corrupt oligarchies and dictatorships. Rather, it was in the people who kept *americanismo* alive, the people who never lost sight of the connections that existed over and above national borders—connections that were deeper and more enduring even than national identities. This *americanismo* was born in the Age of Revolution, and it matured through the first half of the nineteenth century. The rise of Latin American nation states, the turn to economic liberalism, and the emergence of *hispanismo* and Latin race ideology in the late nineteenth century drove *americanismo* underground, yet it persisted. It traveled with Cuban migrants who linked distant ports in and beyond a connected Gulf World as they built a national consciousness and transnational solidarities together. It thrived in the transnational social and political spaces in which Cubans and their Mexican and other Latin American allies envisioned in *Cuba Libre* a Latin American ideal capable of invigorating and reinvigorating their struggles. It persisted in the minds of Cubans like Manuel Márquez Sterling as they made sense in the early twentieth century of a changing world that seemed all too familiar. *Americanismo* was a Latin American invention. As an ideology of solidarity that rejected the imperialism inherent in both Pan-Americanism and Pan-Hispanism, *americanismo* was the forerunner to twentieth-century anti-imperialist *latinoamericanismo*. Martí may have been one of its most eloquent spokesmen, but its custodians in the last decade of the nineteenth century and well into the twentieth were thousands of Cuban and Latin Americans who saw the future of a continent in the fate of an island.

In 1961, as a U.S. invasion force landed at the Bay of Pigs intent on destroying the Cuban Revolution of 1959, former President of Mexico, Lázaro Cárdenas, made a spectacular gesture of solidarity with a new Cuban revolution. The man who had provided support for Castro and his band of rebels when they sought refuge in Mexico in 1955 boarded a plane for Cuba determined to fight on the side of the revolutionary forces. In a recent book about Mexico in the Cold War, Renata Keller tells the story of how Cárdenas was stopped by sitting Mexican president Adolfo López Mateos and reprimanded for his excessive enthusiasm.[21] López Mateos, by contrast, would take a different approach, one that in the long history of Mexican-Cuban relations was broadly familiar. He would profess outward solidarity with the Cuban Revolution because it was consonant with the image of revolutionary Mexico, while working covertly with the United States to undermine it because of the threat it posed in the context of a Cold War that was heating up. Just like Díaz sixty years earlier, López Mateos was caught between Mexico's revolutionary image and conservative reality. In the same year, the Popular Socialist Party (PSP) in Mexico published a call to the Mexican people urging them to support the Cuban Revolutionary struggle. "The revolution of the Spanish colonies in America for political independence was one, from Mexico to Argentina. The revolution for economic emancipation is one from Mexico to Argentina . . . and also from Paraguay to Cuba. . . . The responsibility for what occurs in Cuba will fall on the government of the United States, but also on the democratic forces of Mexico and Latin America. . . . Let's honor the three revolutions . . . which gave shape to our fatherland. . . . Don't let a brother of ours be sacrificed before our eyes by the eternal enemy of our grand Latin American family." The call went on to urge Mexican citizens to volunteer to travel to Cuba to fight for the "respect" and "sovereignty."[22] What is striking about this quote is not the difference it marks between the 1890s and 1960s in Mexico, but rather the continuity it draws between the 1820s and the 1960s. In 1961, Mexican socialists urged the Mexican people to recognize the Age of Revolution as the time when Latin American solidarity was born. The struggle for political independence did not resolve economic inequality, and the revolution continued. In 1961, under attack from the United States, Cuba embodied the vanguard of the revolution for "economic emancipation" for which some Mexicans longed. Also, like their 1890s counterparts, Mexican socialists in the 1960s insisted that it was Mexico's duty to support the Cuban Revolution.

While Mexican statesmen have openly and covertly supported and sought to contain or thwart Cuba's revolutionary movements from the 1820s onward, a current of solidarity between Mexicans and Cubans at least as old and remarkably durable is discernable across the ages as well. The ideas expressed by the PSP—of fraternity born of the Age of Revolution, of Mexico's unique duty toward Cuba, and especially its responsibility to shield Cuba from the United States—are all too familiar. Jacobin liberals of the 1890s were less firm and clear in their opposition to the United States than their counterparts in the 1960s, but they were equally strident about affirming Mexico's role in the hemisphere and its unique responsibility toward Cuba in the context of a Gulf World where the United States bore down on both nations.

Notes

Introduction

1. Márquez Sterling, *La diplomacia en nuestra historia*, 8–9.
2. Ibid., 5.
3. Esteban Borrero y Echeverria to Rafael A. Gutiérrez, 9 April 1898, reproduced in *Correspondencia diplomática de la delegación cubana en nueva york durante la Guerra de independencia de 1895 a 1898*, 5 vols. 2:223.
4. Esteban Borrero y Echeverria to William McKinley, 19 April 1898, copied in *Correspondencia diplomática de la delegación cubana en nueva york durante la Guerra de independencia de 1895 a 1898*, 2:247.
5. See Sartorius, *Ever Faithful*, for an excellent study of how Cubans of African descent sought freedom, rights, and respect through loyalty and under colonialism.
6. See Childs, *The 1812 Aponte Rebellion*. The degree to which the Aponte Rebellion was a concerted plan to liberate Cuba from colonial rule is somewhat unclear, but Aponte was claimed by later Cuban revolutionaries as a liberator. Evidence of this in the 1890s can be found in Veracruz, where one of the first Cuban revolutionary political clubs to be established bore the name "Aponte no. 1."
7. Roy, *La siempre fiel*, 29.
8. Von Grafenstein, Muñoz, and Nelken-Terner, *Un mar de encuentros y confrontaciónes*, 104.
9. Herrera Franyutti, *Martí en México*, 336.
10. See for example Brown, *Costal Encounters*; Guterl, *American Mediterranean, Southern Slave Holders*; Rothman, *Beyond Freedom's Reach*; Landers, *Black Society in Spanish Florida*.
11. See Ernesto Bassi, *An Aqueous Territory*; Renata Keller, *Mexico's Cold War*; Anna Brickhouse, *TransAmerican Literary Relations*; José David Saldivar, *TransAmericanity*; Lara Putnam, *Radical Moves*; Scott, *Degrees of Freedom*; Guridy, *Forging Diaspora*; Luis-Brown, *Waves of Decolonization*.
12. Muñoz, "El Caribe, La diplomacia y la política Mexicana," in Muñoz Mata, *México y el Caribe vínculos, intereses, region*, 173.
13. Dozens of works on the subject are published in Cuba and Spain each year. Important recent works published in the United States include Espinosa, *Epidemic Invasions*; Tone, *War and Genocide*; Prados-Torreira, *Mambisas*; Ferrer, *Insurgent Cuba*; Schwartz, *Lawless Liberators*; Scott, *Slave Emancipation in Cuba* and *Degrees of Freedom*; Pérez, *Cuba Between Empires, 1878–1902*; Sartorius, *Ever Faithful*; Batrell, *A Black Soldier's Story*.

14. For three pioneering works that interrogate these erasures and silences see Ferrer, *Insurgent Cuba*, Pérez, *The War of 1898*, and Tone, *War and Genocide*.

15. Satrorius, *Ever Faithful*, 217–226.

16. See Poyo, *With All, and for the Good of All* and *Exile and Revolution*; Lazo, *Writing to Cuba*; Nancy Raquel Mirabel, *Suspect Freedoms*; Rebecca Scott, *Degrees of Freedom*.

17. This is a large area, but some signature works published in the past two decades in Mexico and Cuba are Morales, *Espacios en disputa*; Bobadilla González, *La revolución Cubana en la diplomacia, prensa y clubes de México*; Herrera Barreda, *Inmigrantes Hispanocubanos en México Durante el Porfiriato*; Rojas, *Cuba Mexicana*; Camacho Navarro, *Siete Vistas de Cuba*; Espinosa Blas, *El Nacional y El Hijo del Ahuizote* and *La política exterior de México hacia Cuba, 1890–1902*; García Díaz and Guerra Vilaboy, *La Habana/Veracruz, Veracruz/La Habana*; Pulido Llano, *Desde Cuba*; Muñoz Mata *México y el Caribe vínculos, intereses, region*; *Mar adentro*.

18. Santí, "'Our America,'" in Belknap and Fernández, *José Martí's "Our America*," 179–190.

19. Pérez, *Cuba and the United States*.

20. Pérez, *The Structure of Cuban History*, 7.

21. Tenenbaum, "Streetwise History," in *Rituals of Rule*, eds. William H. Beezley, Cheryl E. Martin, William E. French (Wilmington: SR Books, 1994), 141.

22. Saldivar, *Trans-Americanity*, 57.

Chapter One

1. De Quesada y Miranda, *The War in Cuba*, 162–165; Collazo, *Cuba Independiente*, 282.

2. ANC, ADPRCNY 12:1915–1920.

3. While numerous studies of Cuban migration to the United States and to a handful of other countries exist for this period, none have systematically reconstructed the migrants' journeys starting with their point of departure. Each applicant to the Association recorded his or her point of origin, point of departure, and date of departure. This critical information allows us to trace the migrants' trajectories and to speculate intelligently about the context and circumstances of their departures.

4. Sorhegui, *La Habana en el Mediterraneo Americano*, 204–205.

5. Basing their theory on linguistic similarities, archeological artifacts, and even colonial travel practices (which may have reflected precolonial travel patterns) by which delegations of native Floridians traveled to Cuba, archeologists speculate that native groups moved between Cuba and Florida in the pre-Columbian period. Rodríguez Ramos and Pagán Jimenez, "Interacciones multivectoriales," 99–139.

6. For an excellent study of Havana's place in the Atlantic World in the sixteenth century and its importance as a regional center of circulation and trade see de la Fuente, *Havana and the Atlantic in the Sixteenth Century*.

7. Sorhegui, *La Habana en el Mediterraneo Americano*, 214, 215.

8. AGA, AHEEM, 233:5. Yucatán and Cuba were also sutured together by people of African descent traveling between them. Matthew Restall documents the cases of six Africans who linked Havana, Campeche, and Mérida between 1740 and 1829. See Matthew Restall, "Manuel's World: Black Yucatán and the Colonial Caribbean," in Jane Landers and Barry Robinson, *Slaves, Subjects and Subversives*, 156–157.

9. Ibid., 190.

10. In a recent book about the history of New Orleans, Ned Sublette argues that the Spanish period in Louisiana might well be referred to as the Cuban period due to the strength of the connection developed between the two colonies. He suggests that Cuban, especially Afro-Cuban musical styles in particular, had a significant impact on the development of music in New Orleans in this period. Sublette, *The World that Made New Orleans*, 86–115. For commercial connections between New Orleans and Veracruz in this period, especially relating to tobacco, see Scott and Hébrard, *Freedom Papers*, 139–40.

11. Guterl, *American Mediterranean*, 18–19.

12. See Rothman, *Beyond Freedom's Reach*; Guterl, *American Mediterranean*; Scott and Hébrard, *Freedom Papers*.

13. Scott, *Degrees of Freedom*.

14. Landers, *Black Society in Spanish Florida*, 246–248.

15. Cornell, "Citizens of Nowhere," 351–374.

16. Trujillo, *El Golfo de Mexico*, 144.

17. Elliott Young's recent transnational study of Chinese migration in the Americas explores the migration pathways and smuggling networks that linked Cuba with the United States and Mexico in the early twentieth century. See Young, *Alien Nation*, 179–188.

18. Kamen, *The Disinherited*.

19. Roniger, Green, and Yankelevich, *Exile and the Politics of Exclusion in the Americas*.

20. Garófalo, *La Vida de José Maria Heredia en México*, 162.

21. López, Rosen, and Argüelles Espinosa, *México y Cuba*, 198.

22. For a pioneering study of Xalapa and that Atlantic World, see Moore, *Forty Miles from the Sea*.

23. Garófalo, *La Vida de José María Heredia en México*, 702.

24. Ibid., 758–762.

25. Ibid., 770.

26. See Lazo, *Writing to Cuba*.

27. Guterl, *American Mediterranean*.

28. Herrera Barreda, *Inmigrantes hispanocubanos en México durante el porfiriato*.

29. López et al., *México y Cuba*, 103.

30. Santacilia, *El Hombre y Su Obra*.

31. Reid-Vázquez, *The Year of the Lash*, 46.

32. Ibid., 82.
33. Cornell, "Citizens of Nowhere," 351–374.
34. Reid-Vázquez, *The Year of the Lash*, 90.
35. Scott, Degrees of Freedom, 76.
36. Pérez, *Essays on Cuban History*, 26.
37. Herrera, *Inmigrantes hispanocubanos en México*, 198–205.
38. Franco, *Antonio Maceo*, 274, 275.
39. Foner, *Antonio Maceo*, 123.
40. Von Grafenstein Gareis and Muñoz Mata, *El Caribe*, 94.
41. Alfonso Herrera Franyutti makes a strong and compelling case for the importance of Martí's time in Mexico in his professional and political formation. Herrera Franyutti, *Martí en México*.
42. Andrés Clemente Vázquez to Ignacio Mariscal, 23 August 1895, AHSREM, Leg. 515.
43. Morales, *Espacios en Disputa*, 244, 249.
44. Ibid., 250.
45. Herrera Barreda, *Inmigrantes hispanocubanos en México*, 86.
46. Ramón Martínez Álvarez, ANC, Donativos y Remisiones (Donativos), Caja 597, Exp. 6; Gerónimo Lobe y Figueroa ANC, Donativos, 594:16; José Castillo Rodríguez, ANC, Donativos, 594:16; Segundo Corvision y Cabello, ANC, Donativos, 595:20; Emilio Cancio Bello, ANC, Donativos, 595:4.
47. Of course, among the ANERC applicants, no one would have been willing to admit that they fled the insurgent advance, as that would have appeared cowardly. It was in the interest of every applicant, whether true or not, to portray himself—and occasionally herself—as a true patriot from the beginning. Legitimate reasons for leaving would have been persecution, protest, and forced exile. Those Cubans fleeing from Havana and other places securely held by the Spanish in 1895 were more likely than not fleeing the insurgent advance, but due to the nature of the documentation, this assertion is difficult to prove.
48. Scott, *Degrees of Freedom*, 132–138.
49. Ibid.; Ferrer, *Insurgent Cuba*; McGillivray, *Blazing Cane*; Tone, *War and Genocide in Cuba, 1895–1898*.
50. Fernando Echermendia Flores, ANC, Donativos, 596:9.
51. Scholars like Rebecca Scott, Ada Ferrer, and Gillian McGillivray have also convincingly argued that the arrival of the insurgents and the destruction of capitalist property were celebrated by those who joined the insurgency as a kind of liberation from exploitation.
52. Scott, *Degrees of Freedom*, 147.
53. Ibid., 147–148; Tone, *War and Genocide*, 145.
54. Scott, "'The Lower Class of Whites' and 'The Negro Element,'" 181.
55. Pérez, *Cuba: Between Reform and Revolution*, 123.
56. Ibid., 125.
57. Zanetti Lecuona and García Alvarez, *Sugar and Railroads*.

58. Andrés Clemente Vázquez to Ignacio Mariscal, 17 January 1896, in Morales, *Espacios en Disputa*, 252.

59. Andrés Clemente Vázquez to Ignacio Mariscal, 31 January 1896, in Morales, *Espacios en Disputa*, 274.

60. The vast majority of applications for admission belonged to émigrés who resided in the United States, followed by those who migrated to Mexico, and, lastly, those who spent time in the Dominican Republic.

61. Andrés Clemente Vázquez to Ignacio Mariscal, 24 June 1896, in Morales, *Espacios en Disputa*, 379.

62. Andrés Clemente Vázquez to Ignacio Mariscal, 26 December 1895, in Morales, *Espacios en Disputa*, 228.

63. See Schwartz, *Lawless*.

64. Andrés Clemente Vázquez to Ignacio Mariscal, AHSREM, Leg. 517.

65. Pérez, *Cuba: Between Reform and Revolution*, 129.

66. The colonial regime commonly used deportation to counter dissent in Cuba and elsewhere in the empire between 1809 and the 1890s. See del Barcia, "Los Deportados de la Guerra."

67. Andrés Clemente Vázquez to Ignacio Mariscal, 4 January 1897. In Morales, *Espacios en Disputa*, 449.

68. According to Rafael Salillas, the term *ñañigo* was synonymous with Afro-Cubans and the public practice of "African" ceremonies. *Nañiquismo* quickly became associated with danger and vagrancy, and the *ñañigo* was seen as a threat to society. This characterization justified their forced deportation to Spain's penal colonies in Africa. Salillas, "Los nanigos en ceuta," 388–389.

69. See Miranda, *Memorias de un Deportado*.

70. Lisardo Muñoz y Sañudo to Eduardo Yero, ANC, ADPRCNY 14:2284. The date on Muñoz y Sañudo's letter is illegible. A subsequent letter that takes up the same topics appears to have been sent in 1897, so the letter cited here was posted in this year or earlier. Ignacio Martín Arbona y Domínguez, ANC, Donativos, 587:4.

71. Barcia, "Los Deportados de la Guerra," 638.

72. José Antonio Caiñas to Tomás Estrada Palma, 13 June 1896, ANC, ADPRCNY, 3:C:640.

73. Ibid., 3:C:644.

74. Tone, *War and Genocide*, 212.

75. F. Villamil to Tomás Estrada Palma, ANC, ADPRCNY, 12 November 1895, 105:14864.

76. Luis Castillo Sánchez, ANC, Donativos, 595:23.

77. Ignacio Martín Arbona y Domínguez, ANC, Donativos, 587:4.

78. Lisardo Muñoz y Sañudo to Eduardo Yero, ANC, ADPRCNY, 14:2284. Date illegible.

79. See Tone, *War and Genocide*, for a brilliant discussion of events in Spain during and after 1897 and their impact on the course of the war in Cuba.

80. Ricardo Sirven to Tomás Estrada Palma, 16 July 1898, ANC, ADPRCNY 21:3285.

Chapter Two

1. Arbona indicates that the delegates from the New York City offices of the Cuban Revolutionary Party were in attendance at the meeting where the expedition was proposed. The visit of these men transpired in September and October of 1897. Furthermore, Arbona remembers that the expedition departed about fifteen days after the meeting. It is safe to assume that the expedition departed sometime in November.

2. Ignacio Martín Arbona y Domínguez, ANC, Donativos, 587:4.

3. Together we discovered that the "rio yons" in Arbona's narrative was the "river john" and hense the now partially filled in Bayou Satin John. Thank you to Lawrence Powell for helping me trace Ignacio's journey on foot and along the Bayou in New Orleans.

4. There is no exact figure for the number of Cuban migrants in Mexico during the 1890s. Bernardo García Díaz posits this number in *La Havana/Veracruz, Veracruz La Habana*. However, census data was unreliable. Also, by 1900, hundreds of Cubans who had sought refuge in Mexico had returned home. The hundreds more that existed in plantations and estates in Yucatan in a state of semi-slavery were not counted.

5. Morales, *Espacios en Disputa*, 118.

6. For a recent study of the historic connections between Cuba and Key West, see Rodríguez et al., *Cuba y Cayo Hueso*.

7. José Martín Bello, ANC, Donativos, 589:7.

8. References to all these businesses appear in the Cuban newspaper *El Grito de Baire* throughout October 1897.

9. Cassasús, *La emigración cubana*, 152.

10. Stebbins, *City of Intrigue*, 95.

11. Greenbaum, *More Than Black*, 61. Also see Hewitt, *Southern Discomfort*.

12. Poyo, *With All, And for the Good of All*, 207.

13. For more information about the growth of the tobacco industry in Florida in relation to Cuba, see Naranjo Orovio, *La nación soñada*; Poyo, *With All, And for the Good of All*; Casanovas, *Bread or Bullets*.

14. González Sierra, *Monopolio del humo*, 75–76.

15. Deans-Smith, *Bureaucrats, Planters, and Workers*, xii and 247.

16. Herrera Barreda, *Inmigrantes hispanocubanos en México durante el porfiriato*, 160.

17. José Brunetti y Gayoso to Arsenio Martínez Campos, 7 March 1895, AGA, AHEEM, 223:10.

18. González Sierra, *Monopolio del humo*, 78–79.

19. *El Grito de Baire*, 13 April 1897.

20. Cassasús, *La emigración cubana*, 152.

21. Poyo, *With All and for the Good of All*, 82.

22. Greenbaum, *More Than Black*, 102.

23. Ibid., 60.

24. For an excellent study of racism and racial democracy in twentieth-century Cuba, see de la Fuente, *A Nation for All*.

25. José Miguel Macias to Tomás Estrada Palma, 10 October 1896, ANC, PRC CD, 123:14816.

26. Helg, *Our Rightful Share*, 55–139.

27. Cañizares Gómez, *De mis recuerdos de México*.

28. *El Continente Americano*, 14 October 1898.

29. Ibid.

30. Erika Pani, *Para pertenecer a la gran familia Mexicana*, 117–118.

31. My observations are based on my review of naturalization records found at ASHREM 329. While the applications of a handful of self-described Cubans of color exist, the photographs and phenotypical descriptions demonstrate that most of the professional Cubans who arrived in Mexico were, or claimed to be, white or nearly white.

32. Domínguez, Pérez Monfort, and Rinaudo, *Circulaciones culturales*.

33. Juárez, "Los aportes de la migración caribeña a la cultural veracruzana," in Muñoz Mata, *México y el Caribe vínculos, intereses, región*, 209–215.

34. This interview is quoted and cited by Christine B. Arce in *Mexico's Nobodies*, 227.

35. See Juárez Hernández, *Persistencias culturales afrocaribeñas en Veracruz*.

36. ANC, Donativos, 589:9

37. Arce, *Mexico's Nobodies*, 246.

38. Ibid., 272.

39. Madrid and Moore, *Danzón*, 1–13.

40. For an excellent discussion of connections between Cuba and Mexico in the realm of art and film in the early twentieth-century see, Arce, *Mexico's Nobodies*.

41. These observations are gleaned from my examination of the 329 naturalization records consulted by Herrera Barreda, housed in Archivo Histórico de la Secretaría de Relaciones Exteriores, Mexico.

42. Estrade, *Jose Martí*, 480.

43. ANC, ADPRCNY, 13:16249.

44. Nicolás Valverde to Tomás Estrada Palma, 23 August 1898, ANC, ADPRCNY, 24:3535.

45. ANC, Donativos, 4:1917.

46. Juan Cañizares to Tomás Estrada Palma, 18 January 1899, ANC, ADPRCNY, 3:C:713.

47. Muñoz, *Mexico y el Caribe*, 165; Bojóquez Urzaiz, *La emigración cubana en Yucatán*, 28.

48. Trujillo Bolio, *El Golfo de México en la centuria decimonica*, 106, 111.

49. Bojórquez Urzaiz, *La emigración cubana en Yucatán*, 27.

50. Ibid., 30.

51. Ricardo Pérez Monfort, "Ecos del Caribe en la Cultura Popular y en la Bohemia Yucateca, 1890–1920," in Von Grafenstein Gareis, Muñoz Mata, and Nelken-Turner, *El Caribe*, 160–186.

52. Madrid and Moore, *Danzón*.

53. *Pittsburgh Post-Gazette*, 11 August 1895. See also César García del Pino, *Expediciónes de la Guerra de independencia*, 29–31.

54. Rodolfo Menéndez Peña to Tomás Estrada Palma, 6 August 1895, ANC, ADPRCNY, 14:2125.

55. Rodolfo Menéndez Peña to Tomás Estrada Palma, 7 August 1895, ANC, ADPRCNY, 14:2126.

56. AGA, AHEEM, Caja 225, Leg 12, Exp. 1.

57. Bojórquez Urzaiz, *La emigración cubana en Yucatán*, 39.

58. Ibid., 147.

59. The exponential growth is reflected in the ANERC documentation as well.

60. Pedro Riguzzi, "Mercados Regionales y Capitales en los Ferrocarriles de Propiedad Mexicana, 1870–1908," in Kuntz Ficker and Connolly, *Ferrocarriles y Obras Publicas*, 39–70.

61. Bojórquez Urzaiz, *La emigración cubana en Yucatán*, 28.

62. Identifying information for Rita Bacallao Vida de Nodarse appears in the ANERC file of José Antonio Pérez y Guichard, also an émigré at the time. See ANC, Donativos, 597:12.

63. Joseph and Wells, *Summer of Discontent*, 112.

64. Cloridiano Betancourt to Tomás Estrada Palma, 26 August 1896, ANC, ADPRCNY, 2B:517; Cloridiano Betancourt, ANC, Donativos 598:15.

65. AGA, AHEEM 2:229:8. Mirabal, *Suspect Freedoms*, 131.

66. AGA, AHEEM 2:229:8.

67. Joseph, *Rediscovering the Past and Mexico's Periphery*, 56.

68. Moises González Navarro briefly addresses the colonization schemes that brought Cuban workers to Mexico in *La colonización en México, 1877–1910*. Herrera Barreda adds some new insight about Cuban laborers in Yucatán in her book *Inmigrantes hispanocubanos en México durante el porfiriato*. Neither González Navarro or Herrera Barreda, however, specifically address the role of the Spanish in bringing workers to Mexico.

69. Juan Ortega Manzano to Governor General John R. Brooke, 24 March 1899, ANC, Estado y Gobierno, Leg. 1, Exp. 5.

70. J. Maresma to Diego Tamayo, 3 January 1900, ANC, Estado y Gobierno, 1:30.

71. Carlos García Vélez to Carlos Zaldo, 16 February 1904, ANC, Estado y Gobierno, 18:517.

72. Lillian Guerra, *The Myth of José Martí*, 77–79.

73. Angela González de Menéndez to Tomás Estrada Palma, 4 September 1897, ANC, ADPRCNY, 7:1379.

74. In *Barbarous Mexico*, John Kenneth Turner describes conditions of semi-slavery in Yucatán and Oaxaca.

75. The exponential growth is reflected in the ANERC documentation as well.
76. Rodolfo Menéndez de la Peña to Tomás Estrada Palma, 22 January 1896, ANC, ADPRCNY, 14:2130.
77. Rodríguez Herrera, *Léxico mayor de Cuba*, 2:70.
78. Rodrigo Menéndez de la Peña to Tomás Estrada Palma, 30 June 1896, ANC, ADPRCNY, 14:2132.
79. Van Hoy, *A Social History of Mexico's Railroads*, 137.
80. See the work of Mauricio Tenorio-Trillo, *Mexico at the World's Fairs*; Pablo Piccato, *The Tyranny of Opinion*; and John Lear, *Workers, Neighbors and Citizens*, among others.
81. Van Hoy, *A Social History of Mexico's Railroads*, 144.
82. Teresa Alfaro-Velcamp writes extensively about immigration laws during the Porfiriato and foreigners' varying access to Mexican citizenship. Notably, she refers to the ability of foreigners who owned property to obtain immediate citizenship under the Ley de Extranjería y Naturalización de 1886). See Alfaro-Velcamp, "When Pernicious Foreigners become Citizens," 46–63.
83. López Mesa, *La Comunidad Cubana en Nueva York*, 11.
84. Ibid., 54.
85. Salazar Anaya, *Imágenes de los inmigrantes*, 227.
86. Alfred Boisse to Tomás Estrada Palma, 19 September 1898, ANC, ADPRCNY, 2B:526.
87. Salazar Anaya, *Imágenes de los inmigrantes*, 235.
88. Antonio Solar to José Antonio González Lanuza, 20 June 1898, ANC, ADPRCNY, 20:3293. Also see Garza, *The Imagined Underworld*, for more information about hotels in Mexico City and links to sex and prostitution.
89. Santacilia, *Pedro Santacilia*.
90. Twenty émigrés who listed multiple places of residence are excluded from these calculations. Nineteen of them listed both a coastal and interior place of residence.
91. Antonio Hevia to Tomás Estrada Palma, 20 April 1897–4 January 1899, ANC, ADPRCNY, 29:13764–1379.
92. Juan Cañizares to Tomás Estrada Palma, 18 January 1899, ANC, ADPRCNY, 3:C:713. Migrant Leandro Cañizarez Gómez estimated that at its peak, there were ninety-two male Cubans in Orizaba, twenty-seven of whom had migrated with their families, which suggests a population of 150 people. See Leandro Cañizarez, *Mis recuerdos de México*, 217–218.
93. One Cuban wrote from Morelia. No other city in Michoacán is registered as a destination for either ANERC applicants or letter writers, so it is plausible that Morelia may have been the destination for this ANERC applicant.
94. See, for example, the logbooks of the Veracruz-based Cuban Association Bartolomé Masó. Recorded in the minutes are numerous references to delegations assembled to travel on club-related missions to neighboring areas. This source is housed in the Archive of the Partido Revolucionario Cubano in the Cuban National Archives.

95. Rodrigo Menéndez Peña to Tomás Estrada Palma, 1 January 1895, ANC, ADPRCNY, 14:2124.

Chapter Three

1. ANC, Donativos, 587:1.
2. ANC, Registro, ANERC, 585:16624:2.
3. Pérez, *On Becoming Cuban*.
4. See Estrade, *José Martí y los fundamentos de la democracia en Latinoamerica*.
5. See also Sábato, *The Many and the Few*; Sanders, *Contentious Republicans* and *The Vanguard of the Atlantic World*; Lasso, *Myths of Harmony*; McGuinness, *Path of Empire*; and Forment, *Democracy in Latin America, 1760–1900*.
6. Hidalgo Paz, *Partido revolucionario cubano*, 37.
7. Cordoví Nuñez, *La emigración cubana en los Estados Unidos*, 20.
8. Poyo, *With All, and for the Good of All*, 100–101.
9. ANC, Veteranos, 1149:24068.
10. Foner, *Our America*, 390–391.
11. Ibid.
12. Ibid.
13. Estrada Palma and Rubens, *Address of Tomás Estrada Palma to the American Public*.
14. Poyo, *With All, and for the Good of All*, 106.
15. Poyo, "The Cuban Experience in the United States," 24–25.
16. Leticia Bobadilla González published an inventory of Cuban political clubs in Mexico based on references to Cuban associations in the press. She came up with the figure of forty-six clubs total. Bobadilla González, *La revolución cubana en al diplomacia, prensa y clubes*, 149–163.
17. These were Veracruz, Mexico City, Mérida, and Puebla.
18. ANC, Registro, ANERC, 584:16614:2. As Lillian Guerra has demonstrated, O'Farrill's commitment to workers' rights was tested in 1902 when as mayor of Havana he faced worker discontent and a major strike. Seeking at first to serve as a mediator, he eventually authorized repressive measures to retrain the workers. Ironically, he was later charged with sedition against the state because his response to the workers was not seen as aggressive enough. The charge resulted in his alienation from Estrada Palma's administration, and he emerged as affiliated to the National Liberal Party that challenged Estrada Palma after 1905. Guerra, *The Myth of José Martí*, 138–146.
19. ANC, Registro, ANERC, 585:16624.
20. Ibid., 585:16622:96.
21. ANC, Donativos, 587:7.
22. ANC, Registro, ANERC, 585:16627, 25.
23. Quiróz, "Free Association and Civil Society in Cuba."
24. Ibid., 57.

25. Recent notable works on the Aponte Rebellion and La Escalera conspiracy include Childs, *The 1812 Aponte Rebellion*, Ada Ferrer, *Freedom's Mirror*, Aisha Finch, *Rethinking Slave Rebellion in Cuba* and Reid-Vazquez, *The Year of the Lash*. Labor-based associations were also important in the nineteenth century. See Casanovas, *Bread or Bullets*. The role of freemasonry and masonic lodges in the development of separatist politics has certainly garnered attention within the study of Cuban history and that of anticolonial struggles across the Americas during the Age of Revolutions. See Torres-Cuevas, *Historia de la masonería Cubana*.

26. Forment, *Democracy in Latin America*, 430, 432.

27. Bobadilla González, *La Revolución Cubana en la diplomacia, prensa y clubes*, 124–134.

28. Cañizares Gómez, *De mis recuerdos de Mexico*, 218–219.

29. Caridad Leon de San Germán to Tomás Estrada Palma, 5 May 1897, ANC, ADPRCNY, 105:14803.

30. ANC, PRC, Libro de Actas Bartolomé Masó, acta 15.

31. López Portillo de Tamayo, *Mexico y Cuba*, 331–332.

32. *El Hijo del Ahuizote*, 15 August 1897.

33. Cancio Alvarez to Tomás Estrada Palma, 18 January 1897, ANC, ADPRCNY, 105:14754.

34. ANC, PRC, Libro de Actas Bartolomé Masó, Acta 1.

35. Ibid., Acta 22.

36. José Miguel Macias to Tomás Estrada Palma, 10 July 1895, ANC, ADPRCNY, 105:14810.

37. Andrés Berrgayaza to Tomás Estrada Palma, 25 August 1897, ANC, ADPRCNY, 105:14796.

38. ANC, ADPRCNY, 105:14867.

39. Fernando Menéndez Capote to Tomás Estrada Palma, 21 July 1898, ANC, ADPRCNY, 29:13778.

40. ANC, Gobierno de la Revolución del 95, Legajo 45, Exp. 6430.

41. ANC, PRC, Libro de Actas Bartolomé Masó, Acta 12.

42. Ibid.

43. Guerra, *The Myth of José Martí*, 252. ANC, Registro, ANERC, 585:16634:2, ANC Registro, ANERC, 585:16624:39.

44. ANC, ANERC, 596:9.

45. *Patria*, 28 October 1896.

46. "La Velada en Honor a Martí," *El Continente Americano*, 28 May 1896.

47. *Las Selvas Cubanas*, 9 September 1897.

48. ANC, Registro, ANERC, 585:16627:25.

49. Ibid., 584:16608:29.

50. ANC, Registro, ANERC 584:16616:19.

51. Staff, "Gacetilla," *Continente Americano*, 10 January 1897.

52. ANC, PRC, Libro de Actas Bartolomé Masó, Acta 6.

53. Bobadilla González, *La Revolución Cubana en la diplomacia, prensa y clubes,* 156.
54. Staff, "Gacetilla," *Continente Americano,* 10 January 1897.
55. AGA, AHEEM, Caja 229, Exp. 30.
56. Cañizares Gómez, *De mis recuerdos de Mexico,* 219.
57. *El Continente Americano,* 4 April 1897.
58. Ibid., 28 March 1897.
59. ANC, ADPRCNY, 105:14872; Mirabal, *Suspect Freedoms,* 177.
60. For discussion of the role of print culture and the formation of national consciousness in Latin America, see Anderson, *Imagined Communities.*
61. *La Estrella Solitaria,* 21 March 1897.
62. *Patria,* 23 September 1896.
63. AGA, AHEEM, Caja 225, Leg 2, Exp. 4.
64. ANC, ADPRCNY, 105:14759.
65. ANC, Donativos, 586:31.
66. ANC, PRC, Bartolomé Masó, Libro de Actas, Actas 13, 14.
67. Nicolás Domínguez Cowan to Tomás Estrada Palma, 6 October 1897, ANC, ADPRCNY, 72:13754.
68. José Miguel Macias to Tomás Estrada Palma, 11 August 1898, ANC, ADPRCNY, 23:16249.
69. I have reason to believe that this was a more generalized practice. Many letters to party leadership included direct information about financial contributions. There are several reasons for this phenomenon. In most cases, clubs and club members wished to establish direct links to the leadership so as to be recognized for their services. There were instances where club members preferred to submit their contributions to the party headquarters because they distrusted the CDC leadership in Veracruz, whom they suspected of corruption. Finally, clubs in areas remote to the city of Veracruz or Mexico City, the only two cities with formal party structures, likely chose to communicate directly with New York out of convenience.
70. ANC, Registro, ANERC, 585:16621:56.
71. Ibid.
72. In the first semester of 1939, 19 pesos were spent on the Comisión de Beneficencia and 30 on émigrés in asylums, compared to the 3–8 pesos that were customary allocations during the mid to late 1920s. The first women appear in elected positions in the ANERC in 1948.
73. Guerra, *The Myth of José Martí,* 138–146.
74. As Lillian Guerra points out, the intervening government worked to ensure that Tomás Estrada Palma would easily win the presidential elections against his rival, Bartolomé Masó, who was much less friendly toward U.S. interests. Estrada Palma's victory confirmed the place and prominence of émigrés in Cuban politics. Guerra, *The Myth of José Martí,* 119.
75. See Prados-Torreira, *Mambisas,* 101–136. Louis Pérez Jr. addresses the role of women in the emigrations. Pérez, *On Becoming Cuban,* 49–51. Lillian Guerra also

discusses the central role women played as cooks, healers, wives, mistresses, and soldiers in the insurgent liberated zones. In fact, she sees these spaces as ones where women enjoyed certain freedoms and were permitted to dream of a different kind of liberation. Even though they remained subject to patriarchy, she argues that there were unique opportunities for women to craft new identities for themselves as *mambisas* within the revolutionary struggle in Cuba. Guerra, *The Myth of José Martí*, 58–62.

76. See Ferrer, *Insurgent Cuba*, 175–176. Guerra also examines the penal code of the revolutionary army and notes that behind the harsh penalties against rape and kidnapping lurked the fear that the largely Afro-Cuban insurgents who populated the revolutionary forces would violate white women. Guerra, *The Myth of José Martí*, 56.

77. In its bylaws and statutes the ANERC was framed as an institution open to all émigrés regardless of race, class, gender, or place of residence. Technically, a Cuban who remained in exile and took on the citizenship of a host country could also become a member of the association. ANC, Registro, ANERC 585:16624.

78. Josefina Betancourt to Tomás Estrada Palma, 7 April 1896, ANC, ADPRCNY, 1:A:5.

79. Magdalena Cabrera to Tomás Estrada Palma, 2 October 1897, ANC, ADPRCNY, 3:C:628.

80. Prados-Torreira, *Mambisas*, 101; Guerra, *The Myth of José Martí*, 47; Pérez, *The Structure of Cuban History*, 89–101.

81. Josefina A. de Betancourt to Tomás Estrada Palma, ANC, ADPRCNY, 1A:7.

82. ANC, Donativos, 587:21.

83. The other three women also should be noted. Carida de Leon y de Quesada resident of Mérida, Yucatán, and member of the two prominent Cuban clubs in that city, Salvador Cisneros and Yucatán y Cuba. De Quesada was nineteen years old when she came to Mexico in 1882. She applied to the association in 1928, at the age of sixty-five. She reported having offered her house for revolutionary meetings. Candida del Rio y Rosas migrated to Mexico in 1880 returning in 1898. She resided in Veracruz and formed part of Protesta de Baraguá and Bartolomé Masó. She said she offered many services to the revolution, including hosting José Martí, Gonzalo de Quesada, and Benjamín Guerra on their visits to Veracruz. Mercedes Perdonio Viuda de Chirino emigrated to Mexico in 1895 and returned in 1898. She was a member of the club Cubano-Mexicano Poesia in Veracruz.

84. Gabriel López Garcia to Joaquín Castillo, 1 July 1897, ANC, ADPRCNY, 12:1917.

85. Ibid.

86. José Antonio Caiñas to Tomás Estrada Palma, ANC, ADPRCNY, 3:C: 640–643.

87. Cubans from Veracruz accounted for the majority of the ANERC applicants and, among these, members of two Cuban political clubs were the most numerous. Caiñas was a member of Bartolomé Masó, one of the two most numerous and most visible clubs in the city. Furthermore, he played an active role in the association and held elected positions. His profile fits that of other émigrés who applied to the

ANERC. His dogged dedication to clearing his name and highlighting his revolutionary activities are also traits common to ANERC applicants, most of whom felt they had a good case to be accepted.

88. Enrique G. Herrera to Tomás Estrada Palma, 15 July 1896, ANC, ADPRCNY, 8:1701; Francisco Campillo to Tomás Estrada Palma, 1 September 1896, ANC, ADPRCNY, 3:C:700.

89. Manuel Ruano to Tomás Estrada Palma, 24 November 1896–27 December 1897, ANC, ADPRCNY, 20:3107–3121.

90. Agustín Meulener's contributions seem excessive, but each of his letters in which he asks for confirmation of his contributions is duly and positively answered by the party secretary. Agustín Meulener to Tomás Estrada Palma, 9 March 1896–3 March 1898, ANC, ADPRCNY, 14:2181–2185; Carlos García y Peñalver to Tomás Estrada Palma, 19 May 1898, ANC, ADPRCNY, CD 7:1414.

91. Extensive review of sixty years of the ANERC's history through the files collected in the Registro de Asociaciones at the Archivo Nacional de Cuba allows me to make this assertion. Further discussion of the exclusive nature of the ANERC will be developed in chapter 6.

92. *El Correo Español*, 11 May 1897.

93. Fernando Cisneros to Tomás Estrada Palma, 23 August 1897, ANC, ADPRCNY, 3:C:878.

94. *La Libertad*, 31 July 1898.

95. Márquez Sterling, "Podemos Gobernarnos," *La Libertad*, 31 July 1898.

96. Sanders, *The Vanguard of the Atlantic World*, 5.

97. Foner, *Our America*, 390–391.

98. Estrada Palma and Rubens, *Address of Tomás Estrada Palma to the American Public*.

99. ANC, Registro, ANERC, 585:16624:1.

Chapter Four

1. José Martí also lived for several years as an exile in Spain and in Guatemala.
2. López, *José Martí*, 89–92.
3. Ibid., 131.
4. Pletcher, "The Building of the Mexican Railway," 26.
5. Herrera Franyutti, *Martí en México*, 27.
6. Ramos, *Divergent Modernities*, 166–167.
7. Ibid.
8. José Martí to Manuel Mercado, 18 May 1895, *Espistolario*, 5:250–251.
9. Numerous scholars across Latin America have explored this topic with a critical concentration in Mexico and Cuba. Among these are Sergio Guerra Vilaboy, Salvador Morales Pérez, Rafael Rojas, Laura Muñoz Mata, Leticia Bobadilla Gonález, Gabriela Pulido Llano, Margarita Espinosa Blas, Maria del Socorro Herrera Barreda, and Yoel Cordovi Nuñez.

10. Yoel Cordovi Nuñez notes the importance of Mexico among the countries where the PRC channeled resources and attention for diplomatic gains. Cordoví, *La emigración cubana en los Estados Unidos*, 52.

11. Garrigó, *Historia documentada*.

12. Regarding the Gran Legión del Aguila Negra plot, see documents in the collection *Mexico y Cuba*. See also Garrigó, *Historia documentada*.

13. Garrigó, *Historia documentada*.

14. Garófalo Mesa, *La Vida de José Maria Heredia*.

15. Pérez Jr., *Cuba in the American Imagination*, 25.

16. Guadalupe Victoria to Lucas Alamán, 28 August 1823, reproduced in López Portillo de Tamayo et. al, *México y Cuba*, 1:23.

17. Vicuña Mackenna, *Diez meses de misión*.

18. Guerra Vilaboy, *La América Latina*.

19. Márquez Sterling, *La diplomacia en nuestra historia*, 116.

20. See Santana and Vilaboy, *Benito Juárez y Cuba*; Sánchez et al., *José Martí y Eloy Alfaro*.

21. For more on the connections between Cuba and various Latin American countries during the 1860s and 1870s, see works on Mexico and Cuba by Salvador E. Morales Pérez, Laura Muñoz Mata, Rafael Rojas, Leticia Bobadilla González, Margarita Espinosa Blás, Guadalupe Álvarez Lloveras, Carlos E. Bojórquez Urzaiz, Sánchez et al. See also Quintana García, *Venezuela y la independencia de Cuba*; and Le Riverend Brusone et al., *Cuba-Colombia*.

22. Varona, *Cuba Contra España*.

23. Archivo Nacional de Cuba, *Correspondencia Diplomática*, 1:xxix.

24. Ferrer, *Freedom's Mirror*, 333.

25. *El Continente Americano*, 23 May 1897.

26. Márquez Sterling, *La diplomacia en nuestra historia*.

27. Tomás Estrada Palma to Aristides Agüero y Betancourt, March 16, 1896, ANC, *Correspondencia diplomática*, 1:14–16.

28. Tone, *War and Genocide*, 150–151. The PRC clubs and organizations established under Martí's leadership were now responsible to a new cadre of representatives appointed by Estrada Palma and approved by the provisional government. The intention was to impose a centralized structure in which the representatives bore the responsibility for both diplomatic labors and the collection of material resources for the war effort. The transition was not necessarily easy, and the new system produced power struggles and conflicts in more than a few places. The older cadre was comprised of faithful Martí followers, whereas the new appointees were largely friends and associates of Estrada Palma.

29. Tomás Estrada Palma to Arístides Agüero y Betancourt, 16 March 1896, ANC, *Correspondencia diplomática*, 1:15.

30. Young, *Catarino Garza's Revolution on the Texas-Mexico Border*, 276.

31. Herrera Franyutti, *Martí en México*, 316.

32. Ibid., 329.

33. Martí, *Obras Completas*, 2:326, 327.
34. Bojórquez Urzaiz, *Entre mayas y patriotas*, 52.
35. Nicolás Domínguez to Tomás Estrada Palma, 7 August 1895, ANC, ADPRCNY, 82:13720.
36. Ibid., 82:13720.
37. Ibid., 82:13721.
38. Ibid., 82:13726.
39. Ibid., 82:13754.
40. Tomás Estrada Palma to Porfirio Díaz, May 1896, reproduced in ANC, *Correspondencia diplomática*, 1:36.
41. Estrada Palma and Rubens, *Address of Tomás Estrada Palma to the American Public*.
42. Matías Romero to Ignacio Mariscal, 16 August 1897, reproduced in López Portillo de Tamayo et al., *Mexico y Cuba*, 307.
43. Morales, *Espacios en Disputa*, 110, 118.
44. Matías Romero to Ignacio Mariscal, 25 March 1898, reproduced in López Portillo de Tamayo et al., *Mexico y Cuba*, 308.
45. Buchenau, *In the Shadow of the Giant*, 43.
46. Ignacio Mariscal to Matías Romero, 30 March 1898, reproduced in López Portillo de Tamayo et al., *Mexico y Cuba*, 308–309.
47. Tomás Estrada Palma to Nicolás Domínguez Cowan, 6 June 1896, *Correspondencia diplomatica*, 1:51.
48. Martí, *Obras completas*, 4:77.
49. Tomás Estrada Palma to Aristides Agüero y Betancourt, 16 March 1896, ANC, *Correspondencia diplomática*, 1:14.
50. Tomás Estrada Palma to Nicolás Cárdenas y Chappotín, 3 June 1896, ANC, *Correspondencia diplomática*, 1:48.
51. Tomás Estrada Palma to Joaquín Alsina, 11 June 1896, ANC, *Correspondencia diplomática*, 1:55.
52. The collection of letters to Estrada Palma that forms part of the archive of the Cuban Revolutionary Party in the Cuban National Archive includes many letters from Cuban émigrés affiliated with the party living in distinct points in Latin America and the Caribbean that describe widespread support for the Cuban independence cause, particularly among working and middle-class Latin Americans.
53. *El Continente Americano*, 23 September 1897.
54. Ibid.
55. The name refers to the proclamations of Mexican and Cuban independence made at Dolores and Yara respectively. Luis E. Puig to Tomás Estrada Palma, 18 October 1896, ANC, ADPRCNY, 105:14759.
56. López Portillo de Tamayo et al., *Mexico y Cuba*, 331–332.
57. *El Continente Americano*, 10 October 1897.

58. José P. Rivera subsequently spoke at a number of other Cuban events including a meeting organized to honor Carlos Manuel de Céspedes held on 10 October 1897; a meeting organized by Morelos y Maceo on 21 February 1897; and the inaugural meeting of the club Cuauhtémoc y Hatuey on 27 March 1897.

59. ANC, PRC, Libro de Actas Bartolomé Masó, Actas 13, 14.

60. Amado Escobar to Tomás Estrada Palma, 25 November 1897, ANC, ADPRCNY, 5:1169.

61. Guayama, Coatepec (Veracruz), Matehuala (San Luis Potosí), Teocelo (Veracruz), Puebla, Mérida (Yucatán), Tangancícuaro (Michoacán), Ayapango and Amecameca (Chalco), Veracruz, Isla del Carmen (Campeche), Valle de Santiago (Guanajuato), Tula (Tamaulipas), Pachuca (Hidalgo), Huitusco (Guerrero), Tampico (Tamaulipas), Azcapotzaltenago, and Zimapan (México).

62. See Anderson, *Outcasts in Their Own Land*.

63. *El Continente Americano*, 1 August 1897.

64. Ibid., 19 December 1897.

65. Piccato, *The Tyranny of Opinion*, 131.

66. Lomnitz, *The Return of Comrade Ricardo Flores Magón*, 56–64.

67. Casals, Donativos 594:85; Pérez, Donativos 590:111; Váldez, Donativos 588:55.

68. ANC, Donativos 585:102.

69. "La subscripción popular Mexicana," *El Continente Americano*, 29 August 1897.

70. Young, *Catarino Garza's Revolution on the Texas–Mexico Border*, 274–277.

71. "La cuestión palpitante y nuestra linea de conducta," *El Continente Americano*, 20 October 1895.

72. The petition from Ozoluama was spearheaded by the Cuban political club Hidalgo y Martí in that city. See "La beligerancia de Cuba," *El Continente Americano*, 15 October 1896. The petition from Pachuca was reprinted in the newspaper as a half page message in a supplement. See "Suplemento al número 68," *El Continente Americano*, 23 August 1896. The petition from Guadalajara was published as "Cuba beligerante," *El Continente Americano*, 22 October 1896.

73. "Cuba beligerante," *El Continente Americano*, 22 October 1896.

74. *Patria*, 13 July 1895.

75. Forment, *Democracy in Latin America*, 201.

76. "Hazaña Quijotesca," *El Continente Americano*, 7 January 1897.

77. *El Continente Americano*, 7 March 1897.

78. Ibid., 20 October 1895.

79. Ibid., 22 December 1895.

80. Ibid., 22 October 1896.

81. López Portillo de Tamayo et al., *Mexico y Cuba*, 309–310.

82. *El Continente Americano*, 28 March 1897.

83. Ibid., 24 June 1897.

Chapter Five

1. For discussion of naturalization among Cubans in Key West, Florida, see Poyo, *Exile and Revolution*, 17–18.
2. See *Patria*, 16 February 1898; Vázquez, *Cuestión de Cuba*.
3. Carlos García Vélez to Carlos de Zaldo, 20 September 1903, ANC, Fondo de Secretaria de Estado y Justicia, 18:525.
4. Ibid.
5. Schell, *Integral Outsiders*.
6. Ibid., xii, xiii.
7. Márquez Sterling, "Podemos Gobernarnos," *La Libertad*, 31 July 1898.
8. Nicolás Domínguez Cowan to Tomás Estrada Palma, 9 September 1895, ANC ADPRCNY, 82:13718.
9. Lida, *Inmigracion y Exilio*.
10. This has been the subject of numerous monographs and collections, some of which include: Rojas, *Cuba Mexicana*; Morales, *Espacios en Disputa*; Zea and Taboada, *España Ultima Colonia de Si Misma*; Pulido Llano, *Desde Cuba*; and Uribe Salas, *México frente al desenlace*.
11. Rojas, *Cuba Mexicana*, 377–378.
12. Buchenau, *In the Shadow of the Giant*, 60.
13. Espinosa Blas, *La política exterior de México hacia Cuba, 1890–1902*, 107–120.
14. Rojas, *Cuba Mexicana*, 387.
15. Espinosa Blas, *La política exterior de México hacia Cuba, 1890–1902*, 107. Also see Buchenau, *In the Shadow of the Giant*.
16. Carlos García Velez to Carlos de Zaldo, 22 October 1904, ANC, Fondo de Secretaria de Estado y Justicia, 18:525.
17. Márquez Sterling, *Los últimos días del Presidente Madero*, 14.
18. Ibid., 11.
19. Sánchez Andres, "La Normalización de las Relaciones," *Historia Mexicana*, 48, 4:1999.
20. Lida, "El Perfil de una inmigración."
21. Lida's study reveals that in 1895 there were 4,124 Spaniards in Mexico City and 2,760 Spaniards in Veracruz, out of a total of 13,000 Spaniards.
22. Rosenzweig, *Un liberal español en el México porfiriano*.
23. See also Pani, *El Segundo Imperio* and *Para mexicanizar el Segundo Imperio*.
24. Schmidt-Nowara, *The Conquest of History*, 2–3.
25. Granados, *Debates sobre España*, 33.
26. Falcón, *Las rasgaduras de la descolonización*, 10.
27. Schmidt-Nowara, *The Conquest of History*, 15–52.
28. Feros, "Spain and America," 109–134.
29. The expulsion of Spaniards became law in 1827 and was more strictly enforced again in 1829. See Sims, *The Expulsion of Mexico's Spaniards*; and Caballero Flores, *La contrarevolución*.

30. Yankelevich, "Hispanofobia y revolución," 29.
31. Falcón, *Las rasgaduras de la descolonización*.
32. Gamboa, "De indios y gachupines." Also see her *Los empresarios de ayer*.
33. Granados, *Debates sobre España*, 34.
34. The importance of honor and of defending one's honor, especially from libel, was a defining characteristic of elite political culture in Mexico during the nineteenth century. Piccato, *The Tyranny of Opinion*.
35. Ibid., 2–3.
36. *Diario del Hogar*, 29 January 1897.
37. Ibid., 22 May 1896.
38. Ibid., 8 August 1896.
39. Granados, *Debates sobre España*, 55–89.
40. *El Correo Español*, 8 April 1896.
41. Ibid., 15 September 1896.
42. Ibid., 22 July 1896.
43. AGA, AHEEM, 229:12.
44. Ibid., 233:5.
45. Ibid., 224:17.
46. AGA, AHEEM, 223:10, 4 April 1895.
47. AGA, AHEEM, 227:2.
48. De Pedro, *La independencia de Cuba*.
49. AGA, AHEEM, 230:1.
50. *Continente Americano*, 28 February 1897.
51. Ibid., 7 January 1897.
52. AGA, AHEEM, 231:1.
53. Ibid.
54. See Picatto, *The Tyranny of Opinion*, 168. For a closer study of penal legislation, see Speckman Guerra, *Crimen y Castigo*.
55. Cosio Villegas, *Historia moderna de Mexico*.
56. José Agustín Escudero to Tomás Estrada Palma, 4 November 1897, ANC, ADPRCNY, 5:1175. *Gachupin* is a derogatory term used to refer to Spaniards since the late colonial period.
57. *El Correo Español*, 19 May 1897.
58. ANC, ADPRCNY 4:1049.
59. Rosenzweig, *Un liberal español en el Mexico porfiriano*.
60. Espinosa Blas, *La política exterior de México hacia Cuba, 1890–1902*, 216.
61. *Continente Americano*, 26 August 1897.
62. These ideas appeared in the newspaper he founded in 1877 titled *La Epoca*. Hale, *The Transformation of Mexican Liberalism*, 89. Among the various official positions he held, Olaguíbel was a tax collector in Guanajuato; a maritime and border customs house inspector in Matamorros; second official, Secretariat of the Treasury, between 1877 and 1878; second official, Secretariat of Foreign Relations; and private secretary of Sebastian Lerdo de Tejada. In addition to his contributions to *La*

Epoca and *La Libertad*, Olaguíbel had a fruitful journalistic career. He was the editor of various newspapers, including *El Observador*, *El País*, and *Periódico oficial del Gran Círculo de Obreros*. He was director of the *Proteccionista* and cofounder of *El País* (1899) with Trinidad Sánchez Santos.

63. Musacchio, *Milenios de México*; Camp, *Mexican Political Biographies*.
64. *El Correo Español*, 12 May 1897.
65. Ibid.
66. Lemus, *Francisco Bulnes, su vida y sus obras*, 56.
67. *El Correo Español*, 4 May 1897.
68. Hale, *The Transformation of Liberalism*, 151.
69. Charles Hale attributes the use of the term Jacobin to the popularity of Hippolyte Taine's *Origin de la France Contemporaine* in Mexico. Taine criticizes the French Revolutionary tradition and the 1871 Paris Commune. Hale, *The Transformation of Liberalism*, 111.
70. *El Correo Español*, 18 May 1897.
71. Schmidt-Nowara, *Empire and Antislavery*, 121, 128, 132.
72. Hale, *The Transformation of Mexican Liberalism*, 224.
73. *El Correo Español*, 12 May 1897.
74. Reséndez, *Changing National Identities at the Frontier*.
75. *El Correo Español*, 18 May 1897.
76. De Pedro, *La independencia de Cuba en relación con el criterio americano y los intereses de México*, 25.
77. The opposition journalists in Mexico City were among the more fortunate. While some journalists were assassinated or imprisoned for long periods of time, the regime generally punished the directors of the main national opposition papers, *El Diario del Hogar* and *El Hijo del Ahuizote*, through a campaign of slow dissuasion, wearing down its targets through constant disruptions and arrests. The directors of both newspapers were thrown in the Belen jail upward of twenty to thirty times in the course of their lives. Cosio Villegas, *Historia moderna de México*, 546–550.

Chapter Six

1. Márquez Sterling, *La Diplomacia en nuestra historia*.
2. Cañizares Gómez, *Don Porfirio*.
3. Nicolás Domínguez Cowan to Tomás Estrada Palma, 9 September 1895, ANC, ADPRCNY, 82:13720.
4. Tomás Estrada Palma to Nicolás Domínguez Cowan, 6 June 1896, ANC, *Correspondencia diplomática*, 1:51.
5. Varona, *Cuba Contra España*.
6. *El Continente Americano*, 10 November 1895.
7. Ibid., 29 October 1896.
8. Cañizares Gómez, *Don Porfirio*, 152–153.
9. Márquez Sterling, "Podemos Gobernarnos," *La Libertad*, 31 July 1898.
10. Foner, *Our America*, 390–391.

11. Mario L. de la Mola to Tomás Estrada Palma, 3 September 1898, ANC, ADPRCNY, 105:14800.

12. ANC, Estado y Gobernación, 1:23:5.

13. Mirabal, *De aquí, de allá*, 197.

14. *El Diario del Hogar*, 16 September 1896.

15. Ibid., 7 October 1896.

16. *El Continente Americano*, 26 May 1899.

17. For a masterful study of Mexican liberalism in transition, see Hale, *The Transformation of Liberalism*.

18. Granados, *Debates sobre España*.

19. *El Continente Americano*, 23 April 1899.

20. Ibid., 29 October 1896.

21. The term *"Alfonsista"* refers to the then king of Spain Alfonso XIII. *El Hijo del Ahuizote*, 26 August 1896.

22. See Voekel, "Liberal Religion," 78.

23. *El Hijo del Ahuizote*, 20 November 1898.

24. *El Continente Americano*, 29 October 1896.

25. *El Hijo del Ahuizote*, 4 June 1899.

26. Ibid.

27. *El Diario del Hogar*, 22 January 1896.

28. *El Continente Americano*, 20 October 1895.

29. *El Hijo del Ahuizote*, 27 September 1896.

30. *El Continente Americano*, 24 October 1897.

31. Ibid., 20 October 1895.

32. Cerefino Sifuentes to Tomás Estrada Palma, 10 January 1898, ANC, ADPRCNY, 21:3272–74.

33. *El Continente Americano*, 30 January 1898.

34. Ibid.

35. It is important to consider that while doctrinaire liberals or *puros* generally admired and sought to emulate the United States, they were, like Martí, not entirely naive about the possible dangers that the States might pose to Latin America. Where liberal conservatives like Olaguíbel believed that a stronger connection to Spain might protect Mexico from the United States, *puros* believed that Mexico needed to be strong and independent within itself in order to stand up to the States if the need occurred.

36. *El Continente Americano*, 22 October 1896.

37. "Programa," *El Continente Americano*, 20 October 1895.

38. The battle of the Cerro de las Campanas was where the French finally capitulated and where French Emperor Maximilian was shot in 1867.

39. The subtitle of the cartoon reads, "Three illustrious Americans reward the triumph of Uncle Sam (Benito Júarez, Xicotencatl, and Cuauhtemoc)."

40. De Pedro, *La Independencia de Cuba en relación con el criterio americano y los intereses de México*, 68.

41. "La Independencia de México," *La Patria*, 7 July 1898.
42. *El Continente Americano*, 22 August 1897.
43. *La Patria*, 7 July 1898.
44. Ibid.
45. *El Hijo del Ahuizote*, 20 May 1902.
46. Louis A. Pérez Jr., *Cuba in the American Imagination*, 122–128.
47. Ibid.
48. Ibid., 19.
49. *El Continente Americano*, 16 September 1896.
50. See Cosio Villegas, *Historia moderna de México*, 629.

Epilogue

1. Márquez Sterling, *Psicología profana*, 152.
2. *El Universal*, Mexico, 15 December 1934. Also collected in ANC, Fondo Secretaria y Ministerio de Estado, Leg. 536, Exp. 6536:111.
3. Lufríu, *Manuel Márquez Sterling, escritor y ciudadano*, 69–124.
4. Márquez Sterling, *La Diplomacia en nuestra historia*, 8–9.
5. Ibid., 13.
6. Ibid., 12–13.
7. Ibid., 13.
8. Ibid., 21.
9. Márquez Sterling, *Los últimos dias del Presidente Madero*, 1–2.
10. Ibid., 7.
11. *El Universal*, 15 December 1934.
12. Lerdo de Tejada, *La revolución y el nacionalismo*, 259.
13. ANC, Fondo Archivo Manuel Márquez Sterling, Caja 684, Exp. 8.
14. Ibid.
15. Yankelevich, *La Revolución Mexicana en América Latina*, 14.
16. Márquez Sterling, *Doctrina de la república*, 46.
17. Arcadio Zentella Jr. to Manuel Márquez Sterling, 21 March 1916, ANC, Fondo Archivo Manuel Márquez Sterling 683:7.
18. Funes, "Slaughterhouse and Milk Consumption," in Steven Palmer et al., *State of Ambiguity*, 121–147.
19. ANC, Archivo Manuel Márquez Sterling, Caja 506, Exp. 23.
20. Lufríu, *Manuel Márquez Sterling, escritor y ciudadano*, 180.
21. Renata Keller, *Mexico's Cold War*, 1–7.
22. Partido Popular Socialista, *Al Pueblo Mexicano*, 10–11.

Bibliography

Archives and Collections

Cuba

Archivo Nacional de Cuba (ANC)
  Archivo de la Delegación del Partido Revolutionario Cubano en Nueva York
    1892–1898 (ADPRCNY)
  Archivo del Partido Revolucionario Cubano (PRC)
  Archivo Manuel Márquez Sterling and Fondo Secretaría de Estado y Justicia
  Donativos y Remisiones (Donativos)
  Fondo Secretaría de Estado y Gobierno (Estado y Gobierno)
  Gobierno de la Revolucion del 95
  Registro de Asociaciones (Registro)
    Asociación Nacional de Veteranos (Veteranos)
    Asociación National de Emigrados Revolucionarios Cubanos (ANERC)
  Biblioteca Nacional José Martí

Mexico

Archivo y Biblioteca Histórico Municipal de Veracruz
Archivo General de la Nación (AGN)
Archivo General del Estado, Yucatán
Archivo Histórico de la Secretaria de Relaciones Exteriores de
    México (AHSREM)
Biblioteca Miguel Lerdo de Tejada
Biblioteca Nacional de Mexico
Casino Español (Mexico City)
Condumex
Hemeroteca Nacional de Mexico

Spain

  Archivo del Ministerio de Asunto Exteriores, Madrid (AMAE)
  Archivo General de la Administración Española (AGA)
    Archivo Histórico de la Embajada de España en Mexico (AHEEM)
  Biblioteca Nacional de España

United States
> The Bancroft Library
> Cuban Heritage Collection, University of Miami
> The New York Public Library

Newspapers

Cuba (Tampa, Fla)
Diario Comercial de Veracruz (Veracruz)
El Continente Americano (Mexico City)
El Correo Español (Mexico City)
El Diario del Hogar (Mexico City)
El Fandango (Pachuca)
El Grito de Baire (Veracruz)
El Hijo del Ahuizote (Mexico City)
El Mundo (Mexico City)
El Universal (Mexico City)
La Epoca (Veracruz)
La Estrella de Panama (Panama)
La Estrella Solitaria (Matamorros)
La Libertad (Mexico City)
La Patria e México (Mexico City)
Los Intereses Sociales (Mérida)
Patria (New York City)
Salvas Cubanas (Veracruz)

Published Primary Sources

Archivo Nacional de Cuba. *Correspondencia diplomática de la delegacion cubana en nueva york durante la Guerra de independencia de 1895 a 1898*. Vol. 1–5. Havana: Archivo Nacional de Cuba, 1943.

Bulnes, Francisco. *El porvenir de las naciones latinoamericanas ante las recientes conquistas de Europa y Norteamérica (estructura y evolución de un continente)*. Mexico City: Imprenta de M. Nava, 1899.

Cañizares Gómez, Leandro. *De mis recuerdos de Mexico, 1896–1900, con notas de un viaje através de ese país*. Havana: Editorial Lex, 1947.

———. *Don Porfirio, el gobernante de mente lúcida, corazón de patriota y mano de hierro: Sinceras consideraciónes de un Cubano queu tuvo escepcionales oportunidades de aquilater su obra*. Havana: Editorial Lex, 1946.

Cassasús, Juan J. *La emigración cubana y la independencia de la patria*. Havana: Editorial Lex, 1953.

Collazo, Enrique. *Cuba Independiente*. Havana: La Moderna Poesía, 1900.

De Pedro, Federico. *La independencia de Cuba en relación con el criterio americano y los intereses de México; colección de notables artículos sobre esta cuestión de distinguidos escritores mexicanos*. México, D.F.: Imprenta Avenida Juárez 624, 1897.

De Quesada y Miranda, Gonzalo. *The War in Cuba, Being a Full Account of Her Struggle for Freedom*. Chicago: National Book Concern, 1896.

Estrada Palma, Tomás, and Horatio S. Rubens. *Address of Tomás Estrada Palma to the American Public: Statement of the Law by Horatio S. Rubens*. New York: 1896.

Garcia, Telesforo. *España y los españoles en México*. México D.F.: Santiago Sierra, Tipógrafo, 1877.

García del Pino, César. *Expediciónes de la guerra de independencia, 1895–1898.* Havana: Editorial de Ciencias Sociales, 1996.

González Alcorta, Leandro. *Que pasa en cuba? Porque crece la insurreción.* Madrid: Leon M. Garzo, 1896.

———. *Vuelta-Abajo, intelectual y mambí: fragmentos y siluetas.* Pinar Del Río: Impr. La Constancia, 1914.

Márquez Sterling, Manuel. *Burla Burlando.* Havana: Impr. Avisador comercial, 1907.

———. *La diplomacia en nuestra historia.* Havana: Impr. Avisador comercial, 1909.

———. *Ideas y Sensaciónes.* Havana: El Figaro, 1903.

———. *Proceso histórico de la enmiendo platt (1897–1934).* Havana: Imprenta El Siglo XX, A. Muñiz y hno., 1941.

———. *Psicologia Profana.* Havana: Impr. Avisador comercial, 1905.

———. *Los últimos días del Presidente Madero (mi gestión diplomático en México).* Havana: Imprenta El Sigo XX, 1917.

Mediz Bolio, Antonio. *Palabras al viento: crónicas de cuba.* Mérida: Talleres tipográficos del Ateneo Peninsular, 1916.

Merchán, Rafael Maria. *Cuba: Justificación de sus guerras de independencia.* Bogotá: La Lúz, 1896.

———. *La Redención de un Mundo.* Bogotá: La Lúz, 1898.

Miranda, Manuel M. *Memorias de un Deportado.* Havana: Imprenta La Luz, 1903.

Ortiz, Fernando. *Rasgos Patrióticos de los emigrados cubanos en Key West (Florida) dedicados a la Mámara de representantes, Senado y ejecutivo de nustra repúbica . . . . los peticionarios de Key West, Fla. Junio, 1902.* Havana: Est. tip. El Arte, 1902.

———. *La reconquista de América, reflexiones sobre el panhispanismo.* Paris, P. Ollendorff, 1911.

Partido Popular Socialista. *Al pueblo Mexicano: Defender a Cuba es defender a México y la América Latina.* Mexico City: Ediciones del Partido Popular Socialista, 1961.

Varona, Enrique José. *Cuba contra España: Manifiesto del artido Revolucionario Cubano a los pueblos Hispano-Americanos.* New York: S. Figueroa, 1895.

Vázquez, Andrés Clemente. *Cuestión de Cuba: Colección de artículos referentes a la independecia de esa isla.* México D.F.: Imprenta en la calle cerrada de Santa Teresa, numero 3, 1871.

Vicuña Mackenna, Benjamín. *Diez meses de misión a los Estados Unidos del norte américa como agente confidencial de Chile,* 2 vols. Santiago, Impr. de la Libertad, 1867.

Secondary Sources

Alfaro-Velcamp, Teresa. "When Pernicious Foreigners become Citizens: Naturalization in Early Twentieth-Century Mexico." *Journal of Politics and Law* 6, no. 1 (March 2013): 46–63.

Anderson, Benedict. *Imagined Communities: Reflections on the Origin and the Spread of Nationalism.* London: Verso, 1991.

Anderson, Rodney. *Outcasts in Their Own Land: Mexican Industrial Workers, 1906–1911.* Dekalb: Northern Illinois University Press, 1976.

Arce, Christine B. *Mexico's Nobidies: The Cultural Legacy of the Soldadera and the Afro-Mexican Woman.* New York: SUNY Press, 2017.

Barcia, Maria del Carmen. "Los Deportados de la Guerra. Cuba 1895–1898." In *La Nación Somñada: Cuba, Puerto Rico y Filipinas ante el 98,* edited by Consuelo Narajo Orovio, Miguel a Puig-Samper, and Luis Miguel García Mora, 635–646. Madrid: Doce Calles, 1996.

Bassi, Ernesto. *An Aqueous Territory: Sailor Geographies and New Granada's Transimperial Greater Caribbean World* (Forthcoming from Duke University Press).

Batrell, Ricardo. *A Black Soldier's Story: The Narrative of Ricardo Batrell and the Cuban War of Independence,* translated by Mark A. Sanders. Minneapolis: University of Minnesota Press, 2010.

Beezley, William H., Cheryl E. Martin, William E. French, eds. *Rituals of Rule: Rituals of Resistance: Public Celebrations and Popular Culture in Mexico.* Wilmington: SR Books, 1994.

Belknap, Jeffrey, and Raúl Fernández, eds. *José Martí's "Our America"; From National to Hemispheric Cultural Studies.* Durham, N.C.: Duke University Press, 1998.

Bobadilla González, Leticia. *La revolución Cubana en la diplomacia, prensa y clubes de México, 1895–1898: Tres visciones de una revolución finisecular.* México: Secretaría de Relaciones Exteriores, 2001.

Bojóquez Urzaiz, Carlos E. *La emigración cubana en Yucatán 1868–1898.* México D.F.: Ediciones Imágen Contemporanea, 2002.

———. *Entre mayas y patriotas: José Martí en Yucatán Mérida.* Mérida: UADY, Facultad de Ciencias Antropológicas, 2008.

Brickhouse, Anna. *TransAmerican Literary Relations and the Nineteenth-Century Public Sphere.* Cambridge: Cambridge University Press, 2009.

Brown, Richmond, ed. *Coastal Encounters: The Transformation of the Gulf South in the Eighteenth Century.* Lincoln: Nebraska University Press, 2007.

Buchenau, Jurgen. *In the Shadow of the Giant: The Making of Mexico's Central American Policy 1876–1930.* Tuscaloosa: University of Alabama Press, 1996.

Caballero Flores, Romeo. *La contrarevolución en la independencia de México; los españoles en la vida política, social y económica de México (1804–1838).* México D.F.: Colegio de México, 1969.

Camacho Navarro, Enrique. *Siete Vistas de Cuba: Interpretaciónes de su Independencia.* México D.F.: UNAM, 2002.

Camp, Roderic A. *Mexican Political Biographies 1884–1935.* Austin: University of Texas Press, 1991.

Casanovas, Joan. *Bread or Bullets: Urban Labor and Spanish Colonialism in Cuba, 1850–1898.* Pittsburgh, Penn.: University of Pittsburgh, 1998.

Childs, Matt. *The 1812 Aponte Rebellion in Cuba and the Struggle Against Atlantic Slavery*. Chapel Hill: University of North Carolina Press, 2007.

Cordoví Nuñez, Yoel. *La emigración cubana en los Estados Unidos: estructuras directivas y Corrientes de pensamiento. 1895-1898*. Santiago de Cuba: Editoriale Oriete, 2012.

Cornell, Sarah. "Citizens of Nowhere: Fugitive Slaves and Free African Americans in Mexico, 1833–1857," *Journal of American History* 100, no. 2 (September 2013): 351–374.

Cosio Villegas, Daniel. *Historia moderna de Mexico. El porfiriato, Vida politica interior*, 2 vols. Mexico City: Hermes, 1972.

Deans-Smith, Susan. *Bureaucrats, Planters, and Workers: The Making of the Tobacco Monopoly in Bourbon Mexico*. Austin: University of Texas Press, 1992.

De la Fuente, Alejandro. *Havana and the Atlantic in the Sixteenth Century*. Chapel Hill: University of North Carolina Press, 2008.

———. *A Nation for All: Race, Inequality and Politics in Twentieth-Century Cuba*. Chapel Hill: University of North Carolina Press, 2001.

Diaz, Delfin, Jeanne Moisand, Romy Sánchez and Juan Luis Simal, et al. *Exils entre deux mondes: migrations et espaces politiques atlantiques au xixe siècle*. Mordelles: Les Persèides editions, 2015.

Domínguez, Freddy Avila, Ricardo Pérez Monfort, and Christian Rinaudo. *Circulaciones culturales: lo afrocaribeño entre Cartagena, Veracruz y La Habana*. México, D.F.: Centro de Investigaciones y Estudios Superiores en Antropología Social (CIESAS, México), 2011.

Espinosa, Mariola. *Epidemic Invasions: Yellow Fever and the Limits of Cuban Independence 1878-1930*. Chicago: Chicago University Press, 2009.

Espinosa Blas, M. Margarita. *El Nacional y El Hijo del Ahuizote: dos visions de la independencia de Cuba, 1895-1898*. Morelia, Michoacán, México: Universidad Michoacana de San Nicolás de Hidalgo, Instituto de Investigaciones Históricas, 1998.

———. *La política exterior de México hacia Cuba, 1890-1902*. In Laura Munoz Mata, México y el caribe: Vínculos, interes, region, vol. 2. México D.F.: Secretaría de Relaciones Exteriores, Mexico, Dirección General del Acervo Histórico Diplomático, 2004.

Estrade, Paul. *La colonia Cubana de Paris, 1895-1898: el combate patriótico de Betances y la solidaridad de los revolucionarios franceses*. Havana: Editorial de Ciencias Sociales, 1984.

———. *José Martí y los fundamentos de la democracia en Latinoamerica*. Madrid: Ediciones Doce Calles, Casa de Velázquez, 2000.

Falcón, Romana. *Las rasgaduras de la descolonización: españoles y mexicanos a mediados del siglo xix*. México D.F.: El Colegio de México, 1996.

Feros, Antonio. "Spain and America: All Is One." In *Interpreting Spanish Colonialism*, edited by Scmidt-Nowara and Nieto-Philips, 109–134. Albuquerque: University of New Mexico Press, 2005.

Ferrer, Ada. *Freedom's Mirror: Cuba and Haiti in the Age of Revolution.* New York: Cambridge University Press, 2014.

——. *Insurgent Cuba: Race, Nation and Revolution, 1868-1898.* Chapel Hill: University of North Carolina Press, 1999.

Finch, Aisha K. *Rethinking Slave Rebellion in Cuba: La Escalera and the Insurgencies of 1841-1844.* Chapel Hill: UNC Press, 2015.

Foner, Philip S. *Antonio Maceo: The Bronze Titan of Cuba's Struggle for Independence.* New York: Monthly Review Press, 1977.

——. *Our America by Jose Martí: Writings on Latin America and the Struggle for Cuban Independence.* New York: Monthly Review Press, 1977.

——. *The Spanish Cuban American War and the Birth of American Imperialism, 1895-1902.* New York: Monthly Review Press, 1972.

Forment, Carlos. *Democracy in Latin America, 1760-1900.* Chicago: University of Chicago Press, 2003.

Franco, José Luciano. *Antonio Maceo, Apuntes Para una Historia de su Vida, Tomo I.* Havana: Editorial de Ciencias Sociales, 1975.

Funes, Reinaldo. "Slaughterhouse and Milk Consumption." In *State of Ambiguity: Civil Life and Culture in Cuba's First Republic*, edited by Steven Paul Palmer, José Antonio Piqueras Areanas, and Amparo Sánchez Cobos. Durham: Duke University Press, 2014.

Gamboa, Leticia. "De indios y gachupines." In *Tiempos de América: revista de historia, cultura y territorio*, núm 3-4: 85-98. Cataluña: España. Universitat Jaume I: Centro de Investigaciones de América Latina (CIAL), 1999.

——. *Los empresarios de ayer: el grupo dominante en la industria textile de Puebla, 1906-1929.* Puebla: Universidad Autonoma de Puebla, 1985.

García Díaz, Bernardo, and Sergio Guerra. *La Habana/Veracruz, Veracruz/La Habana: las dos orillas.* Veracruz: Universidad Veracruzana, 2002.

Garófalo Mesa, Manuel Garcia. *La Vida de José Maria Heredia en México, 1825-1839.* México, D.F., Ediciones Botas, 1945.

Garrigó, Roque E. *Historia documentada de la conspiración de los Soles y rayos de Bolivar.* Havana: El Siglo XX, A. Muniz y hno, 1929.

Garza, James Alex. *The Imagined Underworld: Sex, Crime and Punishment in Porfirian Mexico.* Lincoln: University of Nebraska Press, 2007.

González Barrios, René, E. Rodríguez Mendoza, and Carlos Dublé. *Chile en la Independencia de Cuba.* Havana: Casa Editorial Verde Olivo, 2007.

——. *Cruzada de libertad: Venezuela por Cuba.* Havana: Casa Editorial Verde Olivo, 2005.

González Navarro, Moises. *La colonización en México, 1877-1910.* México D.F.: Talleres de Impresión de Estampillas y Valores, 1960.

González Sierra, José G. *Monopolio del humo: elementos para la historia del tabaco en mexico y algunos conflictos de tabaqueros veracruzanos, 1915-1930.* Xalapa: Universidad Veracruzana, 1987.

Granados, Aimer. *Debates sobre España: el hispanoamericanismo en México a fines del siglo XIX*. México D.F.: El Colegio de México, 2005.
Greenbaum, Susan D. *More Than Black: Afro-Cubans in Tampa*. Gainesville: University of Florida Press, 2002.
Guerra, Lillian. *The Myth of José Martí: Conflicting Nationalisms in Twentieth-Century Cuba*. Chapel Hill: University of North Carolina Press, 2005.
Guerra Vilaboy, Sergio. *La América Latina y la independencia de Cuba*. Caracas: Ediciones Ko'Eyú, 1999.
Guridy, Frank. *Forging Diaspora: Afro-Cubans and African Americans in a World of Empire and Jim Crow*. Chapel Hill: University of North Carolina Press, 2010.
Guterl, Matthew Pratt. *American Mediterranean: Southern Slaveholders in the Age of Emancipation*. Cambridge, Mass.: Harvard University Press, 2008.
Hale, Charles A. *The Transformation of Liberalism in Late Nineteenth-Century Mexico*. Princeton, NJ: Princeton University Press, 2014.
Helg, Aline. *Our Rightful Share: The Afro-Cuban Struggle for Equality, 1886–1912*. Chapel Hill: University of North Carolina Press, 1995.
Herrera Barreda, Maria del Socorro. *Inmigrantes hispanocubanos en México durante el porfiriato*. México, D.F.: Universidad Autónoma Metropolitana, Unidad Iztapalapa, División de Ciencias Sociales y Humanidades, Departamento de Filosofía: M.A. Porrúa Grupo Editorial, 2003.
Herrera Franyutti, Alfonso. *Martí en México*. México, D.F.: Consejo Nacional Para la Cultura y Las Artes, 1996.
Hewitt, Nancy A. *Southern Discomfort: Women's Activism in Tampa Florida, 1880s–1920s*. Chicago: University of Illinois Press, 2001.
Hidalgo Paz, Ibrahim. *Partido revolucionario cubano: independencia y democracia*. Havana: Centro de Estudios Martianos, 2011.
Hoerder, Dirk, and Nora Faires. *Migrants and Migration in Modern North America: Cross-border Lives, Labor Markets and Politics*. Durham, N.C.: Duke University Press, 2011.
Joseph, Gilbert. *Rediscovering the Past and Mexico's Periphery*. Tuscaloosa: University of Alabama Press, 1986.
Joseph, Gilbert, and Allen Wells. *Summer of Discontent, Seasons of Upheaval: Elite Politics and Rural Insurgency in Yucatan, 1876–1915*. Stanford, Calif.: Stanford University Press, 1996.
Juárez Hernández, Yolanda. *Persistencias culturales afrocaribeñas en Veracruz: su proceso de conformación desde la colonia hasta fines del siglo XIX*. Jalapa: Gobierno del Estado de Veracruz, 2006.
Kamen, Henry. *The Disinherited: Exile and the Making of Spanish Culture*. New York: Harper Collins, 2007.
Keller, Renata. *Mexico's Cold War: Cuba, The United States and the Legacy of the Mexican Revolution*. New York: Cambridge University Press, 2015.

Kuntz Ficker, Sandra, and Precilla Connolly, eds. *Ferrocarriles y Obras Publicas.* México D.F.: Instituto Mora, 1999.

Landers, Jane. *Black Society in Spanish Florida.* Urbana: University of Illinois Press, 1999.

Landers, Jane, and Barry Robinson. *Slaves, Subjects and Subversives: Blacks in Colonial Latin America.* Albuquerque: University of New Mexico Press, 2006.

Lasso, Marixa. *Myths of Harmony: Race and Republicanism During the Age of Revolution, Colombia, 1795–1831.* Pittsburgh: University of Pittsburgh Press, 2007.

Lazo, Rodrigo. *Writing to Cuba: Filibustering and Cuban Exiles in the United States.* Chapel Hill: University of North Carolina Press, 2005.

Lear, John. *Workers, Neighbors and Citizens: The Revolution in Mexico City.* Lincoln: University of Nebraska Press, 2001.

Lemus, George. *Francisco Bulnes, su vida y sus obras.* México D.F.: Ediciónes San Andrea. 1965.

Lerdo de Tejada, Carlos Trejo. *La revolución y el nacionalismo: Todo para todos.* Havana: Imprenta Maza y ca., 1916.

Le Riverend Brusone, Julio, et al. *Cuba-Colombia: una historia común.* Bogotá: Editorial Universidad Nacional, 1995.

Lida, Clara E. "El Perfil de una inmigración: 1821–1939." In *Una inmigración privilegiada: comerciantes, empresarios y profesionales españoles en México en los siglos xix y xx.* Clara E. Lida. Madrid: Alianza Editorial, 1994.

———, ed. *Una inmigración privilegiada: comerciantes, empresarios y profesionales españoles en México en los siglos xix y xx.* Madrid, Alianza Editorial, 1994.

———. *Inmigracion y Exilio: Reflexiónes Sobre el Caso Español.* México, D.F.: Siglo Veintiuno Editores en coedición con el Colegio de México, 1997.

Lomnitz, Claudio. *The Return of Comrade Ricardo Flores Magón.* New York: Zone Books, 2014.

López, Alfred J. *José Martí: A Revolutionary Life.* Austin: University of Texas Press, 2014.

López Mesa, Enrique. *La Comunidad Cubana en Nueva York: Siglo XIX.* Havana: Centro de Estudios Martianos, 2002.

López Portillo de Tamayo, Martha, Boris Rosen, Luis Angel Argüelles Espinosa. *Mexico y Cuba: dos pueblos unidos en la historia*, 2 vols. Mexico: Centro de Investigación Científica Jorge L. Tamayo, 1982.

Lufríu, René. *Manuel Márquez Sterling, escritor y ciudadano.* Havana: Imprenta siglo XX, A Muñiz y hno., 1938.

Luis-Brown, David. *Waves of Decolonization: Discourses of Race and Hemispheric Citizenship in Cuba, Mexico and the United States.* Durham, N.C.: Duke University Press, 2008.

Madrid, Alejandro L., and Robin D. Moore. *Danzón: Circum-Caribbean Dialogues in Music and Dance, 1870–1940.* New York: Oxford University Press, 2013.

Márquez Sterling, Manuel. *Doctrina de la república*. Publicaciónes de la secretaría de educación, dirección de cultura. Habana: Cultural, s.a., 1937.
Martí, José. *Epistolario*. Havana: Editorial de Ciencias Sociales, 2003.
———. *Obras Completas*. Havana: Editorial Ciencias Sociales, 1975.
McGillivray, Gillian. *Blazing Cane: Sugar, Communities, Class and State Formation in Cuba, 1868–1959*. Durham, N.C.: Duke University Press, 2009.
McGuinness, Aims. *Path of Empire: Panama and the California Gold Rush*. Ithaca, N.Y.: Cornell University Press, 2008.
Mirabal, Nancy Raquel. *De aquí, de allá: Race, Empire and Nation in the Making of Cuban Migrant Communities in New York and Tampa, 1823–1924*. PhD dissertation, University of Michigan, Ann Arbor, 2001.
———. *Suspect Freedoms: The Racial and Sexual Politics of Cubanidad in New York, 1823–1957*. New York City: NYU Press, 2017.
Moore, E. R. "José Maria Heredia in Mexico and the United States." *Modern Language Notes* 65, no. 1 (January 1950): 41–46.
Moore, Rachel A. *Forty Miles from the Sea: Xalapa, the Public Sphere, and the Atlantic World in Nineteenth-Century Mexico*. Tucson: University of Arizona Press, 2011.
Morales, Salvador E. *Espacios en Disputa: México y la Independencia de Cuba*. Mexico City: Centro de Investigación Científica Ing. Jorge L. Tamayo: Secretaría de Relaciones Exteriores, 1998.
Morales, Salvador E., and Agustín Sánchez Andres. *Diplomacias en conflicto: Cuba y España en el horizonte latinoamericano del 98*. México, D.F.: Centro de Ivestigación Científica Ing. Jorge L. Tamayo, 1998.
Muñoz Mata, Laura. *Mar adentro: espacios y relaciónes en la frontera México-Caribe*. México, D.F.: Instituto Mora, 2008.
———, ed. *México y el Caribe vínculos, intereses, región*. México D.F.: Instituto Mora, 2002.
Musacchio, Humberto. *Milenios de México*. México D.F.: Hoja Casa Editorial, 1999.
Naranjo Orovio, Consuelo. *La nación soñada: Cuba, Puerto Rico y Filipinas*. Madrid: Doce Calles, 1996.
Navarro, Enrique Camacho. *México y Cuba: del porfiriato a la Revolución: diplomaticos, diplomacia e historia política (1900–1920)*. México, D.F.: Universidad Nacional Autónoma de México, 2008.
Nesvig, Martin Austin, ed. *Religious Culture in Modern Mexico*. Lanham, Md.: Rowman & Littlefield Publishers, 2007.
Palmer, Steven Paul, José Antonio Piqueras Arenas, and Amparo Sánchez Cobos. *State of Ambiguity: Civic Life and Culture in Cuba's First Republic*. Durham, N.C.: Duke University Press, 2011.
Pani, Erika. *Para mexicanizar el Segundo imperio: El imaginario politico de los imperialistas*. México D.F.: Colegio de México, Centro de Estudios Históricos: Instituto de Investigación Mora, 2001.

———. *Para pertenecer a la gran familia Mexicana: procesos de naturalización en el siglo XIX*. México D.F.: Colegio de Mexico, 2015.

———. *El Segundo imperio: Pasados de usos multiples*. México D.F.: Centro de Investigación y Docencia Económicas: Fondo de Cultura Económica, 2004.

Pérez Jr., Louis A. *Cuba and the United States: Ties of Singular Intimacy*. Athens: University of Georgia Press, 2003.

———. *Cuba Between Empires, 1878–1902*. Pittsburgh: University of Pittsburgh Press, 1983.

———. *Cuba: Between Reform and Revolution*. New York: Oxford University Press, 2011.

———. *Cuba in the American Imagination: Metaphor and the Imperial Ethos*. Chapel Hill: University of North Carolina Press, 2008.

———. *Essays on Cuban History*. Gainesville: University Press of Florida, 1995.

———. *On Becoming Cuban: Identity, Nationality and Culture*. Chapel Hill: University of North Carolina Press, 1999.

———. *The Structure of Cuban History: Meanings and Purpose of the Past*. Chapel Hill: University of North Carolina Press, 2013.

———. *The War of 1898: The United States and Cuba in History and Historiography*. Chapel Hill: University of North Carolina Press, 1998.

Piccato, Pablo. *The Tyranny of Opinion: Honor in the Construction of the Mexican Public Sphere*. Durham, N.C.: Duke University Press, 2010.

Pletcher, David M. "The Building of the Mexican Railway." *Hispanic American Historical Review* 30, no. 1, (February 1950): 26–62.

Poyo, Gerald E. "The Cuban Experience in the United States: 1865–1940: Migration. Community, and Identity." *Cuban Studies* 21 (1991): 19.

———. *Exile and Revolution: José D. Poyo, Key West and Cuban Independence*. Gainesville: University Press of Florida, 2014.

———. "The Impact of Cuban and Spanish Workers in Labor Organizing in Florida, 1870–1900." *Journal of American Ethnic History* 5, no. 2 (Spring 1986): 46–63.

———. *With All, and for the Good of All: The Emergence of Popular Nationalism in the Cuban Communities of the United States, 1848–1898*. Durham, N.C.: Duke University Press, 1989.

Prados-Torreira, Teresa. *Mambisas: Rebel Women in Nineteenth-Century Cuba*. Gainesville: University Press of Florida, 2005.

Pulido Llano, Gabriela. *Desde Cuba: Escenas en la Diplomacia Porfrista, 1887–1901*. San Juan Mixcoac, México, D.F.: Instituto Mora, 2000.

Putnam, Lara. *Radical Moves: Caribbean Migrants and the Politics of Race in the Jazz Age*. Chapel Hill: University of North Carolina Press, 2013.

Quintana García, José Antonio. *Venezuela y la independencia de Cuba*. Havana: Editorial Pablo de la Torriente, 2005.

Quiróz, Alfonso W. "Free Association and Civil Society in Cuba, 1787–1895." *Journal of Latin American Studies* 43 (2011): 33–64.

Ramos, Julio. *Divergent Modernities: Culture and Politics in Nineteenth-Century Latin America*. Durham: Duke University Press, 2001.

Reid-Vazquez, Michele. *The Year of the Lash: Free People of Color in Cuba and in the Atlantic World*. Athens: University of Georgia Press, 2011.

Reséndez, Andrés. *Changing National Identities at the Frontier: Texas and New Mexico, 1800–1850*. New York: Cambridge University Press, 2005.

Rodríguez, Enrique Sosa, Francisco López Civeira, Antonio Aja Díaz, and Miriam Rodríguez Herrera, Esteban. *Léxico mayor de Cuba*, vol. 2. Havana: Editorial Lex, 1959.

Rodríguez Martínez. *Cuba y Cayo Hueso: Una historia compartida*. Havana: Editorial de Ciencias Sociales, 2006.

Rodríguez Ramos, Reniel, and Jaime Pagán Jiménez. "Interacciones multivectoriales en el Circum-Caribe precolonial: Un vistazo desde las Antillas." *Caribbean Studies* 34, no. 2 (July–December 2006): 99–139.

Rojas, Rafael. *Cuba Mexicana: Historia de una Anexión Imposible*. México D.F.: Secretaría de Relaciones Exteriores, 2001.

Roniger, Luis, James N. Green, and Pablo Yankelevich. *Exile and the Politics of Exclusion in the Americas*. Portland, Or.: Sussex Academic Press, 2012.

Rosenzweig, Gabriel. *Un liberal español en el Mexico porfiriano: Cartas de Telesforo Garcá a Emilio Castelar, 1888–1899*. México D.F.: CONACULTA, 2003.

Rothman, Adam. *Beyond Freedom's Reach: A Kidnapping in the Twilight of Slavery*. Cambridge, Mass.: Harvard University Press, 2015.

Roy, Joaquín. *La siempre fiel: Un siglo de relaciones hispanocubanas, 1898–1998*. Madrid: Instituto Universitario de Desarollo u Cooperación Libros de la Catarata, 1999.

Ruz Menéndez, Rodolfo. *La primera emigración cubana a yucatán*. Mérida: Ediciones de la Universidad de Yucatán, 1969.

Sábato, Hilda. *The Many and the Few: Political Participation in Republican Buenos Aires*. Stanford, Calif.: Stanford University Press, 2001.

Salazar Anaya, Delia. *Imágenes de los inmigrantes en la ciudad de México, 1753–1910*. México: Plaza y Valdés Editores, CONACULTA/INAH, 2002.

Saldivar, José David. *Trans-Americanity: Subaltern Modernities, Global Coloniality and the Cultures of Greater Mexico*. Durham, N.C.: Duke University Press, 2012.

Salillas, Rafael. "Los nanigos en ceuta." In *Revista general de legislación y jurisprudencia* 98. Madrid: Editorial Reus, 1901.

Sánchez Andrés, Agustín. "La Normalización de las Relaciones entre España y México Durante el Porfiriato (1876–1910)," 731–766. *Historia Mexicana* 48, no. 4, 1999.

Sánchez Andrés, Agustín, and Raul Figueroa E. *México y España: diplomacia, relaciones triangulares e imaginarios nacionales*. Michoacán: Universidad Michoacana de San Nicolás de Hidalgo, Instituto de Investigaciones Históricas; México, D.F.: Instituto Tecnológico Autónomo de México, 2003.

Sánchez Parodí, Ramon, et al. *José Martí y Eloy Alfaro: Luchadores inclaudicables por la libertad de nuestra América.* Quito: Escuela de Liderazgo y Oratoria Fidel Castro: Escuela de Sociología y CC PP de la Universidad Central del Ecuador, 2003.

Sanders, James E. *Contentious Republicans: Popular Politics, Race and Class in Nineteenth-Century Colombia.* Durham, N.C.: Duke University Press, 2004.

———. *The Vanguard of the Atlantic World: Creating Modernity, Nation and Democracy in Nineteenth-Century Latin America.* Durham, N.C.: Duke University Press, 2014.

Santacilia, Pedro. *Pedro Santacilia: el hombre y su obra,* edited by Boris Rosen Jélomer. Mexico City: Centro de Investigación Científica Jorge L. Tamayo, 1983.

Santana, Adalberto, and Sergio Guerra Vilaboy, eds. *Benito Juárez y Cuba.* México D.F.: Miguel Angel Porrúa, 2007.

Sartorius, David. *Ever Faithful: Race, Loyalty and the Ends of Empire in Spanish Cuba.* Durham, N.C.: Duke University Press, 2013.

Schell Jr., William. *Integral Outsiders: The American Colony in Mexico City, 1876–1911.* Wilmington, Del.: SRbooks, 2001.

Schmidt-Nowara, Christopher. *The Conquest of History: Spanish Colonialism and National Histories in the Nineteenth-Century.* Pittsburgh, Penn.: University of Pittsburgh Press, 2006.

———. *Empire and Antislavery: Spain, Cuba and Puerto Rico 1833–1874.* Pittsburgh, Penn.: University of Pittsburgh Press, 1999.

Schmidt-Nowara, Christopher, and John M. Nieto-Philips. *Interpreting Spanish Colonialism: Empires, Nations and Legends.* Albuquerque: University of New Mexico Press, 2005.

Scott, Rebecca. *Degrees of Freedom: Louisiana and Cuba After Slavery.* Cambridge, Mass.: Belknap Press of Harvard University Press, 2005.

———. " 'The Lower Class of Whites' and 'The Negro Element': Race, Social Identity and Politics in Central Cuba, 1899–1909." In *La Nacion Soñada: Cuba, Puerto Rico y Filipinas ante el 1898,* edited by Consuelo Naranjo, Miguel A. Puig-Samper, and Luis Miguel García Mora, 179–191. Aranjuez: Editorial Doce Calles, 1996.

———. *Slave Emancipation in Cuba: The Transition to Free Labor, 1860–1899.* Pittsburgh, Penn.: University of Pittsburgh Press, 2000.

Scott, Rebecca, and Jean M. Hébrard. *Freedom Papers: An Atlantic Odyssey in the Age of Emancipation.* Cambridge, Mass.: Harvard University Press, 2012.

Schwartz, Rosalie. *Lawless Liberators: Political Banditry and Cuban Independence.* Durham, N.C.: Duke University Press, 1989.

Sims, Harold. *The Expulsion of Mexico's Spaniards, 1821–1834.* Pittsburgh: University of Pittsburgh Press, 1990.

Sorhegui, Arturo. *La Habana en el Mediterraneo Americano.* Havana: Imagen Contemporáneo, 2007.

Speckman Guerra, Elisa. *Crimen y Castigo: Legislación Penal, Interpretaciones de la Criminalidad y Administración de Justicia (Ciudad de México, 1872–1910).* México D.F.: Colegio de Mexico, 2002.

Stebbins, Consuelo E. *City of Intrigue, Nest of Revolution: A Documentary History of Key West in the Nineteenth Century.* Gainesville: University Press of Florida, 2007.

Sublette, Ned. *The World that Made New Orleans: From Spanish Solver to Congo Square.* Chicago: Lawrence Hill Books, 2008.

Tenenbaum, Barbara A. "Streetwise History: The Paseo de la Reforma and the Profirian State, 1876–1910." In *Rituals of Rule: Rituals of Resistance: Public Celebrations and Popular Culture in Mexico*, edited by William H. Beezley, Cheryl E. Martin, William E. French, 141. Wilmington: SR Books, 1994.

Tenorio-Trillo, Mauricio. *I Speak the City: Mexico City at the Turn of the Twentieth Century.* Chicago: University of Chicago Press, 2012.

———. *Mexico at the World's Fairs: Drafting a Modern Nation.* Berkeley: University of California Press, 1996.

Toledo, Josefina. La madre negra de Martí, Havana: Casa Editorial Verde Olivo, 2009.

———. *Sotero Figueroa, editor de Patria: apuntes para una biografia.* Havana: Editorial Letras Cubanas, 1985.

Tone, John Lawrence. *War and Genocide in Cuba, 1895–1898.* Chapel Hill: University of North Carolina Press, 2008.

Torres-Cuevas, Eduardo. *Historia de la masonería Cubana: seis ensayos.* Havana: Imágen Contemporánea, 2004.

Trujillo Bolio, Mario. *El Golfo de Mexico en la Centuria Decimónica: Entornos Geográficos, Formación Portuaria y Configuración Marítima.* México, D.F.: Cámara de Diputados, LIX Legislatura, Estados Unidos Mexicanos: CIESAS: Porrúa, 2005.

Turner, John Kenneth. *Barbarous Mexico.* Austin: University of Texas Press, 1969.

Uribe Salas, José Alfredo. *México frente al desenlace del 98: la guerra hispanonorteamericana.* Morelia: Universidad Michoacana de San Nicolás de Hidalgo, Instituto de Investigaciones Históricas, Departamento de Historia de México; [Río Piedras, P.R.]: Universidad de Puerto Rico, Recinto de Río Piedras; Morelia, Michoacán, México: Gobierno del Estado de Michoacán de Ocampo, Instituto Michoacano de Cultura, 1999.

Van Hoy, Teresa. *A Social History of Mexico's Railroads: Peons, Prisoners and Priests.* United States: Rowan and Littlefield Publishers, 2008.

Voekel, Pamela. "Liberal Religion: The Schism of 1861." In *Religious Culture in Modern Mexico*, edited by Martin Austin Nesvig, 78–105. Maryland: Rowman and Littlefield Publishers, 2007.

Von Grafenstein Gareis, Johanna, and Laura Muñoz Mata, eds. *El Caribe: región, frontera y relaciones internacionales.* México D.F.: Instituto Mora, 2000.

Von Grafenstein Gareis, Johanna, Laura Muñoz Mata, Antoinette Nelken-Turner. *Un mar de encuentros y confrontaciónes: El golfo-caribe en al historia nacional.*

México D.F.: Secretaría de Relaciones Exteriores, Dirección General de Acervo Histórico Diplomático, 2006.

Yankelevich, Pablo. *Hispanofobia y revolución: Españoles expulsados de México (1911–1940)*. Hispanic American Historical Review 86 (1): 29–60.

———. *La revolución Mexicana en américa Latina: Intereses politicos e itineraries intelectuales*. México D.F.: Instituto Mora, 2003.

Young, Elliott. *Alien Nation: Chinese Migration in the Americas From the Coolie Era Through World War II*. Chapel Hill: University of North Carolina Press, 2014.

———. *Catarino Garza's Revolution on the Texas-Mexico Border*. Durham, N.C.: Duke University Press, 2004.

Zanetti Lecuona, Oscar, and Alejandro García Alvarez. *Sugar and Railroads: A Cuban History, 1837–1959*. Chapel Hill: University of North Carolina Press, 1998.

Zea, Leopoldo, and Hernan Taboada. *España Ultima Colonia de Si Misma*. México D.F.: Instituto Panamericano de Geografía e Historia: Fondo de Cultura Económica, 2001.

Index

1895 War, 3, 16–17, 29–41, 219–20, 250

Abolitionism, 142–43, 203
Africa, 37, 230
African American activists, 27
Afro-Caribbeans, 95
Afro-Cubans: in the 1895 war, 35–36, 37; in ANERC, 95; and the Escalera, 26; in migrant communities, 46–47, 53–56, 57–59, 261n10, 263n68; in opposition to *Cuba Libre*, 202–4; in the PRC, 54–55, 92
Afro-Mestizos, 57
Agachupinados (hispanized Mexicans), 175, 224–25, 229
Age of Revolution, 257–58
Agrupación Cubana de Orizaba, 62–63, 79
Alamán, Lucas, 138
Alvarez de Xiques, Julia, 56
Americanismo: Anglo-Latin struggle in, 141, 211; colonial legacies in, 213–14, 247, 248, 255; common struggle in, 246; in the Gulf World, 5, 256–57; in Latin American politics, 248–49; and the liberal opposition press, 231–40; and Mexican liberals, 211, 213, 222–30, 240–41; of the middle class, 160–61. *See also* solidarity, transnational
Americo Lera, Carlos, 135, 178
Anglo-Latin dualism: in *americanismo*, 141, 211; in *hispanismo*, 6, 181–83, 216; in political cartoons, 244

Annexation: and continental unity, 138; *Cuba Mexicana* project, 177–79; in insurgent diplomacy, 147, 149–50; in rejection of *Cuba Libre*, 202, 208, 218; in revolutionary politics, 129; and slavery, 24
Anti-colonialism: in dehispanicization, 223; in the Gulf world, 18; hispanophobia in, 184; in solidarity, 138–42, 160, 164, 166
Anti-Hispanism: conservative liberals on, 206–7, 230; in Cuban-Mexican solidarity, 158–59; in labor conflicts, 184; of liberal journalists, 213–15, 222–23, 225–28; *Maine* explosion in, 243; rise of, in Mexican history, 11–12; in Spanish-Mexican relations, 223
Arbona y Domínguez, Ignacio Martín, 37–38, 39–40, 43–44, 81, 124–25
Associational culture, 95–96
Authoritarianism, 89–90, 170, 195–96, 205, 222, 225–26
Auxiliaries, revolutionary, 116, 125–27
Avila, Samuel G., 193–94

Barreda, Gabino, 201
Bartolomé Masó, 61–62, 98, 100, 102, 105–6, 109–10, 114, 159–60
Bay of Pigs invasion, 257
Belize, 66
Belligerency rights: in Díaz's Cuban policy, 175; in insurgent diplomacy, 148–49, 152; in legitimation, 250; motions for across Latin America,

Belligerency rights (cont.) 139–40, 144–45; and solidarity, 161–62; student activism on, 164, 232
Bello, José Martín, 50
Boisse, Alfred, 75–76
Bojórquez Urzais, Carlos, 147
Bolívar, Simón, 137
Borrero y Echeverria, Esteban, 1–2
Bravo, Nicolás, 99
Brazil, 142
Britain in the Gulf world, 18, 41
Brook, John R., 69–70
Brunetti y Gayoso, José, 170, 188–93
Bulnes, Francisco, 198–99, 236–37

Caiñas, José Antonio, 38, 39–40, 123–24
California, 205
Cañizares Gómez, Leandro, 55–56, 58, 62–63, 79, 97, 212, 218
Cárdenas, Lázaro, 257
Caribbean region, 7–8, 57–59
Castelar, Emilio, 195–96, 226–27, 228
Castillo Sánchez, Luis, 39–40
Catholic Church and clergy, 223–25, 227, 243
Chile, 139
Cigar workers, 27–28, 158, 160
Cisneros, Fernando, 122, 125, 128
Citizens/citizenship, 91–92, 99, 102–7, 110–15, 117, 168–69
Civilians in the 1895 war, 33, 34, 35–36, 37
Clemente Vázquez, Andrés, 30, 35–37
Cleveland, Grover, 144
Cold War, 257–58
Colegio Unificación (Key West, Florida), 53
Colonialism: in Africa, 230; in *americanismo*, 213, 247, 248, 255; and associational culture, 95; compared to dictatorship, 254; in de-hispanicization, 211, 226; in *hispanismo*, 182, 216; tobacco industry in, 51
Congress of Panama, 137
Connections: in Mérida, 63–67; in Mexico City, 74; of revolutionary diaspora, 83; in Veracruz, 43–45, 48–49, 51, 54–57, 65, 79, 114–15
Conservatism: of the Díaz regime, 197, 213; in rejection of *Cuba Libre*, 10–11, 171, 240–41; rise of, 222–23
Conservative liberalism/liberals: on constitutional monarchy, 205; on de-hispanization, 206–7, 230; opposing *Cuba Libre*, 195–207; in the Porfiriato, 171
Constitutional monarchy, 197–98, 205
Continente Americano, El: and *americanismo*, 229–30, 233–34; in belligerency recognition, 161–62; in Cuban-Mexican solidarity, 153–55, 192–93; in debate over *Cuba España*, 199; donations to, 157; Spanish suppression of, 190–93
Correo Español, El, 186–87, 194, 198
Corruption, 110–12, 113–14, 253–54, 270n68
Cosmes, Francisco G., 224–25
Costa Rica, 152
Cross-gender political clubs, 97–98, 118–19
Cuba Española, 168–80, 195–207, 256
Cuba Libre (Free Cuba): continental relevance of, 1–3, 134–36, 137, 242, 249–50; criminality of, 216, 218; in Cuban history, 8; defending the image of, 127–29; exclusion of non-white Cubans from, 46–47; internationalizing of, 137–45; in Mexican liberalism, 11, 195–207; rejection of, 215–22; transnational dynamics of, 29–30. See also Cuban independence struggle
Cuba Mexicana, 177–79, 256
Cuban history, 8–10

Cuban independence struggle: center of, in Mexico City, 76; connections in, 37–38, 39–40, 43–44, 49; cross border activity in, 20–25; and exiles, 16; and identity, 83; and Latin American solidarity, 135–43, 166, 213, 215–16, 247–49, 255, 258; leaders/heroes of, 98–100, 102–3, 162–64; tobacco workers in, 52. *See also Cuba Libre* (Free Cuba); Latin America; Mexico; Spain; United States
Cuban Legation, 90, 142–43, 147–48
Cuban national flag, 163–64, 187, 190
Cuban nationalist framework, 2
Cubano-Mexicano Poesia political club, 97–98
Cuban Revolutionary Party (PRC): on annexation by Mexico, 177–78; on belligerency rights, 144; diplomacy by, 136; elections in, 110–12; and émigré self-fashioning, 116, 122–26; exclusion in, 87–88, 89, 130–31; fundraising by, 52, 91–92, 100–102; generational conflict in, 59–63, 73; on Haiti, 142–43; history and development of, 88–93; in insurgent diplomacy, 149–50; in Mérida, 66, 68; on Mexican neutrality, 215–16; mission of, 84–85; political clubs in, 91–93, 96–102, 111–12; racial segregation in, 54–55, 92; in repatriation, 221–22; in solidarity, 151–52, 155; women in, 84, 117–18; in Yucatán, 67
Cuban-Spanish migrant conflict, 185–94
Cuerpos de Consejo (CDCs), 54–55, 61–62, 89–90, 92, 110–12
Cultural imperialism, 173, 176–77, 181
Culture: in Díaz's Cuban policy, 172, 173–74; in migrant communities, 46, 50, 53, 57–59, 261n10, 263n68

Danzón, 58–59, 65, 127
Decena trágica, 251

Decolonization, 139, 211, 247–48
Defensive modernization, 173
Dehispanicization of Mexico, 210, 213, 222–30
De la Mole, Mario, 219–20, 221–22
Dellundé, Ulpiano, 142–43
Democracy: and ANERC, 85–86; in political cartoons, 236, 235f6.3; in political clubs, 110–15; and political stability, 201; and the PRC, 91–92; in solidarity, 161, 165–66, 241; in Veracruz, 114–15
Deportation, 25–26, 37–38, 86, 222
"Desespañiolización, La" (Ramríez), 226–27
Diario del Hogar, El, 213, 223–24, 231
Diaspora, Cuban: consciousness of, 80–81; in Cuban history, 9; culture of, 57–59; in the Gulf World, 16; mobility of migrants in, 47–48; PRC and ANERC in, 88–95; in revolutionary politics, 84–85, 87, 88–115; self-fashioning in, 115–30
Díaz, Porfirio: Cuban policy of, 171–80, 213; cult of personality of, 175–76; doctrine of, 233; on *El Continente Americano*, 192–93; and insurgent diplomacy, 136, 145–47, 149–50; in political cartoons, 176, 225
Díaz regime: authoritarianism in, 205, 222; and Catholic clergy, 223–25; conservatism of, 197, 213; and *Cuba Española*, 168–80; and Hispanism, 172–74; hostile passivity of, 212; in Mexican history, 10–11; neutrality of, 169–70, 174–77, 178–80, 216, 231–32; repression by, 38–39, 170, 188–95, 196, 207–8, 241, 242–43, 268n18, 278n77; and U.S. intervention, 232; vulnerability of, 251. *See also* Porfiriato
Dictatorships, Latin American, 248–49, 254. *See also* Díaz regime

Diplomacia en nuestra historia, La (Márquez Sterling), 246–50, 254–55
Dissidents, 20, 24, 112–14, 170, 196
Diversity, 45–46, 77, 84, 105–6
Domínguez Cowan, Nicolás, 147–50, 151, 175, 216, 226

Economic development, 51, 146, 149–50
Economic interests, 53, 149–50, 205–6, 248–49
Economic migrants, 20, 27–28, 35
Economic opportunities, 42, 45
Elites, Cuban: in the 1895 War, 31, 37–38; in ANERC, 13–14, 71–72, 86, 94; in Cuban history, 8–9; in exile and slavery, 23–24, 26; in historical continuity, 254–55; in migrant communities, 41, 45, 68–69; paternalism of, 100; patriotic events of, 103–6; in the PRC, 88; racism of, 46–47; in solidarity, 140–42, 159; in Spanish-Mexican conflict, 191; and working class Cubans, 73, 100
Elites, Latin American, 139–40, 166
Elites, Mexican, 46, 51–52, 57, 64–65, 181
Emancipation of slaves, 18–19, 24
Equality: of American republics, 233–34; of Cuba, 241–42; as goal for ANERC, 85–86
Escobar, Amado, 156
Escudero, José Agustín, 194
Estrada Palma, Tomás: on belligerency rights, 144, 152; on financial contributions, 125; fundraising by in political clubs, 102; on ideal citizens, 91–92; in insurgent diplomacy, 147–51; on neutrality, 216; in PRC history and development, 88–90; and the United States for, 135
Estrella Solitaria de Matamoros, 194
Europe, 27, 214, 229–30
Exclusion: by ANERC, 83–84, 86–88, 94–95, 105, 115, 130–31; by O'Farrill, 113; in the PRC, 87–88, 89, 130–31; from public events, 105; race-based, 46–47, 55, 56–57, 94–95, 131
Exiles, political, 3, 4, 7–9, 16, 20–30

Fandango, El, 159
Federalism, 205
Ferrocarriles Unidos de Yucatán, 67
Filibustering expeditions, 24, 28, 47, 65–66, 123
Financial contributions: and corruption, 270n68; in insurgent diplomacy, 147–48; interregional connections in, 78–80; to political clubs, 91–92, 98, 100–102; in revolutionary politics, 115, 125–26; in solidarity, 156–60; by workers, 71–72
Florida, 27–28, 50, 52–57, 108, 112–13
Florida-Veracruz connections, 48–49, 65, 159
France, 18, 41
Freedmen and women, 19, 25–26, 41, 202–4. *See also* slavery

Gachupines (Spaniards), 11, 224–25, 227–28. *See also* Spanish immigrants in Mexico
García, Gabriel López, 29–30, 122–23
García, Telesforo, 181, 193, 195–96, 207
García Vélez, Carlos, 172–73
Generational tensions, 59–63, 72–73, 75, 110–12, 115, 124–25
Geopolitical dynamics/context: of the 1895 War, 31–32; in Díaz's Cuban policy, 174; in the Gulf world, 4–7, 41; in Mexican-Spanish relations, 171; migrant communities in, 41, 44; in opposition to *Cuba Libre*, 205–6; in U.S. intervention, 237
Gómez, Juan Cañizarez, 62–63
Gómez, Máximo, 27, 28, 98–99, 239

González Alcorta, Leandro, 210–11, 228–29
Gran Legión del Aguila Negra (1824–1829), 137–38
Guatíbaro (person of low social standing), 72–73
Guerra Chiquita (1879–1880), 27
Gulf-Caribbean complex, 7–8
Gulf of Mexico, 4–5, 18–19, 171
Gulf world: 1895 war in, 30–41; as contested space, 256; Cuban migrants and exiles in, 20–30; diaspora in, 16; as framework, 6–8; history of, 17–20; insurgent diplomacy in the, 135; mobility in, 19–20, 77–81, 255–56; solidarity in, 256–57

Haiti, 46, 127, 138, 142–43, 203–4
Havana, Cuba, 17, 30, 31, 38
Henequen industry, 64, 67, 68–70
Heredia, José María, 21–24
Hernández y Fernandez, Pascual, 113–14
Hevia, Antonio, 78
Hijo del Ahuizote, El: anti-Hispanism in, 180, 213–14, 222–23, 226; on Mexican independence, 238; on the Monroe Doctrine, 233–34; on the Platt Amendment, 239; political cartoons in, 99, 174–75, 176, 225; on U.S. intervention, 231, 236
Hispanismo (Hispanism): Anglo-Latin dualism in, 6, 181–83, 216; in Díaz's Cuban policy, 172–74; as ideology, 211; in Mexico-Spanish relations, 170–71; political cartoons on, 225; rise of, 111, 180–95, 223
Hispanophobia, 184, 226–28
Historical continuity: conservative liberals on, 199–200; in Díaz's Cuban policy, 172–73; elites in, 254–55; in solidarity, 140–41, 160, 190–91, 246–47, 255, 258
Humanism, 202–3, 206–7

Ideal émigrés, defined, 116
Ideology: *americanismo as,* 211; Cuban flag symbolic of, 164; and economic interests, 248–49; in Mexican neutrality, 171, 199; in opposition to *Cuba Libre,* 206; in solidarity, 161, 164–66, 195–96, 257; in Spanish-Mexican relations, 180
Image of Cuba/Cubans: in political cartoons, 241–42, 243–44; of revolutionary heroes, 163; in revolutionary politics, 102–7, 115–16, 123, 127–29, 131
Immigration: in Díaz's Cuban policy, 172; during the Porfiriato, 51–52, 267n82; and repatriation, 221–22. *See also* Spanish immigrants in Mexico
Inclusion, 56, 83–84, 98–99
Indentured workers, 69–70, 71
Independence, ideology of, 161
Independence, Mexican, 237–38
Independence clubs, 136
Independence movements, parallels in, 25, 165–66, 199–200, 203–5, 248
Indigenous peoples, 199–200, 203–4, 235
Insurgent army: belligerency rights of, 144–45; Cubans of color in, 55–56; penal code of, 270n75; tactics of, 33–36, 38–39; whitening of, 65, 127, 131
Insurgent diplomacy: and Díaz, 136, 145–47, 149–50; in the Gulf world, 5, 135; and the Mexican state, 145–51; in Mexico City, 47, 75, 77; in solidarity, 137–45, 152–66
Insurgents: in the 1895 War, 29–30, 33–35, 37–38; as ideal patriots, 122–25; in Mexico City, 76; and migrant communities, 81; in migration, 16–17, 28; political clubs funding, 102; in the Ten Years War, 26–27; in Veracruz, 47, 49

Integristas (Spanish residents in Cuba), 40. *See also* Spanish immigrants in Mexico
Inter-American relations in Cuban history, 8
Intercolonial trade, 17–18, 19, 63–64
Interregional connections, 79–80, 98–110
Islas, Daniel M., 193
Isolation of émigré communities, 50, 65, 66, 69, 71–72

Jacobinism, 202, 206, 208
James Woodall expedition, 65–66
Journalists: in Cuban-Spanish conflict, 186–87; as defenders of Cuban civility, 128–29; in Mexican-Spanish conflict, 208; in opposition to the Díaz regime, 10–11, 179–80; repression of, 192–95, 207–8, 241, 242–43; and solidarity, 153–54, 161–64. *See also* liberal opposition press; newspapers
Juárez, Benito, 24–25, 180–81
Junta Promotora de la Libertad de Cuba, 22
Juntas, Cuban, 27
Juntas patrióticas (Spanish political clubs), 183

Key West, Florida, 15, 48–49, 50, 53–54, 92

Lagomasino y Alvarez, Luis, 33, 112, 113–14
La Negra, Toña, 58–59
Latin America: belligerancy rights motions in, 139–40, 144–45; in Cuban history, 9–10; Cuban separateness from, 1–3, 242; Europe as a danger to, 229–30; exile in, 20; PRC fundraising in, 101–2; rejection of *Cuba Libre* by, 215–22; relevance of *Cuba Libre to*, 1–3, 134–36, 137, 242, 249–50; solidarity of, 29, 135–36, 137–43, 247–49, 255–58
Latinamericanismo, 257
Latin race consciousness, 183, 216
Legitimacy of independence struggles, 199–206, 250
Leon y de Quesada, Caridad de, 120–21, 271n82
Lerdo de Trejada, Carlos Trejo: *La revolutión y el nacionalismo,* 252
Liberalism/liberals, Mexican: and *americanismo,* 211, 213, 222–30, 231–41; and *Cuba Española,* 195–207; economic, 166, 222; and foreign aggression, 214–15, 214f6.1; and insurgent diplomacy, 146; meaning of, challenged, 230; on rejection of *Cuba Libre,* 213, 222–30; on socioeconomic reform, 205; and solidarity, 133–34, 166, 211, 222–30; tradition of, 10–11, 27, 139–40, 166; and U.S. intervention, 236
Liberal opposition press: anti-Hispanism in, 180, 213–14, 222–23, 226; on de-hispanicization, 225–28; as reformers, 242; repression of, 193, 241, 278n77; on U.S. intervention, 231–40. *See also* journalists; newspapers
Libertad, La, 197
Little War (1879–1880), 3
López García, Gabriel, 15–16, 32–33, 38, 131
López Mateos, Adolfo, 257–58
Loyalty, 124, 168–69

Maceo, Antonio, 27, 28, 98–99, 163f4.1
Macías, José Miguel, 50, 54, 59, 62–63, 109, 111
Maestre, Angel, 28
Manifesto of Montecristi, 85–86, 87, 90–92, 113, 247

300   Index

Manifesto on Latin American Solidarity, 140–42
Mariscal, Ignacio, 169, 178, 189
Márquez Sterling, Manuel: on corruption and reform, 253–54; on Cuba as "a case apart," 1–2; on Cuban civility, 128–29; on Cuban self-governance, 238; *La diplomacia en nuestra historia*, 246–50, 254–55; on Latin American solidarity, 247–49; in the Mexican Revolution, 250–53; as a migrant, 245–46; on the Platt Amendment, 254; and Porfirio Díaz, 171–74, 179–80; on rejection of *Cuba Libre*, 218–19; *Los Últimos días del Presidente Madero*, 251; on U.S. intervention, 219–20, 241
Martí, José: in insurgent diplomacy, 134, 145–52; on Mexican neutrality, 215–16; on Mexico in the Gulf world, 6, 28–29, 132–33; in revolutionary politics, 88, 91–92, 103–5
Martínez Campos, Arsenio, 36
Masó, Bartolomé, 98–99
Matanzas, Cuba, 31, 35, 38
Mateos, Juan A., 149, 237
Menéndez de la Peña, Rodolfo, 65, 67, 72–73, 80
Merchán, Rafael María, 140, 220, 241
Mérida, Mexico, 45, 47, 63–74, 78, 81, 93
Metaphysical politics, 201, 202–3, 206–7, 208
Mexican Herald, 178
Mexican history, reconsidered, 10–12
Mexican political clubs, 136, 156
Mexican Revolution, 184, 250–53
Mexican-Spanish conflict, 5, 183–88, 189–94, 196, 208
Mexican state. *See* Díaz regime
Mexico: associational culture in, 96; CDC in, 92; and *Cuba Libre*, 6, 132–34, 135, 138; in the Cuban 1895 War, 30, 38–39; Cuban insurgent diplomacy in, 5, 145–51; Cuban revolutionary politics in, 95–115; in geopolitical/geographical context, 4–5, 6–7, 18, 41; and the liberal opposition press, 231–40; political landscape in, 49; rise of *hispanismo in*, 180–95, 223; tobacco industry in, 50–52; travel networks in, 78–79, 109
Mexico City, 29, 45, 74–77, 93, 96
Mexico y Cuba political club, 165
Middle-class: in ANERC, 13, 86; in migrant communities, 47–48; in political stability, 200–201; in revolutionary politics, 86, 88, 91–92; in solidarity, 140, 160–61
Migrant communities: on annexation by Mexico, 177–78; characteristics of, 45–47; conflict with Spanish immigrants, 4, 5, 184–88; connections between, 27, 43–45, 48–49, 51, 63–67, 83, 114–15; in corruption conflicts, 112–14; culture and language in, 46, 48–49, 57–59, 261n10, 263n68; in Díaz's Cuban policy, 176–77; economic opportunities in, 42, 45; in Florida, 50, 53–57, 112–13; generational tension in, 59–63, 72–73; integration of, 80–81; in Mérida, 63–74; in Mexico City, 74–77; mobility between, 47–48; racism in, 53–57; in revolutionary diaspora, 83; tobacco industry in, 50–52; in Veracruz, 49–50
Migrants/migration: in Cuban history, 7–9; in geopolitical context, 7; in the Gulf world, 5, 19–30, 77–81; routes of, 21m1.1; travels of, 3–4, 8; and war, 16–17
Miranda, Manuel M., 37
Mobility: between centers of migration, 47–48; in the Gulf world, 77–81, 255–56. *See also* connections; travel networks

Index   301

Modernization, 68, 129, 133, 166, 173, 184, 196, 211
Monroe Doctrine, 172, 178, 233–34, 237

National Association of Cuban Revolutionary Émigrés (ANERC): in the 1895 war, 31–41; elites in, 13–14, 71–72, 86, 94; exclusion in, 83–84, 86–88, 94–95, 105, 113, 115, 130–31; history and development of, 93–95; inclusion in, 83–84; mission of, 85–86; in revolutionary politics, 83–84, 103, 112–16; self-fashioning in, 117, 262n47, 271n86; women in, 94, 118, 121–22
Nationalism, 9–10, 23, 102–7, 166, 181–82
Nation-state frameworks, 7
Naturalization, 56–57, 59–60, 168–69
Networks, Cuban: in cross-border organizing, 29–30; of political clubs, 107–10; in the Ten Year's War, 26–27
Neutrality, Latin American, 215–22
Neutrality, Mexican: consequences of, 231–32; conservative liberals on, 196–97; Cuban reactions to, 212–13, 215–22; and the Díaz regime, 169–70, 174–77, 178–80, 216, 231–32; ideology in, 171, 199; Spanish elites in, 256
Neutrality agreements, 144, 145
New generation migrants, 63, 111
New Orleans, Louisiana, 24–25, 44, 51, 261n10
New Spain in the Gulf world, 17–18
Newspapers: on Cuban-Spanish migrant conflict, 185–94; as historical record, 13–14; political clubs connected by, 108–9; in solidarity, 14, 152–56, 246. *See also* journalists; liberal opposition press
New York City, 84, 88
Non-white Cubans, 46–47, 54–55, 131

Oaxaca, 52, 71
Obreros de Progreso, 71
Occupations of migrants, 86, *86t3.1*
O'Donnell, Leopoldo, 26
O'Farrill, Juan Ramón, 93, 112–13, 268n18
Olaguíbel y Arista, Carlos, 171, 196–207, 208, 224–25, 236
Ortega Manzano, Juan, 69–70, 71, 131, 222

Pact of Zanjón, 27
Palma, José Joaquín, 140
Pan-Americanism, 12, 211, 213
Pan-Hispanism. *See hispanismo* (Hispanism)
Patria, La, 49, 98–99, 108, 237
Patriotic events and celebrations, 102–7
Patriotism, 46–47, 61–62, 95, 119–20, 125–27, 262n47
Patriots, ideal, 85, 117–29, 122–25
Pérez Gil, Ignacio, 113–14
Persecution in the 1895 war, 33, 34, 36–37
Peru, 139–40, 152
Petitions for belligerency rights, 161–62, 164
Pinar y Pérez, Ignacio, 113–14
Platt Amendment, 1, 220, 238–39, 241, 254
Political cartoons: democracy in, 236, *235f6.3*; Díaz in, 176, 225; images of Cuba in, 241–42, 243–44; on the Monroe Doctrine, 233–35, *234f6.2*; on neutrality, 174–75; on the Platt Amendment, 239; on republicanism, 228; on revolutionary politics, 99; U.S. intervention in, 214–15, *234f6.2*, *235f6.3*
Political clubs: academic conferences of, 105–6; connections between, 98–99, 107–10; cross-national, 96,

302   Index

98, 107–9; democracy and power in, 110–15; financial contributions to, 98, 100–102; founding and creation of, 96–102; fundraising by, 91–92; generational conflict in, 54, 61–63, 72–73, 115; growth of, 92–93; history of, in Cuba, 95–96; inclusivity in, 98–99; membership in, 79–80, 109–10; and mobility, 79–80; in patriotism, 126–27; in the PRC, 89–90, 92–93; as public face of Cuba, 102–7; in revolutionary politics, 95–115; in solidarity, 153, 155–56, 165; Spanish, 183; structure of, 273n28; women in, 97–98, 117–19, 120–21

Political conferences, 105–6

Political exile, 16, 33

Political liberalism. *See* liberalism/liberals, Mexican

Political stability, 196, 200–204, 206, 208, 253–54

Politics, revolutionary: and culture, 58; discourse of, 84–85; inclusion/exclusion in, 83–84; isolation of workers from, 71–72; in Mexico, 95–115; in migration, 42; political parties in, 88–95; self-fashioning of émigrés in, 115–30; socioeconomic class in, 102–7, 122–23, 127; solidarity in, 241. *See also* Cuban Revolutionary Party (PRC); National Association of Cuban Revolutionary Émigrés (ANERC)

Popular Socialist Party (PSP) of Mexico, 258

Population growth, 51–52, 67, 72, 92

Porfirian elites, 181, 196–97, 199, 201, 211, 240–41

Porfiriato: and *hispanismo*, 183–84, 193–95; immigration in, 51–52, 267n82; in Mexican history, 10–12; Mexico City in, 74; and revolutionary politics, 171, 172, 173, 174–75; and solidarity, 251, 254. *See also* Díaz regime

Ports, Gulf, 31–32, *32t1.1*, *32t1.2*, 48–49, 64–67, 79–81

Poverty: and ANERC membership, 86–87, 113, 126; in Mérida, 68–69; and political club membership, 100–101; and repatriation, 86–87, 221–22, 256; in self-fashioning, 122–23

Prado, Mariano Ignacio, 139

Professionals, as migrants, 68, 72, 74–75, 76, 79, 86, *86t3.1*

Progreso, 64–66, 78

Propaganda: Mexican, 175–76; in revolutionary politics, 99, 105–6; in solidarity, 140–42, 153, 162; Spanish, 99, 143, 212, 239

Provisional government of Cuba, 90, 141–42

Public events, 102–7, 119, 154, 189

Public opinion, 135, 136, 152, 189–90, 219–20, 221, 224–25

Puebla, Mexico, 45, 78

Puerto Rico, 20

Puig y Chappotín, Juan, 113–14

Quesada, Gonzalo de, 150

Quesada, Rafael and Manuel, 25

Race/racism: in exclusion, 55, 56–57, 94–95; in *hispanismo*, 182, 183; in insurgent diplomacy, 131, 143; in migrant communities, 46–47, 53–57; in revolutionary politics, 111, 127; in the U.S. Press, 240

Radicalism, social, 88, 159

Railroads, 64, 67, 74, 78–79, 133

Ramríez, Ignacio: "La Desespañi-olización," 226–27

Recolonization, 138–39, 181–82, 208–9

Reconcentración (forced relocation), 38–39, 40

Reconciliation politics, 196, 223–24, 242
Refugees, 3, 20, 30–31, 35–36
Rejection of *Cuba Libre:* conservatism in, 10–11, 171, 240–41; Cuban reaction to, 208–9, 212–13, 215–22; fears of annexation in, 202, 218; Mexican liberal reaction to, 213, 222–30; reconciliation politics in, 242; Spanish-Mexican relations in, 169–70; viability in, 173–74
Repatriation, 86–87, 131, 212–13, 221–22, 256
Repression: in the 1895 War, 38–39; of dissidents, 170, 196; of journalists, 192–95, 207–8, 241, 242–43; of opposition press, 278n77; of solidarity, 187–95; of workers, 268n18
Republicanism, 161, 201, 204, 228, 241
Revolutionary émigrés: defined, 115–16; in the PRC, 92
Revolutionary identity, 87–88
Revolutión y el nacionalismo, La (Lerdo de Trejada), 252
Rio y Rosas, Candida del, 271n82
Rivera, José P., 186
Roosevelt, Theodore, 178
Roosevelt Corollary to the Monroe Doctrine, 172
Royalist connections, 16–17, 37–38, 39–40, 123–25

Sagasta, Práxedes, 40
Sánchez, Serafín, 33–34
Sánchez Azcona, Juan, 246, 251
San José de la Vega, Mexico, 69–70
Santacilia, Pedro, 24–25, 76–77, 140
Santa Clara, Cuba, 33–34, 38
Scientific enquiry into *Cuba Libre,* 196–207
Scorched earth tactics in the 1895 War, 30–31, 33–35
Self-fashioning of émigrés, 115–30, 262n47
Self-governance, 129, 218–19, 220, 237, 238
Sherman, John, 178
Sierra, Justo, 196–98
Sierra y García, Ricardo, 79
Sifuentes, Cerefino, 230, 243
Silvera, Aurelio, 61–63
Sister republic ideal, 212–13, 218–19, 231, 236, 241–42, 248–49
Slave insurrection plot, 138
Slavery, 18–19, 23–24, 25–26, 56–57, 64, 142–43
Slogans, 185–87, 232
Social gatherings, elite, 103–6
Social life in exile, 58, 102
Social reform, 205, 252–54
Sociedad el Progresso (Key West, Florida), 53
Socioeconomic class: in deportations, 37–38; in migrant communities, 45, 46–47, 70–74, 78; in revolutionary politics, 102–7, 122–23, 127; in solidarity, 156–61
Socio-scientific reasoning, 227
Solar, Antonio, 76
Soles y Rayos de Bolivar conspiracy, 22, 137
Solidarity, Cuban-Mexican: *americanismo* in, 6, 161, 230; in club names, 98–99; conservative liberals on, 199–200, 206–7; *hispanismo* in, 188; and insurgent diplomacy, 136, 153–64, 165–66; journalists in, 153–54, 161–64; legacies of, 245–58; migrant communities in, 46, 77; newspapers in, 13–14, 152–55; repression of, 188–95; shared rights and struggle in, 230
Solidarity, transnational: Cuban exiles in, 4, 5; democracy in, 241; diplomacy in, 135, 137–45, 166–67;

304 Index

grassroots, 151–66; in the Gulf world, 256–57; ideology in, 161, 164–66, 195–96, 257; Latin American, 135–43, 166, 213, 215–16, 247–49, 255, 258 (*See also americanismo*); republicanism in, 241; Spanish-Mexican, 183, 195–96, 204–6; transatlantic, 99–100; U.S.-Cuban, 46

Sovereignty: Cuban, 1, 238–39; Mexican, 6, 232

Spain: anti-independence propaganda by, 143; authoritarianism in, 170; colonial mismanagement by, 217–19; and Cuban political clubs, 99–100; in the Gulf world, 4, 17–18, 20, 41; and Mexican independence, 7, 237–38; in neutrality, 216–18; offenses of in Latin America, 141–42, 216–18; public opinion campaign by, 153; recolonization by, 138–39, 181–82, 208–9; in the rise of *hispanismo*, 180–82; and Veracruz, 48–49

Spanish-American war, 40, 44, 174–75, 211–12

Spanish consular records, 66–67

Spanish elites, 200–205, 240–41, 256

Spanish immigrants in Mexico: in *americanismo*, 215; in anti-gachupinismo, 11; in anti-hispanism, 227–28; attacking Cuban civility, 127, 128; in conflict with Cubans and Mexicans, 4, 5, 183–94, 196, 208; in Díaz's Cuban policy, 172; and insurgent diplomacy, 148; and migrant communities, 58, 66, 75, 77; in repression of *Cuba Libre*, 207; response to student propaganda by, 162; scapegoating of, 222–23; in Spanish-Mexican relations, 180–81

Spanish journalists, 186–87

Spanish-Mexican relations: anti-Hispanism in, 223; argument for solidarity in, 204–6; conflict in, 183–88; *hispanismo* in, 170–71, 180–81, 208; as reconciliation politics, 224

Spanish monarchy in de-hispanization, 224–25, 228–29

Spanish officials, 30, 34, 168–69, 176–77, 187–90

Stereotypes of émigrés, 127

Student activism, 158, 161, 164, 232

Student journalists: on the clergy, 224; repression of, 192–93, 207–8, 241, 242–43; in solidarity, 153–54, 161–64; on working-class solidarity, 157–58

Sugar plantations, 33–34, 35

Surveillance, 28, 66–67, 189

Tampa, Florida, 15, 53, 88, 222

Ten Year's War (1868–1878), 3, 16, 25, 26–27, 67, 249–50

Texas, 205

Three Friends expedition, 15

Tizoc, Juan, 222–23, 224, 231, 242

Tobacco workers, 27, 37, 45, 50–52, 159

Trade: intercolonial, 17–18, 19, 27; networks of, 31–32, 41

Transnational dynamics, 8–10, 29–30, 46

Transportation networks, 27, 31–32, 41–42, 44, 64–67

Travel networks, 29, 73–74, 77–81, 107–8. *See also* mobility

Tuxtepecanos (allies of Díaz), 231–32

Últimos días del Presidente Madero, Los: Márquez Sterling, 251

Unión Iberoamericana, 183, 188

United States: in the 1895 war, 250; CDCs in, 89; in *Cuba Española*, 202; dependence on, 172, 173–74, 205; in Díaz's Cuban policy, 171–75; embrace of, 241; in the Gulf world, 6–7, 18–19, 41; and internationalization of *Cuba Libre*, 135, 138, 144

United States imperialism: in *americanismo,* 212; in the Gulf world, 4–5, 7, 18–19; in insurgent diplomacy, 147, 149–50; and Mexican liberalism, 134–35; and the Mexican state, 171, 172–73, 176–77; Platt Amendment as, 238–39; in rejection of *Cuba Libre,* 218; and solidarity, 167, 204–5

United States intervention: Bay of Pigs invasion, 257; and *Cuba Mexicana,* 178; and Mexican independence, 237–38; and the Mexican liberal press, 231–40; migrants and exiles in, 20–30, 42, 45–46; military protectorate as, 171–72; in political cartoons, 234f6.2, 235f6.3; public opinion in, 152; and revolutionary politics, 92, 101; in War of Cuban Independence, 219–20

Unity, 60–62, 84, 137–40

U.S.-Cuban nationalist frameworks, 2

Valdes Corvalles de Muniz, Dominga, 83–84, 121

Valle Nacional de Oaxaca, 52, 71

Varela Felix, 21

Varona, Carlos de, 77

Varona, Enrique José, 140–41, 216–17

Vázquez, Andrés Clemente, 51, 168–69

Veracruz: in the 1895 War, 31, 38; ANERC applications from, 271n86; connectedness of, 43–45, 48–49, 54–57, 65, 79, 114–15, 159; generational tensions in, 59–63, 73–74; in the Gulf world, 17, 77–78; migrant community in, 28, 43, 45, 46–63, 81; and repatriation, 221; in revolutionary politics, 89, 92, 96–97, 114–15

Veterans, 59–63, 90

Viability of *Cuba Libre,* 128–29, 173–74, 218–19, 236–37

Victoria, Guadalupe, 137

Vicuña Mackenna, Benjamín, 139

Villaverde, Constantino R., 217–18

War of Cuban Independence (1895–1898), 3, 16–17, 29, 30–41, 219–20, 250

Wars of Cuban independence, 2–3, 16–17, 25, 26–27, 29–41, 67, 219–20, 249–50

Wealth and patriotism, 125–26

Weyler y Nicolau, Valeriano, 15–17, 36–37, 38, 40

White Creoles, 25–27, 58

White Cubans: in insurgent image, 131; in migrant communities, 45, 53–54, 56; in revolutionary politics, 88, 92, 94, 95

Women in revolutionary politics, 84, 94, 97–98, 107, 110, 117–22, 270n74

Wood, Leonard, 70, 239

Working-class: in migrant communities, 45, 50–52, 68–70, 71–72, 73; in revolutionary politics, 88, 95, 103, 123, 126; in solidarity, 157–58; in Spanish-Mexican conflict, 184, 191

Ybor, V. M., 51, 53

Ybor City, Tampa, Florida, 50, 53

Yucatán, 47, 63–67, 67–72

Zócalo district, Mexico City, 75–76

ENVISIONING CUBA

Dalia Antonia Muller, *Cuban Émigrés and Independence in the Nineteenth-Century Gulf World* (2017).

Jennifer L. Lambe, *Madhouse: Psychiatry and Politics in Cuban History* (2017).

Devyn Spence Benson, *Antiracism in Cuba: The Unfinished Revolution* (2016).

Michelle Chase, *Revolution within the Revolution: Women and Gender Politics in Cuba, 1952–1962* (2015).

Aisha K. Finch, *Rethinking Slave Rebellion in Cuba: La Escalera and the Insurgencies of 1841–1844* (2015).

Christina D. Abreu, *Rhythms of Race: Cuban Musicians and the Making of Latino New York City and Miami, 1940–1960* (2015).

Anita Casavantes Bradford, *The Revolution Is for the Children: The Politics of Childhood in Havana and Miami, 1959–1962* (2014).

Tiffany A. Sippial, *Prostitution, Modernity, and the Making of the Cuban Republic, 1840–1920* (2013).

Kathleen López, *Chinese Cubans: A Transnational History* (2013).

Lillian Guerra, *Visions of Power in Cuba: Revolution, Redemption, and Resistance, 1959–1971* (2012).

Carrie Hamilton, *Sexual Revolutions in Cuba: Passion, Politics, and Memory* (2012).

Sherry Johnson, *Climate and Catastrophe in Cuba and the Atlantic World during the Age of Revolution* (2011).

Melina Pappademos, *Black Political Activism and the Cuban Republic* (2011).

Frank Andre Guridy, *Forging Diaspora: Afro-Cubans and African Americans in a World of Empire and Jim Crow* (2010).

Ann Marie Stock, *On Location in Cuba: Street Filmmaking during Times of Transition* (2009).

Alejandro de la Fuente, *Havana and the Atlantic in the Sixteenth Century* (2008).

Reinaldo Funes Monzote, *From Rainforest to Cane Field in Cuba: An Environmental History since 1492* (2008).

Matt D. Childs, *The 1812 Aponte Rebellion in Cuba and the Struggle against Atlantic Slavery* (2006).

Eduardo González, *Cuba and the Tempest: Literature and Cinema in the Time of Diaspora* (2006).

John Lawrence Tone, *War and Genocide in Cuba, 1895–1898* (2006).

Samuel Farber, *The Origins of the Cuban Revolution Reconsidered* (2006).

Lillian Guerra, *The Myth of José Martí: Conflicting Nationalisms in Early Twentieth-Century Cuba* (2005).

Rodrigo Lazo, *Writing to Cuba: Filibustering and Cuban Exiles in the United States* (2005).

Alejandra Bronfman, *Measures of Equality: Social Science, Citizenship, and Race in Cuba, 1902–1940* (2004).

Edna M. Rodríguez-Mangual, *Lydia Cabrera and the Construction of an Afro-Cuban Cultural Identity* (2004).

Gabino La Rosa Corzo, *Runaway Slave Settlements in Cuba: Resistance and Repression* (2003).

Piero Gleijeses, *Conflicting Missions: Havana, Washington, and Africa, 1959–1976* (2002).

Robert Whitney, *State and Revolution in Cuba: Mass Mobilization and Political Change, 1920–1940* (2001).

Alejandro de la Fuente, *A Nation for All: Race, Inequality, and Politics in Twentieth-Century Cuba* (2001).

www.ingramcontent.com/pod-product-compliance
Lightning Source LLC
Chambersburg PA
CBHW030522230426
43665CB00010B/731